THE DANCE IN INDIA

Bharata Natyam dance costume (traditional nine yards saree). Indrani in an elegant *Nrtta* (Pure Dance) posture from the *Alarippu*. (Photo, H. Rahman.)

ENAKSHI BHAVNANI

THE DANCE IN INDIA

The Origin and History, Foundations,
the Art and Science of the Dance
in India — Classical, Folk and Tribal

FOREWORD BY KAMALADEVI CHATTOPADHYAYA

*With 8 Illustrations in Colour, 415 in Monochrome
Halftone and over 300 Line Drawings*

 **TARAPOREVALA'S**
TREASURE HOUSE OF BOOKS
D. B. Taraporevala Sons & Co. Private Ltd.
210, Dr. D. NAOROJI ROAD, BOMBAY 1.

PRINTED IN INDIA

Printed by Russi J. Taraporevala at Electrographic Industries, Division of D. B. Taraporevala Sons & Co. Private Ltd., Apte Industrial Estate, Worli, Bombay 400 018. and published by him for D. B. Taraporevala Sons & Co. Private Ltd., 210 Dr. Dadabhai Naoroji Rd., Bombay 400 001.

Plates printed by Mr Ajit D. Desai at Print-Em-Up, Unique Industrial Estate, Prabhadevi Bombav-400 025.

To the memory of my husband

MOHAN BHAVNANI

Foreword

Dance may be said to be an instinct, some compelling emotion within us that urges us to find expression in dance, that is, outward rhythmic movements which gradually seem to come to assume certain forms. Dance is obviously an outward mode of a deep inner feeling. On all important occasions man has been moved to dance, on joyous as well as painful. Even birds and animals do, so do children even before they learn the use of all their limbs. There is rhythm manifest in all nature, in the firmaments. It is perhaps the earliest art evolved by man. Dance symbolises an inspiration which elevates us from the earthy bonds that bind us down to higher levels, thus releasing the warped and suppressed feelings, and create even if it be fleetingly, those moments of the soul when we become one with the universe. That is why amongst all peoples and at all times, dancing has occupied a very important place, from the primitive to the highly civilised.

It was believed from earliest times that certain currents generated by repeated rhythmic movements of the body created moods and atmosphere that wrought powerful results affecting man and nature alike. Thus were evolved seasonal dances, festival dances, ritual dances. The man believed he can effect with his mind and emotion what he could not with his physical muscles. Every movement thus became enormously important because it meant something. As man evolved within himself even as without, dance came to be more a spiritual experience, a medium of worship, an experience of the upliftment of the soul. Each step was carefully worked out and every ensemble precisely designed, for every gesture, every eye expression, even the make-up had a special significance.

Indian dance demonstrates the deeply philosophical and the highly religious moods of the Indian people. This is true even of the early folk dances. All the songs that form the clue to the dances are intensely imbued by the same spirit.

With the birth of the industrial age and the growth of a leisure seeking class, dance is becoming a form of entertainment to fill the empty hours. India is no exception. Nevertheless our dances still continue to carry the ancient content. Surprisingly hardly anyone has dared to challenge or change them. Their appeal and power are unquestioned and they continue to reign supreme.

Shrimati Enakshi Bhavnani has in this book tried to describe and present the varied dance forms of India. Each is so distinctive, with its own charm and beauty, that not even the most discerning or critical eye can aspire to improve on them.

There have been no doubt several literary efforts to give an exposition of these dances and their unique qualities. But rarely has there been so elaborate and yet so sensitive and fastidious a presentation as this. A prodigious product of love and labour has resulted in this very valuable presentation. The interpretation is simple though rich in artistry, so that any lay person can be easily initiated into these many forms and yet not be bored. It is indeed an achievement of a technical interpretation of these dances in an elaboration of this length, to be able to maintain a sustained interest.

With the widely growing interest and popularity of Indian dances, the need and search for authentic exposition is pressing and a book of this dimension and character is indeed the need of the hour.

Enakshi Bhavnani, herself a pioneer in this field, has the added advantage of being a dancer, student of art and a well-known writer.

KAMALADEVI CHATTOPADHYAYA

President, Bharatiya Natya Sangh (All India Theatre Centre,
New Delhi) and Chairman, All India Handicrafts Board.

Acknowledgements

My especial thanks are due to Sri E. Krishna Iyer, Guru Gopinath, Natyacharya Banda Kanakalingeshwara Rao and Bharatacharya Chinta Krishnamurthi Bhagavatulu, Kabichandra Kalicharan Patnaik, Srimati Sitara Devi, and Srimati Nayana Jhaveri for their valuable prefaces to my chapters on the main classical schools of the dance of Bharata Natyam, Kathakali, Kuchipudi, Odissi, Kathak and Manipuri respectively, and for their many kind suggestions and advice. And to the late Dr. Verrier Elwin for his kind preface to my chapters on the Tribal Dances of India. Among those who also generously helped me, I would like to thank Sri Bharatha Iyer for his advice on the Kathakali dance art and Guru Bipin Sinha and Nayana Jhaveri in the Manipuri dance art and its hand gestures; and Sri Deba Prasad Das and Sri Korda Narsimha Rao for their advice on the hand gestures of Odissi and Kuchipudi respectively. My thanks also to Guru Gopinath and Sri Gopal Pillai for the material on the Kathakali hand gestures and Srimati Anjali Hora for her patience in demonstrating the Bharata Natyam hand gestures for sketching them.

I also wish to thank Dr. B. S. Keshavan, Director, National Library, Calcutta, for the detailed lists of reference which assisted me in preparing my bibliography; the Andhra Pradesh Sangeeta Natak Akademi, and the Kala Vikash Kendra, Cuttack, Orissa, for the use of their valuable Souvenir numbers on the Dance Arts of Kuchipudi and Odissi respectively; and all those who have so readily contributed the numerous photographs for my book, particularly Dr. Grace Morley, Director of the National Museum, New Delhi, the Archaeological Department of the Government of India, Dr. Shivaramamurthi, National Museum, New Delhi, Srimati Indrani Rahman, Yamuni Krishnamurthi and Mr. M. Krishnamurthi of "Coronet," Madras, Srimati Mrinalini Sarabhai, Sri Mohan Khokar, Ram Gopal, Srimati Sitara Devi, the Jhaveri sisters, Kumari Kamala, Sudha Doraiswamy, Kumaris Cita, Chitra and Lata Pooviah, Sri R. R. Prabhu, Sri Dhiraj Chawda, Sri D. R. D. Wadia, Kumari Sahiar and *Marg* magazine.

My appreciation and grateful thanks to Mr. Jal H. Taraporevala (of Messrs. D. B. Taraporevala Sons & Co. Private Ltd., Bombay) for his great personal interest and encouragement and to Dr. R. J. Mehta who spared no pains in the editing of my manuscript, and thus made possible the publication of my book on the Indian Dance, a contribution which I have long wanted to make to this ancient art of India.

—ENAKSHI BHAVNANI

Prefaces

BHARATA NATYAM

Dance lovers may be proud of the fact that Bharata Natya which was threatened with death or oblivion under a cloud of social prejudice till 35 years ago, has now become immensely popular not only in its home country but also all over the rest of the world. It is due not merely to the propaganda carried on by the earliest cultured pioneers for its revival but also to its own intrinsic worth, vitality and beauty. Historically it had been the most common national and classical dance art of India whose principles and technique had been systematised and codified about 1800 years ago in Bharata's *Natya Sastra* and this ancient treatise has been followed by most writers in later centuries. Copious references to similar principles and technique are to be found in the great Tamil classic *Silappadikaram* of the 2nd century A.D. also.

Though repertoire and modes of presentation might have changed from time to time and from region to region, the basic principles and technique of the art have remained the same to the present day. Hence this 2000-year old art is still as fresh and fascinating as it must have been ages ago. Embodying as it does the wisdom and art experience of ages there is nothing old or new in it. In short it seems to be an art for eternity. No wonder it commands the admiration and reverence of all knowing people both in the East and in the West. On close scrutiny it may be found that Bharata Natya had been the mother art for most of the other classical dance systems of India. It has also been the main source of inspiration for the allied arts of sculpture, painting and icon-making. Though it has been best preserved and developed with system and purity in Tamil Nad, it cannot be dismissed as a mere regional art of a Southern State.

It is rather strange that notwithstanding all its greatness and popularity there are few books in India to explain to the present day dance lovers which is which in Bharata Natya. It is true that everything in art and particularly in dance cannot be fully explained in words. Many things have to be observed, learnt and enjoyed. But books dealing with the principles, basic technique and essential features of any art including Bharata Natya are as much a necessity as learning the technique under masters of authentic traditions. Most of the ancient treatises are in Sanskrit and a few only in one or two regional languages. A few foreign lovers of the art have attempted to give out in their books what impressions they could form in their hurried tours and study in this country about Bharata Natya and other classical dances. Valuable as these are there is still need for Indians to bring out books dealing with the precious heritage of the country in the dance art, as they can be expected to understand the spirit of their own country's tradition better than others. There is also a demand for such books in easily understandable language in India and elsewhere.

Srimathi Enakshi Bhavnani's book dealing not only with the classical but also the folk dances of India has come in time to fulfil this need. In the chapter on Bharata Natya, the authoress has brought out the main features of the art and important points of its technique too and as such I trust that it will be found useful and interesting not only to art lovers in general but also to artistes in the field. I am glad that she has realised also that Bharata Natya is not confined to nor exhausted by the solo lyrical dance of the Devadasi type but has other forms too like the Bhagavata Mela Dance-drama, the Kuravanji ballet and the Navasandhi ritual dances which are still extant. Besides these there had been still other forms which had died out. Mrs. Enakshi Bhavnani, the authoress, is a highly cultured lady who had trained herself in the chief systems of Indian Classical dance and had been on the stage as a dancer of repute and who had travelled also widely in the country and abroad. She is also a writer of note on art and culture. Coming as the book does from such an artiste and writer, it is bound to be of value to all concerned with art and culture. I only hope that books of this kind will bring about better understanding about the various dance systems in India and their kinship to one another and thereby pave the way for cultural integration of the country as a whole. Anyway I congratulate Srimathi Enakshi Bhavnani for her bold and useful venture in the shape of this book.

—E. KRISHNA IYER

KATHAK

The Classical Dance in India is an art that originated more than 2000 years ago, and it has come down through the ages in various forms and styles. This ancient art which fulfils all the rules of a codified technique with a powerful dramatic content as detailed in the Sanskrit treatise the *Natya Sastra* by Bharata Muni, has survived because of its enduring philosophic basis.

In North India, the Classical dance found its fullest interpretation through the Kathak school. Great devotees of the art, deeply versed in the scriptures, and inspired by the Bhakta Cult of giving expression to their love of God through song and dance, like the great masters Bindadin Maharaj and his brother Kalka Prasad Maharaj have been responsible for the preservation of this ancient art and for giving to it much of its lyrical character and brilliant technique respectively. As a direct descendant of this illustrious family, and where my father, sisters and brothers also dedicated their lives to Kathak, I have not only been nurtured in its best traditions since my earliest years, but it became a vital part of my life. For me therefore, the dance is essentially a form of expression which fulfils a deep inner urge.

We in India have a rich heritage in our culture, language, dress and art, which have a fundamental national character. And in our dance, springing as it does from the ancient source the *Natya Sastra*, it has a purposeful affinity one to the other in its many regional forms. In Kathak, we have a dance style that is both skilled and dramatic. In its highly technical aspect, the training has to be rigorous and disciplined in order to master its subtle execution of the Amad, Tukras, Paran and the Chakkardar Paran, with the precision of footwork, many rapid turns, and the perfect exposition of the patterned rhythms with their many varieties of Bol. In its emotional expression, Kathak possesses a fund of subjects and lyrics gleaned from sacred legend and mythology, in the shape of the devotional Dhrupads, Kirtans, Tumri, Ghazals, Gat Bhavas and so on. Much has been written about the dance of India, but with the great renaissance of the arts since Independence, a rediscovery of the dance in its various regional styles has taken place, and everyday more and more research has revealed many hidden treasures of its manifold modes. In writing this comprehensive book on the Indian dance, Enakshi Bhavnani, a devotee of the dance and one of the early non-professional pioneers, is making a notable contribution. In her chapter on Kathak, she has made every effort to emphasise the important aspects and character of this school, so that its special attributes, excellence, manner of performance and affinity to the sister classical schools of the dance are highlighted. She was student of my revered father the late Sukhdeve Maharaj, one of the foremost authorities on Kathak. His deep research and his vast number of original compositions of Tukras, Bhava Parans, Bol and Shabda have added illumination to the school. And it was due to his inspiring guidance and training primarily that I have been able to master this art and win acclaim for it in India and abroad.

—SITARA DEVI

KATHAKALI

The Art of Kathakali, which is indigenous to Kerala, is unique in many respects. It is aptly described as a Drisya Kavya, comprising as it does, a highly specialised dance form that has come to be looked upon as a marvel of perfection in Indian art.

For themes Kathakali draws upon the inexhaustible treasure-trove of the ancient Puranas chronicling the lives, loves and conflicts of the gods and supermen of Indian mythology. For actors and actresses it draws upon the common peasantry of the land, the villager who loves, for one whole night during the dusk-to-dawn performance, to transform himself into malignant demon or benign god, bloodthirsty ogre or dutiful heroine, highlighting, in each case, the emotion characteristic of the role.

And all this achieved with the most meagre "property" and stage effects. The courtyard of a temple or family mansion provides an open air theatre. A patchwork quilt held up by a pair of attendants serves as curtain. A wooden tripod improvises as a throne or seat of honour. And, most important of all is a huge brass oil lamp, the quivering wick flame of which accentuates every shade of expression on the brightly painted face of the actor.

To the accompaniment of the Chenda and the Madalam (typical drums of Kerala), the Chengala (gong) and the Elathalam (cymbals), a pair of musicians sing the theme songs while the actors, mute of word but eloquent of expression, recreate the epic and bring to life a dream world of sheer fantasy. The Kathakali songs, couched in rich poetic diction, are among the gems of Malayalam literature.

Structurally it is based on *Natya Sastra* with added embellishments derived from *Hastalakshana Deepika* and *Abhinaya Darpana*. It presents in a unique manner both the Tandava and Lasya style of dancing. The three fundamentals of Indian dancing laid down in *Natya Sastra*, viz., Nritta, Nritya and Natya, form the basis of Kathakali, as of other forms of dancing in India. Abhinaya (Bhavaprakatana) may be said to be the backbone of Kathakali, and its four varieties, viz., Angikabhinaya, Vachikabhinaya, Aharyabhinaya and Satvikabhinaya are utilised in a remarkable manner to bring out various emotions through the media of gesture or Mudras. In fact these Mudras form "the alphabets," so to speak, of "the language of gestures" employed in such a telling manner in Kathakali.

I am glad that this comprehensive book on The Indian Dance is being written by Enakshi Bhavnani and that in this book Kathakali, the ancient Classical Dance Dramas of Kerala, will find their proper place of importance along with the various other schools of Classical Dance in India. Enakshi Bhavnani has been a devotee of the Dance for many years, and I hope that through this book her deep and earnest desire to see the Classical Dance in its various forms take equal place in our National heritage, will be realised in some measure.

—GOPINATH

ODISSI

Odissi dance which has become so popular in recent years in our country and abroad marks the revival of an old and ancient system of dancing in India which unfortunately could not attain its legitimate place in the field of arts under foreign rule as well as for lack of publicity. The recent recognition that Odissi is another form of classical dances in India fulfils a long felt want. The freedom of India has, no doubt, led to the noble efforts for the revival of our ancient arts and literature both officially and non-officially. It is gratifying to find that artistes and exponents of dance art outside Orissa have been evincing comparatively greater interest in the Odissi dance than those inside Orissa itself. Mrs. Bhavnani's attempt to include a chapter dealing with Odissi dance therefore is quite refreshing to us.

Orissa has been the meeting ground of culture from north and south since ages. The seat of Jagannath on the east coast at Puri has been the symbol of a synthesis of all that is good in every religion or culture. No wonder therefore the dance art of this part of the country should have in it the reflection of these cultures. Quite a good deal of research on the subject needs to be undertaken for a better picture of the system of Odissi dance and a proper form of its performance. Efforts made by Mrs. Bhavnani in her chapter I am sure will go a long way in enthusing other students of this difficult and yet fascinating subject to probe deeper to discover a correct form of this school of dancing so that with years to come, Odissi dance will prove more popular among the art lovers here and elsewhere and benefit the country as a whole.

—KABICHANDRA KALICHARAN PATNAIK
NATYACHARYA

KUCHIPUDI

The recent excavations conducted by the Archaeological Department of Government of India in Andhra Pradesh, reveal rich traditions in the art of dance since the times of the Satavahana Emperors of the Second Century B.C. The sculptures reveal that there were two main schools of dance (1) Devadasi, (2) Kelika, existing under the patronage of Temples and Rulers of the country. It is said that there were three hundred families of Devadasis at Srikakulam, the original Capital of the Satavahana Empire. At Ghantasala, before the onset of the influence of Buddhism, an exclusive street existed consisting of the families of Devadasis and Kelikas. Influenced by the above traditions, Jayapasenani, a commander of the Kakathiya Elephant forces, wrote a treatise on Desi and Margi traditions of dance styles in the 13th century. He originally belonged to Divi Taluk.

All the above places are situated within a radius of 6 miles from Kuchipudi in

the Krishna District. After the fall of the Kakathiya Empire, there was a dark
period for this art in these parts. Later on a great Vaishnava religious leader
Narahari Tirtha came from the Kalinga Royal Court to Srikakulam as regent
of the minor prince and was responsible for the propagation of the Bhagavata cult.
Under this cult Gita Govinda was sung and dances were set to the tunes by the
Brahmin Gurus of Devadasi families. Thus, the Krishna cult was responsible for
the evolution of dance drama (Bhagavata Mela) in Andhra during the 13th Century. One of Narahari Tirtha's disciples or grand disciples, Siddhendra Yogi was
responsible for initiating the Brahmin families of Kuchipudi in the dance drama
of Bhagavata Melas. Till then, the Gurus of these Devadasis were Brahmin scholars who were experts in Bharata Natya, but they did not take to dancing themselves. We are of opinion that Sri Siddhendra Yogi laid the foundation of the
village of Kuchipudi which might have been originally called KUSEELAVAPURI,
which means residence of travelling dancing parties. He commanded the families
to take to the Bhagavata school of dancing and devote themselves to this art.
As a mark of initiation of every child, even today, a small bell is tied round the
waist of every new born child. He further said that no woman shall be allowed
to take part in Bhagavata Melas. He himself composed Bhama Kalapam, a dance
drama which represents the longing of the soul for union with the Infinite.

Kuchipudi Bhagavata Melas were popular all over Andhra. The Vizianagara
Emperor invited the party to his Court. The Golkonda Nawabs granted them
Inam.

The Kuchipudi dancing troupes are called Bhagavata Melas, as the theme of
their performances was taken from the Maha Bhagavatam. *Natya Sastra* mentions
three types of dances, (1) Nritta (pure dance without Rasa but only rhythmic
movement),   (2) Nritya (dancing with a theme full of Rasa, combined with music),
(3) Natya (dancing and Abhinaya adapted in a drama with full Rasa, Bhava and a
suitable theme). All the three styles are adapted in Kuchipudi dance drama. The
Jatis represent the Nritta portion, Sabdams represent the Nritya portion while the
conversational Daravus represent the Natya portion. Thus we feel that the Kuchipudi style is a full fledged dance form. The richness of the style of music, sentimental
display and sway over the audience are the special features of the Kuchipudi style.
In addition, to the Angika, Vachika, and Aharya modes of acting in a drama, the
Sathwika is predominant. There is a place for Lasya and Thandva. There is place
for (detailed gesture) Sukshma Abhinaya and (undetailed gesture) Sthulabhinaya.
There is place for Lokadharmi as well as Natyadharmi (realistic and conventional
acting). This art has been handed down from generation to generation in its traditional form with suitable modifications according to varying requirements. The
great Gurus (1) Vedantam Sambaiah, (2) Vedantam Lakshminarayana Sastri,
(3) Vempati Venkata Narayana, (4) Chinta Venkataramaiah, were responsible
for keeping the torch of this art alive. The present Guru Chinta Krishnamurthi
(one of us) is the son of the late Chinta Venkataramaiah.

A note of warning has to be given. Spurious styles are often propagated as
Kuchipudi styles. This is a dangerous symptom even as all spurious foods are
dangerous to the health of humanity. The soul should not be corrupted. At the
same time we owe our indebtedness to recent exponents of this art who have
created an audience for this rich tradition. A school exists at Kuchipudi near
Vijayawada where genuine Kuchipudi art is imparted to students without taking
any remuneration. Sri Siddhendra Kala Kshetram is the name of this Institution

where modern residential facilities exist for students coming from all over India.

We thank Mrs. Enakshi Bhavnani for having taken great pains to collect information for this chapter and for publishing this book. We are highly indebted to her for having given us an opportunity to write these few lines of introduction to her chapter on the Kuchipudi style.

—NATYACHARYA SRI BANDA
KANAKA LINGESWARA RAO, AND
BHARATACHARYA SRI CHINTA
KRISHNAMURTHI BHAGAVATULU

MANIPURI

Even before the advent of India's independence, the political movement of this country promoted a desire for a cultural renaissance. The need to re-generate the cultural forces of India was nursed by Gurudev Rabindranath Tagore who rediscovered the soul of India through the Fine Arts. Sensitive souls of pioneer dancers like Uday Shankar, Rukmini Devi, Madame Menaka and Enakshi Bhavnani adequately responded to this urge of cultural re-generation.

I not only cherish the spirited devotion of these sensitive souls, but their efforts and contributions in the field of dancing continue to inspire me in my work in the field of Manipuri Dancing.

Manipur, the land of beauty since antiquity has evolved a pattern of living in which it is almost impossible to distinguish art from life. To imbibe the very spirit of Manipuri Dancing, I frequently visit Manipur. I found it extremely difficult to distinguish the art performance from the religious ceremony as these two are magnificently intermingled.

For the purpose of creating aesthetic expressions of dance and music utilised for religious ceremonies, Manipuris not only strictly observe the rules and regulations determined by the religious code, but are also conscious of the need to cultivate highest artistic talent and sensibility.

Music and Dance are the symbols of Manipuris' social instinct to share the pleasure and pain which inspire solidarity between man and man. In Manipur the magic of dance and music and the mystery of religion contribute towards the satisfaction of the spiritual aspiration of man.

I am conscious of the problems, the difficulties and the responsibilities of a dancer, particularly of a traditional dancer. I believe that tradition should not mean mere repetition but a significant creative transformation in terms of modern concepts. New dance compositions must be continuously evolved to suit the numerous demands of the modern stage, without polluting the form and spirit of the traditional dance. All artistic expressions must have their roots in the tradition, however the artist must be alive to create newer interpretations and experiments to justify his or her individual genius.

The process of art is complete only when its communication is achieved. Art being both self-expression and communication, a two-way traffic, is equally dependent on the critical and cultivated audiences. It is here that the critic, the scholar and the writer help the artist in creating such an audience by continuously interpreting and evaluating various experiments in the field of different art forms.

Smt. Enakshi Bhavnani was herself a dancer of merit. She has been associated with this field of Indian Dancing for over three decades. She is one of the few artists extensively travelled not only in India but throughout the world. Her understanding of the subtleties, complexities and intricacies of each dance style and its varied forms is worthwhile sharing. It is needless to add that any comment expressed by such a writer on any dance style of India is more than welcome. Her chapters on Manipuri Dancing not only reveal her technical knowledge but aslo a keen aesthetic experience. I am confident that they will stimulate genuine interest and admiration for the art of Manipuri Dancing.

I consider it a great personal privilege and honour to have been asked to write a Preface to Manipuri Dancing by Smt. Enakshi Bhavnani. Let me take this opportunity to express my gratitude for her kind and continued interest and warm enthusiasm for my dance activities.

—Nayana Jhaveri

TRIBAL DANCES

I have been watching and, when younger, participating in tribal dances for over thirty years, and I have visited very remote places, where nothing was official or "laid on," to do so. I have thus witnessed many of the dances which Mrs. Bhavnani has described with so much charm and insight.

My observations and hers do not always coincide but that is inevitable. For tribal India today is in a ferment. Things vary from place to place and change from year to year. In 1939 I published my first large book on the tribes, *The Baiga*; if I were to write it again now it would be almost unrecognisable. Though the general pattern of the dance often persists, details vary greatly: even in the great Bison-Horn Maria Dance there is much more variety in the steps and rhythm than is generally supposed. It is twenty years since I wrote about the Muria dances and in Mrs. Bhavnani's account there are a number of differences, and yet I am sure that we both are right. It is simply that we have watched dances in different places and at different times.

Although it is common to speak of the "colourful" and "artistic" tribal people, the great majority of them, except when they are dressed up for a folk-dance festival, are not actually colourful—they are too poor to be that—and they are not exceptionally artistic. Many of the pretty things they use are in fact made for them by Hindu craftsmen. Lack of encouragement and difficulty in obtaining raw materials or implements have meant that tribal art has always had to struggle very hard, and with the advance of "civilization" and cheap bazaar products flooding the villages there is a constant temptation to buy something in a shop instead of making it oneself.

The raw materials of tribal creativeness is found in the people's own often very beautiful bodies. Their finest efforts are devoted to decorating themselves and they use their own bodies too to express what they have to say in rhythmic movement. For the tribal people the dance is not an optional luxury : it is a way of life, a source of life. Rhythm and poetry means everything to them. "The tribe that dances does not die." There have indeed been attempts, mainly arising from the sophisticated among the people themselves, to stop dancing on the grounds that it is not respectable, and the life of their villages becomes dull and drab as a result. Happily, the great Folk-Dance Festivals in Delhi and elsewhere have done much to remove the idea that there is something derogatory, something rather low class about dancing and I think we may look forward to a still greater revival of this wonderful art than we have seen already. Books like Mrs. Bhavnani's are not only of academic interest but can have a very practical application in raising the credit of dancers and artists and stimulating them to do more. I am particularly happy that she has not put her tribal dances in a separate book but has integrated them with those of the rest of India.

—VERRIER ELWIN

Contents

Illustrations

LINE DRAWINGS IN THE TEXT

1. Introductory

NATURE HAS inspired man to the noblest ideals and caused him to deify and worship its forces since the earliest recollections of history. In India, the "Revealed Wisdom" of the Hindus, considered the oldest written work known in Sanskrit, placed about 1500 B.C., and consisting of the four *Vedas*, are full of such instances. We find in them that the Rudras (thunder and lightning, the Rudras being the Storm Deities and companions of Indra, Lord of the Firmament), Agni (Fire), Vayu and Varuna (the Wind and Waters), the Sun (Mitra) and the Moon (Soma), are deified into splendid celestial Beings. In many of the beautiful poetic hymns of the oldest *Veda*, the *Rig Veda*, sentiments are expressed showing man's deepest inner response to the glory and wonder of Nature. The roseate hues of early dawn (Usha), the resplendent Sun (known by many names such as Mitra, Twashtri, Pushan and Bhaga) riding across the majestic canopy of the heavens, the Lord of the Firmament (Indra) and the Waters (Varuna) giving nourishment to the earth, are examples. These God-like Immortals gave succour to their devotees from their high dwellings, yet they were like idealised men, tangible to the minds and hearts of those who worshipped them. They were Gods who were noble and all-powerful, and at the same time, they took delight in aesthetic pastimes and were capable of experiencing love, tenderness, anger, rage and the whole gamut of human emotions.

As Sanskrit literature developed, this spirit of Nature worship in all its wonder and mystery remained ever strong. God's hand was in everything, and He became identified with the whole Universe. We read that Heaven has its eternal song of birds; delicious cool winds and crystal springs; forest glades and flower-filled trees and bushes amidst which the bees murmur gently. On the glowing bosom of the lakes, everlasting blue lotuses and water-lilies bloom ceaselessly. Indra, Vedic Lord of Heaven, lives in a paradise that is the acme of peace and happiness, where celestial nymphs called Apsaras dance with ethereal grace, and the divine

1

musicians, the Gandharvas, accompany them with ecstatic music.

Steeped in this heritage, where the mind sought inspiration constantly from Nature, it is no wonder that all Indian thought and art, which is the outcome of man's creative expression, became saturated with the same ideals. "Indian art keeps always in close contact with Nature in all her moods. The sun at its rising, zenith and going-down calls the devout to prayer and meditation and to bring fresh flowers, Nature's own gifts of beauty, to the Creator's Shrine. The beauty of flowers and trees speaks to them in its own intimate language of the Divine Creator's Love." "They regard natural things reverently as symbols of Divine Majesty forming together one great temple of God." "The lotus symbol like all other Indian symbols, had a metaphysical, or subjective, as well as an objective significance. Rooted deep in the mud of a lake or river and pushing its way gradually upwards through the water until its fair flower blossomed in the light of Heaven, the lotus or water-lily was Nature's own symbol of the spiritual process by which the human mind won liberation in Nirvana."[1]

Indian art in all its forms therefore possessed this underlying spirit of understanding of God through the beauties of His natural creation, and became the medium whereby the outward expression connoted a deeply spiritual urge. Taking a glimpse into the distant past, we discover that the history of the dance as an expression of emotion natural to man is almost as old as the history of man himself. Primitive people danced in the forests in simple imitation of Nature as they found it, and laid the basis of great and enduring expressive arts throughout the five continents.

Springing from this common primeval urge for self-expression, before the dawn of civilization began to shape art's differing systems, the Indian dance survives today as one of the world's most fascinating and complex forms. Interpreting the philosophical ideals, myths and legends that grew out of the early Nature worship, it is unique in more senses than one. For it is a Science, an Art and an Exposition at the same time.

Turning to our ancient sacred books the *Vedas*, we find the Hindu dance referred to repeatedly in the *Rig Veda* and often in two of the other *Vedas*, the *Yajur Veda* and the *Atharva Veda*. It nearly always figured in ritual and sacred ceremony. Girls danced round the sacred fire during the purification ceremony and when making a request for rain. At the ancient Aryan ceremony of the horse sacrifice, a ritualistic dance with patterned stepping and accompanied by sacred song was performed by young girls. A sort of ecstasy pervaded this art accompanied as it was by sacred lyrics, more often than not addressed to the great Nature deities.

As we come up through the years, to about 2000 years ago, we have the famous *Natya Sastra* or Science of Dramaturgy (generally placed between the 4th and 1st centuries B.C.). The author, Bharata Muni, has given in this great work, not only a complete repository of theatre craft, its architecture and stage dimensions, but a comprehensive technique of the Hindu dance. Bharata Muni claims a divine origin for the dance. According to him, the God Brahma, Supreme Creator and First of the Hindu Trinity, was the Creator of *Natya* or drama in India.

Indra, Vedic Lord of Heaven, appealed to Brahma to create a pastime worthy of the Gods. Brahma took something precious from each of the *Vedas* and composed the Hindu dramatic art. He took the exquisite lyrical matter called

---

[1] E. B. Havell, *Himalayas in Indian Art*

Paathya from the *Rig Veda* (the *Rig Veda's* hymns extol the grandeur of Nature and its power; and prayers are addressed to Nature's splendour and glory); the expression of gestures from the *Yajur Veda* (the *Yajur Veda* contains Vedic prescribed rituals furnished for reading at sacrificial services); the music from the *Sama Veda* (the *Sama Veda* concentrates on beautiful chants taken from the *Rig Veda* passages); and the aesthetic flavour (*Rasa*) and emotional content from the *Atharva Veda* (in the *Atharva Veda* there is reference to the mystic and mystical aspects of Nature), and He compounded the art of *Natya* or Drama. He named His creation the *Natya Veda*, making it the fifth *Veda*, and endowing it with all the sanctity and dignity attached to the four other *Vedas*. The first drama created by Brahma was said to be *Amrita Manthana*, in which He introduced beautiful dance sequences; and this splendid work He revealed to Bharata Muni.

Vishwakarma, the supreme architect of Heaven, then created a splendid theatre in the hall of Indra's Court for its performance. Having trained his sons and disciples in the various aspects of the drama, in the part that best fitted each of them, Bharata Muni discovered that certain attributes of the dance sequences could only be expounded by women. So he approached Brahma for help, and it is said that the great God overcame the difficulty by creating the celestial nymphs or Apsaras, with divinely feminine grace to perform these delicate aspects of the dance. Thus came into existence the two types of dance, namely, the tender, softly graceful or *Lasya* type for women, and the manly, forceful or *Tandava* type for men.

The drama with its beautiful dance sequences was performed for the first time in the Court of Indra at the ceremony of the worship of the Flagstaff of Heaven at the Indra Dhavaja Festival. When Shiva, the Third of the Hindu Trinity, Creator of Good and Destroyer of Evil, the Origin of Cosmic Movement and Rhythm, Lord of the Dance, saw the special performance which was enacted before Him in the great open amphitheatre of the Himalayas, He was so stirred by it and particularly by the beautiful dance sequences, that He had Bharata Muni further instructed in the art of the dance by His disciple Tandu. Thus Bharata Muni came to learn the basic foundations of the dance comprising the 108 *Karanas*, the 32 *Angaharas*, the 4 *Rechakas* and the various *Pindibhandas*. All this basic dance technique has been described by Bharata Muni in the *Tandava Lakshana* which forms the fourth chapter of his great treatise on Dramaturgy the *Natya Sastra*. In the course of time, Bharata Muni passed this revealed art on to the mortals on earth. Thus one of the most scientifically conceived arts of the world, interpreting a rich and deep philosophy, came to be established with all its refinements, and accoutrements, costume, song and musical accompaniment.

Certainly Bharata Muni's claim of giving the Hindu dance a divine origin will remain amongst our most cherished legends; but at the same time, we must admit that this comprehensive and incomparable treatise on drama, music, dancing and the allied arts, written more than 2000 years ago, justly deserves the reverence with which it is regarded and the sanction it carries for being the work of a profound and great mind—a mind that must have delved deep into the mysteries of knowledge that comes with yogic meditation and contemplation. Indeed, in giving to the world this terpsichorean art so closely associated with the concepts of Hindu philosophy, Bharata Muni has undoubtedly retained in it his inner visions of the beauty, perfect rhythm and noble attributes of the symbolic and divine dances of the Gods.

2. Dances of the Gods

ALL THROUGH the ages and at all times, dancing has been an expression natural to man, and he has utilized this medium to give vent to and to symbolise his inner feelings of joy, sorrow, anger, elation and trance-like bliss as well as his aesthetic emotions. Dance thus became one of the most cogent modes through which an emotion or idea was conveyed by the performer and received by the beholder.

In India, the spiritual trend in both music and dance has all along been present since time immemorial. We find that saintly men (the Bhagavatars, devotees of God), in their unbounded love for the Almighty, sought to gain salvation (*Moksha*) and become one with God, the Infinite and Universal Spirit, through music and dance. Their devotional religious songs were known as *Kirtanas* and though these had their regional flavour and form in various parts of the country, their ennobling and soul-stirring spirit became national.

Great names like Krishna Chaitanya, Purandaradasa, Narayana Tirtha, Bhadrachalam and Ramadasa are known and honoured everywhere in India. *Slokas* (sacred hymns) were also chanted in beautiful *Raga* melodies in praise of God and His multifarious revelations, and benedictory and invocatory hallelujahs were composed, such as are found in the *Astapadis* of Jayadeva's immortal *Git Govinda* (Song Celestial), the *Tarangas* of Narayana Tirtha, and the inspiring devotional compositions of Mira Bai, Gopal Krishna Bharati, Tukaram, Tulsidas and Kabir, to name a few.

Later, in the 19th century, one of the greatest Bhagavatars, Tyagaraja, enriched and added to these past compositions and took them to the people at large. Then, some Bhagavatars felt the need for action with song in their rapturous approach of utter devotion to God and they danced as they sang. The Bhagavata Mela Natakam formed by a group of Brahmin Bhagavatars in their great desire to save the dance when the art began to fall from its high ideals, were of this school. They performed dance dramas, emphasising their religious and philosophical aspects and basing their themes on the stories of the sacred book the *Bhagavata*. Venkatarama Sastri of Melatur, Tanjore District, Madras State, and Siddhendra Yogi of Kuchipudi, Andhra Pradesh, composed such dance dramas.

4

Plate 1

1   2

South Indian bronzes. Dance of Shiva as Nataraja. (1) From Tiruvagalam, early Chola period, 10th century A.D. (2) Chola period, 12th century A.D. (Courtesy, National Museum, New Delhi.)

Plate 2

1

2

3

4

Temple sculptures. Four different powerful dance postures of
Shiva, from the Hoysala temple, Halebid. 12th century A.D.
(Copyright, Department of Archaeology, Government of India.)

Plate 3

1

2

Sculptures from cave temples. (1) Temptation Scene, from Ajanta, Cave No. 26, 7th century A.D. (2) A dance panel, from Bharhut, 2nd century B.C. (3) Panel of dancer with musicians, from Cave No. 7, Aurangabad, 7th century A.D. (Copyright, Department of Archaeology, Government of India.)

3

Plate 4

1

2

3

Temple sculptures. (1) Shiva dancing on an elephant skin, from the Hoysala temple, Halebid, 12th century A.D. (2) Dance of Shiva as Bhairava, from Belur, 12th century A.D (3) Dance of Durga in the Mahisasuramardini theme, from the Surya temple, Chidambaram, 13th century A.D. (Copyright, Department of Archaeology, Government of India.)

One of the most famous themes from the *Bhagavata* being the immortal Gopika-Lila, with its enduring central idea of the Ras Lila dance of Krishna and Radha and the Gopis, expressing symbolically the idea of the *Nayaka-Nayaki Bhava*, the yearning of the individual soul and millions of souls to become one with the Universal Soul or the Infinite. Thus propounding the great truth that God manifests Himself in all beings and the whole Universe. The Bhagavatar (devotee of God), while singing and dancing, felt himself transcend the ego and merge completely with God and realise an inner Bliss. This identification with the Infinite, no matter how brief, was the same as realising God, for God was identified according to the Hindu precepts with the whole Universe, being the One Source, One Essence, One Goal, from which all else springs. In other words, the Bhagavatar experienced "True Reality" or "True Knowledge" (*Vidhya*) as opposed to "Ignorance" (*Avidhya*), caused by being blinded by the transient world of Illusion (*Maya*) in which we live and see around us. His ego thus chastened and ennobled by his moments of ecstasy and bliss, returned to thirst ever after for eternal identification with God. The great Bhagavatars thus used the arts of music and dance for their approach to God.

With art and religious thought seeking the same end, the Hindu allegorical concept of the divine aspects of the dance really represent the manifold activities of God; picturesque parable-modes used by Hindu thinkers to direct mortals on the path of renunciation of the ego and gain true knowledge and salvation. This is the symbolic interpretation of the divine dances of the Gods. The outward forms of many arms, great power, divine and calm radiance, are but symbols of God's Omnipotence, Omnipresence, Omniscience and All-Mercifulness. One who is All-powerful, present in all places at the same time, who can reveal Himself in everything and knowing all things, and possessing unbounded Love.

According to our mythology, the Supreme Lord of the Dance is Shiva, Third of the Hindu Trinity. Brahma is the Creator and the First of the Triad. Vishnu, the Merciful Aspect and Preserver of Mankind, is the Second. Shiva represents that aspect of God who creates good (true knowledge) and destroys evil (ignorance). He is the Source of Cosmic Harmony and Rhythm, and there are three aspects of His dances:

1. The Destructive. 2. The Yogic. 3. The Gift-giving. All these aspects of His dances represent symbolically the manifestation of "primeval rhythmic energy," and the release from the illusions of the ego.

FIRST ASPECT OF SHIVA'S DANCE. This is the *Tandava Tamasic* aspect as Bhairava, when He dances His awe-inspiring dance on the burning grounds. He is ten-armed, denoting great power, celestial and miraculous. Shiva dances as the Destroyer, who destroys the chains that hold each soul to the fleeting world of Illusion. The burning ground or crematorium is symbolic of the hearts of men (His followers), cleansed by fire of the ego, and signifying the state where there is the burning away of all illusions and deeds. Freed of the ego and unhindered, the Soul gains eternal Liberation.

SECOND ASPECT OF SHIVA'S DANCE. This is the Lord's Divine Yogic Evening Dance performed on Mount Kailasha (Mount Golden), the Himalayan Hermitage of the Lord. He is two-armed, and His dance is one of calm and beauty, when the sun is setting and there is a magical contemplative stillness resting like a mantle on the world. It is described as follows in the *Shiva Pradosha Stotra*:

"Placing the Mother of the Three Worlds upon a golden throne, studded with precious gems, Shulapani dances on the heights of Kailasa, and all the gods gather round Him.

"Sarasvati plays on the *Vina*, Indra on the flute, Brahma holds the time-marking cymbals, Lakshmi begins a song, Vishnu plays on a drum, and all the gods stand round about.

"Gandharvas, Yakshas, Patagas, Uragas, Siddhas, Sadhyas, Vidyadharas, Amaras, Apsaras, and all the beings dwelling in the three worlds assemble there to witness the celestial dance and hear the music of the divine choir at the hour of twilight."[1]

Shiva dances with divine almost expressionless face, calling to His followers to worship Him with peace in their hearts. At His feet, there are no wordly ambitions, sorrow or argument; no fear nor destruction; no pride nor mockery; only peace and the beauty of contemplation. The mind of man drinks deep of the essence of Yogic self-forgetfulness and is cleansed and purified not by force or destruction, but by the renunciation of the ego. Here is Shiva's noble, grace-giving dance signifying the granting of spiritual Bliss to those who seek to realise Him, known as the *Sandhya Nrtya* Dance.

THIRD ASPECT OF SHIVA'S DANCE. The gift-giving. According to the Patanjali myth of the *Yoga Sutra*, as related in the *Koyil Puranam*, it is said that one day, Vishnu went to Mount Kailasha in the Himalayas to visit Shiva. The great God Shiva told Vishnu that a group of heretic rishis (sages), living in the forest of Taragam, refused to recognise the existence of God. He was therefore going there to convert them. Shiva, disguised as a mendicant, Vishnu as His wife, and accompanied by the great Serpent Ati Sesha, on whom the world is said to rest, they came to the forest. Suspecting some danger, the rishis created a sacrificial fire to destroy the intruders. A fierce tiger emerged from the fire and rushed at Shiva, who caught it, tore off its skin and wore it as a mantle. The rishis continued their sacrifice and rituals, and there came out a huge serpent which Shiva seized and coiled around His neck as an ornament. Then Lord Shiva began His Mystic Dance. Undismayed by the futility of their attempts, the rishis continued their incantations, which brought into existence the black dwarf Muyalagam. Shiva crushed the vile creature under His Sacred Foot, and keeping it writhing on the ground, continued His dance, which was witnessed by all the Gods. The heretic rishis, overcome with awe, acknowledged Shiva as their Lord, and became His fervent devotees. Then Ati Sesha worshipped Shiva and prayed above all things for the gift of once again seeing this Mystic Dance. Lord Shiva promised that he would see the dance again in Sacred Tillai—the Centre of the Universe, signifying the heart of Man.

This is the Mystic Cosmic Dance of Shiva known as the Nadanta dance of the Nataraja, danced before the golden assembly in the Golden Hall of Chidambaram or Tillai, the Centre of the Universe. Here, Shiva is dancing with four hands. One right hand sounds the drum (sound representing the primal creative force and the intervals of the beat in the time process); the other right hand in the pose of *Abhaya Hasta*, giving protection to His devotees; one left hand holds the Sacred Flame, which represents the Fire of Sacrifice; and the other left hand is in the *Danda*

[1] Ananda Coomaraswamy, *The Dance of Shiva and Fourteen Other Essays*

Hasta pose, stretched across the body and pointing to the upraised foot, signifying blissful refuge to those who seek His Love and Grace. The right foot tramples down the dwarf Muyalagam, signifying the stamping down of evil; the left foot raised in the *Kancita Pader*, showing that He showers Grace on all who seek it.

A beatific expression on His face, His eyes smiling radiantly, and emanating love and mercy bountiful, He spreads His Glory over the entire world, graciously granting release to the countless souls that seek Him. To the imagination, Shiva in the dance of the Nataraja is a most glorious vision. "In His hair may be seen a wreathing cobra, a skull, and a mermaid figure of Ganga; upon it rests the crescent moon, and it is crowned with a wreath of Cassia leaves. In His right ear He wears a man's earring, a woman's in the left; He is adorned with necklaces and armlets, a jewelled belt, anklets, bracelets, finger and toe-rings......and He wears also a fluttering scarf and a sacred thread."[1]

"Shiva in this dance is the dual personality of God and Goddess, the gentle gracious entity with the powerful nobleness. He is the Source of all life and movement with His divine flaming arch that vibrates during His dance. Through His dance He will destroy all evil, freeing the souls of mankind from the illusions that keep him tied to the earth."[2]

"This dance has a dual significance. On the one hand it represents the material processes of Nature; on the other, the subjective spiritual processes by which worldly passions, evil thinking and wickedness are destroyed or transmuted in the alembic of the Divine Alchemist."

"In the night of Brahma, Nature is inert and cannot dance till Shiva wills it. He rises from His rapture, and dancing sends through inert matter, pulsing waves of awakening sound, and lo! matter also dances appearing as a glory around Him. Dancing, He sustains its manifold phenomenon. In the fullness of time, still dancing, He destroys all forms and names by fire and gives a new rest. This is poetry but none the less science."[3]

A glance at some of the beautiful prayers said in the South Indian Shiva temples, will illustrate the beauty of faith and love of God. "Oh Lord of the Dance, who calls by beat of drum all those who are absorbed in worldly things, and dispels the fear of the humble and comforts them with His love Divine: who points with His uplifted Lotus foot as the refuge of Salvation; who carries the fire of sacrifice and dances in the Hall of the Universe, do Thou protect us!"

And again, "Oh my Lord, Thy hand holding the sacred drum hath made and ordered the heavens and earth and other worlds and souls innumerable. Thy uplifted hand protects the multifarious animate and inanimate extended universe. Thy sacred foot, planted on the ground, gives abode to the tired soul struggling in the toils of Karma. It is Thy uplifted foot that grants eternal bliss to those that approach Thee. These Five Actions are indeed Thy handiwork."[4]

The great Gods have their twin aspects in Hindu mythology, their active principle or energy being considered feminine and symbolically called the Consort (*Shakti*). . The consort of Shiva takes many forms and represents many diverse qualities. Well known among her names are Sati, Uma, Parvathi, Meenakshi, Durga and Kali. Sati, according to the many legends and myths, was re-born as Uma, Daughter of Himavan (the Himalayas), taking the added name of Parvathi

---

[1] Ananda Coomaraswamy, *The Dance of Shiva and Fourteen Other Essays*

[2] Sir John Woodroffe (Arthur Avalon), *Tantra-Tattva* [3] Ananda Coomaraswamy, *ibid*

[4] (Chidambara Mummai Kovai) O. C. Gangoly, *South Indian Bronzes*

(meaning "born of a mountain"), and is the acme of the perfect woman, virtuous and courageous. Durga is the embodiment of the powerful aspect of Shiva in feminine form. She is the destroyer of evil and makes war upon evil beings who are harmful to mankind. In the form of the slayer of the *asuras*, enemies of the Gods, she is also known as Chamundi. Kali is another powerful terrifying aspect, representing that twin aspect of Shiva as Destroyer of evil and the releasing of the soul from the chains of illusion. She is the power behind world upheavals.

KALI'S DANCE. Kali is also associated with the dance, and dances on the burning grounds, which are symbolically speaking the hearts of men cleansed of all illusions and the ego. "Kali is set in such a scene, for She is that aspect of Great Power which draws all things unto Herself at and by the dissolution of the universe. He alone worships without fear who has abandoned all worldly desires and seeks union with Her as the One Blissful and perfect Experience. On the burning ground all worldly desires are burned away. She is naked and dark like a threatening rain-cloud, for She who is Herself beyond mind and speech reduces all living things into that worldly "nothingness" which, as the Void (*Shunya*) of all we know, is at the same time the All (*Purna*) which is Light and Peace. She is naked, being clothed in space alone (*Digambara*), because Great Power is unlimited; further She is Herself beyond *Maya* (*Mayatita*); that Power of Herself with which She covers Her own nature and so creates all universes. She stands upon the white corpse-like (*Shavarupa*) body of Shiva. He is white, because He is the illuminating (*Prakesha*), transcendental aspect of Consciousness. He is inert because the Changeless aspect of the Supreme, and She the apparently Changing aspect of the same. In truth She and He are one and the same, being twin aspects of the One who is Changelessness in, and exists as Change. Clothed in Infinite Space."[1]

The same deeply philosophical and religious symbolism pervades the picturesque dances of Sri Krishna, incarnation of Vishnu, the Merciful aspect of God; Krishna, who was born of royal blood, yet grew up amongst the simple, laughter-loving pastoral people of Brindaban in Gokula. He played with the lively Gopas (cowherds) and Gopis (milkmaids), but early showed His divine grace and power. As a boy he accompanied the Gopas as they went to graze their cattle, and as He grew into a handsome youth, He was the beloved of the Gopis with whom He sang and danced in the countryside. Later, He was variously King, Diplomat, and Soldier-Philosopher, and the Charioteer of Arjuna in the battle of Kurukshetra. Author of the immortal lyrical sacred book of the Hindus, the *Bhagavat Gita* (Song of God), He emphasised the immortality of the soul, the magnitude of duty and the freeing of oneself of the ego. He who seeks God need not cut himself away from his fellow men. He can indeed achieve the supreme end of becoming one with God, the Universal Soul, in the very midst of his allotted place in life, wherever it might be, as the hindrances which must be overcome in order to gain that perfect identification are not to be found in the world around us but within us. This is the central lesson always surrounding the teachings of Sri Krishna. Though Sri Krishna danced on many occasions, three important dance themes will explain the philosophical truths reflected through them.

[1]   Sir John Woodroffe (Arthur Avalon), *Garland of Letters*

Plate 5

1

2

3

Some of the old dance bas-reliefs, recently rediscovered in the Brihdeshwara temple. Tanjore (10th-11th century A.D.), of Shiva's Tandava dance. (Copyright, Department of Archaeology, Government of India.)

Plate 6

1

2

3

4

Temple sculptures. (1) Dancing goddess, from the Kesava temple, Somnathpur, 13th century A.D. (2) Tandava dance of Shiva, from Andel temple, Belur, 12th century A.D. (3) A dancer, from Markanda temple, Andhra Pradesh. (4) Dance scene. Gwalior Museum. (Copyright, Department of Archaeology, Government of India.)

Plate 7

1

2

Temple sculptures from the Hoysala temple, Halebid, 12th century A.D. (1) Vishnu dancing in the guise of Mohini. (2) Dancing Saraswati. (3) Krishna dancing on the serpent Kaliya (4) Dancing Ganapathi. (Copyright, Department of Archaeology, Government of India.)

3

4

Plate 8

1

2

3

4

Temple sculptures of dancing goddesses, from the Hoysala temple, Halebid, 12th century A.D. (Copyright, Department of Archaeology, Government of India.)

KRISHNA'S TANDAVA DANCE. When Krishna was a boy, living in Gokula with His foster parents Nanda and Yashoda, the serpent Kaliya lived in the river Kalinda (Jamuna) that flowed through this little village. Soon this hundred-headed monster became a menace to the harmless herdsmen and their cattle. They appealed to Krishna to help them get rid of this wicked creature. Krishna, recognising by His divine power, that Kaliya really represented the forces of evil, jumped on the serpent and with upraised foot, danced His famous Tandava Dance. Moving with forceful determination, He leapt from one head to another of this monster and overcame it. Having subjugated it, He made it leave the Jamuna for ever. Thus in this youthful dance, Krishna symbolised that aspect of God who destroys evil and subjugates the enemies of the innocent.

NAYAKA-NAYAKI BHAVA—KRISHNA LILAS. All the dances in which Radha His Beloved participates, represent the eternal yearning of the individual soul to join the Divine Soul, love being regarded as the path to devotion. The dance gives us the eternal lesson of the perfect harmony of the spiritual life by the conquering of earthly passions and ties. All souls must ultimately become one with the Universal Soul, till they vibrate in perfect unison with the Supreme and Absolute. Man's heart is the place of sacrifice where the fire of love for God burns ceaselessly. All his deeds and thoughts are offerings offered as sacrifice and renounced for ever. It is a dance of renunciation of the ego by love and devotion to God; and it indicates the state of realising that peace and yogic calm with the release from attachments to the world and its illusions, which one can achieve while carrying out the duties one is called upon to perform in one's allotted place in life.

THE MAHA RAS. Krishna's beautiful symbolic dances at Brindaban on the banks of the Jamuna river with the Gopis, and particularly the grand Maha Ras performed on the night of the full moon, are picturesque representations of a deeply philosophical meaning. He is the divine lover, dancer and musician. The Gopis allegorically represent the countless souls of mankind in search of the Divine Soul. These are dances of ecstasy, and the Gopis leave their husbands and parents to follow Him, indicating the freedom of the individual souls from all earthly attachments for the path of renunciation of self. Thus these dances, surrounded by an aura of love and devotion, represent allegorically a realisation of True Reality (*Vidhya*). Reality of the spiritual truths and of God (Krishna). The Gopis are the countless souls of mankind yearning for Him. And the pastoral beauty and quiet of Brindaban represent the peace and calm state of one's thoughts and feelings of contemplation. The Gopis dancing with Krishna, searching for the Divine Soul, give their all to Him willingly, without so much as question or hope of reward. Thus should men love God. This is the philosophical theme underlying the picturesque dances of Krishna and the Gopis.

To the imagination, Krishna presents as glorious a vision as Shiva in His dance of Nataraja. "His azure breast glittered with pearls of unblemished lustre, like the full bed of the cerulean Yamuna, interspersed with curls of white foam. From his graceful waist flowed a pale yellow robe, which resembled the golden dust of the water-lily, scattered over its blue petals....Bright earrings, like two suns, displayed in full expansion, the flowers of His cheeks and lips, which glistened with the liquid radiance of smiles. His locks interwoven with blossoms, were like a cloud variegated with moonbeams; and on His forehead shone a circle of odorous oils, extracted from the sandal of Malaya—like the moon just appearing on the dusky horizon; while His whole body seemed in a flame, from the blaze of un-numbered gems."[1]

Shiva's Gift-giving dance of the Nataraja "represents His Five Activities, (*Pancakritya*), *Shristi* (overlooking, creation and evolution), *Sthiti* (preservation, support), *Samhara* (destruction, evolution), *Tirobhava* (veiling, embodiment, illusion and also giving rest), *Anugraha* (release, salvation, grace)."[2]

These activities are represented through the many revelations of God. So also it is believed that Krishna, the eighth incarnation of Vishnu, the Merciful aspect of God, is the essence of all. He represents "the verse of hymns, the rhythm of metres, the tune of mouths, the flowers of the seasons. He is the Path, Husband, Lord, Witness, Abode, Shelter, Lover, Origin, Dissolution, Foundation, Treasure House and Seed Imperishable."

Therefore God is One, no matter in what form He reveals Himself and under what Name He is known. The human imagination which has devised these inspiring ecstatic divine dances, explains that "beauty alone can bring to the hearts of man goodness, and love can move them to compassion. His great Self which dwells within ourselves, destroying ignorance-born darkness by the shining lamp of wisdom."

DANCE OF PARVATHI. According to legend, the twin aspect or energy of Shiva was Sati. Once when her father Daksha, spiritual son of Brahma, did not invite Shiva to a sacred ceremony, she took it so much to heart that she cast herself into the sacrificial fire and perished. When Shiva came to know of this, He appeared on the scene and putting Daksha and the other adversaries to flight, He picked up Sati in His arms and danced seven times round the world. Such was the forcefulness of His grief and the movements expressing His sorrow that the world and all its creatures trembled. Vishnu, fearing for the catastrophic results of Shiva's tremendous power, is said according to legend to have severed Sati's body into pieces and thus released Shiva from His agonising rage. The Gods then beseeched Shiva to be calm. The great God retired to Mount Kailasha, His Himalayan hermitage, where He became lost in meditation, grieving for the loss of Sati. Then she was re-born as Uma, daughter of Himavan (the Himalayas), taking the added name of Parvathi (meaning, born of a mountain). Parvathi was exceedingly beautiful, full of grace and endowed with all the qualities that Sati possessed—the essence of a perfect woman. She sought to become again the consort of Shiva, and to win Him, she danced and sang divinely, He being the Creator of the Dance and its mode of portrayal, her person exquisitely adorned with jewels and ornaments. The dance is poetically described in lyrical verse and rhythms and interpreted in one of the *Shiv Tandava Nrityas* of the Kathak school of the classical dance of North India.

"Jata Joot Madh Ganga Kalak Katha
Sesh Chandra Lalit Jhalak Katha
Roond Malah Galay
Sesah Dharani Dhara

[1] Edward Moore, *Hindu Pantheon*   [2] Ananda Coomaraswamy, *Dance of Shiva and Fourteen Other Essays*

Parvathi Shiva Har Har, Parvathi Shiva Har Har.
Parvathi Pathi Parvathi Shiva Har Har Har Har Har.

"Ee Jee Ka Tha, Jee Jee Ka Joo Ka Tha,
Koocha Ha La Ha La,
Chooka Chamaka
Chapala See Da Mee Nee See, Da Ma Ka Tha,
Mooka Mangtha Hasatha,
Shri Parvathi, Shri Parvathi, Shri Parvathi.

"Chama Chama Nachata, Sangeet Rita,
Beebee Dha Bathi Gathi Nyee Nyee,
Tho diga diga Tram tram Thayee Thaka,
Tho diga diga Tram tram Thayee Thaka,
Tho diga diga Tram tram Thayee.

"Uma Rachi Chika Nachata Parvathi,
Thaka Chome Thaka Chome,
Kookoo Jana Nana Jana Nana,
Hava Bhava Sangeet Lasya Ko,
Na Diga Dig, Tho Diga Dig, Diga Diga,
Theeah, Heeah, Theeah, Heeah, Theeah, Heeha.

"Daga Maga Dhimitha Dhimi, Ka Dhimi,
Madal,
Roonoo Jhoonoo Manjeera Bajata Bol,
Kinkeenee Rana Ranee
Noopoora Dhone Gathee, Athee Ana Mola,
Ghay Thee thay Ghay thee thay Mirdang Garajatha,
Dhimi Dhimi Bajata Gaga Na Nishan,
Chi chi chome Cha na ka ri diga dig,
Chi chi chome Cha na ka ri diga dig,
Chi chi chome Cha na ka ri.

"Chi chi chome Chi chi chome Bajata Noopoora,
Niratata Giri Kailash Shikara Para,
Narada, Sharada Shookalah Deva Milee,
Gavata, Nachata, Dye dye Karata Ree,
Gavata, Nachata, Dye dye Karata Ree,
Dye dye Karata Ree, Dye dye Karata Ree."
                              —*the late Sukhdeve Maharaj*

A broad translation of the meaning explains that:

He with the matted locks from which flows the Ganges
In a sparkling cascade; on His brow, the serpent and
The crescent Moon.   With a garland of skulls, He dances
On the earth upheld by the great Snake.
Parvathi's Lord, Shiva, Shiva.

In sparkling raiment she is clothed,
Her gentle breast rises and falls with tender thrill,
Her little feet with music stress rhythmic ecstasy.
A smile divine lights her face faintly and all
The colour of Nature has painted her with heavenly hue
To please the assembly of Gods and Goddesses
Parvathi, Parvathi, Parvathi.

Her twinkling feet speak almost words,
A lilting song they form,
Parvathi, the pale Uma dances as in a dream,
Her mood sweeps all those present
And fills the winds of Heaven.
So gentle is the flow of her body
Like a serenade it joins the music
And every cadence strikes sweet harmony
With the words of the drum.

The Madole drum rings forth its low bass notes,
The cymbals clink lightly,
And in the music join her little ankle bells,
While the Gods and Goddesses and Sages
Narada and Sharada and the company of Heaven sit
Transfixed by the chorus of instruments and
Spiritual dance and song.

Once more we have in this picture of Parvathi, dancing and singing to become again the consort of Shiva, the idea of the dual personality of God and Goddess, "the gentle gracious entity with the powerful nobleness." So we find Sati re-born as Uma (Parvathi), being "the twin aspects of the One who is Changelessness in, and exists as Change." Legend goes on to say that it was Uma's meditation and austerities for many ages that eventually helped her become once again the consort of Shiva. This lends us the idea again that in order to gain the final achievement of becoming one with the Godhead, one must pursue the path of love and devotion through renunciation of the ego.

DANCES OF THE APSARAS. According to mythology, these are the pure spirits, the celestial fairies or heavenly nymphs who danced in the Court of Indra, Vedic Lord of Heaven. "The lissom bodies of the pure spirits who know divine ecstasy and heavenly bliss, float through space with the effortless ease of the winged denizens of the air."[1]

The Apsaras represent a symbolic conception of ecstasy. An ecstasy of pure joy and rapture born of contemplation of God. It is again the parable picture of "a soul saturated with goodness and the desire to impart to countless souls on earth that indescribable bliss of being with God." And again, "The pure ecstasy of the dance, the *joie de vivre* which lifts the body out of itself into the realms of heavenly bliss, is nowhere shown better in Indian art than in the portrayal of the demi-gods and goddesses, the *Siddhas* and *Siddhis* of the upper air, who hover round the sum-

[1] E. B. Havell, *Himalayas in Indian Art*

mits of stupas or holy mountains and take part as messengers, dancers and musicians in divine ceremonials."[1]

All divine aspects of dancing therefore have this central theme of the love of God for the countless souls that seek Him and the constant seeking and striving of man to become one with the Infinite and Universal Soul. This leads to the renunciation of the ego and the casting off of the shackles of earthly ties and illusions and the gaining of Salvation (*Moksha*).

These enduring mental pictures of the divine dances made perfect subjects for some of the greatest works of Indian art. Thus Dance in Imagery was created and caught the imagination of not only the craftsmen who executed them, but also of art connoisseurs and devotees alike . And especially of the simple minded people, who found inspiration and something tangible in these splendid themes so vividly conceived.

[1] *Ibid*

3. Dance in Imagery

SCULPTURE

THE DEEP and abiding ideals of philosophy and aesthetics on which the Hindu dance has been built, have also profoundly influenced the allied arts of sculpture, metal casting, frescoes and painting in India.

Ever since the early Buddhist builders started using stone for constructing their monuments about 272-231 B.C., architecture and sculpture took on an important place among the Indian arts. The Buddhists, we are told, were really the first to use this material in the Stupas or semi-spherical monuments containing relics of the Buddha, followed by the Cathedrals (*Chaityas*) and Monasteries (*Viharas*), of which there are numerous examples in the Buddhist caves found in the various parts of our country. It was the Buddhists too, we are told, who from the 2nd century A.D. onwards, first used representations of Hindu deities like Shiva, Vishnu, Lakshmi and Indra in their sculptural art. And it was from them that Hindu religious sculptural and architectural arts took their inspiration, commencing from about the 6th century A.D. and reaching their zenith in the 13th century A.D.

The temples very naturally became the centres not only of religious worship but of art and learning. Sanskrit was studied by the few, who gained knowledge of the high philosophical precepts by learning the *Vedas*, *Puranas* and other sacred books. But art was meant for all, and through it, Hindu religious thought and philosophy were conveyed to all classes of society. To make these abstract theological teachings understood by the average person, symbols were created which clarified the inner meaning of these precepts. And there developed a great art and culture wherein the abstruse, highly ethical philosophies were put into concrete explicit form.

The ancient Indian sculptors, due to whose genius such prolific and splendid works have come to posterity, held a recognised position in society. They belonged

14

to guilds which were protected and acknowledged by royal patronage. They were trained in this hereditary calling by their fathers, whose devout disciples they became. In addition, they had to study the thirty-two *Silpa Sastras* or Rules for Craftsmen, and were expected according to some sources to understand also the *Atharva Veda* and the mystic Vedic prayers (*Mantras*) by which the deities are invoked. After thorough study of the *Silpa Sastras*, the artisans and craftsmen came to know and understand the distinctive features of the various deities and the other minute details about them and their mythological vehicles. This knowledge proved a valuable guide to craftsmen, who meditated on what they had learned and got the mental images fixed in their minds. Noble, ideal, divine visions were born of their contemplation and imagination and transferred to stone.

Thus from very early times in India, the urge for worship of God through an image became established. And worshippers came to associate, recognise and become devotees of a particular revelation of the Creator by a sculptured form born of the imagination of these hereditary sculptors after study and meditation. Hence we find such texts as Sukracharya's : "Let the imager establish images in temples by meditation on the deities who are the objects of his devotion. For the successful achievement of this Yoga, the lineaments of the image are described in the books to be dwelt upon in detail. In no other way, not even by direct and immediate vision of an actual object, is it possible to be so absorbed in contemplation, as thus in the making of images."[1]

Mythology also played its part in inspiring the craftsmen, who meditated on these allegorical parable stories of God's divine perfection and revelations and incorporated these precepts into their marvellous sculptures. It followed then that the art of the dance with its expressive forms of rhythmic movement and dramatic content, as well as the mystic allegorical divine dances representing the various aspects of God, became the subject of some of the most beautiful sculptures. One can literally see in many pillared halls of the temples throughout India, hundreds of examples of the magnificence of the mental images that sculptors of old must have drawn upon for the many dance sculptures they created. It will be interesting to substantiate this with some representative examples.

During the Buddhist period (500 B.C. to about A.D. 6), and in what is called the Classic Age (2nd century A.D. to about the 8th century A.D.), in spite of injunctions against family members studying, performing or encouraging the dance, both the sculptures and frescoes bear witness to the popularity of the art. We find fine examples of dance sculptures at Bharhut, Amaravati, Aurangabad, Ajanta, Ellora, Khandagiri and Udayagiri rock-cut cave temples. Situated half-way between Allahabad (Uttar Pradesh) and Jabalpur (Madhya Pradesh), the Bharhut cave temples belong to 200 B.C. Many sculptures on the pillars show dancing figures, one in particular being different and unique. It represents the legend of the peacock dancing proudly his vainglorious dance which eventually lost him the hand of the Swan King's beautiful daughter. At Amaravati (Andhra Pradesh), belonging to the 3rd and 4th centuries A.D., delicately executed dancing Apsaras are depicted performing gracefully in the Royal Court. While in Ajanta and Ellora, there are beautifully sculptured dancing Natarajas. Again, in the Khandagiri and Udayagiri caves (placed at just before the beginning of the Christian era, Orissa State), both the friezes and bas-reliefs depict not only a series of dancers in graceful poses, but men and women dancers have been sculptured making offerings

---

[1] Ananda Coomaraswamy, *Dance of Shiva and Fourteen Other Essays*

to the Jain shrine.   In fact, the dancing Apsaras take an important place in Buddhist, Brahamanical and Jain sculptural art, and they are shown to represent the the grace and tender spirit of the feminine personality devoid of earthly attachments.

The earliest sculptures of Shiva's Nadanta dance of the Nataraja in the Golden Hall at Chidambaram or Tillai, are said to be placed about the 6th century A.D. In the famed Nataraja temple at Chidambaram (Madras State), there are impressive sculptures of this dance which represent Creation, Preservation, and Destruction. While in the great Brihadeswara temple at Tanjore (Madras State), and in the Hoysala temple at Halebid (Mysore State), bas-reliefs portray many instances of Shiva as Lord of the Dance.   These marvellous works of art reveal Shiva's rhythmic dance as the Source of all movement in the Universe.   Here we find a tremendous sense of power and a wonderful balance expressed by the genius of these ancient sculptors.   More of these magnificent sculptures representing this mystic dance can be seen in the Shiva temples at Tiruchirapalli (Trichinopoly), and Rameshwaram (Madras State), the Jagannath temple at Puri, the Lingaraj temple at Bhubaneshwar and the Sun temple at Konarak, all last three in Orissa State.

For examples of Shiva's Forceful Tandava dance in His *Tamasic* aspect as Bhairava or Vira-Bhadra, one has only to visit the rock-cut temples at Elephanta and Ellora (Maharashtra State), both placed about the 8th century A.D., as well as the main temple at Bhubaneshwar; emphasising the power and glory of the great deity, these sculptures are perfect examples of how the imagination and artistry of the sculptors of old combined to produce the most vivid forms in plastic art to denote these qualities of God.   Again, in one of the reliefs at Kailashnatha Shiva temple at Kanchipuram (Madras State) this dance is so illustrated that one gets a lasting impression from the whole ensemble of posture, hands and lineaments of the stupendous speed and force that underlay this aspect of Shiva's dance.

Further examples of Shiva's Tandava dance as Bhairava can be seen in the large sculpture in the Hoysala temple at Halebid (Mysore State), the many portrayals in the Sri Andel temple at Belur (Mysore State), and in the recently re-discovered series of bas-reliefs which depict various postures of this dance in the Brihadeswara temple at Tanjore (Madras State).   The Kailashnatha temple at Kanchipuram (Madras State) is famed for the large sculpture of Shiva's Yogic Evening dance, the *Sandhya-Nrtta-Murti*, with its gentle rhythms, harmoniously set at glorious eventide.   The dance can also be seen almost at its best in the 8th century Chalukya temple of Malikarjuna at Pattadakal (Maharashtra State).

The dances of the Goddesses Durga and Kali, twin aspects of Shiva, are best seen in the temples of the South.   At the temple at Belur (Mysore State), Durga is six-handed and dances her dance of Destruction of Evil; while at the Devi temple at Chidambaram (Madras State), she slays the evil asura, known as the *Mahisasura-mardini* theme.   Posture, rhythmic line and gesture are expressive of dance in all its power of harmonious, emotional, interpretive qualities.   Kali's dance of Destruction of Evil is splendidly represented in the Hoysala temple at Halebid (Mysore State).   Here too can be seen a unique sculpture of Ganapathi (Ganesha), the elephant-headed God and spiritual son of Shiva and Parvathi.

For examples of the legendary dances of Saraswati (Goddess of Learning and Music), of Sri Krishna, and of Vishnu in the guise of Mohini, there are classic sculptures in the 12th century temples of Belur and Halebid, built by the Hoysala King Bittige.   The dancing Goddess Saraswati connotes the acme of grace and

Plate 9

1

2

Temple sculptures. Dancing bracket figures from Belur, 12th century A.D.
(Copyringht, Department of Archaeology, Government of India.)

3

4

Plate 10

1

2

3

4

Temple sculptures. Dancing bracket figures from Belur, 12th century A.D. (Copyright, Department of Archaeology. Government of India.)

Plate 11

1   2   3

South Indian bronzes. (1) Krishna in dance posture, 17th-18th century A.D. (2) Krishna in dance posture, 10th century A.D. (3) Tandava dance of Krishna as a boy (Balakrishna), 15th century A.D. (Courtesy, National Museum, New Delhi.)

Plate 12

1   2   3

South Indian bronzes. (1) Goddess Kali in dance posture, 12th century A.D. (2) Goddess Parvati in dance posture. (3) Goddess Devi in dance posture. (Courtesy, National Museum, New Delhi.)

beauty, from whom elegance, delicacy of line and rhythm flow graciously like the soft sound waves of some gentle *Raga* melody.   These are two of the few places where this Goddess, who according to legend is the consort of Brahma the Creator, is shown as a dancer.   In these two temples too, there are sculptures of Sri Krishna in His Tandava dance subduing Kaliya, the hundred-headed serpent.

The sculptures representing Vishnu (the Merciful Aspect), depicts the myth that Vishnu took the form of the Goddess Mohini, representing Delusion, and danced in order to defeat the Asura Bhasmasura, representing Evil.   According to the legend, this demon had the power to kill anyone over whom he held his magical hand.   Mohini lured him to a dance contest and suddenly took a pose in which she held her hand over her head.   In his wild dance, the evil creature imitated her and destroyed himself, as he placed his hand over his own head.   The legend portrays how God will destroy evil doers in order to protect the innocent.

Turning to examples of the classical dance itself, there are scores of examples readily available in the many temples all over the country.   In the Nataraja temple at Chidambaram, on the seven inset pillars which flank the entrance of each *gopuram* (temple-tower gateway), there are carvings of the 108 *Karanas* or basic dance postures; and underneath each sculpture is engraved a Sanskrit verse describing it in detail that corresponds to the same text and *Karana* as given in the *Natya Sastra* by Bharata Muni.

Dance sculptures abound in the temples of Ambarnath (Maharashtra State), at Puri and Bhubaneshwar (Orissa), and in the medieval temples of Khajuraho (Madhya Pradesh); those in the last named temples have many sculptures that are similar to the postures as practised today in the Bharata Natyam classical dance of the South.   While in the temples of Orissa, particularly in the famous shrine of Konarak (Orissa), belonging to about the 13th century A.D., the sculptures represent almost every important dance pose and gesture found in the *Karanas,* in the form of reliefs; and hundreds of these reliefs of women in various dancing poses decorate the Hall of Dance, the *Natya Mandapam.*   Numerous other sculptures in this ornate temple of Konarak show the dances of deities such as Shiva in the dance of the Nataraja, Parvathi, Ganesha, the Apsaras and dancing girls.

For more figures of feminine dancers, one can visit the Jagannath Vishnu temple at Puri, and the Virupaksha, Papanatha and Kashanatha temples at Pattadakal.   Within the richly sculptured pillared halls at Belur and Halebid Hoysala temples, bracket figures show dancers and the famous queen Shantaladevi (Hoysala, 12th century A.D.) who was a renowned dancer.   Outside, the walls are ornamented with dances of this artistic queen.   Mobile and perfect in line and expression, these are among some of the finest examples of the dance in temple sculpture. More examples of the classical dance poses performed by female dancers abound in the Ramappa temple at Palampet (Andhra Pradesh), at the Nataraja, Surya and Devi temples at Chidambaram, in the Brihadeswara temple at Tanjore, and in the main temple at Udaipur (Rajasthan), where there are friezes inside and on the temple tower, depicting dancers and musicians.

In each magnificent work of art, the whole idea underlying each dance has been vividly expressed, and whether it be the parable-stories of the Gods, or the graceful dances of the Apsaras, or depictions of the classical dance, these many sculptures come to posterity as repositories of the dance in India.   The nobility of form, grace and rhythmic flow of these sculptures inspire the lover of aesthetics and the arts with a deep sense of admiration.   The uplifting philosophical concepts they symbolise, impel a feeling of reverence in the beholder, as though their creation was motivated by divine influence.   Indeed, their appeal is universal, for they are true masterpieces in every sense of the term.

METAL CASTING

Turning to the dance in the art of metal casting in bronze and copper, the picture is the same.   Not only are the philosophical ideals put into concrete form through the dance, but the art itself reached the highest conceptions.   Mobile, graceful line, perfect placement of arms and feet, the rhythmic balance of the body (*Bhangas*) convey ecstatic raptures and spiritual moods of the craftsmen. In addition, these ancient *Sthapatis* (organised guild of skilled sculptors and bronze founders) utilized a highly formalised and cultivated gesture language to enhance the dramatic and interpretive context of each work of art.   In some cases they used the dance gestures as explained in the *Natya Sastra* by Bharata Muni, and in others, they invented a symbol or sign of their own with particular spiritual meaning. These special gestures known as *Mudras* have been called *Divyakriya* or divine actions by Sukracharya, having special significance.

Southern Indian sculptors have particularly excelled in transferring the special attributes of the dances of the Gods to bronze.   And we have many examples, particularly of those placed in the period between the 9th and 13th centuries A.D., belonging to the Chola period.   There is Shiva's Cosmic dance of the Nataraja, the most favourite subject still to be seen in many of the large temples of the South; notably the Brihadeswara temple at Tanjore, the Shiva temples at Kanchipuram, the Nataraja temple at Chidambaram and the Meenakshi Sundaram temple at Madurai, to name a few.   The Government Museum at Madras, the National Museum at New Delhi, the Calcutta Museum and the Art Gallery at Tanjore have some splendid bronzes of this subject.   The *Tandava* Forceful dance of Sri Krishna on the hundred-headed serpent Kaliya is another ever popular subject that the old bronze casters found joy in executing.   There are examples of this subject to be found in all the leading museums of India.

Besides bronze, we find some very interesting figures of dancers in terracotta, belonging to the ancient Dravidian culture of about 5000 years ago, about the same period as the figure of the dancing girl in metal found in the excavations of the Indus Valley civilization at Mohenjodaro.   In fact, one finds that all through the ages, not only metal, but wood, terracotta, clay, ivory, and pith have been the raw materials for the expression of great artistic objects created by our craftsmen. Right from the Mauryan dynasty (4th century B.C. - 3rd century B.C.), extending to the 10th and 11th centuries A.D., when they reached their zenith, this has been the case.   Notable examples are Shiva's dance of the Nataraja and the Forceful *Tandava* dance of Sri Krishna on the serpent Kaliya.

These early traditions have come down to posterity, and we find today examples of dancing figures in the red wood from Tirupatti (Andhra Pradesh), in mellow wood and stone figures from Orissa; an assortment of dancing dolls in clay and glazed and painted terracotta from Bengal; dancing figurines in ivory from Kerala, and in sandalwood from Mysore and Rajasthan.   Examples too can be found in the beautiful Nirmal work from Hyderabad (Andhra Pradesh), where paintings are done on wood or metal comprising white clay and dry tamarind seed with vegetable dyes for producing the vivid colours, or with the use of white metal, tamarind seed

Plate 13

1

2

Miniature paintings. (1) Krishna dancing, Malwa School, late 17th century A.D. (Courtesy, National Museum, New Delhi.) (2) Vasanta Ragini, Krishna dancing accompanied by musicians, Malwa School, mid.-17th century A.D. (Courtesy, Bharat Kala Bhavan.)

3

Miniature painting. Vasanta Ragini, the Melody of Spring. Krishna dancing with musicians, Rajasthan School, 17th century A.D. (Courtesy, National Museum, New Delhi.)

Plate 14

1

2

Miniature paintings. (1) Krishna Lila (Maha Ras), Jodhpur, early 19th century A.D.
(2) Hamviri Ragini; line drawing of dancing girls, Rajasthan, 18th century A.D. (3)
A *Nayika*; dance pose with hands in *Kartari hasta* (separation from her lover in
distress), Rajasthan School. (4) Vasanta Ragini; Krishna dancing accompanied by
musicians, Mewar, 17th century A.D. (Courtesy, National Museum, New Delhi.)

3

4

and vegetable juices to produce the effect of gold or silver. The dance has also invaded the field of textiles, and in the various museums in India there are fine specimens of colourful prints depicting the Krishna dances with the Gopis, as well as folk dance motifs, hailing mostly from Bengal, Rajasthan, Andhra and Assam.

FRESCOES AND PAINTINGS

One finds the identical attention paid to the spiritual beauty, the grace and philosophical meaning of the dance subjects in Indian frescoes and paintings. Here, however, artists have used their imagination more freely, and in the process of introducing colour, they have incorporated a moving humanism and a deep inspiration from Nature. As in the sculptures and metal castings, one can see in these artistic forms, the same restful poise, perfect balance and foot placement, detail of gestures and both the *Tandava* and *Lasya* types of the Indian dance. Dress and ornament too are conspicuous for the meticulous detail and correctness with which they have been executed. An outstanding dance theme in fresco painting is to be seen in Cave I at Ajanta. The story is from the Mahajanaka Jataka (the temptation scene), placed about the 7th century A.D. It shows a scene of girl musicians with tapering flutes, in delicate poses, with the dancer in rhythmic movement. Her head is bent graciously with tilted chin; the right arm curved and the wrist bent, the left arm also curved, the two arms forming a movement of entwining tendrils (denoting enticement); and the wrists turned back, with the fingers in the gesture of holding a flower. This is a perfect example of the Gentle or *Lasya* dance style.

Not far from Ajanta, in the Ellora rock-cut cave temples, Shiva's Tandava dance is depicted on the ceiling of the temple of Kailash. He is seen dancing with upraised foot, holding in His right hands the trident, drum, and bowl of renunciation; while in one of His left hands is a skull, the other being at rest. In this old fresco painting, powerful line and balance of figure are perfectly obtained with the additional beauty of colour.

Again, in the Brihadeswara temple in Tanjore, built about the 11th century A.D., there is a fresco of dancing Apsaras and musicians. Half hidden by fleecy clouds, they are showering lotus petals on the audience as they dance. Their arms are bent and raised in statuesque pose, their figures showing the exotic movements of heavenly beings on joyous occasions. Lotus blossoms are held alluringly in their left hands. This again is an example of the *Lasya* style of the dance.

In this same temple, there are two panels which describe in rich and pure colour tones, two of Shiva's dances. The first explains the whirling figure of the Lord of the Dance as the Nataraja with the Sacred Fire in His upraised hand. The dance indicates Shiva as the Source of all movement, rhythm and harmony in the Cosmos. The second scene shows Shiva's vigorous dance of Destruction, which legend says was performed on the occasion when the enemies of the Gods, the asuras, attacked the city of Three Worlds called Tripura, and were completely destroyed by the Gods. This fine portrayal of the destruction of what metaphorically stands for evil, and the triumph of good, is an outstanding example of what a high standard of artistic achievement was reached in the art of fresco painting.

In the ancient palace at Padmanabhapuram in Travancore, Kerala, there are several dancing figures in expressive postures, showing the rhythmic harmony of the dance. Besides, one can see in beautifully mellow colours the dance of Shiva in the Cosmic dance of the Nataraja, with the right foot trampling on the evil dwarf Muyalagam, the left foot raised to give release. In His hands are the drum and the flame.

Coming to medieval times, of the colourful Rajput period, we have the delicate miniature paintings, in which there are innumerable examples of both music and dance. Several series of the *Ragas* and *Raginis* have been most exquisitely executed representing these melodic themes detailed in our classical music. These *Ragas* and *Raginis* visualised in the miniature paintings, illustrate the emotions each melody awoke in the heart of the artist who heard it. A *Raga* is "the traditional melody into which the Indian musician has woven his improvisations, and it is a selection of five, six or seven notes distributed along the scale, each *Raga* symbolising in rhythmic form some emotion, elemental force or particular aspect of Nature when it may be appropriately sung or played." The *Ragini* is the feminine form of the *Raga*, and suggests a condensation of the main theme of the melody. In the dance themes, though there are some paintings of Shiva in His Cosmic dance of the Nataraja, we find that most of the subjects centre around the dances of Sri Krishna, covering the lively childhood merry-making dances with the Gopis and Gopas; the famous *Tandava* dance on the hundred-headed serpent Kaliya; and the devotional group dances with the Gopis and Radha the beloved, set on the banks of the Jamuna river in Brindaban, against a background of flower-filled bowers and blossoming trees. Kangra and the various Rajasthani schools of painting have many delightful examples of these pastoral and devotional dances, done with all the excellence of colour, delicate line and finesse of subject matter.

Many of the postures and gestures as well as the general style of dress and composition of the dances depicted in these paintings can find their counterparts in the Kathak style of the classical dance of North India.

With these few representative examples of Dance in Imagery, as found in the sculptures, bronzes, frescoes and paintings, one can see that art and philosophy have been closely associated in India since time immemorial, thereby giving them a strong and common link. And the dance, because of its peculiarly lovely rhythmic stances, coupled with its deeply philosophical background, has contributed dynamically towards enriching the fine arts—a dance-art based on solid technical foundations, scientifically prepared with rules and regulations for its performance.

4. Foundations of the Dance

BASICALLY, the Indian dance is one on which almost any accepted style can be modelled, and among the many facets of its make-up are to be detected extraordinary parallels with the dance as it has been developed in the West. Yet, in its many classical and folk interpretations, it constitutes a unique art, not the least intriguing aspect of which is its complete "language" of physical gestures, comparable in expressiveness and subtlety with a spoken tongue and firmly based upon its own regular "grammar" of sign and symbol.

As already mentioned, the *Natya Sastra* or Science of Dramaturgy by Bharata Muni is the most important and comprehensive source. It is, we are told, generally placed between the 4th and 1st centuries B.C. The other important source is the ancient treatise, dealing with gestures and emotional expression, called the *Abhinaya Dharpana* by Nandikeshwara, and translated into English by Ananda Coomaraswamy and Duggirala Gopalakrishnayya, under the title of *The Mirror of Gestures.*

COMPONENT PARTS OF THE DANCE

In the *Natya Sastra*, it is made clear that drama and acting are considered inseparable from the dance and from music. They are interdependent. The dance itself may be divided into three main parts.

NATYA: The combination of both dancing and acting.

NRTTA: Pure dance. Movements without any special meaning or mood, and used to show pure technique, and the intricacies of complicated timing, rhythms, posture and footwork.

21

NRTYA: That form of the dance, comprising movements of the body, hands, limbs, together with facial expressions, and filled with *Rasa* or Flavour, which may express small episodes, just a sentence, or a whole drama.

This then is the foundation of the dance.

The Science of Dramaturgy further showed that the dance was composed of a series of enchanting combinations of Three Main Elements of Bodily Gesture, namely:

THE LIMBS
THE WHOLE BODY
THE FACE

These three main components had to express between them one uniform whole in which speed, delicacy, symmetry, body control, versatility, eye expressions, facial expressions, thought, word and song followed in a natural stream of harmony. The meaning of the dance was further detailed in the Three Forms:

BHAVA OR MOOD: This part of the dance was to be tenderly described by the glances and play of the eyes and eyebrows; the *Hastas* or hand gestures, accompanied by the relevant facial expression.

RAGA OR MELODY: Song and melody.

TALA OR RHYTHMIC   The technique of the feet guided by the set timing of the
TIMING: drum.

Rules and regulations for the performance of the Indian dance made it an exact science and art, where nothing was left to the arbitrary whim of the dancer. Yet, it could be mastered so perfectly that each dancer's individuality and ability in expression, grace, technical knowledge and personality, emotional feeling and confidence, gave distinction to her performance. In other words, "The danseuse or *Nartaki* had to be very lovely, young, with full round breasts, self-confident, charming, agreeable, dextrous in handling the critical passages; skilled in steps and rhythms; adorned with costly jewels, with a charming face, neither very stout nor very thin, nor very tall, nor very short."[1]

BUILDING UP OF THE DANCE

Technically, the dance was evolved step by step in stages.   First came what is known as a *Karana* or Single Posture.   This is the source and origin of all movement.   In it, the body as a whole is in one fixed position, with certain positions of the hands, arms, legs and feet.   There are 108 *Karanas* upon which the dance movements are founded.

The *Karanas* may therefore be considered as comprising the alphabet on which all the dance movements have been built up.   Each *Karana* is a co-ordination of the prescribed position (*Sthanka*), the gait (*Cari*), and hand gesture (*Nrtta Hasta*). There are 6 kinds of *Sthanakas*, 32 *Caris*, and 27 *Nrtta Hastas*. When two such *Karanas* are combined, one Unit of Action takes place —called a *Matrika*.

[1] Ananda Coomaraswamy and Duggirala Gopalakrishnayya, *The Mirror of Gestures*

When six or eight *Karanas* are combined, that is, three or four Units of Action, an *Angahara* is evolved.   There are 32 such *Angaharas*.

It will be helpful to give here three examples of how and which *Karanas* when combined make particular *Angaharas* or Units of Action.

According to the *Natya Sastra* or Science of Dramaturgy, to make the *Angahara* called *Aksipta*, meaning "Scattering Round,' the following *Karanas* have to be combined:

There are eight *Karanas* required to make the *Angahara Aksipta*, known as *Angahara* No. 5 (Plate 15):

1. *Karana 36, Nupura*. (Meaning "the Anklet Bells").   The basis of this is, the feet are crossed on the toes with the legs bent at the knees.   The arms are stretched out on either side with the hands drooping at the wrists.   Then there are three movements.   (i) The hip is moved in a circular manner.   (ii) The left hand is stretched down at an angle.   (iii) And the right hand is circled; while the legs are placed apart on the toes and are moved.

2. *Karana 21, Viksipta*. (Meaning "Thrown Over").   The legs are bent at the knees, the feet a little apart with the toes facing outwards.   The left hand is placed at the hip, and the right arm stretched downwards at an angle.   Then four movements take place.   (i) The hands are stretched straight down and are circled from down to up again.   (ii) The legs are taken back with the toes facing back and kept apart, and then brought to the ground.   (iii) The feet are crossed on the toes, with the legs apart and knees bent.   The hand and leg movements are done together.   (iv) The legs are then bent, raised and moved down, and the fingers of the hands are bent one by one, first finger, second, third and little fingers.

3. *Karana 18, Alata*. (Meaning "Circling").   The left leg is placed bent on the ground with the foot facing flat outwards.   The right foot is raised toes downwards about a foot above the ground.   Legs are outspread.   The right hand rests on the knee of the right foot, and the left hand is stretched downwards at a slant.   Then there are three movements.   (i) The right leg is taken back, raised straight, moved round from right to left and then placed with the heel resting on the ground.   (ii) The right hand is raised upwards at an angle.   (iii) Finally, the right leg is raised, bent and kept with the knee near the chest.

4. *Karana 55, Aksipta*. (Meaning "Scattering All Round").   The left leg is bent with the flat foot on the ground, the toes turned outwards.   The right foot is raised toes downwards with the heel touching the left ankle.   The left hand is raised to the shoulder level in the *Pataka* gesture, that is, all the fingers and the thumb stretched straight close together.   The right hand is kept hanging down at a slight angle.   Then there are four movements.   (i) The right leg is bent, raised and moved about.   (ii) Then the same is done with the left leg.   (iii) The right hand is kept straight and still.   (iv) The fingers of the left hand are bent slightly, one by one, the little finger, third, second, and first fingers consecutively.

5. *Karana 54, Uromandala*. (Meaning "Chest Region").   The legs are crossed on the toes at the ankles, and are kept outspread.   The body is slightly bent and the arms allowed to hang down at an angle.   Then there are five movements.   (i) The feet are crossed on the toes and re-crossed.   (ii) Again the legs are crossed with the calves touching.   (iii) The fingers of the right hand which are bent into the palm are softly stretched one by one, the first, second, third and little fingers, and the wrist is turned round with delicacy of movement.   (iv) The fingers of the left hand which are straight are bent into the palm, one by one, the

first, second, third and little fingers in succession. (v) The hands are then circled near the chest.

6. *Karana* 85, *Nitamba*. (Meaning "Posteriors"). The legs are crossed at the ankles on the toes, and the legs are spread out. The right and left arms are bent and the hands are held close together towards the right near the waist. Then there are four movements. (i) The hands are in *Pataka*, that is, all the fingers and thumb are stretched close together, and are raised upwards, and bent at the elbows. (ii) The palms of the hands are faced inwards, with the fingers towards one another. (iii) The feet are crossed on the toes with the calves touching. (iv) The legs are bent and spread out, with the right knee slightly turned towards the left.

7. *Karana* 87, *Kari Hasta*. (Meaning "Elephant Trunk"). The left arm is bent so that the finger tips of the hand almost rest on the shoulder over the ear. The right arm is flung across the body downwards to the left, with the fingers pointing downwards. The legs are placed apart, bent at the knees, left foot flat, toes pointing outwards, the right foot resting on the heel and turned outwards too. Then there are four movements. (i) The right hand is held at chest level. (ii) The left hand is placed so that the finger tips almost rest on the shoulder over the ear, the hand in *Tri-pataka*, that is, the third finger is bent parallel to the palm, and the first, second and little fingers stretched straight with the thumb close together. (iii) Delicately the right hand is turned and the fingers which are bent into the palm opened one by one, the first, second, third and little fingers in succession, with the finger tips pointing down. (iv) The legs are apart with the toes spread.

8. *Karana* 11, *Katicchinna*. (Meaning "Split Waist"). The legs are apart, bent at the knees, resting on the toes, with the feet facing outwards. The arms are stretched out and raised shoulder level and the hands are dropped at the wrists with the fingers pointing downwards. Then there are four movements. (i) The waist is moved in a circular manner. (ii) The arms are raised and crossed above the head, palms facing outwards. The hands are in *Pataka*, that is, all the fingers and thumb stretched close together. (iii) The hands are brought down, still in the same gesture. (iv) In this *Karana*, (i), (ii), and (iii) are repeated over and over again as the dancer pirouettes rapidly.

When these eight *Karanas* have been combined, then these series of movements make one *Angahara*—the *Angahara Aksipta* No. 5.

A second example gives the *Angahara Bhramara* (The Bee) No. 14. The following eight *Karanas* have to be combined to form it (Plate 16).

1. *Karana* 36, *Nupura*. (Meaning "Ankle Bells").
2. *Karana* 55, *Aksipta*. (Meaning "Scattering All Round").
3. *Karana* 11, *Katticchinna*. ("Meaning "Split Waist").
4. *Karana* 78, *Sucividdha*. (Meaning "Needle Probing"). Seated, resting on the toes of the feet, the knees apart, the left knee more in a slightly horizontal position turning outwards. The arms bent to either side, almost touching the shoulders with their backs. The left hand with all the fingers closed into the palm and the thumb stretched up. The right hand in *Pataka*, that is, all the fingers and thumb stretched close together, palms of both facing outwards. Then there are three movements. (i) The right foot is placed on the heel. (ii) The left foot with the sole of the foot facing back is raised on the big toe and touching the right foot. (iii) The hands rest gracefully on the waist and are moved and placed on the chest.

Plate 15

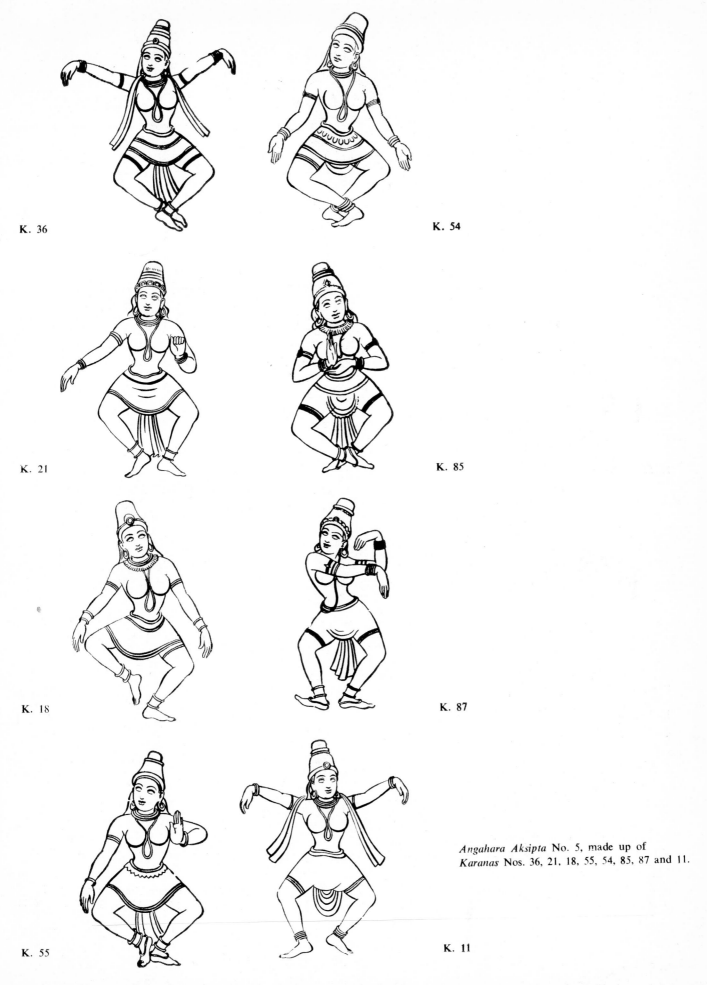

K. 36

K. 54

K. 21

K. 85

K. 18

K. 87

K. 55

Angahara Aksipta No. 5, made up of
Karanas Nos. 36, 21, 18, 55, 54, 85, 87 and 11.

K. 11

Plate 16

K. 36

K. 85

K. 55

K. 87

K. 11

K. 54

K. 78

K. 11

Angahara Bhramara No. 14, made up of *Karana* Nos. 36, 55, 11, 78, 85, 87, 54 and 11.

Plate 17

K. 18

K. 21

K. 25

K. 55

K. 26

K. 87

Angahara Alata No. 22, made up of *Karanas* Nos. 18, 25, 26, 77, 21, 55, 87 and 11.

K. 77

K. 11

Plate 18

1

a

b

2

a

b

4

3

Examples of *Karanas*, the Alphabet of Postures, from the Nataraja
temple, Chidambaram, 13th century A.D. (1) K83, Harinapluta
(deer flight); (2a) K24, Bhujanga Trasita (Serpent fright);
(2b) K23, Ancita (placing); (3) K39, Catura (four fingers);
(4a) K71, Ganda Suci (cheek needle); (4b) K31, Valita (folded in).
(Copyright, Department of Archaeology, Government of India.)

Plate 19

a

b

c

1　　　　　2　　　　　3　　　　　4

Examples of *Karanas*, the Alphabet of Postures, from the Nataraja temple, Chidambaram, 13th century A.D. (1a) K68, Gajakridita (elephant sport); (1b) K96, Nivesa (settling); (1c) K70, Garuda pluta (kite's flight); (2a) K75, Sannata (hands well bent); (2b) K55, Aksipta (scattering all round); (2c) K81, Danda Pada (serpent creeping); (3a) K38, Bhramara (bee); (3b) K80, Mayuralita (peacock's grace); (3c) K63, Parsva Kranta (side-transit); (4a) K66, Ataikranta (step beyond); (4b) K83, Harinapluta (deer flight); (4c) K78, Sucividdha (needle probing). (Copyright, Department of Archaeology, Government of India.)

Plate 20

a

b

1

2

a

b

3

4

Examples of *Karanas*, the Alphabet of Postures, from the Nataraja temple, Chidam-baram, 13th century A.D. (1) K23, Ancita (placing); (2a) K48, Vyamsita (beguiled); (2b) K47, Vrscika (Scorpion); (3) K96, Nivesa (Settling); (4a) K40, Bhujangancita (Serpent touch); (4b) K39, Catura (four fingers). (Copyright, Department of Archaeology, Government of India.)

5. *Karana 85, Nitamba.* (Meaning "Posteriors").

6. *Karana 87, Kari Hasta.* (Meaning "Elephant Trunk").

7. *Karana 54, Uromandala.* (Meaning "Chest Region").

8. Again *Karana 11, Katticchinna.* (Meaning "Split Waist").

When these eight *Karanas* are combined, then these series of movements make one *Angahara*—the *Angahara Bhramara* No. 14.

A third example gives *Angahara Alata* ("Circling") No. 22.

The following eight *Karanas* have to be combined to form it (Plate 17).

1. *Karana 18, Alata.* (Meaning "Circling").

2. *Karana 25, Urdhva Janu.* (Meaning "Raised Knees"). The left foot is placed flat with the toes facing outwards. The right foot is raised with the heel at knee level of the left foot, and the toes pointing down. The right arm is raised straight to shoulder level, slightly bent at the elbow; the hand is in *Pataka*, that is, all the fingers and the thumb stretched straight close together, and the fingers pointing down. The left hand is held at shoulder level in *Pataka* also, with the palm facing outwards. Then there are two movements. (i) The leg is bent and raised to chest level. (ii) The hands are moved delicately.

3. *Karana 26, Nikuncita.* (Meaning "Bent"). The left foot is flat, toes facing outwards, the right leg raised right back, with the heel almost touching the back of the head near the ear. The right hand is stretched across the body to the left, the hand in *Pataka*, that is, all the fingers and the thumb stretched straight close together, with the fingers pointing to the ground. The left hand is also in *Pataka* gesture, with the fingers pointing up, and the palm on the side of the left cheek. Then there are two movements. (i) The right leg is kept raised upwards. (ii) The left hand is kept in position and the right hand is moved to touch the tip of the nose.

4. *Karana 77, Urdhvacuci (Ardha-Suci).* (Meaning "Needle Probing"). The feet are crossed at the ankles, with the left foot in front of the right. The left foot is on the flat and the right foot has the back of the toes touching the ground. The right arm is bent with the palm facing outwards, held near the arm-pit in the *Pataka* gesture, that is, all the fingers and thumb are stretched straight close together; the left arm is bent with the hand at chest level, also in the *Pataka* gesture, palms facing inwards and the fingers pointing down. Then there are two movements. (i) The hands with the backs pointing outwards are raised and held above the head. (ii) The right foot is raised so that it balances on the big toe.

5. *Karana 21, Viksipta.* (Meaning "Thrown Over").

6. *Karana 55. Aksipta.* (Meaning "Scattering All Round").

7. *Karana 87, Kari Hasta.* (Meaning "Elephant Trunk").

8. *Karana 11, Katicchinna.* (Meaning "Split Waist").

When these eight *Karanas* are combined, then these series of movements make one *Angahara*, the *Angahara Alata No. 22.*

At the beginning of *Angahara Alata* No 22, before commencing the eight *Karanas* that are combined to form it, certain hand movements are done. First, make *Svastika*, that is, the two hands are in *Kataka Mukha* gesture; the second, third and little fingers are bent almost touching the palm, and the first finger and thumb touch at the tips. The hands are held with the finger tips pointing outwards and placed about chest level in front. Then this gesture is changed to *Hamsapaksha*, the four fingers are stretched, palm very slightly hollow, and the thumb bent to touch the second finger at the base. The wrists are crossed in the form of a *Svastika*, and then the hands are moved around. After this, place the hands with the palms facing each other in front at chest level at a slight angle. Second, *Vyamsita* is done, that is, between each completed *Svastika* movement as described above, the hands are moved round and round and brought back to position. After these preliminary movements of the hands, the eight *Karanas* are done in the order described to make *Angahara Alata* No. 22.

In these three examples of *Angaharas*, it can be seen that they have several *Karanas* in common. For instance:

a) *Angahara Aksipta No.* 5 equals *Karanas* 36, 21, 18, 55, 54, 85, 87 and 11.

b) *Angahara Bhramara No.* 14 equals *Karanas* 36, 55, 11, 78, 85, 87, 54 and 11.

These two *Angaharas* have six *Karanas* in common, namely, 36, 55, 54, 85, 87 and 11.

c) *Angahara Alata No.* 22 equals *Karanas* 18, 25, 26, 77, 21, 55, 87 and 11.

Angahara Alata has five *Karanas* in common with *Angahara Aksipta*, namely, 18, 21, 55, 87 and 11.

Angahara Alata has three *Karanas* in common with *Angahara Bhramara*, namely, 55, 87 and 11.

In this manner, the 32 *Angaharas* are formed by the various combinations of different and common *Karanas*, and sometimes other hand and leg and foot movements are added. This makes the pattern of postures and hand gestures. Together with these *Karanas* and *Angaharas*, the *Rechakas* are studied. These are special foot, waist, neck and arm movements and hand gestures. Finally, the *Pindibhandas* are studied. These are the completed whole bodily movements achieved from particular sequences of the dance.

Having seen how the basic postures the *Karanas* are utilized for the various *Angaharas*, and noted that the *Rechakas* and *Pindibhandas* complete the technique of the dance, we go finally into the portrayal of feeling and expression in the dance. This is known as *Abhinaya*.

Abhinaya is fourfold:

a. ANGIKA   or the expression through the limbs and body.
b. VACHIKA   or the expression through the voice.
c. SATTVIKA   or the mental expression of feeling and emotion by facial expression and use of eyes.
d. AHARYA   or the expression through the dress, ornaments, and other aids.

Thus it is that with the combination of the five main items, the *Karanas*, *Angaharas*, *Rechakas*, *Pindibhandas*, and *Abhinaya*, dance takes shape and resolves into a meaningful art. From every posture of the head; the placement of the body; from the hands full of lucid gestures; from the position of the waistline and hips, the legs and feet; from the eloquent facial expressions supported by the eyes and eyebrows; and with the particular dress, ornaments, voice and melody, the whole is evolved. Every part of the body must be brought into studied control, and every gesture, expression and unit of movement must be rightly studied.

By the same token, exactly designed physical movements of the dance must be in perfect harmony with each beat of the drum in the musical accompaniment. Every single step must find its counterpart in the drum beats, and with ever-varying poses of bodily movement combined with hand gestures, the feet maintain a great frequence of cunningly intricate steps which pass rapidly from the flat of the foot to the toes; from the toes to the heels; from the heels to the ball of the foot; and again to the edges of the soles of the feet.

In all Indian dancing there must be the contrast in styles too—the *Lasya* or Gentle feminine type and the *Tandava* or Forceful manly type. The next step now is to see how the classical dance is actually practised in India, in the south, north, south-west, north-east, and east of the country, where it is known as the Bharata Natyam, Kathak, Kathakali, Orissi (Odissi), Manipuri, and Kuchipudi, respectively.

The traditional dance based on some of the important aspects of the classical dance form is also followed by the Chau masked dancers of Bihar, and the Mohini Atam and Krishna Atam of Kerala.

5. *Main Schools of the Classical Dance*

BHARATA NATYAM

THE classical dance is practised in South India, Tamil Nad, under the name of Bharata Natyam, and the centres where it is most active are Tanjore and Madras.

Tamil Nad or the Tamil country, in which this ancient dance art has been preserved in all its purity and arranged into its present form, is the possessor of some of the finest temples to be found in our country. Standing in many instances to a height of over 200 feet, their elaborately carved massive temple-tower gateways called *Gopurams* are heavily ornamented with sculptures of Gods and Goddesses representing various aspects of the Creator, and mythological figures and kings and heroes from legend and sacred history. These places of worship rise like giant sentinels into vivid blue skies radiant with a brilliant sun, and in many of these temples, we find a great profusion of dance sculptures that add to the beauty of form and design.

In the magnificent pillared halls and corridors, all heavily ornamented, the pavilions and lotus tanks, the atmosphere of ancient India lingers with a compelling fragrance. Creating landmarks wherever they rise above the cities, these seats of religion, art and learning make a fascinating picture as they stand towering over trees aflame with bud and blossom.

Far inside the corridors, initiates chant and study Sanskrit and classic Tamil. At the shrines, worshippers bend low with their offerings, walking the age-old passageways that are lighted with flickering oil lamps. Outside, the country is warm and alive with the scent of the mango blossom, jasmine and temple flowers; and warmth radiates everywhere—in the brilliant sarees and flowers, the rich tones of the old mellow language and the strains of music from the oldest instruments known in India.

There is little doubt that the present prescribed form in which the Bharata Natyam is performed was set in this particular order about a century ago by the

28

Plate 21

1

2

3

4

5

6

7

8

9

Temple sculptures. Classical dance postures, inspired by the
Karanas, from the Devi temple, Chidambaram, 13th century A.D.
(Copyright, Department of Archaeology, Government of India.)

Plate 22

1

2

3

4

5

Temple sculptures. Classical dance postures, inspired by the *Karanas*, from .the Devi temple, Chidambaram, 13th century A.D. (Copyright, Department of Archaeology, Government of India.)

Plate 23

1

2

3

4

5

6

Sudha Doraiswamy (now Sudha Sekhar) in Bharata Natyam
Nrtta poses (Pure Dance). A series of *Karana-adavus* in the
"Tat Thai Tha" series. (Courtesy, Sudha Sekhar.)

Plate 24

1

2

3

Indrani in Bharata Nat-
yam *Nrtta* (Pure Dance)
postures.
(Photos, H. Rahman.)

Bharata Natyam dance costume (a brocaded temple saree). Mrinalini Sarabhai in a statuesque posture showing the clear-cut lines typical of *Nrtta* (Pure Dance) of Bharata Natyam. (Photo, Hemendra A. Shah. By courtesy of Mrinalini Sarabhai.

Plate 25

1

2

Yamini Krishnamurti in Bharata Natyam *Nrtta* (Pure Dance) postures. (Courtesy, Coronet, Madras.)

Yamini Krishnamurti in Bharata Natyam, pausing between a Pure Dance interlude. (Photo, Coronet, Madras.)

3

Plate 26

1

2

3

4

M. K. Saroja in Bharata Natyam *Nrtta* (Pure Dance) postures. (Photos copyright, Mohan Khokar.)

Plate 27

1

2

3

4

Mrinalini Sarabhai in Bharata Natyam *Nrtta* (Pure Dance)
postures. From the (1) *Jatisvaram,* (2) *Sabdam,* (3) *Varnam,*
(4) *Tillana.* (Courtesy, Mrinalini Sarabhai.)

Plate 28

1

2

Kumari Kamala in Bharata Natyam *Nrtta* (Pure Dance) postures.
(Courtesy, Kumari Kamala.)

Shirin Vajifdar in Bharata Natyam *Nrtta* (Pure Dance) postures.
(Courtesy, Shirin Vajifdar.)

3

4

adepts and teachers (*gurus*) of the South, known as Nattuvanars.   Among them may be mentioned illustrious names like Vadivelu Pillai, Chinniah, Ponniah and Sivanandum, and their revered guru Muttuswami Dikshitar, all of whom were Sanskrit and Tamil scholars and masters of music and the dance.   It is to these Nattuvanars, their descendants like Pandanallur Meenakshisunduram Pillai and their pupils the Devadasis (the handmaidens of God), that we really owe a debt of gratitude for having so assiduously preserved the purity of the classical dance techniques in the South.

As far as we are able to glean from some of the inscriptions placed between the 9th and 11th centuries A.D., the institution of Devadasis became established with the great temple building period of the Chola kings, especially Rajaraja I. With the close interrelation between the higher philosophies, dance and the temples which were the centres of religion as well as art and culture, it was only natural that the system of having Devadasis became established.

In those early times, we read, the Devadasis enjoyed a high social status and were very accomplished.   They could sing, read the classics, play on a variety of musical instruments and write on philosophical subjects.   The girls generally fell into two categories, namely, those who were voluntarily dedicated by their parents in a feeling of religious fervour, and those who were dedicated owing to circumstances of stress.   Their duties were to use the fan (*Chamara*) on the deities and to carry the Sacred Light (*Kumbarti*), as well as to sing and dance before the Gods when they were carried in procession. The Devadasis received a fixed salary for these religious duties.   Their training in the art of the dance was very thorough, so that for the most part, they started their studies at the tender age of five.   Tamil inscriptions mention that in the 11th century A.D., about four hundred such dancers were attached to the great Shiva temple at Tanjore, and about a hundred to the temple at Kanchipuram.

The *Silppadhikaram* ("The Epic of the Anklet") by Illango, a classic Tamil literary work of about the 2nd century A.D., describes the beauty and allure of the art of the dance as performed by the beautiful dancer Madhavi, who won the love and devotion of the merchant prince Kovalan.   In this tragically sad and touching story, there is a description of the manner in which Madhavi performed her *Avinaya Koothu* or the emotional expression of her *Abhinayam* and her capabilities in her *Nrtya*, that form of the dance comprising movements of the body, hands, limbs, together with facial expressions, and filled with *Rasa* or Flavour, which is perfect for dramatic interpretation.   From this classic, one gets a true picture of how the dance can be translated into the poetry of movement through the grace and talent of a beautiful woman.   The flexibility and flow of her hands; her gait, sometimes smooth and swan-like, sometimes elegantly alive as singing bees; the emotional abandon, sometimes sensuous, sometimes deeply withdrawn, express an over-powering rapture.   Thus did Madhavi, a queen in emotional expression, conquer the heart of the noble Kovalan.   Such too was the standard and accomplishment of some of the dancers of that early period.

Unfortunately, in the South, under the influence of Western culture and the social reform movement, cultured Indian social reformers began to associate Bharata Natyam with the so called life of the Devadasis, and an anti-Natya movement was started in about the third quarter of the 19th century.   This movement, together with the economic deterioration of the Devadasis, gave Bharata Natyam a great set-back from this time till about 1925.   It was at this juncture that the well known authority E. Krishna Iyer learnt Bharata Natyam from the great Natya-charya Melatur Natesa Iyer, and worked tirelessly for its revival both by precept and practice for seven long years. His noble work and propaganda started the initial renaissance of this great classical dance tradition of the South.

Although Bharata Natyam is performed today in solo by women, it took many forms, such as the dance dramas of the Bhagavata Mela Natakas of Melatur (Tamil Nad), the Kuruvanji dance ballet, and the Navasandhi ritual dance of the temples. Each temple too had its own distinctive form of the Bharata Natyam, "such as the Ahamargam, Chindi, Varikolam, and Sokkam of the Thiruvenaivoyal; the Suraguru Natakam of Tirukazhikunrum; the Thiru Natakam of Pattamadai in the Tirunelveli district and the Rajaraeswari Natakam of Tanjore."[1]

Really, therefore, the Bharata Natyam embraces a wide and comprehensive system of classical dancing based on the *Natya Sastra* by Bharata Muni and the *Abhinaya Dharpana* by Nandikeshwara.

The Nattuvanaras and Devadasis became great adepts in the Bharata Natyam, and while the Nattuvanars confined themselves chiefly to imparting and preserving the art, the Devadasis performed it. The Nattuvanars were mostly non-Brahmins who were well versed in Sanskrit and the *Sastras*. On the other hand, the art was also practised and preserved in the form of dance dramas by the Bhagavatars, men generally of the Brahmin caste, who sang the praise of God, and formed a system called the Bhagavata Melas. Forceful, statuesque in posture and full of a philo-sophical content, these dance dramas were beautifully dramatised and danced.

The Bhagavatars found the dance drama the best medium for interpreting the great philosophic teachings of the *Puranas*. And in utilizing drama with classical music and the Bharata Natyam dance techniques, they created an art which truly expounded dance as Bharata Muni had conceived it in his *Natya Sastra*.

Throughout these dance dramas of the Bhagavata Mela, dramatic action, lyrical composition, choice music and classical dance were subtly mingled one into the other to interpret the highly emotional and appealing stories which were enacted; and as characterisation became an important feature also in this form of the dance, many artistes participated. Only men took part and they excelled in the art. These devotees of the dance drama were responsible for handing the art down through the generations.

The Nattuvanars on the other hand concentrated on the solo form of Bharata Natyam which until recently was known as Dasi Atam or Sadir Atam. They arranged the dance in such a way that its performance took place in certain stages. This was probably done in order to gradually bring before audiences the full strength of its technique and dramatic value through a variety of sequences. Today, in spite of the fact that the art first gained honour in the temples where it took the form of dances of ritual and devotion, it is very popular on the secular stage.

The word "Bharata" as used in this form of the classical dance, is believed to be composed of the first syllable of each of its Three Main Elements:

BHAVA	or	Mood.	
RAGA	or	Melody, Song.	Bharata
TALA	or	Rhythmic Timing	

---

[1] E. Krishna Iyer, *The Illustrated Weekly of India*, 20th November, 1960. Article on Bharata Natyam

Natyam means the combination of both dancing and acting.

The dance being composed of these Three Elements, commences with *Nrtta* or pure dance movements to emphasise the importance of timing and rhythm. Timing is based on time measures, that is, beats of equal length. There are five special separate types of time measures or units that are commonly used, known as *Jatis*, namely, *Tisram, Chatsura, Khanda, Misram* or *Sathwaisira,* and *Sankirna*; consisting of units of 3,4,5,7 and 9 *Matras* or sub-divisions of the steady beat respectively. In other words, *Tisram* (ta-ka-ta) equals 3 beats; *Chatsura* (ta-ka-dhi-mi) equals 4 beats; *Khanda* (ta-ka-ta-ki-ta) equals 5 beats; *Misram* or *Sathwaisira* (Ta-ka-dhi-mi-ta-ka-ta) equals 7 beats; and *Sankirna* (ta-ka-dhi-mi-ta-ka-ta-ki-ta) equals 9 beats. The dance is generally arranged to one or more of these basic timings.

The cymbal player and one *Mirdanga* drum player keep the main basic timing or *Talam*[1] with its regular intervals of time beats. Another *Mirdanga* player is employed to play an intricate combination of drum syllables which are fitted into the main timing to give it pattern. These drum syllables correspond to word syllables which are recited or chanted by a musician. Each step that the dancer takes has to correspond with the syllable which is simultaneously played by the drummer and recited by the musician. The patterned sound syllables which the drummer plays are called *Chollu* in Bharata Natyam, and the corresponding word syllables which are recited by the musician are known as *Sollu-kuttu.* Both the drum sound syllables and the corresponding word syllables that are recited, are put into verse form, each verse lasting a few seconds, a quarter of a minute, or half a minute; and these verses are strung together into little poems, just as in poetry so many verses make a complete poem. These dance syllabic poems, as we might well call them, have a wonderful rhythmic flow, and their length depends on the composition of the particular pure dance or *Nrtta* sequences required in the various stages of the dance.

Here are three distinct sets of sounds beautifully co-ordinated in perfect harmony—the patterned drum syllables, the corresponding recited word syllables, and the steps of the dancer which follow these closely step by step. The dance syllabic poems are played and danced in three speeds, namely, the starting speed which is generally slow (*Vilamba*); double the starting speed, but still at medium tempo (*Madhya*); and then at four times the starting speed, which is quick (*Drut*). This is necessary for contrast and variety.

Great heights of technical brilliance can be achieved by the accomplished dancer as her feet beat their intricate patterns exactly synchronising with the patterned syllables of drum and recitation—all in perfect rhythm with the basic timing. The result is very beautiful, for as the dancer performs her design of steps, her arms and hands are used effectively, her neck and head are moved gracefully, and she bends and turns, advances and retreats in absolute concord, to unfold sequence after sequence of pure dance.

Grace, speed, versatility and complete mastery of the art are necessary to do full justice to technique such as this. And skilful team-work must be obtained all through between the drum player, the musician and the dancer. Indeed, so close is the affinity between the accompanists and the dancer, that according to some sources, even timing or *Tala* is derived from a philosophical concept like the dance. And we have the Tender or *Lasya* content and the strong Forceful content in it;

[1] *Talam* in South India; *Tala* in Sanskrit

it being believed that the word *Tala* has been evolved from the first syllables of *Tandava* and *Lasya*. Bharata Natyam as practised in Tamil Nad in its solo form is mainly *Lasya* in style.

I have already described in some detail, with a few illustrations, how from the *Karanas* or the origin and basic postures of all dance movement, the *Angaharas*, a combination of several *Karanas*, are formed; and from these, the pattern of the dance is evolved. These are the fundamental postures or alphabet of dance movement as detailed in the ancient treatise the *Natya Sastra* by Bharata Muni. When the actual practical performance of the Bharata Natyam was evolved, however, it was probably found that these *Karanas* and *Angaharas* had to be adapted to suit the capabilities of the human body. Whereas the *Karanas* and *Angaharas* envisage every possible movement and posture the human body can take theoretically, for practical application, many of them had to be adapted and the closest possible replica to each *Karana* was evolved and used as the basis for the dance style that has come down to posterity and performed in the particular techniques of order and form.

In the Bharata Natyam, therefore, the dance technique of pure dance or *Nrtta* consists of a number of *Adavus* or phrases of combinations of postures in which the body, waist, arm, hand, leg and foot, head and neck movements are done to various set dance syllable wordings. Like the *Karana*, the *Adavu* is the basic foundation and unit of the dance step patterns and postured movements, each *Adavu* involving a basic pose or *Sthanka*. A combination of *Adavus* makes what is known as an *Adavu-jati*. Some beautiful gestures and arm positions combine to ornament the general beauty of postures; and we find among these, the use of the classical hand gestures with the arms stretched forwards, sideways and bent in varying manner. According to experts, there are ten different groups of *Adavus*, each having twelve different Modes, making in all 120 basic dance arrangements which can be further combined into hundreds of varieties of patterned dance movements. Dancers, however, generally learn about forty to seventy-two *Adavus*, and then study the intricate dance techniques of pure dance and *Abhinayam*.[1]

The *Abhinayam* comprises the interpretation of the classic Sanskrit, Tamil and Telugu lyrics and songs, by gestures, facial expressions, postures and acting. These songs are either devotional like the *Geetam*, *Sabdam* and *Kirtana*, or love themes like the *Padams* or *Javeli*. In the *Abhinayam* also, timing or *Talam* plays an important part, just as it does in the pure dance techniques. The movements of the neck, the hand gestures, the swing of the arms and the gait, are all controlled by the main basic timing or *Talam*.

As the dance unfolds, we see that the Bharata Natyam has incorporated in it the important aspects of the dance as detailed in the *Natya Sastra*, namely, *Nrtta* or pure dance, *Natya* or the combination of both acting and dancing, and *Nrtya* or that form of the dance comprising movements of the body, hands, limbs, together with facial expressions, and filled with *Rasa* or Flavour, and may express small episodes, just a sentence or a whole dramatic story or sequence.

The dance moves in a very methodical manner. The movements of posture, arms, hands and rhythmic patterns of the feet, proceed gradually from simple to difficult and thence to very difficult techniques in set stages. Finally it ends with a dramatic finale, in which the feet move very swiftly; arms take various angles and lines, with the hands in varying gestures, the dancer finally making a graceful

---

[1] *Abhinayam* in South India; *Abhinaya* in Sanskrit

circular movement of the arm over the head and bringing the arm downwards so that the hand points straight down in front before the feet. This finale is known as the *Thirmana*, and it not only lends a perfect climax to each series of movements in each stage of the dance, but is also often used most effectively in between alternate short and long sequences of the dance. The *Thirmana* is usually repeated three times, and done in three speeds, each time the dancer moving faster. Although I have mentioned that usually five or six different main *Talams* or timings are used in the actual performance, a finished dancer studies at least thirty various *Talas* and her repertoire may go up to as many as the whole 120 or a hundred different rhythmic patterned step and postural designs or *Adavus*, and more than a dozen finales or *Thirmanas*.

The Bharata Natyam is usually performed in the following stages, namely:

1. Alarippu. The dance usually begins with the *Alarippu*, meaning the "opening of the bud into blossom." *Alarippu* literally is the Temple Flower or Oleander, used as an offering at the beginning of devotional worship. The *Alarippu*, which is the first stage of the dance, is not generally accompanied by music, but is danced to the accompaniment of *Sollu-kuttu* or the rhythmic syllables recited by the singer. These are set to a particular time measure of *Tisram* (3 beats) or *Misram* (7 beats), played on the *Mirdanga* and cymbals. The dancer starts with the feet a little apart, knees bent outwards, the hands folded above the head, and goes into some slow movements to the recitation of the word syllables of pure dance and the corresponding drum wordings. The deliberate fanwise movements of the head from right to left, lightly upwards and again to the right and left, with pleasing eye glances and lift of eyebrows, serve as an introduction to what follows in this stage of the dance. These preliminary movements are done with the dancer standing, and then the same movements are repeated after she has changed her position to squatting on the toes, knees outspread. As the dance continues, the hand movements and footwork increase in speed and become more complicated, moving in lines and patterns. It finally ends with a very quick set of movements, terminating at a high speed with the finale or *Thirmana*.

The *Alarippu* is short and sweet; its rhythm is very beautiful. Dancers usually study at least two *Alarippus*, in which there are slight variations of movement and postures. The most popular timings are *Tisram* and *Misram*. As its name indicates, the *Alarippu* is a sort of introduction and invocation making a prelude to the *Jatisvaram*, the next stage of the dance, and introducing a general outline of form and technique of all that is to follow.

2. Jatisvaram. Following the *Alarippu* comes the *Jatisvaram*. *Jatis* are time measures, and *Svaram* is the musical notation. Stress is laid on these two aspects— time and musical score. It is danced to the accompaniment of *Svara* passages composed of *Ragas*.

At this stage, the background music, the timing and dance movements become highly technical. It is pure dance composition at its best with accompanying sequences of the scale and the timing elaborately combined. Beautiful movements of the neck, arms, gestures, feet, and bodily sculpturesque postures are combined in a fascinating design. The dance rises as it were to a state of technical brilliance, in which more of the wonderfully patterned stepping, the pretty changes of posture and graceful weaving of arm movements are co-ordinated with a charming pattern of the drum beats.

3. Sabdam. Third comes the *Sabdam*. Here, emphasis is on interpretation. This stage of the dance usually commences with a few pure dance movements that are very lovely, yet subtly different from what has gone previously, followed by a *Thirmana*. Then comes the rendering in gesture language and emotional acting, the explanation of a song or *Sahitya* which are devotional sentiments in lyrical verse form and are the text to be interpreted. A religious, heroic or philosophical theme, based either on sacred legend or story, is interpreted, generally in a metre of seven beats. The *Sabdam* is really the prelude to the *Varnam*, the next stage, and is similar but less elaborate and intense. The dancer has ample scope here to show her art of interpretation by the use of gesture language and acting, her facial expressions, eloquent eye and eyebrow play, mobility of lips and the manner in which she moves on the stage. The neck is used constantly in its varying modes as it is moved to and fro to help the inclinations of the head and assist her acting. As she translates her song into dance expression, she walks gracefully in certain prescribed modes as directed by a simple rhythm.

In between the gestural interpretation and mime, the dancer adds an alluring touch by introducing some lovely pure dance movements. The dance performance has now reached the stage where the audience has been introduced to the Three Elements of the Bharata Natyam, namely, *Bhava* or Mood, *Raga* or Melody, Song, *Tala* or Rhythmic Timing; and *Natya*, the combination of both dancing and acting.

4. Varnam (Colour). *Varnam* comes after the *Sabdam*, and is one of the most beautiful and highly elaborate dance conceptions, incorporating technical brilliance, richness of melody and artful interpretation. It gives form and shape to the soul and true intentions of Bharata Natyam, and is the most complete example of the art of Bharata Natyam. Usually, one of the well known musical compositions, selected from an important *Raga* that is perfect for showing great technical skill in the performance of music, is chosen as the theme for the *Varnam*.

The *Varnam* is composed of emotional acting with rhythmic cadences and can be compared to a musical composition or sonata, wherein exquisite and elaborate pure dance is performed in a series of interludes amidst a display of song interpretation. Succession after succession of dance sequences are enriched in between by passages of emotional interpretation of the song. Each sequence finishes with an intricate finale or *Thirmana*—with an exhibition of great skill and power. The emotional passages are done three times each, and every time it is different, to show the variety of the gesture language. In this fourth stage of the dance, we find therefore all the three components of the complete dance magnificently displayed, namely, *Natya* or the combination of both dancing and acting, *Nrtta* or pure dance and rhythm, and *Nrtya* or body movements with facial expressions and acting filled with *Rasa* or Flavour.

5. Padam. To soften the high pitch that the dance has now reached, the dancer glides into the *Padams*. These are finely chanted seven-line lyrical songs of mother love or romantic theme, in Tamil, Telugu or Sanskrit, as immortalised in the Classics, or telling of Gods and Goddesses in the *Sringara Bhava* or Mood of Love. Sometimes the theme speaks of the separation of lovers (*Viraha*); sometimes of lovers and their bliss (*Sambhoga*); and sometimes of mother love, as when Yeshoda fondles the baby Krishna.

The dancer interprets these themes in soft flowing gestures and emotional acting. Sometimes she interprets the dialogues of more than one character in the poem or song. Usually, in the *Padams*, one of the important lines which forms the

Plate 29

2

4

5

6

Sudha Doraiswamy (now Sudha Sekhar) in Bharata Natyam.
(1, 3, 4, 5, 6) *Nrtta* (Pure Dance) postures. (2) Pose depicting
Madan (the God of Love) with his bow ready to shoot his flowery
arrows—from the *Varnam*. (Courtesy, Sudha Sekhar.)

Plate 30

1

2

3

4

Ritha Devi in Bharata Natyam *Nrtta* (Pure Dance) postures.
(Photos, B. Bhansali.)

Plate 31

Ram Gopal in *Natanam Adinar*, the Dance of Shiva, a part of the Bharata Natyam performance. (Courtesy, Ram Gopal.)

Plate 32

1

"O Lord! Who danceth with one leg raised...."

2

"Who art the father of Subrahmanya, the bearer of the Sacred lance!"

3

"Who danced in the Golden Hall of Chidambaram...."

4

"Who hath Ganga issuing from Thy locks...."

Plate 33

5

6

"Who art both man . . . .

. . . .and woman."

7

8

"Invisible to Brahma and Vishnu."

"Nandi plays the Mirdanga . . . ."

M. K. Saroja in *Abhinayam* portraying the Bharata Natyam *Kirtanam* "Kalai Thooki," a sacred song addressed to Lord Shiva. (Photos copyright, Mohan Khokar.)

Plate 34

9

"Vishnu gives rhythm on the cymbals...."

10

"Narada, the Veena...."

11

"O Thou, who danceth on the subdued Muyalahan...."   M. K. Saroja in *Abhinayam* portraying the Bharata Natyam *Kirtanam* "Kalai Thooki." (Photos copyright, Mohan Khokar.)

Plate 35

1

2

3

The "Sarabhendra Bhoopala Kuruvanji" dance drama of Bharata
Natyam. (1) The three *Sakhis* (girl attendants) introduce the
heroine Madanavalli. (2) Mrinalini Sarabhai as Madanavalli, the
heroine, tells her *Sakhis* of her deep longing to be united with
her Lord. (3) Mrinalini Sarabhai as Madanavalli, the heroine,
wonders what fate has in store for her as the *Kurati* (Gipsy fortune-
teller) studies her palm. (Courtesy, Mrinalini Sarabhai.)

Plate 36

1

2

3

4

5

6

(1) Chitra Pooviah in one of the important postures of the *Nrtta* or Pure Dance of the *Paran* in Kathak. (2) Lata Pooviah in a characteristic posture of the *Nrtta* or Pure Dance in Kathak. (3) *Abhinaya-Gat Bhava*—three different poses of the Gopis looking for Sri Krishna ; (*left to right*), Chitra Pooviah showing "peeping", Lata Pooviah showing "raising of the *Ghunghat* above the face," Cita Pooviah showing "moving the *Ghunghat* sideways." (4) Chitra Pooviah in one of the important postures of the *Nrtta* or Pure Dance seen in the *Paran* and other sequences in Kathak. (5) Cita Pooviah in the first characteristic position of *Hastak* as taken at the starting of the *Thata* and the *Amad* in Kathak. (6) Cita Pooviah in the second characteristic position or *Hastak* as taken in the *Thata*, the *Sangeet* and at the beginning of any dance sequences. (Courtesy, Misses Pooviah.)

main theme or burden of the song (*Pallavi*) is repeated over and over again by the singer and interpreted each time by the dancer with variations of different gestures and emotional acting. Following the *Pallavi* interpretations, comes the *Anu-Pallavi*, where two lines of the song are then similarly interpreted. This mode of interpretation creates for the audience a series of mental pictures or conceptions (*Sanchari Bhava*), that are replete with very many aspects of the motif (*Sthayi Bhava*). In the *Padams*, the song or lyric may well be likened to the bud, and the *Sanchari Bhava* to the fully open flower of many petals and beautiful attributes. The idyllic love lyrics of the Krishna legends and the poetic *Git Govinda* by Jayadeva are perfect subjects for this particular interpretive style of the *Padams*. Well known *Ragas* like Bhairivi, Kalyani, Khambodi, Saviri, and Vasanta are generally selected for the *Padam* songs.

6. **Tillana.** The final stage of the performance is *Tillana* or pure dance with statuesque postures, intricate rhythms and a complete unison between the technique and touches of emotional acting. It is a picture of all the feminine charm, with a woman's airs and graces, and the intricate patterns of dance and footwork with swiftly moving arms, the tilt and fanwise jerks of the head and neck, the play of the eyes and eyebrows, coquetry and lilting grace. This stage of the dance, though the acme of *Lasya* and feminine beauty, is done at a fast tempo with all the confidence of a virtuoso. The music and song accompanying it are haunting, the melody repeated over and over again, its alluring rhythms marked by liveliness.

These then are the six stages in which the Bharata Natyam is usually and conventionally done. The performance ends with a sort of benediction in the form of a recitation of a short *Sloka* (Sanskrit sacred verse dedicated to God).

Often, just before this concluding item, there may be a short chant from the *Git Govinda* (the Song Celestial), the immortal poetic work by Jayadeva, which describes the philosophical story of the love of Radha and Krishna. During the chanting of these *Slokas*, which are unaccompanied by music or drum, the dancer stands in one position and interprets the poetic chant with gesture language and *Abhinayam*.

Many of the Bharata Natyam programmes today are considered incomplete without the additional item of the grand and stirring *Natanam Adinar*. This depicts the Dance of Shiva on the occasion when according to legend He called the great rishis into His presence in the Golden Hall on Mount Kailasha in the Himalayas and danced the Dance of Creation and Destruction of the World. The Light Spheres of the Universe vibrated tremulously, the great Serpent upon whose head the world is believed to rest swerved and swayed, and caused the four ends of the earth to shake and quiver, so that great cascades gushed forth from the tortured waters of the Ganga....Coiled with hooded serpents, Shiva's hair waved gloriously as He moved in rhythmic perfection and His dance brought salvation to the world.

This is the theme of this item, and the dancer introduces in the course of its interpretation, some magnificent *Tandava* postures reminiscent of the sculptures of Shiva's dance of the Nataraja, found in many temples in India. Both *Tandava* and *Lasya* intermingle, as the chanting leads the dancer into the intricacies of the pure dance stances and the descriptive analysis of it, through the play of gestures and mime. Full of dignity, yet forceful, the *Natinam Adinar* fittingly expresses both the dramatic and technical excellence of the concepts of the South Indian classical dance art.

KURUVANJI

This subject forms a part of characteristic Tamil literature in poetry and song. The earliest *Kuruvanji* composed by Thirukutarajappa Kaviyar about three hundred years ago was the *Kutrala Kuruvanji*.   Nearly thirty other *Kuruvanjis* were written after this, and are still current.   In all these various *Kuruvanjis*, the theme is the same, usually having the main character of a heroine who is either a Goddess, a princess, or a woman of good family who is in love with a God, a good king, or a virtuous nobleman respectively.   The *Kuruvanji* or gipsy is the other important character who is introduced as the fortune teller who foretells whether or not the heroine will win the love of her beloved.   Among the various *Kuruvanji* subjects may be mentioned the *Kutrala*, the *Viralimalai*, the *Alagar*, the *Chitrambala* and the *Sarabhoji Kuruvanjis*.   The last named closely follows the style of the early *Kutrala Kuruvanji*.

The *Kuruvanji* is performed in dance ballet form with Bharata Natyam techniques.   A number of very fine select pure dance sequences (*Nrtta*) and *Abhinayam* are utilised with excellent *Adavu-jati* modes by the gipsy dancer.   These have a lilting rhythm and are of a lighter classical vein appropriate to her character and personaity, which are gay and charming.

The most popular and frequently performed *Kuruvanji* that is included at the end of a Bharata Natyam programme is generally the *Sarabhoji Kuruvanji*.   This dance drama tells of the beautiful woman Madanavalli and her love for the Raja Sarabhoji.   The heroine Madanavalli, who is a woman of culture and of good family, enacts her love for Raja Sarabhoji, under whose patronage music, dance and poetry flourished, and she tells of his many virtues.   In the course of the dance drama, the gipsy fortune teller (*Kuruvanji*) assures her that she will win the love she desires and paves the way for the romance to be fulfilled.   It is an appealing theme, beautifully suited to the dramatic character of Bharata Natyam and its wonderful display of *Abhinayam*.

Gifted and dedicated Nattuvanars and dancers have preserved this style of dance drama for posterity.   Pandanallur Meenakshisundaram Pillai's troupe, Nattuvanar Sri Dandayudhapani Pillai, Rukmani Devi, Balasaraswathi, Mrinalini Sarabhai, the Nrityodaya Troupe of Madras and the Tamil Isai Sangam, under the direction of Professor P. Sambamoorty, have most successfully performed *Kuruvanji* dance ballets.

In conclusion, it can be seen that the art of Bharata Natyam as practised in Tamil Nad is deeply emotional, intense and graciously appealing.   Added to its strength of form and enduring beauty, it has come down through the ages still maintaining its power and purity: now deeply religious in content, now enchanting and sculptural, now noble in form and expression and now gentle and enticing. It is no wonder that it has become one of our most cherished dance forms, and one that continues to enchant both performer and audience alike.   Indeed, one can truly say of the Bharata Natyam that age has not withered it nor custom staled its infinite variety.

KATHAK

The classical dance as it is practised in North India, is known as Kathak. The actual source of both Bharata Natyam and Kathak has obviously been the same, namely, the *Natya Sastra* by Bharata Muni.   In fact, the *Natya Sastra*

...thak dance costume (mythological). Sitara Devi Radha in the *Abhinaya* of one of the Krishna *Tandava Nrityas*.

Kathak dance costume (Moghul). Sitara Devi, the celebrated dancer, showing the *Chakkar* (fast turns) from one of the *Thoras* in a *Nrtta* (Pure Dance) sequence.

(Photos, **S. R.** Mundkur. By courtesy of Sitara Devi)

mentions that the classical dance in India was first performed in the Himalayas, and from other sources we read that the classical dance in northern India was known to have flourished for centuries in the form of solos, duets and dance drama. The word Kathak literally means "story teller," referring probably to the old bards and story narrators who used to travel over the country entertaining the people with sacred legend, folk lore and mythology as part of the cultural programmes. This very old form of entertainment later incorporated music, dance and mime, and became clear-cut and distinct as a dance form. Besides, communities of dancers performed various types of dances; among them were the Kathaks who were both dancers and musicians, and whose performance in all probability came to be styled as Kathak.

With the spread of the worship of Vishnu and Krishna, sacred songs and hymns, dance, lyrical compositions, painting and literary works were composed and dedicated to God. The beautiful parable modes of the Krishna Lilas came into being, and Sri Krishna was associated with the term "Natavara," the Divine Dancer. The Ras Lilas were danced in the style of an operatic dance drama with much of the classical modes in them, and were enacted by a community of artistes known as the Rasudharis, who were devotees of Krishna. Sacred dances (*Dadhi*) were performed on particular days in the temples.

Turning to the old treatises on music, the *Kurtanas*, we find that they had among them special texts which dealt with dance compositions and their accompanying techniques. These dance *Kurtanas* gave details of the postures (*Mandalas*), the fast turns (*Bhramaris*), the steppings (*Gatis*), the hand gestures (*Hastas*), the emotional interpretive aspect (*Abhinaya*) and special dance syllable rhythms to be played on the *Mirdanga*. Thus we find in the traditional dance as practised in the north, all the elements of the classical dance as detailed in the *Natya Sastra*, namely, *Nrtta* or pure dance, *Natya* or the combination of both dancing and acting, and *Nrtya* or that form of the dance comprising movements of the body, hands, limbs, together with facial expressions and filled with *Rasa* or Flavour, which may express small episodes, just a sentence or a whole dramatic story or sequence.

The Kathak became famous and has been best preserved in the cities of Lucknow (Uttar Pradesh) and Jaipur (Rajasthan). In Uttar Pradesh, there are innumerable fine old temples, which were the centres of the arts and learning. The historic and sacred Ganges river feeds its plains, curving through a number of its cities which have been associated with learning, religious festival and philosophic thought since earliest times. In this land of great rivers and historical and religious monuments, it is not surprising that music, poetry, and dance flowered to their fullest beauty.

In Rajasthan, colour and artistic endeavour are abundantly apparent in the picturesque costumes of the people, in the old palaces, forts and temples that are noted for their striking architecture either in mellow rose sandstone or chaste marble. Rajput history abounds in deeds of chivalry, and the innate love of the people for ornament and pageantry, festival and celebration, so that art in many forms flourished, not the least being music, dance, delicate miniature painting and folk art.

The Kathak in its present form was established in Lucknow about a century and a half ago by the two distinguished masters, Prakashji and his son Thakur Prasad, who hailed from Rajasthan. They were scholars of note and belonged to the Rasudhari tradition of Kathak. Thakur Prasad's three sons, Bindadin Maharaj, Kalka Prasad and Bhairon Prasad, carried on the great work started by their father, and it is mainly due to the marvellous combination of the genius of the gifted dancers Bindadin Maharaj and Kalka Prasad that the famous Lucknow Gharana or School of the Kathak dance earned both name and fame throughout India.

Bindadin Maharaj was a devotee of Sri Krishna, and he composed some of the most beautiful lyrics, particularly his *Bhajans* (sacred songs dedicated to God); and Kalka Prasad became famous for his virtuosity in the techniques of pure dance and its wonderful rhythms. What Bindadin Maharaj did for Kathak is history now. He endowed the technique with new forms, variety and vitality, and by his emphasis on the beauty of Mood (*Bhava*), he enriched its dramatic content. He created lyrical compositions like the *Thumri, Dadra, Ghazal* and *Gaths*, with their many subtleties of Mood (*Bhava*), pronounced features of the Lucknow school. Kalka Prasad's three famous sons, Achhan Maharaj, Lachhu Maharaj and Shambu Maharaj, became great adepts and exponents of Kathak; the late Achhan Maharaj was largely responsible for spreading the art and fully retaining all the valuable technique and beauty of composition that his uncle the great Bindadin Maharaj gave to Kathak. Another eminent master, composer and dancer was the late Sukhdeve Maharaj, father of Sitara Devi.

In the Jaipur Gharana or School of Kathak, the famed old master Girdhariji was one of the greatest exponents. His sons Hari Prasad and Hanuman Prasad (a great devotee of God), continued to retain the beauty of form and musical compositions of Kathak at their highest aesthetic level. They were followed by many eminent dancers such as Jaya Lal, Narayan Prasad and Sunder Prasad, Mohan Lal, Chiranji Lal and Guru Narayan Prasad, winner of the Sangeet Natak Akademi award in 1959, to name only a few of the famous *gurus*.

The Kathak as practised both in Lucknow and Jaipur has become known on a nation-wide scale today. And although it is generally conceded that the Lucknow school lays more emphasis on Mood and *Abhinaya*, there are really no strict set differences between the two schools, and they have much in common.

Like the Bharata Natyam, Kathak embodies fully the three composite parts of the classical dance, namely *Bhava* or Mood, *Raga* or Melody and *Tala* or Rhythmic Timing. However, although the *Natya Sastra* by Bharata Muni is the main source of both the Bharata Natyam and the Kathak, it will be found that due to differences of language, custom, environment and the influence of history, dress and music, the Kathak differs from the Bharata Natyam in certain important aspects. But at the same time, the adherance to a code of rules and regulations for their performance, the philosophical background and trends, the beautiful devotional subjects of many of the interpretive songs and lyrics are similar. Kathak follows its own tabulated set of hand gestures denoting a basic language of signs, but the manner in which they have been adapted in the *Abhinaya*, the way in which each mood is portrayed through the combination of gesture and bodily expression, and the variety of ways in which the mood is described (*Gat Bhavas* in Kathak, similar to the *Sanchari Bhava* in Bharata Natyam) are different. The footwork in Kathak is not as designed as that of the southern school, the swift feet rhythms being done for the most part on the flat of foot and toes, with very many turns (*Chakkar*) on the toes and flat of foot.

Here too the dance commences with *Nrtta* or pure dance movements to emphasise the importance of timing and rhythm. As in the Bharata Natyam, timing is based on time measures, that is, beats of equal length with five special types of time measures or units known as *Jatis*, namely, *Tisra, Chatasra, Khanda, Misra* and *Sankirna*, consisting of units of 3, 4, 5, 7, and 9.

.The dance is arranged to various main drum timings or *Talas*, such as *Adi Tal, Juptal, Dadra, Dhamar, Keherwa, Dhrupad, Teen Tal*, and so on, consisting of 3, 5, 6, 7, 8, 12 and 16 *Matras* or sub-divisions of beats in the main timing respectively. Further, to beautify the dance and rhythms, the main basic timing is embellished by means of *Bol* or little syllabic drum words like the *Chollu* of Bharata Natyam, that correspond with the feet patterns like the *Jatis* of the south, together with the recitation of the word syllables by the musicians, *Padhant* in Kathak and *Sollu-kuttu* in Bharata Natyam.

Music lends the background to the dance and keeps in tune with the main basic timing. The drummer plays the rhythmic fractional syllabic words (*Bol*) into the main timing at three-quarters the speed (*Paun*), one and a quarter times the speed (*Sawai*) or at one and a half times the speed (*Dedhi*). Thus while maintaining the basic timing or *Tala* he creates further varieties of *Tal* by using multiples of the main timing (*Kala*), for technical excellence. When the rhythmic syllabic words (*Bol*) are put into verse form they make *Thoras* or *Thukadas*. Each *Thora* includes in its composition a rhythmic finale or *Tahai* done three times. These *Tahais* are of many varieties and embellish the *Thoras*, being generally done by spinning round in one spot at great speed.

So here also, as in the Bharat Natyam, the intricate and harmonious balance of the main timing of regular beats of the *Tal*, the *Thoras* with their patterned syllabic sounds on the drum, the recitation of these *Thoras* by the musicians (*Padhant*) and the repetition step by step by the dancer as she follows the recitation create a perfect co-ordination of sound harmonies.

There are literally hundreds of such *Thoras* that differ subtly one from the other, both in the combinations of their syllable sounds (*Bol*) and in their translation into dance movement. Each set of *Bol* is specially created for a particular type of *Nrtta* or pure dance, and are classified accordingly. As in Bharata Natyam, the dance syllabic verses or *Thoras* are danced and played in three speeds or *Laya*, namely, slow (*Vilambit*), double the starting speed but still at medium tempo (*Madhya*), and four times the starting speed, which is fast (*Druta*). In dance parlance, *Vilambit* is *Tha*, *Madhya* is *Doon*, and *Druta* is *Chaugan*.

It is interesting to note that some of the *Thoras* of Kathak closely resemble the word syllables used in the same manner in Bharata Natyam. Each *Thora* is also done three times to complete one cycle of movement.

Example of the type of syllable wordings used in the Bharata Natyam rhythms:
    Tha, Dhim-thaka, Naka—Janu, Thaka—Dhim, Dhim—
    Thaka, Thaka—Digi, Digi, Thaka, Thari Thom.
    Thalangu, Thaka, Dhimi—Thatingana, Thom,
    Thalangu, Thaka Ninu, Nammithi—Nanu.

Example of the type of syllable wordings used in Kathak rhythms:
    Tha, Thoonga —Thaka Thoonga—
    Thaka Diga Diga Diga Diga Thoonga—
    Tha, Thoonga—Thaka Thoonga—
    Thaka Diga Diga Diga Diga Thayee—

Thaka Thaka Diga Diga Thaka Thaka Gadi Gina Thome—
Thaka Thaka Diga Diga Thaka Thaka Gadi Gina Thome—
Thaka Thaka Diga Diga Thaka Thaka Gadi Gina Thome—

Not only has the dancer to master the pure dance or *Nrtta* of Kathak, but he or she must become expert in the *Abhinaya*. Songs and lyrics in the old *Brij Bhasha*, or Hindi or Urdu with either devotional, heroic or love themes are interpreted through gestures, facial expressions, acting and postures. It has been shown that in the Bharata Natyam performance, there are various stages, proceeding from the simple and introductory to the more technically difficult stages, with the inter-play of emotional interpretive sequences to balance the tempo and structure. In the Kathak performance, generally no rigid stages are adhered to in a particular order. The technique of pure dance or *Nrtta* consists of several important features each with its distinctive and different facets of technique. *Abhinaya* may be shown between pure dance items or in the second half of the programme.

All classical dancing contains the devotional element. Traditionally, the Kathak performance commences with the invocation just as Bharata Natyam does.

Ganesha Vandana. This is the dance of invocation and salutation to Lord Ganesha, the elephant-headed God, remover of obstacles. In the musical accompaniment there is the unique combination of the lyrical sacred words of the text with fine rhythmic syllable wordings (*Bol*) set in perfect rhythm. Beauty of posture, movement, stepping and devotional attitude with expressive gestures and interpretation are combined in this introductory sequence of Kathak.

Thata. The dancer takes an elegant posture, with the characteristic position or *Hastak*, in which the right hand is held at right angles to the body, bent at the elbow, and the left hand is held vertical and stretched out. The feet are crossed, with the right foot slightly bent behind the left, and placed on the toes. To the beats of the drum played at a slow tempo, the dancer keeps the rhythm by touching and re-touching the first finger and thumb tips of each hand, the other fingers being kept straight. The neck, eyes, eyebrows, chest and shoulders are moved rhythmically. The hands are then brought into the second characteristic position or *Hastak* with both hands held at chest level in the same hand gesture, forearms parallel to the chest, palms facing down and the finger tips of each hand tip to tip. The neck, eyes, eyebrows, chest and shoulders are moved rhythmically and the dancer commences with the introduction to the technique of the dance or *Nrtta*.

Amad. The dancer casts her arms outwards and forwards, as her feet punctuate the steps, moving forwards and backwards and then circling. The *Thoras* here have a special type of rhythmic syllabic words or *Bol* peculiar to the *Amad*. This part of the dance is a coming to life or leading up to all that is to follow in *Nrtta*, and paves the way for the *Sangeet*. One may say in this sense that the *Amad* corresponds to the *Alarippu* of Bharata Natyam. Series of fine *Thoras* are danced in a striking rhythm and as the dance continues, there are many quick turns and deft syncopated movements. Intricate word syllables or *Bol* played on the *Pakhavaj* and other drums blend together and the dancers feet coincide with exactitude.

Sangeet. *Sangeet* in Kathak, we may say, generally corresponds to the *Jatisvaram* of Bharata Natyam, for here too the stress is laid on time and musical notation. The rhythmic word syllables or *Bol* of the *Thoras* is recited in *Svaras*,

Plate 37

1

2

Sitara Devi (1) as Mirabai in a devotional attitude of prayer to Lord Krishna, from the *Abhinaya* in Kathak;
(2) in Natwari—dance of Shri Krishna with the flute, as performed in the Kathak; (3) In a *Tandava* pose
representing Lord Shiva in the dance showing in the *Bol* or rhythmic syllables of the drum in the Kathak;
(4) in the dance of the Nataraja in Kathak. (Courtesy, Sitara Devi.)

3

4

Plate 38

1. *"I'll pull you by the hand . . . ."*

2. *"Removing the ghunghat (veil) to one side shyly seeing . . . ."*

3. *"Covering the face with the ghunghat and seeing through it . . . ."*

Guru Shambhu Maharaj, the noted exponent of Kathak, showing Kathak *Bhava* in *Abhinaya*. (1) From a *Dadra* (2, 3) From the *Gat Bhava*. (Photos copyright, Mohan Khokar.)

Plate 39

1. *"His mother beckons him . . . ."*

2. *" . . . .but he indulges in play . . . ."*

3. *" . . . .and childish pranks . . . ."*

4. *"He who fought Kansa and slew him . . . ."*

Briju Maharaj in *Abhinaya* portraying in Kathak the *Bhajan*, "Pragate Braj Nandalal". (Photos copyright, Mohan Khokar.)

Plate 40

1. *"Krishna playfully takes a stone to throw it at a Gopi."*

2. *"The stone reaches its aim and the Gopi is visibly annoyed."*

Rani Karna portraying *Abhinaya* in Kathak, a *Gat* from the Krishna legends. (Photos copyright, Mohan Khokar.)

Gopi Krishna showing one of the types of walk from the Kathak. (Courtesy, Sitara Devi)

and the *Nrtta* or pure dance style of the Kathak is further elaborated as the mode of musical recitation reaches a high degree of beauty and excellence.

Paran.   Now comes a wonderful and subtle variety of *Thoras* played on the *Pakhavaj*.   The compositions are various, with intricate rhythms and the technique becomes more forceful or *Tandava* with complicated patterns of movement.   The dance rises to great heights of technical virtuosity and the *Paran* is considered the *piece de résistance* of the *Nrtta* or pure dance of Kathak.

Like the *Jatis* of Bharata Natyam, the metrical syllables are complex here and each *Paran* or technical piece seems to outbeat the next in speed and intricacy of rhythms.

Just as a good Bharata Natyam dancer should try to learn a maximum of the 120 basic dance arrangements that are derived from the ten different groups of *Adavus*, each with twelve different modes, so in Kathak, a good dancer must know at least 100 *Parans*, comprising different main time measures and varying complicated syllabic verses or *Thoras*, composed of a series of *Bol* combinations.   At this part of the dance therefore several *Parans*, each different and perfect in timing, are done; the drummer's word syllables and the dancer's feet working in perfect unison.   The technicalities of pure dance here are superb, with the *Bol* arranged at slow and fast tempo (*Yati*) in a splendid form, counterbalancing one another. Sometimes there are cross rhythms and tempo, rendered in a fascinating complexity of *Thoras*, all working together and proceeding to end precisely at the climax of the *Sum* or the last beat of the pattern of beats (*Graha*).

Instead of the statuesque posturing of the Bharata Natyam, the Kathak dancer moves up and down and sideways, whirls and pirouettes, punctuating each *Paran* with a perfectly timed precision.   Each time the dancer starts a fresh *Paran*, she takes again the characteristic first basic position or *Hastak*, where the hands are placed as at the start of the *Thata*, with the first fingers touching and re-touching the thumb tips in each hand, a position also resorted to between the sequences of the dance.

From the *Hastak* position, the dancer turns round very fast to the right or left, spinning dizzily as her arms move in time, going sideways and forwards. And from rotating in these tremendous turns (*Chakkar*), stamping her feet, she will change and advance, move in lines parallel to the stage, as her flat of feet, toes, and ball of the foot beat and re-echo the series of complicated *Thoras*.

Although the dance has reached an exciting tempo, no good Kathak dancer will conclude her or his performance without doing some very thrilling *Parans* at four times the speed of the basic timing.   Seeming to tread on air, the dancer's feet sounds mingle with those of her ankle bells in a fantasy of patterned sounds that harmonise dramatically with the resounding drum syllables.

Tarana.   The *Tarana* like the *Tillana* of Bharata Natyam again, is pure dance with wonderful intricate rhythms and patterned movements.   It is full of grace and charm, and the complicated foot rhythms, the speed and design of arms moving sideways, forwards and upwards, and the scintillating combinations of all these, lend this part of the dance a vivid beauty.   The *Tarana* is done in a fast tempo, the movements and feet of the dancer sparkling in a finished syncopation with the verve of the recited and drum beat rhythmic syllables.

Turning to the interpretive aspect of Kathak, we find here a rich and dramatic repertoire.   *Abhinaya* in *Nrtya* of Kathak may be said to correspond to the

Sabdam and *Padams* of Bharata Natyam.   Kathak has a number of types of lyrical song compositions that lend themselves most aptly to the art of *Abhinaya*.   These songs are either devotional and addressed to some deity like the *Dhrupads,Kirthanas, Dhamar, Pada* and *Bhajan, Tandava, Gat Bhava* and *Gatis*; or love lyrics, in the *Sringara Bhava* like some of the *Dhrupads*, the *Thumri, Dadra, Ghazals* and *Kavita*.   Emotional acting is shown with a great deal of variety of interpretation. Standing or sitting, the dancer interprets her theme.   The music is soft and plaintively accompanied on the *Sarangi*, the words being sung in chaste *Brij Bhasa*, Hindi or Urdu.   In the *Dhrupads*, each lyrical composition consists of two to four verses in praise and glory of one of the deities.   The *Kirthanas*, sung in chorus, have the Krishna Lilas as their main theme, with fine rhythmic syllabic words incorporated into the text.   While in the *Dhamar*, there is again the theme of the Krishna legends with much scope for poetic metaphors.   *Raga* melody is shown at its best in the *Pada* and the *Bhajans* with their devotional trends; and the *Tandavas* like the *Natanam Adinar* of Bharata Natyam introduce the rhythmic word syllables with mime in a descriptive analysis of Shiva or Krishna.   Lovely are the *Gat Bhava* and the *Gatis*, each *Gat Bhava* having a different theme, where a dancer, as a Gopi shows in a variety of ways the use of the veil (*Ghungat*), or any episode from the sacred legends; while in the *Gatis*, she shows her art of impersonation. In the love themes, the *Thumri*, composed of three or four lines of lyric, has each line repeated to reveal a different meaning.   With the *Dadra* and *Ghazal*, the love theme is emphasised; while in the *Kavita* the dancer beautifully blends the interpretation of the text that tells some legend of the Gods with rhythmic word syllables.   Indeed the *Abhinaya* in Kathak is rich and dramatic.

To further emphasise technical virtuosity, a finished Kathak dancer can trace a peacock or elephant, blind-folded, with her feet on a floor covered with rice powder.   If the rice is multi-coloured, she can place the right colours in the proper places for the fan-tailed bird.   She can also while dancing make just one or seven or twelve bells tinkle from the whole circlet of a hundred bells worn around each ankle.

Expressive, alluring, sharp and precise, balancing beautifully the *Tandava* and *Lasya* styles, the Kathak lives today as one of the important schools of the classical dance.   Both men and women perform it, for it has grace and strength, softness where required and affords great scope for the art of interpretation.

KATHAKALI—THE CLASSICAL DANCE DRAMAS OF KERALA

This school of the classical dance, performed in Kerala, south-west India, presents the art in dance drama form.   Kathakali actually means "story-play," and it has come down through the ages in a highly specialised mode.

These dance dramas usually take place on a sketchy stage, under the canopy of a star spangled sky, lit by a great shining brass oil lamp.   The performances generally start after dinner and continue through the whole night.   Entire episodes are danced and enacted from the ancient epic poems, the *Ramayana* and the *Mahabharata*, with a detailed gesture language for their interpretation.   Kathakali is deeply religious being based on some of the richest literature of Kerala that has been inspired by the beautiful and highly ethical stories of the *Puranas*, which tell of Gods and Goddesses, heroes and their enemies.

Kathakali has been considerably influenced by the old Sanskrit dramas of

Plate C

Kathakali dance drama costumes (traditional). Mrinalini Sarabhai as Sita and Chattuni Pannicker as Rama (using the Pachcha facial make-up typical of a noble character) from a sequence of the dance drama from the *Ramayana*. (Photo, Hemendra A. Shah. By courtesy of Mrinalini Sarabhai.)

Kerala called *Kudiyattam*, and also the *Krishna Atam* or the dramatic stories of Sri Krishna, which came into being about A.D. 1650.   The Malayali poet, the Raja of Kottarakkara (North Kottayam), first introduced into Malayalam literature the dramatic lyrical compositions so perfectly interpreted through the art of Kathakali.   The themes of these compositions were based on the stories of the *Puranas* with their beauty of parable and moral lesson.   Intensity of dance technique, dramatic acting, powerful expression, religious fervour and pantomime mark these dance dramas, as they unfold to tell the age-old sacred stories.

The village people of Kerala have a hereditary aptitude for Kathakali, and it is impossible in speaking of this form of the dance to disassociate oneself with the background of the village, and the beauty that its background provides.   The parallel of the Passion Play at Oberammergau suggests itself.   One has only to look at the natural scene in Kerala to be impressed by its inspiring charm.   The waving palms along the backwaters and blue lagoons, the rolling azure sea and the lofty rugged Western Ghats give it a character all its own; while the many flowering trees and bushes, the boats gliding along the serene backwaters, and the pretty, extremely clean villages with their gardens of banana, mango, jack-fruit and coconut trees create a pattern of colour amidst the rich green of the rice fields. Into this colourful picture, the spotless white costumes worn by the men and women blend most harmoniously.   Indeed, the beauty of ther natural surroundings has inspired the people of Kerala to create many enduring arts in the shape of magnificent temples with their galaxy of sculptures, dance and drama, music and poetry, and several traditional handicrafts.

The temples in Kerala have played an important part in the cultural life of the people through the ages.   The Cakkayars, a community of actors and story tellers have been attached to the temples since ancient times, and used to perform the old Sanskrit dramas of Kerala, the *Kudiyattam* in the ornate temple-theatres or *Kuttambalams*.   The ornamental outer temple-courtyards afford the setting for the Kathakali dance dramas to be enacted at festival time.   During the important celebrations, like the Arat festival, loud drumming announces these performances that take place nightly for about ten days.

Kathakali is traditional and has been conceived by a learned and philosophical mind, and then given to the people.   It contains therefore much of the set rules and regulations of the classical dance as enjoined in the *Natya Sastra* by Bharata Muni, and the famous Kathakali text, the *Hastalakshana Dipika*.   The dance dramas contain the Three Main Elements of the classical dance, namely :

> BHAVA   or   Mood
> RAGA   or   Melody, Song
> TALA   or   Rhythmic Timing

Although the main character of Kathakali is its dramatic interpretive content (*Nrtya*), it pays a great deal of attention to the importance of the rhythmic time measures.   The pure dance movements are arranged to the various timings or *Talams*, and are embellished by means of little pieces in syllabic poetry-form, like the *Jatis* of Bharata Natyam and the *Thoras* of Kathak.   These syllabic words are played by the drummer (as the *Chollu* in Bharata Natyam) and recited simultaneously by the musicians (as the *Sollu-kuttu* in Bharata Natyam) and closely followed by the dancer step by step.   In the Bharata Natyam, each series of dance movements in each stage of the dance, ends with a dramatic finale known as the *Thirmana*. In Kathakali, at the end of every four lines of the song (*Khanda* or *Carana*), which have been interpreted in acting and dance movements, there is a climax or finale known as the *Kalasam*.

Foot rhythms are very important and are employed between long conversations of the dramatic sequences, whenever pure dance is used. Here is an example of the syllabic rhythmic wordings in Kathakali, which resemble quite closely those used in the Bharata Natyam and Kathak.

> Thaka dee, Thaka Thagada dee; Thaka dee, Thaka Thagada dee;
> Thaka dee, Thaka Thagada dee; Thaka dee, Thaka Thagada dee;
> That Thagada, Thaga Thagada Thagada;
> Thit Thigadee, Thiga Thigadee Thigadee;
> Thagada Thagada That Tha; Thigadee Thigadee Thit thee;
> Thayee Thayee Dhit Thee Thayee;
> Dhit Thayee Thee, Dhit Thee, Thigada Thayee.

To aid dramatic interpretation, there are the expressions of the eyes, eyebrows, the whole face including the facial muscles, the movements of the neck, the hand gestures with a complete language of signs, and the swing and postures of the arms and body. In Kathakali, the use of the eyes and eyebrows is far more evolved and involved than in either the Bharata Natyam or the Kathak or any other school of the classical dance. Eyes and eyebrows are constantly used to aid the process of communication in the most effective manner and with great intensity. This art employs a rich vocabulary of more than eight hundred language signs based on an alphabet of twenty-four Single and Combined Hand Gestures.

To learn the elaborate techniques of these dance dramas, the Kathakali dancer has to go through an intensive and disciplined course that takes about twelve years for him to perfect. He therefore usually starts his training at about ten or twelve years of age, beginning with massage and oil baths to make his body and muscles supple. He is then ready to start the very strenuous and extremely difficult postures and techniques that the art of Kathakali demands. Traditionally, only men take part in a Kathakali performance in the villages, the feminine roles being played by young handsome men or grown boys in their late teens; but today, with the dance performances being staged in the cities, girls and young women frequently play their appropriate roles.

The Kathakali dance dramas are enacted with great virtuosity and aplomb, for the actors taking part are excellently trained, confident, and dedicated to the art. Besides, they have been nurtured in a region where every temple and landmark is enshrouded in sacred myth and legend. From their earliest years, they have been inspired by these dance dramas which expound their noble and familiar philosophical stories. The dancers have also been imbued with the exuberant and elevating musical compositions and the ecstatic and lyrical texts that have been woven into the fabric of these dance dramas. Therefore, the dancers do not act their roles, but actually become the characters they portray.

In the musical accompaniment to the dance dramas, the story is expounded through the *Pattus*, which consist of *Slokas* and *Padams*. The *Sloka* is the recitation of certain incidents of the story generally not acted. It ushers in a particular situation or scene. The *Padams* represent the dialogues of the characters. The songs are composed in the mode of the Karnatic or Southern school of classical music, and drums play a very important part. They announce the performances, and control the whole rhythm, technique and tempo of the dance dramas.

Kathakali—The Actual Dance Drama

The Kathakali dance drama is usually announced with what is known as the *Keli-Kottu* or loud drumming on the *Chenda*, a drum which is played on one side only, either beaten with two sticks or drummed with one stick in the right hand and the palm of the left hand. It is loud and penetrating. In addition, there is the *Madala*, which is a large drum, but softer and more mellow in tone than the *Chenda*; and large cymbals. All these instruments combine to announce the performance. This is followed by the *Suddha Madala*, that is, pure drumming on *Madalas*, and just after this ends, sacred verses are chanted and prayers are offered as an invocation to the Gods for the success of the performance. After this, a finely designed curtain is raised on the stage by two ushers, and two artistes hidden behind it, dance a devotional dance called *Todayam*. They go through various timings or *Talams*, usually of five varieties, consisting of 6, 7, 8, 10 and 14 sub-divisions of the main timing. It is pure dance and rhythm. Presently, the curtain is lowered half-way, revealing the dancers who represent noble characters. Louder drumming follows and introductory songs and *Padams* in praise and worship of God. The curtain is then removed.

Now comes the *Purappadu*, the commencement or starting point, in which the pure dance style and technique of Kathakali is performed. Fine rhythmic movements are made to the accompaniment of drums and the conch shell. Here we see the intricate footwork, bodily posture, the spreading of the legs with the knees bent, the standing on the edges of the feet, fluttering eyebrows, the quick darting eye movements and the fanwise neck movements, all done to perfect timing. Marvellous body control and powerful technique are the characteristics of this introduction to the dance drama. The audience sits spellbound, watching the technical excellence and virtuosity of the dancers. The style of the technique of Kathakali is admirably exhibited here and much of these pure dance movements are later employed in the actual drama, between the long conversations and sequences, and as the various characters take the stage.

The chief singer, acting as the conductor, keeps time on a bronze plate to regulate the tempo of the show. A song is sung from the *Git Govinda*, the Song Celestial, by poet Jayadeva, telling of the love of Krishna and Radha. This is followed by the *Melappadam* that is, beautiful drumming after the song from the *Git Govinda* is over.

After all these preliminaries, the actual dance drama begins, and the subject for the day may be any episode or episodes from the *Puranas*, the *Mahabharata* or the *Ramayana*. Once the performance commences, everyone is completely absorbed by the intensity of the acting, the rhythmic precision of the footwork as the dancers use their heels, flat of foot, the sides of the feet, jumping, circling and walking in a magnificent display of the Forceful or *Tandava* style of the dance, with the *Lasya* or Gentle style introduced when the feminine character enters.

All through the singer continues to play a very important part, as he really leads the dancers. One can feel the very fine harmony that exists between the acting and the dancing on the one hand and the beauty of melody and rhythm on the other.   As one is lost in the drama being enacted, with the singing and the accompanying orchestra, the old-world costumes and make-up, the technical brilliance and dramatic content, one is carried away far back into the fascinating realm of legend and sacred mythology.   The imagination is fired with excitement, as every scene, every event, and every passion and emotion is vividly described in gesture and supported by the most carefully created mime.   Battle scenes are portrayed with great realism and war cries are shouted by the warriors.   Sometimes one hears the evil vengeful laughter of a wicked character, or sees a fantastic acrobatic feat performed as a dancer leaps into the air in a heroic action.   Actors imitate perfectly an elephant, a tiger, a deer, or other animal; a peacock or other bird; or even an inanimate object like a chariot drawn by stampeding horses; or the actor may step into a chariot the shape of which has been described in gestures, and then taking the reins drive furiously off the stage.   The whole style of Kathakali is vigorous and stirring, and when it is well performed, there is a magnificence and grandeur about it that is most impressive.   A deeply philosophical and purposeful meaning is given to explain the form and arrangement in which these dance dramas are performed.   A beautiful parallel is drawn between the significance of the Kathakali performance and Creation.   I can best give it in the words of the authoritative writer on Kathakali, K. Bharatha Iyer.   "The stage represents the world that has come into being in space by the primal act of the Creator.   The thick blazing wick of the oil lamp set towards the stage and the thinner one facing the audience symbolises the sun and the moon.   Sound is heard in the drumming which first vibrates 'Pralaya, Pralaya dimmurdala' announcing the end of the Great Deluge and the coming of the 'New Age'.   The curtain is rajani or tamas (the darkness that divides).   Behind it a couple of dancers execute an invocative dance Todayam.   They stand for Maya and Sakti.[1] The dancers remain unseen by the spectators, just as these forces work beyond the ken of human perception; their activities represent the Lila, the endless play of cosmic forces.   There is no background for the stage, for life emerges from the dark, unknown void and there can be no background to the sport of the gods which transcends time and space.   In this endless process of the advent of the gods and mythological heroes, there is only an un-veiling or falling off of the veils that obstruct vision.   Therefore, the curtain is not fixed but held up by human agency (two men hold it up) and it falls away the moment reality approaches. The musical prelude with rhythmical drumming and singing symbolises the development of sound into language.   Light, life and letters having been manifested, prayers are offered to the gods and the gurus (teachers).   The next stage in the structure of the play is Purappad (literally going forth), signifying the grand pageant of life on earth; what follows is the depiction of the world in its various phases and modes."[2]

Actor's Make-Up

To enhance the dramatic effect of the dance performance, and aid the wonderful facial expressions, the Kathakali dancers have an elaborate make-up of various types which takes several hours to put on.   Each particular facial mask represents a different type of character.   The base of the make-up used is rice powder enhanced by lime and certain paints.

[1]   Primal energy and creative power.   [2]   K. Bharatha Iyer, Kathakali, The Sacred Dance-Drama of Malabar

Plate 41

1

2

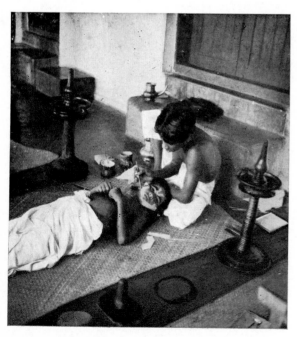

3

(1) The character of Sri Krishna, the Noble One, with his crown of peacock feathers and typical make-up as portrayed in the Kathakali dance dramas. (2) A powerful and fierce character using the Red *Tadi* (Red Beard type) in the typical make-up and magnificent headdress as portrayed in the Kathakali. (3) Kathakali make-up being applied on the face, with the dancer in a recumbent position. (Photos copyright, R. R. Prabhu.)

Plate 42

1

2

3

4

5

Five important characters in characteristic make-up and costume as seen in a Kathakali dance drama. (1) Ravana, a wicked character. (2) Sri Krishna, a noble character. (3) Sita, female character. (4) Rama, the heroic character. (5) Valmiki, a saint, (Photos, Author.)

Plate 43

3

1

(1) A noble character and a female character from a Kathakali dance drama in typical headdress and make-up. (Courtesy, Stanley Jepson.) (2) A scene from one of the Kathakali dance dramas showing two noble characters and a female character in their typical dress and make-up. (Photo, R. R. Prabhu.) (3) Hanuman and Rama from the Kathakali dance drama "Rama Charitam." (Photo, B. Bhansali.)

2

Plate 44

1. *The Brahmin and his wife are in deep sorrow. The Brahmin laments his Fate. He has no one to send to Baka. If the truce with Baka is not honoured, he will destroy all.*

2. *The Brahmin volunteers to go himself and requests his wife to let him go and sacrifice himself for their sake. Kunthi enters and overhears this.*

3. *Kunthi tells the Brahmin and his wife that she has a son, Bhima, who is very strong and that she will send Bhima to Baka.*

The Kathakali dance drama "Baka Vadham," a story from the *Mahabharata*. The Kathakali play has been written by the Raja of Kottayam, Kerala. The story runs as follows : "In a forest dwells the mighty demon Baka. A glutton, he freely preyed upon the inhabitants of nearby villages. Eventually, the people made a truce with Baka that they would send him a hundred pots of food and a man for him to eat every day and he, in turn, would leave them alone. Finally the turn came of the Brahmin's family where the Pandavas lived, and one man had to be sent from here as food for Baka . . . . ." (Photos copyright, Mohan Khokar.)

Plate 45

4. *The Brahmin and his wife are reluctant to accept Kunthi's offer, for they fear the worst. But Kunthi argues and tells them not to fear for Bhima.*

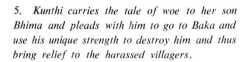

5. *Kunthi carries the tale of woe to her son Bhima and pleads with him to go to Baka and use his unique strength to destroy him and thus bring relief to the harassed villagers.*

6. *Bhima willingly accepts the order and the challenge and asks Kunthi for blessings before leaving.*

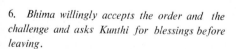

The Kathakali dance drama "Baka Vadham"—Continued. (Photos copyright, Mohan Khokar.)

Plate 46

7. *The Brahmin loads the cart with food and Bhima prepares to leave for the demon's place.*

8. *The Brahmin shows the direction Bhima is to take to reach Baka's abode.*

9. *Baka, as is his temper, is full of fury and raves. He grunts, too, (Curtain look introduces Baka in the play.)*

The Kathakali dance drama "Baka Vadham"—Continued. (Photos copyright, Mohan Khokar.)

Plate 47

10. *After the food arrives, Baka partakes of some of it and begins to sway in contentment. Meanwhile Bhima prepares himself for a fight with Baka, for he is intent on destroying him.*

11. *The fight ensues.*

12. *Eventually, Bhima strikes a fatal blow which sends Baka spinning and reeling to his death.*

The Kathakali dance drama "Baka Vadham"—Continued. (Photos copyright, Mohan Khokar.)

Plate 48

Traditional Kathakali dance drama "Nala Charitam." (1) The marriage of Nala (Chattuni Panicker) and Damayanti (Mrinalini Sarabhai). (2) King Nala (Chattuni Panicker) and Hamsa, the Swan (Shivashankar). (3) Chattuni Panicker as Nala. (4) Chattuni Panicker as Nala and Mrinalini Sarabhai as Damayanti in a dramatic sequence. (Courtesy, Mrinalini Sarabhai.)

Minuku. In this, the face is painted with yellowish-pink pigment, and black unguent is applied to the eyelashes, eyebrows, and to greatly enlarge the eyes. The lips are painted red. This particular type of make-up is used generally by women characters and sages in the play.

Pachcha. Here, green paint is applied to the face, with blackened eyes, red lips and a white *Chutti* made of a mixture of rice flour and *chunnam* (lime), fixed to stand out from the chin and lower sides of the face in fluted lines. This type of make-up is adopted by noble characters, like Sri Krishna, Rama, all the heroes, and eminent kings.

Kathi. In this, red paint is used on either side of the nose and over the eyebrows, and green paint on the rest of the face. A large blob of white on the tip of the nose and on the forehead indicates that this represents a ferocious or wicked character, like the Asuras, the enemies of the Gods. Ravana, the demon king of Lanka, and the villain of the play are made up in this way.

Tadi (*Beards*). There are three types of *Tadi*—the Red, the White and the Black Tadi. The Red Tadi, uses a red beard, white and black on the face, white pith on either cheek and black lips. White bristles stretch from the top of the lips to the eyebrows. The Red Tadi is used by grotesque characters like Baka the demon, or even by physically powerful and fierce characters like the monky general Bali, and Surgiva, one of the great characters of the *Ramayana*. The characters who use the Red Tadi frequently wear a furred coat.

The White Tadi has the face painted half red and half black, with a green nose, white moustache and woolly white beard. It is used by good and strong characters like Hanuman, friend of Rama. The White Tadi character generally wears a white coat.

The Black Tadi has a black painted face, white around the eyes, white bristling hair for a beard and red painted lips. This make-up is usually worn by forest dwellers and tribal hunstmen.

Kari. In this, the face is painted black, with a crescent shape drawn in red on the cheek bones, and the eyes are elongated with black. This type of make-up is used when the actor is impersonating female demons like Surpanakha and Simhika.

The make-up used in Kathakali is a highly developed art, involving great skill in the application of the paints. Meticulous care is taken to see that each mask is perfectly applied on the face, with each colour in its right place. Dammer (pitch) is mixed into the paints to make the skin glitter and intensify the dramatic effect. A mild irritant dropped in the eyes causes the whites to become red and glowing. This gives prominence to the eyes, so that the rapid and varying expressions may be clearly discerned.

I have witnessed night-long sessions of the Kathakali dance dramas, both in the village in the open air, as well as during the Arat festival in Travancore, in the magnificent courtyard of the ornamental Padmanabha temple. The setting of the ornate walls and columns of stone, the blazing oil lamps, the atmosphere of ancient sculptural glory, gave the performances a grandeur and power that are most impressive. Particularly excellent were the two performances of the entire episode of the exile of the Pandava princes with Draupadi, one of the most exhilarating and emotional stories from the *Mahabharata*; and the enactment of the long sequence of Sri Krishna consoling Arjuna before entering the battle against his cousins the Kauravas, and the battle scenes, ending with the great battle of Kuruk-shetra.   It was a wonderful experience.   Here was stylised, highly technical dance, with the added art of pantomime and mimicry—noble, powerful and full of vigour. Now it was an actor representing a variety of characters, now an animal, now a bird, now a charioteer and his chariot with prancing horses.   Sometimes battles raged, sometimes tender love scenes or passages of rare and exquisite lyricism were interpreted with all the dramatic effects possible.   This is Kerala's rich contri-bution to the Indian classical dramatic dance art.

Great names have been associated with the preservation and teaching as well as the performance of Kathakali through the years.   Among them are the dis-tinguished masters, Kunju Kurup, Ravunni Menon, Kavalappara Narayanan Nair, Bali Othikkan Nambudri, Parasu Pattar, Eswara Pillai, Nalan Unni, Kunju-Krishna Pannikar, Kesava Kurup, Sankaran Nambudri, Vechoor Raman Pillai, Kalamandalam Krishnan, Kunjun Pannikar and Gopinath.

Kummi

Traditionally, the Kathakali dance dramas have always been enacted and danced only by men.   The style is *Tandava* and therefore very vigorous.   The feminine gentler aspect of Kathakali dancing is found in the Kummi.   In this popular dance form of Kerala, the themes are from mythology, and the general mode and technique as well as the traditional timings and rhythms of Kathakali are followed.   The Kummi however is essentially *Lasya* in style, with grace, softness of gestures, and a fine balance between the swift movements and the more elegant lilting pace taken while interpreting the *Abhinayam* or emotional expression, evident all the time.   The Kummi, in fact, may well be compared to the dances of the Apsaras with their gentle alluring charm.

Some of the well known and most popular subjects of the Kathakali dance dramas are, *Rukmani Kalayanam, Prahlada Charitam, Bhagavat Doothu, Lalita, Krishna-Arjuna Moksham, Shiva-Dakshayagam, Harischandra, Poothana Moksham, Sita Kalayanam, Rama Charitam* and the *Wamana-Mahabali* theme.

6. *The Main Schools of the Classical Dance*
—Continued

ORISSI OR ODISSI

The classical dance as practised in Orissa, a State on the mid-north-eastern coast of India, is known as Orissi or Odissi. The centres where the art is best known are Puri and Bhubaneshwar.

Orissa is one of the most picturesque and historically rich regions in our country. With its rivers and luxuriant vegetation, hills and forests, and many magnificent ancient monuments and temples, it presents a picture of all the essentials that are required for lovers of both Nature and the Arts.

From earliest times, eminent writers, scholars, dancers, musicians and gifted artisans have given of their talents to foster and enrich Orissa's cultural traditions, and they continue today to add lustre to the renaissance of the arts in India.

The ancient Jain rock-cut temples of Khandagiri and Udayagiri are notable for their fine friezes and bas-reliefs, many representing the dance; the great temples of Bhubaneshwar, especially the Rajarani and Venkateswar temples, and the Jagannath temple at Puri, as well as the *Nat Mandapa* of the Sun temple at Konarak, with their high ornate towers and beautifully carved and ornamental halls and courtyards, are perfect examples of how these many places were not only religious centres, but were also centres of culture and the arts. Both music and dance became closely connected with rituals and worship with the establishment of these places of religious veneration.

The Orissi dance has been preserved not only by the great *gurus*, their descendants, and their pupils the Maharis or Devadasis, but the temples themselves have brought to posterity thousands of examples in sculpture that are a prolific orientation of the techniques of the art.

The institution of the Maharis, who were temple dancers and worked in the service of these religious centres, goes back almost to the 2nd century A.D., and it is clear from inscriptions and literature that with the establishment of the great Shiva temples at Bhubaneshwar these handmaidens of God were encouraged and helped to preserve the classical dance right from the 7th century A.D. About the 6th or 7th century A.D., the Vishnu temple of Jagannath (Lord of the Universe) at Puri, also introduced this institution of temple dancers. In the fine large dance halls (*Natya Mandapa*), attached to these places of worship, and particularly at Konarak, dance performances took place with all the grace, technical brilliance and atmosphere of devotion and honour that existed in the Sanskrit era. For in the olden days, the Maharis were held in great esteem and enjoyed a good social status, girls of good family including royalty (like Chandrika Devi), taking the dance as an honourable profession. Besides the Maharis, there were the Gotipuas or boy dancers who came to be attached to the temples about the 16th century A.D. They helped to protect the temples, saw that the rituals were regularly performed in the Jagannath temple at Puri and danced during religious festivals and at social gatherings. But whereas Orissi as performed by the Maharis and their *gurus* has come down to posterity, having been preserved through the generations, that of the Gotipuas has been kept up with great difficulty.

The Orissi dance has its roots in devotional ritual, and though it really consists of one long theme, starting from the invocation to the deities, the Earth and the *gurus*, and ending with a highly technical finale of pure dance, it is generally done in stages like the Bharata Natyam of the south, so as to bring to the fullest its very beautiful stances of posture and the art of interpretation. Every aspect of Orissi is based on the *Sastras*, the *Natya Sastra* by Bharata Muni, where it is actually mentioned that in the eastern region Odhradesa (Orissa), the classical dance was practised in the *Odhramagadha Prabriti* or style; the *Abhinaya Dharpana* by Nandikeshwara; and several other treatises in Orissi, such as the *Abhinaya Dharpana Prakash* by Jadunath Sinha, the then ruler of Tigiria State of Orissa, which gives in detail the invocatory dance, the style and technique, the hand gestures and expression, music and timing, which closely follow the *Natya Sastra* and the *Sangeet Ratnakar* by Sarngadeva; and the two *Abhinaya Chandrikas*, one by Maheshwara Mahapatra and the other by Rajamani Patra. Orissi also contains the Three Main Elements of the classical dance, perfectly compounded, namely:

BHAVA   or   Mood
RAGA   or   Melody, Song
TALA   or   Rhythmic Timing

as well as *Natya*, which entails the combination of both dancing and acting.

Here again the dance is arranged to various main drum *Talas* or timings such as *Ektal, Pahapata, Jhula, Aditala, Atha, Jhampa*, and so on, consisting of 4, 4 quick (*drut*), 6, 8, 7 and 10 *Matras* or sub-divisions of beats respectively in the main timing. Intricate patterns of rhythmic syllables are woven into the main drum beats in all possible series of arrangements to create poetic syllabic verses. The rhythmic patterned syllables that are recited and played on the drum are called *Bani* or *Ukuttas*, and the rhythmic patterns of the feet are known as *Chali* in Orissi. This is in the same manner as one finds in the Bharata Natyam of the south, where the patterned sound syllables of the drum are known as *Chollu* and the recited syllabic words of the musician are known as *Sollu-kuttu*, followed by the patterned feet rhythms or *Jatis*. Once again the mode of the classical dance is here; where

Orissi or Odissi dance costume (traditional). Indrani in the classical *Karihasta Karana* posture. (Photo, H. Rahman.)

there is the perfect co-ordination of sound harmonies on the one side and the different co-ordination of movements on the other, by the threefold play of maintaining within the main basic timing or *Tala*, the patterned sounds of the drum, the recited syllables of the musicians and the rhythmic patterns of the feet of the dancer.

Bani or *Ukuttas* of Orissi resemble the syllable patterns of the Bharata Natyam of the south at certain places, and here is an example:

Kadtak, ta Jhenu, ta Jhenu tak jhen jhen kita kukandari,
Ta Jhenu ta kad tak jhenu ta aa
Ta Jhenu ta kad tak jhenu ta aa,
Ta Jhenu ta kad tak jhenu
Tingine dha, thingine dha,
Dha gadi ghene dha.

Note, that there are also certain similarities to the syllable wordings of the Kathak.

Orissi, like the Bharata Natyam of the south, bases its *Nrtta* or pure dance technique on the *Karanas* or basic dance units which are the origin or alphabet of all dance movement. The *Karanas* are known in Orissi as *Sthanaks*. Carefully founded on the *Karanas* of the classical treatises, the experts have evolved what are known as *Belis* or fundamental bodily positions combined with basic dance movements, and the *Bhangis*, which are the principal dance positions more highly elaborated.

The *Belis* are therefore like the *Adavus* of the Bharata Natyam and are the first basic stances to be studied by the dancer. They constitute such basic positions and movements as *Sthanaka*, the act of standing still on the flat of the feet with the feet together or apart, or on the toes, or on the heels with one foot flat and the other resting on the toes; *Baitha*, squatting on the flat of feet or on the toes or with one leg stretched to one side; *Utha*, movements of rising or jumping on either one foot or both feet, backwards and sideways or at the same place; *Chali* or *Chari* or *Chalan*, the style of walk, various directions of the steps backwards, forwards, sideways, and fast circular movements with the hands and arms; *Bhasa*, bending to left and right backwards and forwards and spreading the arms outwards; *Bhaunri*, pirouetting with one foot raised to the knees and the other stamping the ground, the hands and arms stretched (*Bhramari-Natya Sastra*); *Pali*, the retreating movements to be done at the end of each sequence of the dance, going backwards in any direction. The stretched foot resting on the heel and dancing on the heels is a marked mode of the Orissi.

The principal *Bhangis* add more distinctive technical touches to the *Belis*, such as the curve of the hips with the head inclined and the legs bent at the knees. They include some of the main postures and movements that make up the style of the dance. It can be explained here that in the Bharata Natyam as done in the south, the dancer bends the waist to give beauty of form to the postures, whereas in the Orissi style of the dance emphasis is given to bending the hips to accentuate the rounded curves of the posture. In Hindu plastic art, there are actually four bends of the body for beauty of line and posture. These have been incorporated into the dance in various stances, some schools emphasising one or more modes. The four bends are, *Sama Bhanga* or equal bend with hardly any noticeable bend to any one side; *Abhanga* or the state of slightly bending the figure to either side;

Atibhanga or the exaggerated bend; and the *Tribhanga* or what is called the triple bend, in which there is emphasis on curvature of the hips. This last posture is common in the Orissi dance style. The *Atibhanga* or greatly bent attitude is also found in many sequences of the Orissi dance, wherein the upper part of the body is rhythmically moved to the left and to the right alternately, with the knees greatly bent and the arms stretched to either side at the same time.

The dancer learns in the *Bhangis* the exact method of performing the introduction of salutation to *Bhumi* (the Earth), and to the *guru*; the starting position of the actual dance by using the traditional stance of standing with the legs apart and posture of arms in an almost horseshoe shape; followed by the squatting position, the use of the stretched leg and interchanging of feet positions with the hands in different gestural forms; and then goes on to the other stances of the particular method of using the toes, bending the legs, waist, and hip movements; feet and heels and the stamping of the feet as the dancer raises the leg and finally whirls. In other words, the *Bhangis* prepare the dancer for the main techniques which will come into the actual dance performance in the various sequences. The dance unfolds itself in a methodical and pleasing manner, bringing in all the fine flexions of arms and hands, the rhythmic feet patterns, the turns and twists of the body and hips, and the very fast whirling. Based on the *Belis* and *Bhangis*, the *Pada Bhedas* (the various ways in which the feet can be used), the *Bhumis* (the ways in which the dancer moves on the stage, namely, in a square, circle, straight lines, tracing a small semi-circle with the foot, standing with the feet in one place); together with the study of hand gestures, and the expressions of the face, eyes and eyebrows constitute the *Abhinaya*. Then the dance unfolds. *Abhinaya* (*Hastabhinaya*) in Orissi is known as *Parija* or *Lakshyana*. The favourite subject for this interpretive quality of the dance is the *Git Govinda*, the immortal poem by poet Jayadeva, who himself was born in Orissa, and which tells of the philosophical love of Krishna and Radha. This subject has been popular in the annals of Orissi classical dance since round about the 13th century A.D. when it was interpreted in dance by the Maharis or Devadasis of Orissa in the Vishnu temples. In addition, songs sung by ancient bards in Orissi, like Kabi-Samrat Upendra Bhanji, Kabi-Surya Baladeva Rath, and Gopal Krishna, are interpreted. The music used is akin to the Hindustani or Northern school.

An Orissi classical dance performance may be done in the following stages for its perfect interpretation and unfolding of style.

1. Patra Prabesh. Entrance of the dancer.

2. Bhumi Pranam. The dance usually begins with the *Bhumi Pranam*, or invocation to Mother Earth and salutation (*Jagarana Nrtya*). It is accompanied by the rhythmic recitation of verse syllables by the musicians and the drum verse syllables (*Bani* or *Ukuttas*). The dancer commences by standing still with hands clasped and feet close together, so that the big toe of the right foot rests on that of the left. To the chant-like recitation of the word syllables and the drum sounds, the dancer inclines forward and touches the earth (*Bhumi*) with the hands in a prayerful attitude (*Vandana*), and then retreats and salutes the *guru*; following which come some beautiful preliminary pure dance movements. The *Bhumi Pranam* is introductory and invocatory, and hence it is short and sweet, and its rhythm gracious; surrounded by an atmosphere of devout ritual, propitiating as it does, Mother Earth, Ganesha the Remover of Obstacles, and other deities presiding over the Dance (*Pancha Debata*).

3. Vighnaraj Puja. The invocation continues, now addressed to the deity Vigheshwara. A Sanskrit *Sloka* is recited and interpreted by the dancer, who also sometimes chants the *Sloka* while interpreting it, rhythmically stamping the right foot in perfect time.

4. Batu Nrtya. The dance proceeds to the worship of Shiva (*Batu-Keswar*), this stage being known as the *Batunata*. Here, one is introduced to both pure dance (*Nrtta*) and to emotional expression and acting (*Nrtya*), offsetting each other in alternate sequences. In this highly elaborate item, the dancer is able to show the techniques of pure dance incorporated in the *Belis*, *Bhangis* and basic units of the *Karanas*, as well as the art of interpretation, a rich part of Orissi, accompanied by complicated patterns of rhythmic word syllables, which are chanted in a choice *Raga*, or recited to the melody being played on a musical instrument. No song is sung.

This stage of the dance is certainly a complete picture of Orissi; successive passages of interpretive acting with gestures depict the various rituals performed for worship, such as playing on a musical instrument for the deity, making offerings, getting ready to seat the God in a special place and bowing to the Almighty. Full play is given to facial expressions, eye and eyebrow movements, and gesture language, which interpret the words of the chant, this being done between pure dance sequences. Movements are performed in a fast tempo, combining both the *Tandava* or strongly defined and *Lasya* or gentle modes. The dancer spreads and bends her legs, stamping on one foot as she pirouettes, raising the other foot to the knee as she whirls, moving first in one direction and then round in the other, arms stretched horizontally or to the front, matchless grace and speed marking the movements. Finally, this stage ends with the dancer making an obeisance and performing an intricate piece of pure dance (*Nrtta*) done to the timing or *Tala* of six *Matras* or sub-divisions of beats (*Jhula Tala*). Statuesque, full of vigour and speed, the three components of the classical dance are evident, namely, *Nrtta* or pure dance, *Nrtya* or bodily movements with facial expressions filled with *Rasa* or Flavour, and *Natya* or the combination of both dancing and acting.

5. Ishta Deva Bandana. The ritualistic character of Orissi is ever present and at this stage the dancer offers worship to a favourite God or Goddess. A soft appealing *Sloka* in Orissi or in Sanskrit is chanted to the deity or a verse from the *Git Govinda*, which is interpreted with great emotional depth of feeling. Like the *Sabdam* of the Bharata Natyam, a few pure dance movements are introduced either after every couplet of the lyric (*Charana*), or after every two couplets, or even sometimes at the end of the lyric. Emphasis is on the interpretation of the chosen devotional lyric addressed to God. One can notice here a similarity in gesture language, facial expressions, and eloquent use of eyes and eyebrows, with the *Abhinaya* of the Bharata Natyam as practised in the south.

6. Swara Pallabi Nrtta. After the softened tempo which the dance has taken in the previous stage, it moves into the graceful poetic form of this part of the dance, where once again pure dance (*Nrtta*) and *Abhinaya* are introduced together. Stress is laid equally on both music and rhythm.   The dancer sings the melody of a choice *Raga* which introduces the mood, and interprets it with explicit facial, eye and eyebrow expressions (*Nakhi*), followed by pure dance.

7. Abhinaya Nrtya.   As the name suggests, quiet descends again on the dance performance and song and interpretation take over, as in the case of the *Padams* of the Bharata Natyam.   The dancer interprets a romantic poem, usually on the Radha-Krishna theme, with the underlying philosophical concept of the lover and the loved (*Nayaka-Nayik)*, emphasising the *Sringara Rasa* or love mood.   Or a lyrical verse from the *Git Govinda*, denoting the worship of God through love and devotion (*Bhakti*) may be interpreted.   Once again, after every couplet (*Charana*) or two couplets of the lyric, some very fast dance sequences are done. Often *Parhis* are introduced, that is, the dancer shows a command of skill and elaborate technique by cleverly changing from the basic timing on which the *Abhinaya Nrtya* has started to one or more other timings or *Talas*, smoothly slipping from one to the other and back into the original timing.   Finally it ends with a pure dance sequence called the *Tarijhamo* that highlights and balances the softness and grace of the *Abhinaya* that has gone before, and at the same time lends a finish to this stage of the dance.

8. Tarijhamo (also called Ananda Nrtya or Natangi).   This is really a continuation of the previous stage, and like the *Tillana* of the Bharata Natyam is pure dance showing all the allure, statuesque postures and variety of movement of the Orissi style.   Fine patterned feet rhythms with swift movements of the arms, the tilt of the head and fanwise jerks of the neck, are accompanied by a fanfare of the rhythmic patterned playing of the drum syllables set to a basic timing of either four beats or *Ektal*, or six beats or *Jhula Tala*.   The dance reaches a climax in a very rapid finale, the *Tihai* or *Mukti*—done three times.

This usually ends a full performance of Orissi.   But sometimes in order to maintain the spirit of devotional and ritualistic mood, the *Trikhandi Majure* is done at the end.   Gracious, reverent and calm, the dancer once more pays homage to Mother Earth, the Gods and to the *guru* in a final salutation.

Just as the Bharata Natyam has its highly dramatic item called the *Natanam Adinar*, the dance of Shiva, in Orissi, there are the *Shiva Sabda Svarpata* and the *Ganesha Sabda Svarpata*.   The difference is mainly in the fact that the *Natanam Adinar* is done by women in their programme of Bharata Natyam, whereas the *Shiva Sabda Svarpata* and the *Ganesha Sabda Svarpata* are traditionally danced by men only.

Shiva Sabda Svarpata and Ganesha Sabda Svarpata.   *Tandava* in style and performance, the *Shiva Sabda Svarpata* interprets a lyrical Sanskrit *Sloka* that describes Shiva, Lord of the Dance and Cosmic Harmony, Destroyer of Evil, and Third of the Hindu Trinity.   Between the *Abhinaya* that interprets the qualities of the great God, fine passages of pure dance in Orissi style are introduced.   If the *Ganesha Sabda Svarpata* is being performed, the Sanskrit *Sloka* tells of this wise, sagacious elephant-headed God, spiritual son of Shiva and Parvathi, and Giver of Good Fortune and Success.   The same procedure of interpretation of the *Sloka* and interspersing the emotional passages with sequences of pure dance is followed.

Plate 49

2

1

3

(1) Indrani in a classic posture from the Orissi dance demonstrating the action of ornamenting the forehead before a hand mirror.
(2) Indrani in a posture based on the classical *Karanas*, one of the fundamental movements in Orissi (Photos, H. Rahman).
(3) Indrani showing the perfect *Tri-bhanga* or Triple Bend with curvature of the hips ; a plastic motif in the Orissi dance.
(Photo copyright, Mohan Khokar.)

Plate 50

1

2

(1, 2) Yamini Krishnamurti in expressive and characteristic postures from the Odissi school of the dance. (Courtesy, Coronet, Madras.) (3) A dance sequence in Odissi Style. (Courtesy, Ritha Devi. (Photo, S. Santhanam.)

3

Plate 51

1

2

4

3

(1) A difficult posture from a *Nrtta* or Pure Dance sequence in the Orissi classical dance. (2) The *Mardala Karana* from the Pure Dance technique of Orissi which is based on the *Karanas*. (3) The *Lahunia Bandha*, a unique posture from the *Nrtta* or Pure Dance of Orissi, (4) *Chira Bhangi*, one of the highly elaborate dance positions in Orissi. (Photos copyright, Mohan Khokar.)

Plate 52

1

Kuchipudi dance dramas of Andhra Pradesh. (1) Vedantam Satyanarayana Sharma, the celebrated exponent, in the title role of the dance drama "Bhama Kalapam." (2) A *Nrtta* or Pure Dance posture from one of the Kuchipudi dance dramas. (3) An interlude from the dance drama "Usha Parinayam." (Photos copyright, Mohan Khokar.)

2

3

After having seen a performance of Orissi, the captivating, statuesque, plastic character of the postures lingers long in one's memory. The art reflects a fluid flow of rhythmic poise and graceful flexibility. Appealing, devotional and lyrical, it possesses brilliance of technique. Indeed, India is all the richer with the national renaissance of this ancient and dynamic classical dance form.

Great *gurus* in the past have enriched this dance school, and among them may be mentioned Prataprudra Dev, a great patron of the dance and music whose authoritative knowledge helped preserve it in its pristine purity; Ramananda Pattanaik and Kelucharan Mohapatra, distinguished authorities and specialists in the mode and manner of performance of the Orissi dance school. Under royal patronage, the dance became closely associated not only with the temples but with festival and ceremonial, and this gave a great impetus to the art as well as encouraged illustrious *gurus* to enrich and preserve its essential qualities.

KUCHIPUDI

The classical dance as practised in Andhra Pradesh, a State on the mid-eastern coast of India is known as Kuchipudi, and it gets its name from the village of the same name, near Masulipatam in the Krishna district. Springing from the comprehensive principles, system and techniques of the classical dance as expounded in the *Natya Sastra* by Bharata Muni, this highly developed form of the classical dance has come down to posterity in the purposeful dance drama form. Through these dance dramas, the full beauty of lyric, music and dance composition are unfolded to tell a story pregnant with emotional expression and high ethical intent. Andhra's classical music follows the Karnatic or Southern mode and many of the beautiful Telugu songs and lyrics are used attractively and often in the *Padams* and *Sabdam* of the Bharata Natyam of Tamil Nad.

Andhra has a rich heritage of culture and the arts, and is historically important as one of the great Empires of ancient India which held sway over a large portion of the south as well. It presents a very picturesque scene. The two large rivers, the Godaveri and the Krishna, flow through this region, creating vast green and fertile tracts, while on its east, sun and shadow play on the deep blue sea as it ebbs and flows, its white crested waves whispering mystically.

A profusion of colour appears in the dress, the festivals and the natural scene. In the midst of these delights, magnificent old temples and historical monuments with their rich architectural glory, stand like many jewels of ancient design and origin, constant reminders of the vital role that aesthetics played in Andhra's history. Indeed, under royal patronage, the arts and crafts flourished through the centuries, and have come down through the ages to reflect the artistic trends of the people both past and present.

Superb and delicate dance sculptures of young dancers, Apsaras, the heavenly nymphs, and Gods and Goddesses, together with the exquisite examples of musicians playing musical instruments, decorate the temples of Amaravati, the excavations of Nagarjunakonda and the cave-temples of Bhairvani Konda in the Nellore district and many other famed temples such as the Ramappa temples in Palampet, Warangal District, (belonging to the 13th century A.D.), to name a few examples. As the temples became the centres of the arts and learning, the classical dance was performed before the Shrine in all its pristine beauty and religious content. The dance in fact took several forms in Andhra, noted for its many celebrated artistes and musicians. And aesthetics reached a high standard as is evident in the detailed descriptions of the many forms of entertainment and cultural activities given by Palkuriki Somnatha in his famous *Panditaradhya Charitara*.

Three different types of dances were prevalent in Andhra, each distinct one from the other, yet all based on the classical modes and trends. These were the devotional dances of the Devadasis, the religious dance dramas of classical Yakshagana of the Brahmins, and the secular dances of the Raja Nartakis. The dances of the Devadasis were dances of devotion and dedication to God. They were performed before the Shrine and on the polished stone slab placed behind the Nandi bull which faced the Shrine. They were ritualistic dances that corresponded to the *Aradhana Nrityas* described in the old 13th century A.D. treatise written on palm leaves, the *Nrittaratnavali* by Jayapa Senani of the Kakathiya dynasty of Warangal. The very fine dance sculptures in the Ramappa temples closely follow this treatise. The dance dramas of religious Yakshagana performed by the Brahmins in the temple *mandapas* took shape from the early dance dramas of indigenous origin called *Bahu Natakas* that portrayed the ten varieties of *Shiva Leela Natayams* or Shiva Legends. These showed the various manifestations of Lord Shiva—*Garala Kantha* (Shiva as the Saviour of the World who drinks poison to save mankind), *Mrutyam Jaya* (Shiva as the Destroyer of the God of Death), *Tripura Samhara* (Shiva who saves the three cities from the Asuras), *Satvika Ananda Rupa* (Shiva as half-man half-woman who creates harmony and unity in the world process), *Palonetra* (Shiva as destroyer of Kama, the cupid of Hindu mythology), *Aradhanari* (Shiva as half-man half-woman, signifying the dual processes), *Atavika Rupa* (Shiva as the Hunter who tests Arjuna's strength and valour), *Kala Bhairava Rupa* (Shiva in His dance of Anger, as He destroyed Daksha and His enemies), *Nataraja* (Shiva as the God who controls the harmony and rhythm of the Universe); and *Sandhya Nritya* (Shiva in His gift-giving noble dance that calls to men to worship Him with peace in their hearts). Taking shape as the religious Yakshagana dance dramas, they were dedicated to the presiding deity of the temple and enacted in the *Kalayana Mandapa* pavilions of the Shiva temples for the entertainment of the worshippers. Lastly, there were the secular dances performed by the professional women dancers, the Raja Nartakis, who danced outside the temples and in the royal courts.

When the high and austere order of the Devadasis deteriorated, mainly owing to economic stress, famed Brahmin *gurus* and experts of the dance assembled in Kuchipudi village and formed into groups in order to preserve the art of the classical dance in all its purity and original quality and pass it on to posterity. Brahmins deeply versed in the *Sastras* thus became the custodians of the classical dance in Andhra and formed themselves into the Brahmana Melas that were entirely composed of men of the highest integrity and character.

The earliest reference to the Brahmana Melas, we are told, is about A.D. 1502, in the reign of King Viranarsimha Raya of Vijayanagar. At first, the Brahmana Melas travelled from Kuchipudi village where they had established themselves, to various parts of the State, entertaining the people with dance dramas based on the themes from the *Shiva Puranas*, the *Ramayana* and the *Mahabharata*; and later, under the influence of Vaishnavism (the worship of Lord Vishnu), they began to enact also dance dramas based on the *Bhagavata Purana*. Devoting themselves to the worship of God through song and dance, they came to be called Bhagavatulus, and it is owing to these great exponents and devotees of the art that the clas-

Kuchipudi dance costume (traditional). Yamini Krishnamurti demonstrating a graceful posture from a solo sequence in *Nrtta* or Pure Dance. (Courtesy, Coronet, Madras.)

sical dance was preserved in its purity and high quality in Andhra.

With the fall of the Vijayanagar Empire in Andhra, many of the Brahmin Bhagavatulus who were well versed in the dance, scholars and musicians of note, migrated to the Tanjore District in Tamil Nad where they were given shelter and land by the Nayak King. They formed a colony, and called the place Achutapuram after King Achutappa Nayak (1561-1614) who was their patron. Later, this centre became known as Melatur, and still retains this name today. At the same time that these Bhagavatulus came to Tanjore, a number of secular professional dancers, the Raja Nartakis, also migrated there, all bringing their arts of the dance and music with them. The Raja Nartakis, it is historically mentioned, performed several interesting types of solo dances known as Durupada, Chaupada, Pada Kila, Madomabela Dyutam, and so on, in the royal Nayak *durbars*.

Among the distinguished composers and masters of music and lyrics who migrated to the Tanjore District from Andhra were Bhakta Kshetragna and Bhakta Tirthanarayana Yati, both noble and saintly men and strong devotees of God. Kshetragna, who came from the village of Muvva near Kuchipudi, composed *Padams* which brought him both honour and reverence, particularly the *Muvva Gopala Padams*, the deeply appealing and poetic love lyrics dedicated to Sri Krishna. When he went to Tanjore, he took with him his wonderful compositions and *Abhinayas* with their highly emotional expression, full of *Rasa* or Flavour, and certainly influenced the trend of the classical traditions there. Then, the other great composer and lyricist from Andhra, Bhakta Tirthanarayana Yati (1620-1700), migrated to Tanjore where he became famous as the author of the *Krishna Leela Tarangani* in Sanskrit, a very soulful and dramatic form of the classical dance drama of Yakshagana, in which were combined fine techniques of patterned rhythms of *Laya Venyasams* (the *Raga Venyasams*), so perfectly created for *Nrtya*, being that form of the dance comprising movements of the body and limbs together with facial expressions and filled with *Rasa* or Flavour. Here he composed a number of dance dramas in Telugu, well known among them being the *Parijataharanam* and the *Rukmangada*. Closely adhering to the teachings and methods of God's devotees as shown in the *Bhagavata* traditions, he composed his beautiful songs and dance dramas, and through them he expressed his utter devotion to God. He kept strictly to the classical modes in the music, dance and *Abhinaya*. With the settling of Bhakta Tirthanarayana Yati in Tanjore District, the tradition of the Bhagavata Mela Nataka appears to have taken on importance, and he had many followers for years to come.

However, although some of these notable personalities and other scholars and dancers migrated to Tanjore, many remained in Andhra, to stabilise the important cultural art centre that had already been established by the Bhagavata Mela Nataka groups in Kuchipudi village. Among these distinguished pesonalities was the ascetic composer Bhakta Siddhendra Yogi, who composed the *Parijata Harana*, a *Kavya* in the *Sringara* Mood, based on the dance drama by Bhakta Tirthanarayana Yati, and inspired by the theme of the early Sanskrit play *Parijatam* written by Umapathi of Bharhut in the early 14th century A.D.

Being an ascetic Bhagavatulu who believed that one could best achieve spiritual union with God by devotion and love through the singing of hymns of praise and glory, Bhakta Siddhendra Yogi was inspired to produce his composition in dance drama form, and had the Bhagavatulus and artistes of Kuchipudi village interpret it. The theme, which was taken from the sacred teachings of the

Bhagavata Purana, tells of the incident in which Satyabhama, consort of Sri Krishna, asks Him to get her the celestial Parijata flowering tree to plant in her garden. Her request stems from that fact that she knows that Sri Krishna has already presented to Rukmani the Parijata flower which the seer Narada has obtained from the heavenly garden of Indra, and given to Krishna. In the dance drama however the incident of the Parijata flower is given secondary place and the theme centres round the great love and devotion of the proud and beautiful Satyabhama for Lord Krishna, and her suffering when He leaves her for having displeased Him. It is full of emotional intensity and is symbolic of the yearning of the individual Soul to become one with God, and the trials and tribulations the individual must go through before realising the Infinite. This dance drama by Bhakta Siddhendra Yogi, based on the Kuchipudi classical dance techniques, became the best item in this style of the dance and remains so today.

It is interesting to note at this point how the classical dance in Andhra, now taking the general name of Kuchipudi after the village of that name, became enriched and further developed. As mentioned previously, there were three distinct groups of dancers: the Devadasis who danced their devotional dances in the temples, the Brahmins with their devotional dance dramas, and the Raja Nartakis who performed their secular dances outside the temples and at the royal court and social gatherings. Naturally the modes of all these three groups came to influence one another. The Devadasis, for instance, who danced in the Vishnu temples learnt the fine intricacies of the Parijata Harana of the Kuchipudi dance dramas and enacted it in the temples during festivals. The Raja Nartakis were influenced by the Yakshagana techniques that were at first prevalent and performed in secular Yakshagana dance dramas on their own; and the Kuchipudi dance dramas, with their devotional trend, had something new incorporated into them. Thus there was an exchange of dance techniques among the three groups, each adapting and retaining certain fundamental characteristics of its own and creating richer modes all round.

The Kuchipudi dance drama of Parijata Harana was for instance remodelled, and became the Bhama Kalapam. In this new form, the character of the heroine was elaborated and more stress was laid on the *Abhinaya* or emotional dramatic aspect, namely, her *Viraha* or mime of the sorrows and tribulations she undergoes when she is parted from Lord Krishna. In addition to this, many new modes of the pure dance of the classical techniques or *Nrtta* were added. Bhama Kalapam then became the most perfect item in the Kuchipudi repertoire and was so popular that dance experts from other parts of Andhra came to learn it at the Kuchipudi centre and then they composed their own versions of it.

It will be appropriate here to first describe the technique, form and story of the Kuchipudi dance dramas, and then to discuss briefly some of the fundamental differences between them and that of the solo performers.

The Kuchipudi dancers of the Brahmana Melas were well versed in the precepts of the ancient Sanskrit treatises the *Natya Sastra* by Bharata Muni, the *Abhinaya Dharpana* by Nandikeshwara, and the *Nrittaratnavalli* by Jayapa Senani among others, and so they were able to retain all the fine points that these authoritative books enjoined. Their dance dramas therefore had in them the Three Main Elements of the classical dance beautifully incorporated, namely, *Natya* or the combination of both acting and dancing, *Nrtta* or pure dance, and *Nrtya* or that form of the dance comprising movements of the body, hands, limbs, together with facial expressions and use of eyes, eyebrows, and filled with *Rasa* or Flavour, which may be perfectly expressed in the use of dramatic theme and characterization; as well as *Abhinaya* or emotional acting with mime. They further elaborated and enhanced the dance dramas by the introduction of *Daruvus*, this being the entrance dance of each character in the drama, in which the dancers introduce themselves by starting with a song (*Pravesha Daru*), followed by pure dance interludes, postures and hand gestures which are accompanied by the chant-recitation of the *Sollakath* (word syllables chanted by the musicians for each step that the dancer takes), or rhythmic dance syllables. Finally they introduced the *Sabdas*, which are dramatic lyrics based on the theme and rendered in a particular musical form called *Paathya*, which includes the chant recitation of the *Sollakath* or rhythmic dance syllables, song with text (*Sahitya*), and beautifully chanted *Slokas* describing the story of the characters.

The addition of *Daruvus* and *Sabdas* gave the dance dramas full scope for the four types of *Abhinaya* or expressive emotional content, namely, *Angikabhinaya* or the expression through the limbs and body, *Vachikabhinaya* or the expression through the voice, *Sattvikabhinaya* or the expression through feeling and emotion, and *Aharyabhinaya* or the expression through dress, make-up, ornaments and other aids. Then there emerged a perfect fusion of lyrical verse, music and dance. Although the emphasis remained on the dramatic interpretive aspect, the importance of all the three components of *Bhava*, *Raga* and *Tala* are clear cut and necessary, that is, Mood, Melody and Song, and Rhythmic Timing. As we shall see presently while giving the story and enactment of the actual dance drama of Bhama Kalapam, the mood of the drama is wonderfully carried right through by the correct emphasis on the central theme of Satyabhama's suffering and the dramatic events that bring it to its climax; the right selection of the *Raga* melodies that bring to the fullest effect the songs that both the dancers and musicians sing in the unfolding of the story, and the use of many interesting *Talas* not only for the songs, but for the perfect maintenance of the highly technical pure dance sequences and interludes.

Here, too, as in the other schools of the classical dance in India, the pure dance movements are arranged to various timings or *Talas* and are embellished by means of little "pieces" in poetic form, like the *Jatis* of the Bharata Natyam of Tamil Nad, the *Thoras* of Kathak and the *Ukuttas* of Orissi. Here also, music and song lend the background to the dance and keep the main timing, in which there are the regular short metrical intervals of time of equal length. The drummer then plays fascinating "pieces" which fit in in a pattern, and these rhythmic drum syllables coincide exactly, syllable for syllable, with word syllables which are chanted or recited by the musicians and echoed by the dancer's feet. For greater effect, the use of finales or *Thirmanas* in the pure dance sequences is important. The foot rhythms of the dancer, matching the recited word syllables and the drum syllables, are seen to advantage between verses of the song and with the entrance of pure dance sequences, as well as in the *Thirmanas*. Here is an example of a foot rhythm word syllable piece in the Kuchipudi school that resembles quite closely those which are used in the other classical dance styles.

Dhigu Tangu Taka, Tang Takita Taka,
Dhi Talangu Taka, Talangu Dhi Taka,
Nam Kita Kita Taka, Tari Kita Kita Taka,

Thom, Kita Kita Taka, Tari Kita Kita Taka,
Tata Kita Taka, Ta Dinginatom,
Ta Dinginatom, Ta Dinginatom.

With emphasis on the principles of the *Karanas*, with the swing and placements of the arms and the statuesque postures; with great grace and purity of line and pose, the style truly and beautifully counterbalances both *Lasya* and *Tandava*. Being highly dramatic, the emotional side is fully developed, and there are the expressions of the eyes and eyebrows and face, supported by the use of hand gestures with a language of signs closely following the *Natya Sastra* by Bharata Muni and the *Abhinaya Dharpana* by Nandikeshwara, as well as the *Nrittanatnavalli* by Jayapa Senani.

Traditionally, only men take part in the Kuchipudi dance dramas, the feminine roles being played by young men as in Kathakali. Yet, the whole impression left by these performances is one that is gracious and intensely moving: their compelling aim and purpose being the interpretation of devotional themes through music and dance.

In all these dance dramas, the *Suthradhara* or Stage Director plays a most important role. He is a *guru*, well-versed in dance, music and the *Sastras*, and it is he who really conducts the dance dramas. He introduces the characters before they come on the stage, provides humour if required, and even sings and enacts *Abhinaya* when necessary.

The Kuchipudi school has many dance dramas to its credit, the most important being the *Bhama Kalapam*. The *Golla Kalapam* is another favourite, the philosophic musings of a Gopi. Later on, mention will be made of some of the important subjects that are well known and have been produced with conspicuous success by this dramatic school of the classical dance.

1. Kuchipudi Bhama Kalapam. This dance drama embraces as already explained the main theme of the great love of Satyabhama, consort of Krishna, for her Lord, and the pangs of tribulation that she has to suffer when she is parted from Him till He re-joins her. This is known as the *Viprlambha Sringara*, the "Sorrowful Pangs of Love."

The Bhama Kalapam is the *Parijata Apaharana* theme and the story in short is:

Once Krishna was adorning Satyabhama with all her jewels, and taking a mirror, He asks her who she thinks is the more truly beautiful, she or He. Satyabhama proudly and unthinkingly declares herself more beautiful than her Lord (*Pranaya Kalaham*). Lord Krishna is displeased at her hauteur and leaves her (*Manam*) to go to another consort, Rukmani. Realising her folly, Satyabhama suffers the pangs of regret and separation (*Vihara*), and to add to her sufferings, she has constant visions of Krishna giving His love to the other women who seek Him, and also visualises the incident of Krishna giving the celestial Parajita flower to Rukmani. She sends a messenger (*Duti*) to Krishna, begging Him to come back to her (*Dautya*). Finally, the Lord relents and returns to her (*Samagama*). There is an additional episode introduced called the *Savatula Kayyam*, to further dramatise Satyabhama's suffering and make her feel the pangs of jealousy as well. Another character is introduced in the form of Rukmani who is presented to Krishna as His bride. This results in an altercation between the two women, but in the end when they both realise that all have the right to love Him only and neither of them can live without His love, they become reconciled. The linking character in the dance drama is Vidhusaka, who plays the dual role of Madhavi (the girl messenger who goes to Krishna to intercede on Satyabhama's behalf and as Madhava, the man who gives Rukmani as bride to Krishna.

This is the story in general—the form is somewhat like the classical Kathakali dance dramas of Kerala.

The dance drama commences with a prologue—the playing of the *Mirdanga* and *Madala* drums accompanied by cymbals. This is followed by a prayer song to Bala Gopala (Lord Krishna); and then comes the worship of the Flagstaff of Indra (Vedic Lord of Heaven), *Arangam* as performed on the ancient Sanskrit stage and described in the *Natya Sastra*. The *Sutradhara* (Stage Director) now sings and announces the theme of the play, introduces the characters and invites the audience to enjoy the drama. All this takes place behind a curtain that has been raised by two attendants as in Kathakali. Satyabhama now looks over the top of the curtain (*Mukha Darshana*), and performs a beautiful dance of invocation, full of expression and filled with *Rasa* or Flavour. Her *Rechakas* (special foot, waist, neck and postural movements and hand gestures) are eloquent. Towards the end of her song, she takes hold of her magnificent braided plait and throws it over the curtain towards the audience, as a sort of challenge to anyone to rule out her supremacy in the art. If anyone present succeeds in winning the challenge after having accepted it, Satyabhama accepts defeat and the play commences again with another dancer playing the role of Satyabhama. This however is mere convention now. Satyabhama casts her braid over the curtain as a symbol and no challenge actually takes place. The *Sutradhara* now performs another *puja* (worship) as the curtain is half lowered, and Satyabhama sings a song introducing herself (*Druva Pravesika Druva*), and once again dances pure dance to perfection. The *Sutradhara* discourses with Narada the sage; while Madhavi the girl messenger performs with attractive gait (*Charis*) and acting and dance movements. The curtain is lowered; Krishna appears and receives from Madhavi (who is now impersonating Madhava, personifying the wisdom of the inner Self), the hand of Rukmani. The introduction now being over with all these preliminaries, the real theme begins.

Satyabhama introduces herself to Madhavi through song, and pleads with her to intercede on her behalf with Krishna. Madhavi asks Satyabhama to describe her Lord. And this is the opportunity in the dance drama to introduce the highly intricate *Dasavatarabhinayam*, when the ten *Avatars* or Incarnations of Krishna are portrayed, namely, *Matsya* (the Fish), *Kurma* (the Tortoise), *Varaha* (the Boar), *Narsimha* (the Man-Lion), *Vamana* (the Dwarf), *Parsurama* (the Warrior with the Axe), *Rama* (the Archer and Heroic Prince), *Balarama* (the Man with the Plough), *Buddha* (the Enlightened One), and *Kalki* (the Protector of the Horse).

Madhavi, perseveres steadfastly in her appeal to Krishna and succeeds in bringing Him back to Satyabhama. There follows three very fine dance sequences full of *Rasa* or Flavour, between Satyabhama and Madhavi, between Satyabhama and Krishna, and between Satyabhama and Rukmani. With this, there is a happy ending and Krishna is reconciled with Satyabhama. There is superb characterization and emotional acting throughout the dance drama. Each artiste appears with a *Daru*, first singing the song of introduction of herself or himself, and then dancing to interpret the sentiments expressed in the accompanying song.

Both the dancers and the musicians sing the songs in choice *Raga* melodies of the Karnatic or Southern school of music, with the use of many interesting *Talas*, accompanied by the *Mirdanga*, the flute, and the *Thiti*, a wind bag instrument with a reed mouth-piece.

The Bhama Kalapam is essentially a love theme with dance and drama beautifully balanced and expressed through dramatic acting and intricate pure dance sequences done to complicated time measures. Possessing nearly eighty *Daruvus*, each sequence ends with a fine *Thirmana* or finale, in which the footwork and timing are rhythmically patterned in the Kuchipudi techniques. There is every element in it of the dance as described in the *Natya Sastra*, every form of *Lasya* or graceful soft bodily movements, pure dance, *Padams* and *Abhinaya*. Besides the *Lasya* feminine grace, there are the forceful *Tandava* men's postural stances (*Nata Lakshmanams*), excellent footwork (*Padabhinayam*) expressing the importance of *Tala*, and finely acted mime (*Natya*). Above all, it is philosophical, symbolic of *Satyabhama* (the individual Soul) yearning to become one with God, and to achieve this the individual must go through much suffering and tribulations. The individual Soul (*Satyabhama*) utilizes Madhavi (personifying the wisdom of the inner Self) to help overcome trials and tribulations.

2. Golla Kalapam. The theme of this Kalapam in Kuchipudi is an ethical satirical conversation between a Gopi and a Brahmin, in which she asserts that she is in no way lower in position or learning or worthiness than he is. All are born the same and the Brahmin gains his status only after he has been taught the fundamentals of knowledge. Other popular themes of the dance dramas in Kuchipudi include, *Prahlada Charitam, Sarangadhara Charitam, Jalakridalu, Harishchandra, Rukmani Kalayanam, Usha Parinayam, Codigani Kalapam, Mohini Rukmangada*, and *Rama Natakam*.

As mentioned before, the dance drama is really the most complete form of all that Bharata Muni has described for the rules that encompass the classical dance in India. For it not only embraces all that can be done by a solo dancer, but also has the added richness of perfect dramatic characterization. In the Bhama Kalapam of Kuchipudi, it can be noted that all the five main items of Bharata Natyam are included, namely, the *Alarippu, Jatisvaram, Sabdam, Varnam* and the *Padams*.

1. The first performance of Satyabhama in the dance drama as she looks over the top of the raised curtain (*Mukha Darshana*). She does here what is really the opening sequence and it is a preliminary introduction, a prelude to the entire performance and the theme to follow. Her pure dance movements and special foot rhythms, movements of the waist, neck, postural and hand gestures (*Rechakas*), may in their entirety be compared to the *Alarippu*.

2. Satyabhama's pure dance following her introductory song (*Pravesika Daruva*), with the curtain half lowered, corresponds to the *Jatisvaram*. This pure dance composition, done to elaborate timing with patterned stepping, graceful arm and neck movements and postures, show the stress on rhythmic *Tala* or timing and musical score as in the *Jatisvaram*.

3. The *Sabdas*, as they are called in Kuchipudi, are dramatic lyrics based on the theme and rendered in a particular musical form called *Paathya*, which includes the chant-recitation of the *Sollakath* or dance syllables, song with text (*Sahitya*), which is religious, and beautiful chanted *Slokas* describing the story and character. This is done as Satyabhama introduces herself (*Druva Prasesika*

Druva), and then enacts the meaning of the *Slokas*. This corresponds to the expressive interpretive *Sabdam*.

4. When the real theme begins in the dance drama, and Satyabhama introduces herself to Madhavi, the messenger girl, through song and pleads with her to intercede on her behalf with Krishna. Here, there is richness of melody and fine interpretation. There is as in the *Varnam* of Bharata Natyam, emotional acting with rhythmic cadences and pure dance interludes between the song verses. Each sequence finishes with an intricate finale or *Thirmana*, and it possesses all the three components of complete dance displayed, *Natya, Nrtta*, and *Nrtya*, as in the *Varnam*.

5. The whole sequence of Satyabhama's *Viraha* or the emotional acting of the pangs of separation and sorrowful love and yearning as she is parted from her Lord, is filled with very dramatic *Abhinaya*. She interprets her feelings with soft flowing gestures and this sequence forms the main theme of the dance drama. In the Bharata Natyam, the idyllic love lyrics of the Krishna legends are perfect subjects for the *Padams*, so here also, Satyabhama's love for Krishna provides the same suitability and the lyrics are comparable to the *Padams*.

6. In place of the *Tillana*, there is the interesting scene in the dance drama when Satyabhama meets Rukmani and there is a quarrel between them for the love of Krishna. Each one performs with the acme of perfection and elegance, combining intricate dance sequences to show her particular attributes coupled with emotional acting. This part in Kuchipudi is called *Uktapratyuktaka* in the form of the *Savatula Kayyam* or the quarrel scene between Satyabhama and Rukmani. Its characteristics may be compared in general with the gentle grace and yet temperamental attributes of the *Tillana*.

7. The *Dasavatarabhinayam* is an additional dramatic part with *Abhinaya* and dance combined of the Kuchipudi dance drama, and is alive with mime and drama. Satyabhama here depcts the ten *Avatars* or Incarnations of Krishna, when describing her Lord to Madhavi.

It may be mentioned here that today dancers enact the *Sabdas* in solo, thus giving scope for the solo performance of Kuchipudi on the modern stage. Each particular character in a particular chosen theme may enact a part, and so the whole detailed form of the actual dance drama is being curtailed for urban stages. There may be just two main characters, or three, or even one dancer enacting more than one role. There are both feminine and masculine *Daruvus*, and this makes the characterization more understandable.

It has already been explained how the Brahmana Melas, the Devadasis and the Raja Nartakis exchanged and retained certain aspects of the dance modes in Andhra, and in this connection, it will be appropriate to explain here some of the differences. When the Devadasis exchanged and adapted certain techniques of the Brahmana Melas, they finally had different *Daruvus*, that is, the entrance dance of each character in which they introduces themselves by starting with a song (*Pravesha Daru*) followed by dance expressing the meaning of the song, with fine combinations of pure dance interludes (*Nrtta*), postures and hand gestures accompanied by the chant-recitation of *Sollukath* or rhythmic dance syllables. The Devadasis also had a different mode of interpretation of the *Bhava* or Mood of the song, and in the expression through the body and limbs or the *Angikabhinaya* of the narrative lyrics. There were many variations too in the pure dance sequences with their dance word syllables (*Sollukath*) and in the finales or *Thirmanas*, which were all in very *Lasya* or feminine style and the dances were very fast in tempo and more patterned on the whole. The Brahmana Melas for their part not only remodelled the dance drama of Parijata Harana into the Bhama Kalapam, but they created pure dance techniques which could be incorporated into either solo or dance drama at relevent places. These were very technical and consisted of complicated foot patterns in the *Vibayaka Tala* with seventy-two *Matras* or beats in the main metrical timing; and also in the *Simhananda Tala* with 108 *Matras* or beats in the main metrical timing.

The dance organised and arranged by the Nattuva Melas are again quite distinct from those of the Brahmana Melas. The Nattuva Melas were the *gurus* and experts who about a little over a hundred years ago taught the dance to various women dancers, and these formed the *Bhoga Melan* or *Natya Melas*. These comprised three categories, namely, the Melan or the actual Devadasis, who danced in duty in the temples before the Shrine and when the deity was taken in procession. The Mejuvani, who specialised in the *Abhinayam* and in the rendering of the *Padams*, the interpretation in gesture language and facial expressions with emotional acting of lyrical *Ragas* to which the songs in the romantic mood were set. Their performances were very correctly classical in mode and were therefore of much cultural value. And, lastly, the Kelika, the dancers who performed in solo, doing dances more or less conforming to the solo Bharata Natyam done in the Tanjore Durbars by the Raja Nartakis. This form of the dance differed slightly in the various families in Andhra in which the art was practised and preserved. In the dance of the Kelika, stress was laid on the *Padams* and the complex beauty of the *Varnam*, the most complete and highly emotional and technical item in the Bharata Natyam; *Nrtya* and *Abhinaya* were very important, particularly well known *Abhinayams* being the benedictory and invocatory songs of praise to God of the *Taranga Nritya*, the *Ashtapadi* and the *Kshetragna Padas* in *Abhinaya*.

Among the famous names in Kuchipudi is the well known authority on the art Jayapa Senani, author of the *Nrittaratnavalli*, and disciple of the Brahmana Natyacharya Gundamatya. Another great teacher was Vennalakanti Suryamata, a specialist on the classical techniques; Pasumarti Sitayya, a distinguished scholar, actor and director of the dance; Chinta Venkataratnam and his brother Chinta Venkataramaiah, who were disciples of Pasumarti Sitayya. The former became famous in the role of Narada Maharshi and other dramatic characterizations, and the latter distinguished himself in the role of Satyabhama and in many other dance dramas. He revived and improved on the old dance dramas and re-shaped the special *Sabdas* and *Daruvus*. Chinta Narayanamurti is yet another well known and remembered name in the interpretation of the Bhama Kalapam dance drama, particularly in the exposition of the *Kshetragna Padams* and the general *Abhinaya*.

With the renaissance of the art of Kuchipudi, the classical dance forms practised in India have become greatly enriched. Dramatic in its intensity and possessing an abundance of variety within its many facets, Kuchipudi is at the same time philosophic in character and deeply emotional in its dramatic presentation. It has a great appeal not only because of the beauty of its vibrant, subtle and enduring qualities, but because it is truly a complete dramatic dance form. Indeed, one can see as these dance dramas unfold, exactly how the classical dance was the forerunner of the Sanskrit plays, and how much this art has contributed

Plate 53

Yamini Krishnamurti as Satyabhama in the ...ipudi dance drama "Bhama Kalapam" ... she makes her first appearance in the ... (2) Yamini in "The Dance of the Braid" ...-Bharatam) which precedes the entry of ...abhama in the dance drama "Bhama ...pam." Yamini excels in this most difficult ...ure. (3) Yamini Krishnamurti as Satya-...na, heroine of the dance drama "Bhama ...pam," wearing the elaborate braid (Naga-...); this particular braid was presented to the ... by the Siddhendra Kuchipudi Academy ... her great accomplishment in this school ...e dance. (Courtesy, Coronet, Madras.)

1

2

Plate 54

1

2

(1, 2) Yamini Krishnamurti in two expressive and characteristic postures from the Kuchipudi school of the dance. (Courtesy, Coronet, Madras.)

(3) Indrani Rahman in graceful posture depicting the beauty of bodily lines as seen in the Kuchipudi dance style. (Photo, H.Rahman.)

3

Plate 55

2   3

5   6

Kuchipudi *Sabda* (*Abhinayam*) from the subject, the *Manduka Sabda*. Sudha Doraiswamy (now Sudha Sekhar) in : (1) A characteristic pose depicting the *Manduka*
or "frog" with her hands in the *Manduka Mudra*. (2) Sudha as Mandodari, the
frog-queen, who emerges from the womb of a frog and whom Ravana marries
according to legend. (3) A *Nrtta* or Pure Dance pose in the *Manduka Sabda* depicting
the swan pose (*Hansa Sthanaka*). (4) The beautiful frog-queen Mandodari in the
Lasya or Gentle posture of this *Sabda*. (5) A characteristic *Nrtta* or Pure Dance
pose. (6) A posture showing Ravana, the demon king of Lanka, with his sword,
(Courtesy, Sudha Sekhar.)

1   2   3   4

5

The Lai Haraoba dance drama of Manipur—*Abhinaya* : Rajni Maibi demonstrating with classical Manipuri hand gestures (1) "Holding a child" (use of *Ardha-chandra Hasta*), (2) "Invocation" (use of *Chatura Hasta*), (3) "Holding a string" (use of *Hansasya Hasta*). (Photos, Narayan Sharma.)
The Lai Haraoba dance drama of Manipur—Khamba and Thoibi sequence. (4) Premlata Devi as Thoibi. (Photo, Narayan Sharma.) (5) *Left to right*, Bino Kumari Devi, Sudhir Singh, Thambal Angaobi and Tondon Devi in a scene from the Lai Haraoba dance drama. (Photo, Darshan Lall.)

towards the artistry, characterization and dramatic purpose found in the classic dramas of old.

DANCE OF MANIPUR

The classical dance of Manipur is an ancient art based on the noblest traditions and possessing a deeply philosophical content. The chief centre where it is performed is Imphal, the capital of Manipur, and its many varieties of dance and religious ceremonial are together known as the Manipuri Nartana.

Situated on the eastern frontier of Assam, on the north-east of India, Manipur presents a picture of great natural beauty and charm. Artistically constructed homesteads are set amidst lush tropical vegetation and green rice fields, with the added attraction of two or three temples in each village. The country abounds in myth and legend, and these are closely associated with Manipur's art and culture. Since earliest times, the people have shown an innate love and a gift for expressing their emotional and religious fervour through dance and music.

At first the people followed the Shaivite faith, worshipping Lord Shiva, Third of the Hindu Trinity, and His twin aspect Parvathi. But later, with the advent of Vaishnavism, Krishna and Radha became and are today the principal divinities whom they worship.

Legend says that once when Shiva and Parvathi visited the earth, they came to this beautiful region. Parvathi saw Krishna and Radha dancing the *Ras* (with its philosophical symbolism representing the eternal longing of the individual soul to become one with the Infinite Soul), and she wished to dance in the same manner with her Lord. Shiva found an ideal spot, covered by water, set like a gem within the hills. It is said that He pierced one of the hills and released the water, leaving a wonderful lush valley. Here, He danced with Parvathi for many nights and days, with supreme joy, accompanied by heavenly musicians; the darkness of the nights lit by the glowing gem provided by Nagadev, the great Serpent god. From that time this sacred place came to be known as the "land of the gem" (*Mani*, "jewel" and *pur*, "place"). Ritualistic dances dedicated to Shiva (Nong-pok-ningthou) and Parvathi (Panthoibi), were then composed by the people since those early times. One of the most famous dance dramas is the Lai Haraoba, which was believed to have been inspired by and based on the Ras Lila of Shiva and Parvathi. Later, the romantic and tragic story of the immortal lovers Khamba and Thoibi, a princess of the Moirang dynasty of Manipur, as told in the well known epic of Manipur the *Moirang Parba*, was incorporated into it. Khamba and Thoibi were gifted dancers and because of their undying love for each other, they were believed to have been re-incarnations of Shiva and Parvathi.

According to the annals of Manipur, one of the earliest dance forms prevalent there was the Leisem Jagoi, which was a ritualistic dance based on the theme of the old legend that the earth came into existence when nine gods brought its substance from heaven, and seven goddesses shaped it. This was followed by the Laibou dance of the Lai Haraoba dance drama, in which the three styles of the old Chappa dance, the Konglei and the Moirang dance were to be found. The Laibou tells of the creation and continuity of man by divine power.

The Lai Haraoba Dance Drama (Meaning Invocation and Providing Pleasure for the Gods).

This is a ritualistic, Shaivite and cosmological dance drama performed for ten days annually in the month of May. It tells of the invocation to the Gods, the creation of man, birth, youth, adult life and marriage, and of the arts and learning. This ancient dance drama contains pure dance sequences or *Nrtta* (much of which has been adapted in the *Bhangi Parengs* of the later Vaishnavite Ras Lilas), *Abhinaya* with explicit hand gestures (also adapted in the Ras Lilas), songs and musical accompaniment.

As it is ritualistic, the Lai Haraoba is directed and led by a high priest (*Maiba*) and a high priestess (*Maibi*), who are like all the *Maibas* and *Maibis* dedicated to the service of God and to the dance. This long and interesting dance drama commences with a procession, ceremonial, invocation and dance addressed to the deities by the *Maibas* and *Maibis* to call them to be present at the celebrations. They then intimate that the Gods have arrived and announce the commencement of the dance drama. The dances of the *Maibas* and *Maibis* are inspired by religious fervour and hence are full of emotion and feeling.

Groups of women dancers arrive now in front of the village deity, dancing and singing songs that explain symbolically the glory of creation and the birth of a child. Each group of dancers, swaying and circling with graceful movements and expressive hand gestures, succeed the previous group without a break; while opposite them, a group of men commence singing and dancing and chanting words of praise to God.

As this continues, three *Maibas* and *Maibis* start dancing, while a large circle of women dancers introduce the Spring dance, symbolic of the birth of new life. A dancing procession meanwhile emerges carrying the emblems for worship and dedication, ending with a ritualistic dance characterizing the life processes. Some of the interesting dances of the Lai Haraoba dance drama, besides depicting the ritualistic theme of fertility and birth and life, describe spinning and weaving, sowing and harvesting, playing ball and fishing. The dance drama ends with the dance symbolic of the boat in which the invoked deities will return to heaven, to be invoked again in the late spring the next year. Perhaps the most beautiful part of the Lai Haraoba festival is when dancers perform in duets the *Moirang Parva*—the romantic and tragic story of Khamba and Thoibi. The Lai Haraoba dance drama contains both the *Lasya* or the Gentle type and the *Tandava* or Forceful type of dancing, but the movements are graceful and flowing, symbolising the ancient beliefs and sacred legends of the people of Manipur.

About the 15th century A.D., however, Vaishnavism came to Manipur, and was adopted as the State religion by the then ruler. One of the great names associated with the worship of God through love and devotion (the *Bhakti* cult or Gaudiya Vaishnavism) was Maharaja Jai Singh, also known as Bhagya Chandra, who ruled in Manipur in the latter half of the 18th century. He became a great devotee of Sri Krishna, following the teachings of Chaitanya Mahaprabhu of Bengal. Baghya Chandra was also a patron of the arts, and it is believed that Sri Krishna appeared to him and revealed the mystic Ras Lila dance, asking him to have it performed in a special pavilion known as the *Ras Mandapa*, which was to be attached to the Govindji temple at Imphal. Bhagya Chandra was thus inspired to have the Ras Lilas created. They were codified and systematised on a strictly classical basis by well known *gurus*, who gleaned the material from all the existing dances of Manipur and created many new compositions. During his time, the *Maha Ras*, the *Vasanta Ras*, the *Kunj Ras* and the *Achouba Bhangi Pareng*, an important technical part of all the Ras Lilas were composed. Later rulers followed

Manipuri dance costume (traditional). Darshana Jhaveri as Krishna and Suverna Jhaveri as Radha in an expressive mood from one of the Ras Lila dance dramas. (Photo, Dhiraj Chawda. By courtesy of Nayana Jhaveri.)

his precepts, and under Maharaja Gambir Singh, the *Ghostha Bhangi Pareng* was composed by the *gurus*; and in Maharaja Kirti Chandra Singh's reign the *Brindavan* and the *Khurumba Bhangi Parengs* and the *Nitya Ras* were composed.

The dances of Manipur have retained their pristine beauty and rich content owing to the fact that they have been the outcome of a deeply religious faith, with a strict discipline for their performance.   Intimately connected with religious and social ceremony and festival, the dance lives through its people as a vital part of their lives and spiritual existence.   Becoming absorbed in the teachings of their scriptures, they have transferred to their dance and music all the sacred legends and parable stories centring round the lives of Krishna, Radha, Balarama, the Gopis and Gopas, as they lived and danced on the banks of the Jamuna river at Brindavan.

In its many forms, the dance of Manipur presents a richness of choreography, purity of rhythmic law and a moving intensity of worshipful ritual.   Every gesture, every subtle inflection of the body, is calculated to convey an inner grace of meaning. Indeed, in this most graceful school, we have the *Bhava* (Mood), *Raga* (Melody, Song), *Tala* (Rhythmic Timing), and *Natya* (Drama), propounding together a rare harmony through which its inner spiritual urge and its outward lyrical movements are perfectly delineated.   Being classical in form and intention, the dance of Manipur is based on the ancient Manipur texts the *Laithak Leika Jagoi* (in the old Meitheli language), the *Govindasangeetsleelavilasa* by Maharaja Bhagya Chandra, the *Sri Krishnarasasangeetasamgraha* and others, and also the Sanskrit treatises like the *Sangeeta Damodar* and *Sangeetasara Samgraha* from Bengal, all of which have been inspired by the *Natya Sastra* by Bharata Muni.

Like all Indian classical dancing, there is here also the *Nrtta* or pure dance technique to emphasise the importance of timing and rhythm, and the *Abhinaya* to express the interpretive quality and emotional content.   Its music is mainly inspired by the Hindustani or Northern school, though it has some kinship with the Karnatic or Southern school.   At the same time, it retains its special regional beauty, embellished by its own code of tonal compositions.   The dance expounds these intrinsic qualities, graciously imparting a mosaic of movement to the many intricate *Talas* or timings and the patterned rhythms.   Much of the variety in the creation of ever new and richer syllable patterns of dance that are being added is due to the virtuosity of the *gurus* of Manipur.

Here again, the dance is arranged to various main drum timings or *Talas*, such as *Tanchep, Menkup, Tintalmacha, Tintalmel, Meital-Surfac, Tanjao, Chartal*, and so on, consisting of 4, 6, 7, 8, 10, 12, and 14 *Matras* or sub-divisions of beats in the main timing respectively.   There are a great number of such main timings, comprising up to sixty-four *Matras* or sub-divisions of beats.   Intricate patterns of rhythmic syllables are woven in these main beats in a multitude of permutations and combinations to create innumerable poetic syllabic verses or *Alankar Punglol*, like the *Chollu* of Bharata Natyam.   These correspond with dance patterns or *Nrttalankar* (*Jatis* of Bharata Natyam), and coincide with the recitation of the musicians (*Sollu-kuttu* in Bharata Natyam).   Music supports the dance and keeps in tune with the main timing.   And these rhythmic syllabic verses or *Alankar Punglol* are played into the main basic timing to exactly coincide with all its *Matras* or sub-divisions of the beats, or to match the main stress and unstress of the basic timing, or to flow smoothly through the basic timing.   Thus while maintaining the basic timing or *Tala*, the *Mirdanga* player creates these many varieties of sound harmonies.   There are literally hundreds of such dance syllabic verses

(*Alankar Punglol*) that differ subtly one from the other, both in the combinations of their syllable sounds and in their translation into dance movement (*Nrttalankar*). These dance syllabic verses can be played and danced in three speeds or *Laya*, namely, slow (*Vilambit*), double the starting speed but still at medium tempo (*Madhya*), and four times the starting speed, which is fast (*Druta*). To add to the variety, these syllabic verses are utilized variously. For instance, when two or more of these *Alankar Punglol* are composed on the same timing and used together, they form what is known as a *Pareng*. If the *Alankar Punglol* composed on two or more *Talas* or timings are used together, a *Tal Prabandha* is created. Further embellishment is made possible when the *Alankar Punglol* instead of having its particular composition keeping to one rhythm in a particular *Tala* or timing, is set so that all the three speeds of slow, medium and fast are utilized (*Yati*), as well as introduced in different metric arrangements (*Jati*). When this is done the composition is known as the *Bol* variety. Here is an example of the syllabic wordings used in the Manipur school of the dance:

Ritujati *Ektal* *Menkup*, Six *Matras* or sub-divisions.

Dhentra Khraten Ta Tentra Khraten Ta
Dhentra Khraten Ta Tentra Khraten Ta
Tang Tata Khita Takhi Tata Khita
Tat Gragra Dhen Tat Krang Khit

Similarity in some of the word syllables between the *Thora* or syllabic verse of the Manipur dance and those as used in the Kathak can be noted.

Not only has the dancer to master the *Nrtta* or pure dance of the Manipur school, but he or she must become expert in the *Abhinaya*. Songs and poetic lyrics composed by the great saint-poets Jayadeva, Vidyapati, Chandidas and Govindas are interpreted through facial expressions, acting and postures.

The dance of Manipur contains both the *Lasya* or Gentle and graceful style (*Sukumar Naubathotpa*) and the *Tandava* or Forceful style (*Uddhata-Akanba*). So there are the soft graceful dances and the strong forceful dances, each style created to suit a particular theme.

Rules and regulations have been created for instance in the *Lasya* style which determine that there should be no exaggerated movements or postures, but a balanced flexibility is necessary, with the hips and body moving up and down, feet and legs close together, the movements filled with a rare grace with lilting sway of the body, and a gentle turn of the head in a semi-circular manner, forming a rhythmic unison with hands, arms and body. So that the general impression of the whole dance as it unfolds is as though the elements composing it flow like soft unbroken cadences in a legato musical piece. These *Lasya* movements are done either in a slow tempo with gracious and perfect equilibrium of posture (*Simitangam*), or in a medium-fast speed where the patterned footwork becomes more intricate and the movements are less restricted (*Sfuritangam*).

In the *Tandava* dances, one finds the same flow of movements as in the *Lasya*, but they are more virile and strong, and the dancers sit, jump and whirl to add the forceful element (*Gunthanam*). In addition there are the strong decisive free movements, with raised legs and great jumps and stamping to accentuate strength (*Chalanam*).

Plate 57

2

3

5

The *Nrtta* or Pure Dance of Manipur. Darshana Jhaveri in *Sthanakas* or basic postures. (Photos, Miss D. Sahiar.)

Plate 58

6 7 8

9 10 11

The *Nrtta* of Manipur—Continued. (6, 7, 8, 9) Ranjana Jhaveri showing postures from the *Chali*. (10) Darshana Jhaveri showing the *Ublai* (spiral movement) in *Lasya* style. (11) Darshana Jhaveri showing the *Longelei-Matek* (spiral movement) in *Lasya* style (Photos, Shri Marjadi.)

Plate 59

12

13

The *Nrtta* of Manipur—Continued. (12) Darshana Jhaveri showing the *Longelei-Matek* (spiral movement) in *Tandava* style. (13) Darshana Jhaveri showing the *Achongbi* (jumping movement) in *Tandava* style. (Photos, Shri Marjadi.)

14

15

The *Nrtta* of Manipur. (14, 15) Thouranisabi Devi demonstrating two graceful pure dance movements. (Photos, Narayan Sharma.)

Plate 60

16

17

18

The *Nrtta* of Manipur—Continued. *Bhangi Parengs :* (16) *Left to right*, Nayana, Ranjana, Darshana and Suverna Jhaveri showing the flow of movement from the *Achauba Bhangi Pareng*. (17) Vinodini Devi (*left*) and Kalavati Devi (*right*) showing a posture from the *Goshtha Bhangi Pareng* in *Tandava* style. (18) *Left to right*, Suverna, Darshana and Ranjana Jhaveri in a *Lasya* movement of the *Brindavan Pareng*. (Photos, Nos. 16 and 18 by Dhiraj Chawda ; No. 17 by Rajdutt.)

Plate 61

1

2

3

4

5

Abhinaya in the Manipuri school. Gambini Devi in the *Nayikabheda* (emotional expression): (1) As Madan Mohan — Sri Krishna as lover, (2) as Prathayati Putanikaiva — the female demon Putana holding the child Krishna in her arms, (3) Aisare Amar Pranera Vachha — Yashoda calling Krishna. Kshetritombi Devi in *Ras Abhinaya* showing (4) Gunjata Alikule—the humming bee over the flower, (5) Marakata Manju Mukura—Krishna's face is brilliant as a diamond-like mirror. (Photos, Narayan Sharma. Courtesy, *Marg* for 1, 4 and 5.)

Plate 62

1

2

3

Vasanta Ras—*Abhinaya* of Manipur. Suverna Jhaveri demonstrating (1) "Doe-eyed" (*Mriganayani*), (2) "Behold his beautiful face" (*Heri Mukha Mandala*), (3) "Singing" (*Gavata*). (Photos, Miss D. Sahiar.)

Plate 63

1

2

Nitya Ras—*Abhinaya* of Manipur (in praise of Radha). Nayana Jhaveri demonstrating (1) "Holding the blue lotus" (*Rayer Kare Neelakamal*), (2) "Jingling of the bracelet" (*Kankana Nod*), (3) "Armlet" (*Taraka*). (Photos, Rajdutt.)

3

Plate 64

1

2

Ras Lila of Manipur—the *Goshtha* (Gopa Ras). (1, 2) Vinodini Devi and Kalavati Devi in the Krishna Balaram Nartan (duet dance). (Photos, Rajdutt.)

3

Ras Lila of Manipur—the Nitya Ras performed at festival time in the temple courtyard at Manipur. (Photo, Narayan Sharma. Courtesy, Manipur Administration and *Marg*.)

Plate 65

1   2   3

The Khabakishei Ras (Clap Dance)—*Abhinaya*, Ranjana Jhaveri demonstrating (1) "If you go to Madhupure" (*Tumi Gela Madhupure*), (2) "Do not desert me" (*Anathini Karo Na*), (3) "Stop the chariot" (*Radha Rakho*). (Photos, Shri Marjadi.)

1   2   3

The Ulukhal Ras (Damodar Ras)—*Abhinaya*. Theme, "Stealing of the butter (*Makhanchori*). Darshana Jhaveri demonstrating (1) "Climbing to take the curds," (2) "Striking the pot of curds with a stick," (3) "Frightened that He has been seen." (Photos, Shri Marjadi.)

Plate 66

1

2

3

4

5

The Kartal Cholom (Cymbal Dance) of Manipur. (1) A group of *Kartal* players with *guru* Maibam Ibohal (second from right) as Duhar (leader) accompanied by two drummers. (Photo, Narayan Sharma. Courtesy, Manipur Administration). (2) Vijay Singh. (3) Priya Gopal Singh. (Photos, Miss D. Sahiar.)

The Pung Cholom (Drum Dance) of Manipur. (4) Amuyaima and Nipa Macha Singh. (5) Nipa Macha Singh. (6) *Left to right*, Amuyaima, Nipa Macha, and Virmangal Singh. (Photos, Miss D. Sahiar.)

6

Plate 67

1

2

3

4

5

Classical Chau dancers of Seraikela, Bihar. (1) The dance of Shiva-Parvati (*Hara-Parvati*). (2) Dance of the Fisherman (*Dheebar*). (3) Dance of the Sun-god and the maiden in the duet *Chandrabhaga*. (4) Dance of the Flower and the Bee (*Phool-o-Bhramara*). (Photos copyright, Mohan Khokar). (5) Mask of a Rajput warrior in the Chau folk design. (Courtesy, Bharatiya Natya Sangh, New Delhi.)

Plate 68

1

2

3

(1, 2) Mrinalini Sarabhai in the Mohini Atam of Kerala. (Courtesy, Mrinalini Sarabhai.) (3) Two dancers performing in the Mohini Atam. (Photo copyright, Mohan Khokar.)

One can better understand the nature of the various compositions to be found in the technique of the Manipur dance style, if a brief survey is made of them.

Technique of Pure Dance or Nrtta

1. *CHALI.* This forms intrinsic and traditional dance compositions used in the *Lasya* and *Tandava* dances. Usually it is danced in *Madhya* or medium tempo on the *Tintal Mel* comprising eight *Matras* or sub-divisions of the main basic time.

The *Chali* is short and precise, its rhythm gentle, unfolding the beauty of this school. It is also used as a finale or ending of the five important *Bhangi Parengs* or series of bodily postures of the dance. The *Bhangi Parengs* are the basic postural flexions comprising the various bends of the classical mode as already explained, such as the *Sama Bhanga* (equal bend with hardly any bend to any side), the *Abhanga* (state of slightly bending the figure to either side), *Atibhanga* (exaggerated bend), *Tribhanga* (the triple bend or emphasis on curvature of the hips), and so on. In the *Bhangi Parengs* we find therefore the essence of pure dance composition, with varied movements in each *Pareng*. They introduce a fundamental structure of form and technique of the Manipur dance.

Bhangi Parengs (Lasya)

(a) *The Achauba Bhangi Pareng.* Grace of movement flowing in soft rhythmic cadences of posture and composition. It fulfils the spirit and intentions of this school with its special stress on delicacy of motion. It is a basic dance composition, mainly composed on a timing of seven *Matras* or sub-divisions of beats (*Tal Rajmel*).

(b) *Brindavan Fareng.* A variation of the *Achauba Bhangi Pareng.* It is composed mainly on a timing of eight *Matras* or sub-divisions of beats (*Tintal Achauba*).

(c) *Khurumba Pareng.* Another variation of the *Achauba Bhangi Pareng*, comprising devotional postures and movements such as the worship of Sri Krishna and honour to Radha. It is mainly composed on a timing of seven *Matras* or sub-divisions of beats (*Tal Rejmel*).

Bhangi Parengs (Tandava)

(a) *Goshtha Bhangi Pareng.* A basic dance composition with its strength and flow of postures fulfilling a series of basic body movements. It is mainly composed on a timing of seven *Matras* or sub-divisions of beats (*Tal Rajmel*).

(b) *Goshthabrindavan Pareng.* A variation of the *Ghostha Bhangi Pareng*, based on the Brindavan theme. It is mainly composed on a timing of eight *Matras* or sub-divisions of beats (*Tintal Achauba*).

The *Lasya Bhangi Parengs* are composed on a slow (*Vilambit*) rhythm and end on (*Tanchep*) which is four *Matras* or sub-divisions of beats and the (*Menkup*) which is six *Matras* or sub-divisions of beats; the *Tandava Bhangi Parengs* are composed on a medium (*Madhya*) rhythm, but they end on the same timings as the *Lasya Bhangi Parengs*. Like the *Adavus* of Bharata Natyam, the *Chali* and *Bhangi Parengs* form the foundation and essentials of the style and expression of the Manipur dance. Each *Bhangi Pareng* has a character of its own which distinguishes it; and as one *Bhangi Pareng* graciously moves into the other, great finesse of form and posture is achieved.

2. *TALLINA or TELANA*.   Here, like the *Tillana* of Bharata Natyam, technique is enhanced by a dance composition based on an intricate system of word arrangements sung in a selected *Raga* melody, with the beats of the *Mirdanga* blending harmoniously in tune to the syncopation of the word sounds.   The *Tallina* or *Telana* is classed under the *Nirgeeta* type, emphasis being on the beauty of word composition and its interpretation through dance.

3. *SWARMALA*.   As the name indicates, like the *Jatisvaram* of Bharata Natyam, stress is laid on musical notation (*Svara*) and time measures, so that the dance movements are directed by excellence of highly intricate *Svara* passages composed of *Ragas*.

4. *CHATURANGA*.   This is one of the most attractive and elaborate dance conceptions in the Manipur school, incorporating lyrical verse, song and *Svara* passages (*Swarmala*) and word composition (*Nirgeeta*).   Wonderful successive dance sequences are exhibited to the accompaniment of poetic and song compositions with rhythmic word arrangements.

5. *KIRTIPRABANDHA*.   Now comes the highlight of this dance school. The *Kirtiprabandha* lends the true expression and soul of pure dance composition. Again lyrical verse, song and *Svara* passages with word composition support the dance with their rhythmic syncopation of *Mirdanga* play and recitation or chant of the lyric (*Mukhabol*).

These are the five types of dance composition which form the basis and fundamentals of the technique of pure dance or *Nrtta* of the Manipur school.

Abhinaya

Turning to the interpretive aspect of the dance, we find here richness of expression and emotional content. The Radha-Krishna idylls with their parable stories of the eternal longing of the individual soul to become one with the Universal Soul through love and devotion pervade all their sentiments. The *Sringara Rasa* or Mood of Love (*Nayaka-Nayika Bhava*) is pre-eminent, though the other eight sentiments are also employed.   For the fullest expression of these sentiments (*Rasa*), all the fourfold forms of the *Abhinaya* come into play: the *Angikabhinaya* (expression through the limbs and body), *Sattvikabhinaya* (expression through feeling and emotion by facial expression and use of hands and eyes), *Vachikabhinaya* (expression through the voice), and *Aharyabhinaya* (expression through dress, ornaments, and other aids). Vaishnav Manipur classical texts like the *Ujjvalanila-mani* have elaborated the *Sringara Rasa*, so that every subtle inflection of mood and sentiment is fully expressed in the emotional aspects (*Nayika Bhedas*). Dancers go through a long and disciplined training not only to learn all the technical aspects of expression, but to understand fully and be able to interpret each mood with deep feeling and emotion.   And apart from the sympathetic accompaniment of the music, lyrics and songs, the dance itself must be a graphic pulsating art expressing every inner feeling (*Swanguta*).   This is shown to great effect for instance in

the lighter themes of the dance depicting Krishna playing a ball game with his brother Balarama (*Kandukakrida*). When the importance is to be on the lyric or song or sacred verse, then the dance flowers into its full beauty mirroring every sentiment expressed in the texts (*Anugata*). Sometimes again, the dance is so subtle, it merely indirectly paraphrases the song or lyric (*Gamaka*). Thus many exquisite dance compositions (*Nritya Bandha*) have been evolved to show *Abhinaya* with its many facets and to illustrate the special interpretive qualities of the dance.

According to the ancient treatises like the *Natya Sastra* by Bharata Muni, there are what are known as *Rasakas* or group dances which may be performed in a circle, with the dancers either clapping their hands (*Tal Rasaka*); or using the play of short sticks (*Danda Rasaka*); or grouped in a circle (*Mandala Rasaka*), with the circle formed of girls and a boy dancer in the centre (*Hallisaka*, which is simple); and the more developed *Ras*.

In Manipur all these three types of *Rasaka* are done, but in order to give full scope to *Nrtta* (pure dance), *Nritya* (that form of the dance comprising movements of body, limbs, hands, together with facial expressions and filled with *Rasa* or Flavour and sentiment which may express small episodes), and *Natya* (the combination of both dancing and dramatic acting), the *Rasakas* have been developed with all these three elements of *Nrtta* , *Nritya* and *Natya* in them and have become the Ras Lila dance dramas, the subjects of which are devotional and centre round the themes of the Radha-Krishna idylls. The Ras Lilas are classified into six types, each to be performed on a special occasion.

1. *THE MAHA RAS.* This is performed on the full moon day in the month of Kartik (October). The theme is based on the story from the *Bhagawat Purana*, that one night when Lord Krishna was aroused by the beauty of the full moon, he decided to keep his promise and dance the Ras Lila with Radha and the Gopis. So He began to play sweet music on His magical flute beside the shimmering sands of the Jamuna river. They heard it and came forth to dance with Him in rapture. When pride entered their hearts at dancing with Him, He vanished. But as soon as they became humble and bowed to His Divine Will, He joined them again, duplicating himself many times. And they danced again in rapture. So Sri Krishna seemed to be throughout the circle yet in reality remained One. Although this Ras is one continuous dance drama, it is perfectly composed to bring out story, dance and characterization. Krishna, Radha, and twelve Gopis are introduced (the Gopis included represent Rupavali, sister of Radha, and two of the chief Gopis, Ananda Manjuri and Brinda Saki). Lilting movements follow a main pattern of form and procedure, starting with the singing of a *Kirtan* or sacred song of praise, followed by introducing the *Krishna Abhisar* (comprising emotional expression and interpretation), introducing Radha and the Gopis in their *Abhisar* and then proceeding step by step to tell the story. Fine technique of pure dance (*Achauba Bhangi Pareng* and *Brindavan Bhangi Pareng*), solos (of Krishna and Radha), group patterns of movement (the dances of the Gopis), melody with chorus, chanting and song, with *Abhinaya* to interpret the feelings of Radha and the Gopis and their longing to be with Him, are all combined as the dance drama unfolds. It ends with the offering of flowers (*Pushpanjali*) and the prayer with the sacred fire (*Arati*).

2. *THE VASANTA RAS.* This charming dance drama is also performed

on the full moon day in the month of Chaitra (March) in the *Ras Mandala* (palace temple).　It celebrates the Holi or the springtime festival of the Carnival of Colours. It tells of the episode of how Sri Krishna according to legend gained Radha's displeasure for dancing only with Chandrabali, one of the Gopis.　Finding that she has left the *Ras Mandala* after discarding her blue veil, symbolic of her love for Krishna, He relents, receives her forgiveness and enters the bower with her.　Then all the Gopis dance.　The general pattern of the first half of the Maha Ras is enacted, followed by the dancers throwing the colours (*Fagukhel*).　Once again there is a display of pure dance (*Achauba Bhangi Pareng* and *Khurumba Bhangi Pareng*), duet (Krishna and Chandrabali), group patterns of movements (dances of the Gopis), melody, chorus, chanting and song, with *Abhinaya* to interpret the drama of the Radha-Krishna misunderstanding.　It ends as usual with the offering of flowers and prayer.

3. *KUNJA RAS*.　This dance drama is performed on the day of the new moon in the month of Asvin (August).　The theme depicts the divine joy that Krishna, Radha and the chief Gopis experience when they meet in the floral bower (*Kunja*) which the Gopis have built for Him in which to rest.　It is less detailed than the Maha Ras, and its chief components lie in the fine and expressive *Abhisar* (showing the joy and the preparations of the Gopis and Radha going to meet Sri Krishna).　This is followed by the joyous group dance of Radha and the Gopis, done in a great circle with Krishna in the centre.

4. *NITYA RAS*.　We have in this again the theme of Krishna with Radha and the Gopis, and it is danced on almost all occasions of social and festive celebration.　Simple, more recent in composition, with the introductory *Abhisar* of the main theme in *Abhinaya*, accompanied by *Kirtanas* followed by the introduction of Krishna, Radha and the Gopis in the order of their importance, they dance finally in the big circle, with Krishna in the centre.

5. *GOSHTHA or THE GOPA RASA*.　In this Ras done in the *Tandava* style, Sri Krishna and His brother Balarama, having been taught by the sage Narada how to tend the cows, join the Gopas in grazing their herds on Mount Govardhan. On one occasion, after Krishna, Balarama and the Gopas had danced the *Kanduk-Khel* (the game of ball), they go to the forest of Tadavana to eat the fruit from the trees.　They are attacked by the demon Dhenukasur who holds sway there. Balarama engages the evil creature in a fight and kills him.　Then, when they all reach Brindavan, as they dance together, they are attacked by Bakasur, another demon.　Krishna being challenged, engages the demon in a fight and destroys him. This thrilling dance drama is performed also in Kartik (October), either in the famed Govindji temple *Mandapa* or the village temple *Mandapa*.　After the sacred *Kirtana* is sung to Saint Chaitanya Mahaprabhu (considered a re-incarnation of Sri Krishna), the story unfolds in dance and *Abhinaya* step by step.　It is a Ras of joy and vigour, and the swift turns, jumps, eloquent postures of interpretation, all harmonise with the general spirit of devotional ecstasy.

6. *ULUKHAL RAS*.　We have here the ever popular and lovable theme of the childhood mischief of Krishna.　Joining with His companions the Gopas, He teases the Gopis, breaks their pots of curds and steals the butter.　When they

report to Krishna's mother Yeshoda, she binds him to the *Ulukhal* (stone mortar) where she pounds rice. But Krishna escapes and starts His playful pranks again. In this group dance with the Gopas, Gopis, Krishna and Yeshoda, there is fine *Abhinaya*, a lilting melody and the exposition of the lighter appealing pure dance movements.

The Ras Lilas are a true exposition of the classical dance in its various facets. The sweetness of melody of the classical *Ragas*, the rhythmic play of the *Mirdanga*, songs, chorus and the soft notes of the flute and *Esraj*, the syncopated play of the *Manjiras* (small cymbals) and conches, add great devotional flavour. The whole ceremonial, decor, costumes, place of performance the *Nat Mandapa*, the recitation of *Slokas*, the dedication to God, all create an atmosphere of reverence and consecration, for these deeply religious dances which commence after dark and continue all night. The ancient Shri Govindji temple, which has been traditionally patronised by royalty, has been closely associated with the art and religion of Manipur since ages past, and all the social, cultural and religious ceremonials and festivals are performed under royal patronage. Groups of *gurus* and artistes of distinction (*Palaloisang*) are encouraged by the Maharaja and they participate in all the festivals that are celebrated in the precincts of this temple.

The religious and ritualistic spirit of devotion that pervades the Ras Lila performances, giving them a sublime mysticism, is present in all other forms of the dance in Manipur. During festival time, the whole day is devoted to the singing of sacred *Kirtans* by groups of men who play the *Kartals* (large cymbals) to the accompaniment of *Mirdangas*. As they become lost in ecstasy, drummers and singers commence dancing rapturously. This has developed into some of the most thrilling and technically brilliant dance compositions, in which either the *Kartal* (*Kartal Cholom*) or the drum (*Pung Cholom*) play the significant part. Here too, as in the Ras Lilas, there is a traditional recognised form for their technique of pure dance or *Nrtta*, and play of the *Kartals* or *Mirdangas* as the case may be, with their wonderful intricate timings and rhythmic syllable wordings, the accompanying song and the theme.

Kartal Cholom (*Tandava* Dance of Cymbals)

In this dance, men dancers play intricate *Talas* or timings on their *Kartals* (large cymbals) in perfect harmony with the rhythmic patterns of the accompanying *Mirdanga* (*Kartal Marol*). Grace and emotional feeling radiate as the dancers stand in correct posture (*Sthanka*) in a semi-circle, jump, perform sinewy movements (*Bhramaras*), whirl, turn to the right and left in tune with the music that is punctuated by the drum beats and the song that tells the theme. Though essentially *Tandava*, the tempo and verve of movements are contrasted by the lissom salient undulation of arms and body, the sway and turn of the head, and the picturesqueness of the tassels at the end of their *Kartals* tossing gently in rhythmic unison. Dancers can raise the dance tempo to a climax of emotional abandon as they move sometimes clockwise and sometimes anti-clockwise in a circle; sometimes moving forwards and backwards seeming to imitate Nature's own grace of movement of the *Kapote* (crane), *Mayur* (peacock), *Khanjan* (wagtail) or *Hansa* (swan). The subjects of the Kartal Cholom vary with the particular festival day when it is performed and the number taking part also varies accordingly. The usual group in the Kartal Cholom comprises the dancers, two *Mirdanga* players and the singers. Here again as in the Ras Lilas, the uplifting devotional lyrics of Jayadeva, Vidyapati, Chandidas and Govindas are sung in Sanskrit, Bengali, the old Meitheli language and in one of the Manipur dialects, in choice *Raga* melodies.

Manjira Cholom (Small-Cymbal Dance)

This is usually performed during the festival of the Jhulan Yatra (Ceremony of the Swing—*Dola*), when the images of Sri Krishna and Radha are placed on a beautifully decorated seat before a musically playing fountain, and rocked. A group of dancers as Gopis sing and dance playing *Manjiras*. Very graceful with expressive gestures, this dance is one of the light festival dances.

Khubakishei (The Clap Dance)

This particular dance is performed during the festival of the Rath Yatra (ceremony of the sacred temple chariot). Lively and graceful, it is very picturesque, connected as it is with processions and chanting and ritual.

Pung Cholom

In this *Tandava* drum dance unique to Manipur, there is the perfect synchronization of timing with varying patterns of footwork that offset the harmony of the intricate drum rhythmic syllables. The *Mirdanga* drums are suspended across the right shoulder, and the dancers form a semi-circle, sway, whirl, perform spiral movements, bend and turn, sit and move in a fast pace, playing their drums. There are some splendid drum rhythms in which the word syllables ring forth, just as in the Kartal Cholom the *Duhar* as the chief *Kartal* player plays splendid syncopated word soundings in varied patterns on his cymbals.

In the Pung Cholom, as in the case of the Kartal Cholom, the number who participate, including dancers and musicians, vary with the particular day on which it is performed. In the Dhrumel, for instance, the group comprises from fourteen to one hundred drummers. Dancers in both Choloms are dressed in spotless white waist cloths (*dhoties*), scarves and turbans, and as they move with lithe yet manly grace, there is a sense of strength and flexibility beautifully harmonising with the drum sounds in their balance of a rising crescendo and a falling gentleness. It is like an imitation of Nature, sometimes seeming to echo a thunder storm or lightning flashes and sometimes gentle as a summer breeze or the flight of a bird.

The dance of Manipur has for many years become familiar with audiences all over India. Its special grace, delicacy, subtle nuances of mood, and its most beautiful costume have given it a place of honour and distinction among the classical dance styles in India.

The creative genius and expert knowledge of many distinguished *gurus* and artistes have been responsible for maintaining and enriching the choreography, compositions and unique qualities of the Manipur classical dance. Through their dedicated devotion to the art, it has come to be understood and appreciated all over India. Among the many illustrious names are Nabhakumar Singha, one of the great exponents and *gurus* who came from his native region at the invitation of the late poet Rabindranath Tagore to teach at Shantiniketan.   Nabhakumar's special gifts in the techniques and *Abhinaya* and his many compositions have won him a unique place amongst dance experts. Well known in Bombay, Delhi, Ahmedabad and Calcutta, where he has taught the dance for many years, I had the privilege of having had him as my *guru*.   Ambui Maisnam, *guru*, specialist in the classical Ras dances, winner of the 1956 Akademi Award for the Manipur dance; noted for his creative talents, Ambui Maisnam is another *guru* who has done valuable work in Calcutta, Ahmedabad, and Almora where he was associated with the Uday Shankar school, and Imphal, where he is at present the senior teacher at the Manipur Dance College sponsored by the Sangeet Natak Akademi.   Tomba Haobam, famous expert in the Ras and the purity of this classical school, also went to Shantiniketan at the invitation of poet Tagore.   Winner of the 1958 Akademi Award for the Manipur dance, his special work is known in Calcutta and Shillong and in Imphal where he teaches at the Manipur Dance College.   Amudon Sharma, the third recipient of the Akademi Award for Manipur Dance in 1960, is an expert in the Manipur *Mirdanga* and known for his scientific approach to the dance.   Bipin Singh, teacher, scholar, noted exponent of the Imphal, Cacher and Tripura Schools of the Manipur dance, has also a deep understanding of the other classical schools of the dance.   His research into the ancient texts, his beautiful compositions in the strictly classical modes, have won him acclaim.   He is now the Principal of the Sri Govindji Nartanalaya, of which the Maharaja of Manipur is the patron. He also heads the dance section of the palace, as *Hanjaba*.   Bipin *guru* has a great many distinguished artistes whom he has taught to his credit both in Manipur and in Bombay.   Meitei-Tomba-Sarangtham is an expert *guru* of Pung Cholom and a recipient of an award of *Hanjaba* (Head) of *Senapala* (the royal group of artistes in Manipur).   Chaoba Thangyam has distinguished himself in the *Tandava* style of Manipur, and is considered one of the finest exponents of the Kartal Cholom, as well as of the sacred *Kirtans* and the *Abhinaya*.   Tombi Kshetri is an authority on the Ras Lilas and in her performance of *Abhinaya*.   One of the oldest experts, she teaches in the Sri Govindji Nartanalaya at Manipur.   Rajani Devi is a *Maibi* (priestess) and is therefore a dedicated dancer and specialist in the Lai Haraoba traditional dance style of Manipur, taking the lead in the Lai Haraoba festival performances.   Tompok Singh, who teaches in the Sri Govindji Natranalaya of Manipur, is a specialist in *Ras* composition and choreography.   Among other famous personages are Kumar Maibi, specialist in the Lai Haraoba, who teaches in the Sri Govindji Nartanalaya at Manipur, Shri Nilkant Singh who is a well known scholar and critic on the Manipur dance, and M. Chandra Singh Pandit, scholar and authority on the Lai Haraoba.

CHAU DANCERS OF SERAIKELA, BIHAR

This former princely State originally in Orissa and now in Bihar has earned fame through its ancient dance form known as the Chau Masked Dances of Seraikela.   "Chau" literally means a "Mask," and these traditional dances are performed exclusively by men.   Princes of the royal family have always taken part along with other dancers in the grand spectacle of the Chaitra Parta (Spring Festival) dedicated to Ardhanarisvara (*Ardha Nari*)—the twin aspect of Shiva, the Shiva-Shakti motif of half-male half-female.   The dance festival is the final celebration of the three-day ceremonial worship in the Shiva temple, and then there is a grand procession of the Sacred Pitcher, followed by the dance performances which go on for four nights in the palace courtyard. Finely staged, and lighted by brilliant displays of torches, lanterns and many flickering oil lamps, these dances done in solo, duet and dance drama form, interpret mythology, sacred history, legend and Nature subjects.

The art of the Chau dancers has come down through the generations and is studied in great detail; special exercises are done from an early age, to enable the dancers to become adepts.

Chau dancing follows certain fundamental traditions of the classical modes as detailed in the ancient treatises. In it therefore are to be found the Three Main Elements of the classical dance, namely:

BHAVA   or   Mood
RAGA   or   Melody, Song
TALA   or   Rhythmic Timing

Paying great attention to the rules of timing and time measures, the dancing is accompanied by two *Dhols* (small drums), two *Nagaras*, the *Mirdanga* and cymbals for rhythm, and the *Sanai* and *Drone* for the melody and to accompany the picturesque songs that describe the incidents of the story being enacted. The style is precise and vigorous, and the rhythmic patterned footwork of the dances comprising intricate steps, jumps, quick turns, gliding walks and various gaits (*Gati*), as well as their compositions and choreography are well thought out and impressive.

Embodying all this, the dances are a national feature of Seraikela, and the art is taken so seriously that competitions are regularly arranged between various groups to stimulate and attain the high standard of technical excellence that prevails. Special banners are presented by the ruler to the best dancers.

Using many of the hand gestures described in the classical treatises, the *Natya Sastra* and the *Abhinaya Dharpana*, the dancers also use many created gestures peculiar to this school, and they are able to express and interpret each chosen motif vividly. All the nine moods of the classical dance are also relevently used— *Shringa* (Love), *Vir* (Valour), *Karuna* (Compassion), *Allrida* (Wonder), *Bhayana* (Fear), *Bhibhalsa* (Repulsion), *Dryndra* (Wrath), and *Shanti* (Peace). Expression fills the eyes and adds distinction to the masks worn by each character.

Wearing beautiful gold and silver brocaded costumes in rich colours, with gorgeous head-dresses and delicately moulded and painted masks made from papier maché and wood, for their historical and mythological roles, the dancers create a picture of colourful beauty as they depict their many themes. Among these subjects, one may mention the introductory Arati dance done by a priest who waves a lighted lamp and sounding a bell, performs this sacred preface to the items to follow. Among the mythological subjects are the *Tandava* dance of Shiva, the dance of Narada, the Heavenly Musician and spiritual son of Brahma, the story of the dancer and Rishya Sringa from the *Ramayana* and the Gadda Yuddha that tells of the battle between the noble Pandava Bhim and Duryodhana. Based on the 108 *Karanas* or basic dance movements, these dances are performed with all the vigour, power and precision of the *Tandava* style. The striking Astra Danda or Sword Dance and the famous legendary theme of the young girl Chandraprabha who is pursued by the Sun God and in fright rushes headlong into the river are very typical. Among the dance dramas that are popularly performed are subjects from

the classics, such as *Meghdoot* (The Cloud Messenger) by Kalidasa.

Nature subjects such as the Sabara or Dance of the Hunter, complete with feathered cap, spear and simple costume; the Phul Basant or dance of love in springtime; the Peacock Dance done in brilliant costume with resplendent head-dress, are beautifully rendered. There are also dances of ritual and worship, more delicate and devotional in character, and accompanied by music and lyrical songs.

There is something very ethereal about these dances in spite of the fact that that they are performed entirely by men, and the strength of the rhythmic precision of the movements done to the vivid drum beats, because of the delicacy of the masks and costumes and the grace of the dancers.

MOHINI ATAM

This is one of the important forms of the classical dance tradition of Kerala, presenting a perfect mode for solo performance that incorporates both the *Lasya* and *Tandava* styles. The technique is based on the Kathakali mode, which includes the peculiar manner of dancing with the feet and legs apart, knees greatly bent, and utilizing similar fine rhythmic syllable words in the recitation and play of the drum, with perfect synchronization of the dancer's feet. Starting at a medium tempo, and increasing the speed gradually to reach a thrilling climax, the series of pure dance sequences blossom into a superb pattern of movements, grace and strength combining in the design of footwork, posture, varied arm movements and hand gestures.

Such is the flawless manner in which this style of the classical dance has been conceived, that technique and interpretation are most skilfully merged while maintaining the same tempo, and sustaining beauty of posture. As the lyrical story is chanted, and the dancer interprets the theme, one is struck by the unique arrangement where the pitch of the exciting speed and rhythm full of verve of the pure dance sequences continues smoothly into the dramatic, where the dancer expresses by gestures, emotional acting and specially created mime, each mood and sentiment of the story being told. The mode of the *Abhinayam* in the Mohini Atam is based on that of the Kathakali dance dramas, and the themes are just as varied, telling as they do the age-old stirring tales from the *Ramayana*, the *Mahabharata* and the *Puranas*.

Mohini Atam presents a dance style that is thrilling and full of allure, beautifully blending *Nrtta* or pure dance, *Nrtya* or that form of the dance comprising movements of the body, hands, limbs, together with facial expressions and use of eyes, eyebrows and filled with *Rasa* or Flavour, perfect for dramatic characterization, and *Natya* or the combination of both dancing and acting. Very aptly too, according to legend, when Vishnu wanted to defeat the Asura Bhasmasura, He took the form of Mohini representing Delusion, and lured the evil creature to a dance contest through which the asura was entranced and destroyed.

KRISHNA ATAM

The Krishna Atam as the name suggests is drama associated with Krishna and the Krishna legends. Actually it is the earlier form of indigenous classical dance drama of Kerala, from which the Kathakali dance dramas have been inspired. Sometime in the middle of the 17th century A.D., the Zamorin Manadevan Raja of Calicut, who was a poet of distinction and a votary of Lord Krishna, composed eight dramatic lyrical plays dealing with the various episodes of Krishna's life on earth, and he incorporated them into one ensemble which he named the Krishna Atam.   The plays were written in Sanskrit, in devotion and dedication to Lord Krishna.

Krishna Atam is similar in dance style and technique to that of Kathakali, since the latter was inspired by it.   There are, however, certain fundamental differences, which can be noticed when seeing a performance.   Whereas Kathakali stresses dramatic acting and mime, the Krishna Atam emphasises very beautiful pure dance stances that are often long and performed in solo.   Vigorous, stylised, with a strict code of rhythms and timing just the same as the other classical dance forms, it contains the Three Elements of the classical dance, namely:

BHAVA   or   Mood
RAGA   or   Melody, Song
TALA   or   Rhythmic Timing

In it are also to be found *Nrtta* or pure dance, *Nrtya* which comprises movements of the body, hands, limbs, together with facial expressions and use of eyes, eyebrows and filled with *Rasa* or Flavour, perfect for dramatic characterization and *Natya* or the combination of dancing and acting.   This gives it its fine pure dance sequences, acting and emotional expression.   The pure dance in the Krishna Atam is arranged to the same *Talams* or Timings as used in Kathakali, but whereas in Kathakali, there is at the end of every four lines of song (*Khanda* or *Carana*), which have been interpreted with acting and dance, a climax or finale called the *Kalasam* (as the *Thirmana* of Bharata Natyam), in the Krishna Atam, the *Kalasams* are not short pure dance finales.   They are solo performances of pure dance with rhythmic patterned stepping and splendid postural stances that come either at the end of a dramatic scene or continue it.   On the emotional side, there is mime, the use of a studied gesture language, dramatic acting and significant stress on facial expression.

A Krishna Atam dance drama commences with the prologue of the *Kelikayya* or loud intricate drumming played on two *Madala* drums.   Behind a raised curtain, as in the Kathakali, two boy artistes dressed as Krishna's companions the Gopis, with their hair in top knots, and decorated with feathers and flowers and scintillating bands around the hair near the forehead, dance a dance of devotion accompanied by song and the rhythmic word syllables.   A Sanskrit *Sloka* in praise of God is then chanted.   More songs of glory follow, and then the actual drama begins.

Each play, covering a different episode in Krishna's life, commencing from the thrilling incidents surrounding His birth, telling of the various incidents during His boyhood, early and later manhood, and finally His return to Heaven, are enacted.   His ten *Avatars*, His conquest of the hundred-headed Serpent Kaliya, His dances with the Gopis and Radha on the banks of the Jamuna river, His destroying of His wicked uncle Kamsa; the story of the Pandavas and Kauravas that lead to the Battle of Kurukshetra, and His sacred teachings to Arjuna as He played the role of charioteer, and His final return to Heaven, are all meticulously and beautifully played and portrayed.

Once the play begins, one is transported to a realm of myth and legend,

Plate 69

1

2

3

Krishna Atam dance drama of Kerala
(1) Four actors in full costume and make-up: *from right to left*: Sri Krishna, Balarama, and two other noble characters. (2) Characters from the dance drama of *Banayudha; extreme left*, Sri Krishna. (3) A masked monkey character (Jambavan) from one of the dance dramas. (Courtesy, Ragini Devi.)

Plate 70

1

2

3

Bhagavata Mela Natakam dance drama of Melatur, Tamil Nad. (1) Actors in the dance drama *Harischandra*. (2) The gipsy girl from the dance drama *Rukmangada*. (3) Two characters in the Bhagavata Mela Natakam of Kuchipudi, Andhra, in the famous dance drama *Usha Parinayam*. (Photos copyright, Mohan Khokar.)

Plate 71

1

2

3

Yakshagana dance drama. (1) Close-up of two good characters in full costume and make-up. (2) Group of dancers from the southern region. (Courtesy, Publications Division, Government of India.) (3) Yakshagana group from Mangalore, Karnataka State, showing the varied and interesting costume and make-up. (Courtesy, Ragini Devi.)

Plate 72

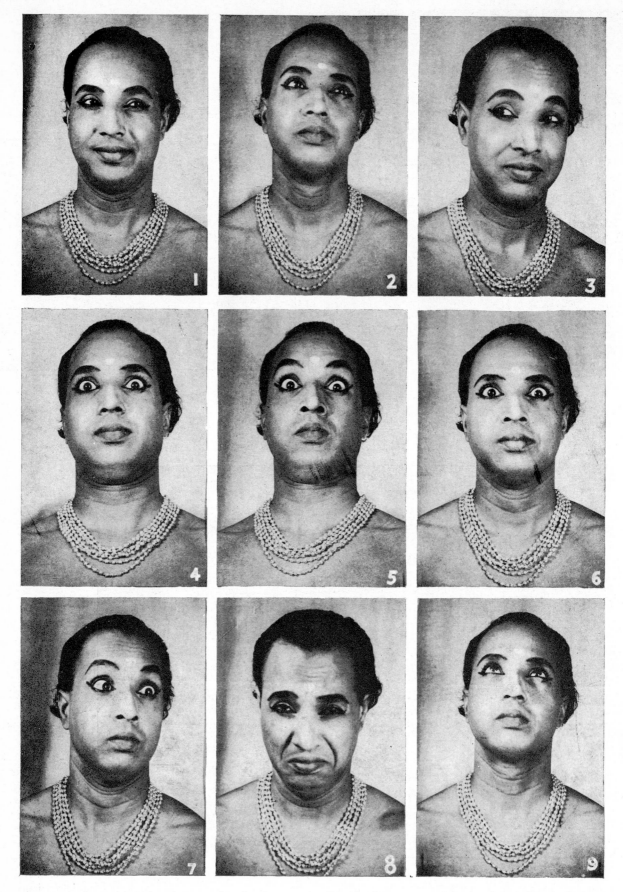

Chatunni Panicker demonstrating the *Navarasa* or Nine Moods as expressed in the Kathakali school of the dance. (1) *Sringara* (love); (2) *Karuna* (compassion); (3) *Hasya* (laughter); (4) *Veera* (valour); (5) *Raudra* (anger); (6) *Adbhuta* (wonder); (7) *Bhyanaka* (fear); (8) *Bibhatsa* (disgust); (9) *Shanta* (peace). (Photos copyright, Mohan Khokar.)

and the characters of Krishna, Arjuna, Brahma, Shiva, Yeshoda, Radha, Bala-rama, Satyabhama, and a host of other characters pass in cavalcade.   The charac-ters come alive in mime, excellent rhythmic movement and footwork, walking, talking, turning, jumping, as the stories unfold.   Strong, well defined, dramatic, the Krishna Atam moves smoothly to the slow gracious music of cymbals, gongs and the voices of the singers, punctuated by the two resounding *Madala* drums, one small and the other large.

The various actors, some wearing carved wooden ornamental masks, and others with their facial make-up in the Kathakali style of rice flour, *chunnam* (lime) and paints, create a world that is at once real and illusive, thrilling and awesome. Many of the familiar Kathakali make-ups are recognisable, like the *Minnukku*, where the face is painted with a yellowish-pink pigment, black unguent to the eyes and eyelashes, and red lips; the *Pachcha*, where green paint is used on the face with blackened eyes, red lips, and a white *Chutti* standing out from the chin and face in fluted lines, made of rice flour and *chunnam*; and the *Tadi* (Red, White and Black), with these particular colours prominent in the particular type; and also the Garuda bird with his beak and bird face.

Particularly lovely in the Krishna Atam is the *Rasa Kreeda*, which shows a group dance of Krishna and the Gopis called the *Mallipu Chital* or the Jasmine Flower Dance.   Pretty and lively, forming patterns as they weave in and out, the circle moves sometimes in a single round and sometimes in a double ring.   The pace is fast, there is ecstatic excitement and some very beautiful foot stepping and postures as the dance develops.   This sequence shows the richness of Krishna Atam, and the fact that though it is *Tandava* in style, still there is some very charm-ing and subtle *Lasya* introduced in the relevant portions to perfectly balance both types of the dance.

THE BHAGAVATA MELA DANCE DRAMAS OF TAMIL NAD

The Bhagavata Mela dance dramas of Tamil Nad appear to have gained import-ance about 300 years ago, when Bhakta Tirtha-Narayana Yati, author of the *Krishna Lila Tarangani* in Sanskrit, migrated from Andhra to Varahur in the Tanjore District.   He began the Bhagavata Mela tradition on the pattern of the *Natya* or dance drama as expounded in the *Natya Sastra* by Bharata Muni.   It was his belief that true devotion to God was achieved when the great philosophic truths of the *Bhagavata Purana* were enacted in drama, with classical music and Bharata Natyam dance and *Abhinayam*.   With these ideals before him, he composed several dance dramas like *Parijataharanam* and *Rukmangada*.

After him, the art was continued through the generations, and among his followers was Gopala Krishna Sastri of Melatur, author of dance dramas like *Sita Kalayanam*, *Rukmani Kalayanam*, *Dhruva* and *Gauri*.   But it was his son Venkata-rama Sastri of Melatur who brought the art to its highest peak of honour and fame. His celebrated dance drama compositions like *Prahlada*, *Harishchandra*, *Usha Parinayam* and *Gollabhama*, were not only enacted in Melatur, but many of them were performed in Sulamangalam, Uttukkad, Saliamangalam, Nallur and Tepperu-manallur villages; and it is these dance dramas that are enacted at Melatur today.

The Bhagavata Mela dance dramas became a part of the life of the people, and were performed annually at the great festival dedicated to God Narsimhan (Vishnu in the form of the Man-Lion).

The performance took place on a modest stage in front of the temple and lasted through the night.   Traditionally, the dances followed a distinctive and characteristic mode and form.   They started with the entrance of the *Konangi* or comedian who danced briefly, and then called on the audience to enjoy the show.   A group of musicians then sang an invocation song, the *Todaymangalam*, immediately followed by the *Sabdam*, dramatic lyrics based on the theme with classical dance movements done to alluring syllable chant recitations (*Sollu-kuttu*).   The prologue ended with the entrance of a young boy wearing a mask representing Lord Ganesha who blessed the drama for its success.

The Actual Drama.   The principal dancers were now assembled before a raised curtain, and on its being lowered, they introduced themselves by singing and dancing the *Patrapravesan*.   As the story unfolded, dramatic acting was beautifully interspersed with Bharata Natyam pure dance interludes of postural beauty, hand gestures and technique, and *Abhinayam*.   Sometimes, items like the *Alarippu* and *Tillana* were introduced in specific instances.   Indeed, dance entered at every stage of the performance, ornamenting the rhythm and grace, and the charm of form and movement, as the theme of man's devotion to God was delineated through lyrical dialogues, narrative, and melodiously sung songs in choice *Raga* melodies. Refinement of phrase and sentiment, depth of emotion and perfection of dance techniques marked these dance dramas of old.

All through the years, distinguished devotees like Sitarama Bhagavatar and Vaidyayanatha Bhagavatar at Sulamangalam, Swami Bhagavatar at Uttukkadu, Guru Natesa Iyer at Melatur, and his disciple Kinchin Kodandarama Iyer kept the art alive in the best traditions.

However, due to economic circumstances, Nallur gave up the art about 1900, Uttukkadu in 1930, and Sulamangalam in 1943.   In Melatur, after the death of Guru Melatur Natesa Iyer, the art suffered somewhat and was kept up as a religious formality before the temple till 1950.   From 1951, Sri E. Krishna Iyer, distinguished authority on the classical dance and disciple of Guru Melatur Natesa Iyer, worked for its revival and reform, and his assiduous labours brought it again to prominence and popularity.   Today, the tradition survives in good form in Melatur headed by Vidhwan Balu Bhagavatar.   In the words of Shri E. Krishna Iyer, "As a classical Dance-Drama according to the conception of *Natya Sastra*, the Melatur Bhagavata Mela art happens to be the only surviving link that connects us of the present day with our ancient national theatre tradition.   As such, its national importance and value have to be adequately recognised and realised by the art circles in India that count."[1]

With the general all-India revival of the classical dance in all its forms, this is certainly necessary.   One very encouraging fact is that Shrimati Rukmani Devi, who has done such valuable work in the revival and renaissance of the Bharata Natyam, is now encouraging proper research and study of the Melatur art at her centre Kalakshetra, in Adyar, Madras.

YAKSHAGANA

In Andhra, one of the very early forms of indigenous musical drama known

[1] E. Krishna Iyer, "The Melatur Bhagavata Mela Dance-Drama," *Bulletin of the Institute of Traditional Cultures*, Madras, Part II, 1959.

as *Bahu Nataka* was composed by Pakkuriki Somnatha in about A.D. 1250, and portrayed as already explained, the ten varieties of the Shiva-Leela episodes. In time, these took the form of the Yakshagana plays, common to many regions of India. The Yakshagana plays of Andhra were largely descriptive in style and at first only one artiste danced and sang the whole story, playing the various roles in it.

Three well known Yakshagana plays belonging to the 15th and 16th centuries are *Garudachalam* by Obayya Mantri, *Krishna-Hiramani* by Srinddha (both 15th century) and *Sugriva Vijayam* by Rudra Kavi (16th century).

The name Yakshagana, according to some sources, springs from the fact that the solo player was usually a woman who wore the costume of a Yaksha and interpreted the story through song and dance. The dancers came from a particular community known as Jakkula Varu, that is, of the Jakkula families of Andhra who specialised in Yakshagana.

And we find that the prototype of what is Yakshagana in Andhra, Karnataka and Tamil Nad, is known as Lalita in Maharashtra, Bhavai in Gujerat, Yatra in Bengal, and Gandharva Gana in Nepal.

From being a musical play with dance interpreted by only one artiste, the Yakshagana developed further and two principal characters were introduced on the stage, and then two more characters were added, namely, the clown for the comic element and a fortune teller or *Yerukala Sani*. There was thus a gradual development of Yakshagana into a regular dramatic dance form with a number of artistes playing the various characters in the story. The subjects were taken from mythology, and those plays in which the themes were dedicated to the presiding deity of the temple, were enacted by Brahmin artistes as religious Yakshagana dance dramas in the *Kalayana Mandapa* pavilions for the entertainment of worshippers and devotees. This religious form of the Yakshagana dance dramas was taken up by the Bhagavatulu Brahmana Melas of Kuchipudi and enriched, improved and brought to a classical level by the introduction of beautiful classical dance modes, hand gestures, *Karana* and *Angahara* postures and *Abhinaya* as detailed in the *Natya Sastra* and other classical treatises. By the further addition of special *Sabdas* and *Daruvus* as already explained when dealing with the Kuchipudi dance, artistes were given full scope to express the four types of *Abhinaya*. These technically brilliant and correctly classical dance dramas that emerged under the artistic and masterly treatment of the Kuchipudi Brahmana Melas became known as the Kuchipudi dance dramas or the classical Bhagavata Mela Natakam of Kuchipudi, Andhra.

The Yakshagana of the original simpler musical dance drama form had as already mentioned its prototype in other regions of India. Today these different forms of Yakshagana in Andhra and other regions of India as well as the classical Bhagavata Mela Natakam of Kuchipudi, Andhra, retain the use of facial make-up masks with the use of paints and in some cases masks made of papier maché for certain characters.

Every one of the main schools of the classical dance however has its own intrinsic and characteristic mode of arm movements and hand gestures. The hand gestures which are used in the *Nrtta* or pure dance sequences are known as *Nrtta Hastas* and ornament the general beauty and pattern of arm movements, postures and techniques. But in the *Abhinaya* or emotional interpretive aspect of the dance, the hand gestures (*Asamyuta* and *Samyuta Hastas*) have special meanings (*Viniyogas*) based on an alphabet constituting a complete language of sign and symbol and hence play an interpretative role in this dramatic part of the dance.

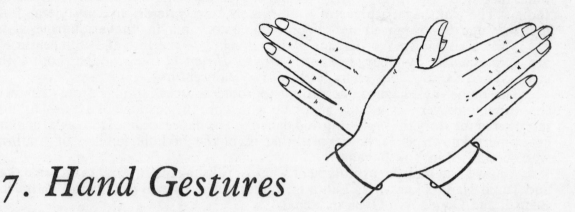

7. Hand Gestures

In the foregoing chapters, emphasis has been laid on the importance played by the hands in the interpretive aspect of the dance. Just as the technique of pure dance has been evolved from a basic foundation or Alphabet of Postures known as *Karanas*, so a comprehensive system of language signs or Hand Gestures has been evolved from an Alphabet of Basic Hand Poses or *Hastas* in the same manner in which the written and spoken language has been established from the ABC. To further elucidate meanings, the hands are not just held up to express the meaning, but the fingers are formed into the required position, the wrists are subtly used, and the arms co-ordinated for mobility and mood.

In this way, the hands become the vehicle of "Dance Speech," and to those initiated in the art, whole conversations can be communicated which closely translate song-words into sign-words. These can be followed like utterances of words in a conversation. Adjectives, nouns, verbs, proper names, and adverbs can all be shown and clearly expressed along with the relevant facial expressions. Each school of the classical dance has made use of this Alphabet of Language Signs in a particular mode and built up their own code of Hand Gestures.

According to the classical treatises like the *Natya Sastra* by Bharata Muni and the *Abhinaya Dharpana* by Nandikeshwara, we find about thirty-one Single Hand Gestures; that is, thirty-one different poses of the single hand, and twenty-seven Combined Hand Gestures, that is, varied combinations of these basic thirty-one single hand poses to change meanings and enrich the "Dance Speech." These hand gestures, both singly and combined (either the same pose in both hands or one gesture in one hand and another with the other), constitute the complete language of signs or *Hastas*.

It will be observed further that each gesture indicates a multitude of ideas or objects, and one might feel a little puzzled to note how very different and numerous these ideas or objects may be. In reality, a hand gesture which by itself may mean one or a multitude of things, can by well established conventions of using the arms, wrists, positions of the body and with the relevant facial expressions, single out one particular meaning from the available meanings attached to it as the one interpretation which best fits the particular context. Consider the analogy of speech; while speaking, by the mere change of intonation, words can be made to change their meanings; and just as in the spoken tongue there are synonyms for nearly every word, which give richness and beauty to the language and its literature, so it is with regard to the use of gestures and their varied meanings in the dance. As there are word-combinations in the spoken language, in the same manner, the combinations of Hand Gestures are present in the grammar of the dance, affording a dictionary of Language Signs. Single Hand Gestures are known as *Asamyuta Hastas*; the Combined Hand or Double Hand Gestures are called *Samyuta Hastas*. Their meanings are known as *Viniyogas*.

ALPHABET OF SINGLE HANDS. From the Treatises on the Classical Dance

1. *PATAKA* (The Flag). The open palm is held facing outwards, the four fingers and thumb held all close together. It is used at the beginning of a dance, and to denote clouds, a forest, things, bosom, might, peace, a river, heaven, prowess, moonlight, strong, sunlight, wave, entering, silence, an oath, the sea, sword, a palmyra leaf.

2. *TRI-PATAKA* (Three Parts of the Flag). The palm faces outwards. The thumb and first, second and little fingers are kept straight. The third finger is bent into the palm. It is used to express the holding of a trident, turning round, crown, tree, flower, light, arrow, invocation, book, stroking the hair, doubt, lamp, etc.

3. *ARDHA-PATAKA* (Half Flag). The hand is rested with the palm facing outwards. The thumb, first and second fingers are extended straight, the third and little fingers are bent into the palm. It is used to express two or both, knife, horn, tower, etc.

4. *KARTARI MUKHA* (Face of the Arrow Shaft). The hand is raised with the palm facing outwards. The first, second and little fingers are extended straight up; the third finger is bent into the palm and the thumb is placed to touch the tip of the third finger. It is used to express opposition, disagreement, falling, separation (of lovers), a creeper, yearning, buffalo, deer, fly, hill-top, elephant.

5. *MAYURA* (Peacock). The hand is raised with the palm outwards. The first, second and little fingers are extended straight, the third finger is bent to touch it at the tip. It is used to express the peacock's beak, wiping away something, wiping away tears, stroking the hair, the forehead mark, etc.

6. *ARDHA-CHANDRA* or *ARDHA-CANDRA* (Half-moon). The palm faces upwards slightly. The four fingers are stretched together and the thumb is stretched to its fullest away from the rest of the fingers. It is used to express the moon (on the eighth day), anxiety, prayer, greeting, meditation, bangle, wrist, mirror, ear of an elephant, bow.

7. *ARALA* (Bent). The palm is raised and faces outward. The second, third and little fingers are stretched straight, the first finger crooked or curved and the thumb a little bent beside it and almost touching the tip of the finger. It is used to express nectar, drinking poison, benediction, dressing the hair, decorating the face, etc.

8. *SUKUTANDA* or *SUKUTUNDAKA* (Parrot's Beak). The palm is raised facing outwards. The second and little fingers are stretched, and the third

and first fingers are curved forward, while the thumb is bent a little beside them. It is used to express the sense of shooting an arrow, mystery, anger, Brahma the Creator, fighting, bow, abandonment, refusal.

9. *MUSHTI* (Fist). Depicts the four fingers bent into the palm, and the thumb set on them. It is used to express steadfastness, holding or grasping things, stronghold, holding a book, holding a shield or spear, order, imprisonment, Yama (the God of Death), etc.

10. *SIKHARA* (Spire). The palm is raised outwards. The four fingers are bent into the palm, and the thumb is extended straight out. It is used to express silence, questioning, sound of a bell, pillar, husband, saying No, embrace, steadfastness, hero, friend, the number four, sapphire, intensity.

11. *KAPITHA or KAPIDDHA* (Elephant Apple). The palm is raised outwards. The second, third and little fingers are bent into the palm and the first finger is bent forward; the thumb is bent to touch the tip of the first finger. It is used to express the holding of cymbals, holding flowers, holding a rope, offering incense or offering lights, Lakshmi (Goddess of Wealth), Saraswati (Goddess of Learning), milk, showing a dance, pounding seed, winding.

12. *KATAKA MUKHA or KHATAKA MUKHA* (Opening in a Link). The palm is raised outwards. The third and little fingers are extended and bent very slightly, the first finger and thumb curved forwards to touch at the tips, and the second finger bent to touch the base of the thumb. It is used to express the picking of flowers, holding a pearl necklace, holding a garland, flowers, giving betel leaves, applying scent, drawing a bow slowly, glancing, holding a mirror, breaking a twig, holding a fan.

13. *SUCI or SUCYASYA* (Needle). The palm is raised outwards. The third and little fingers are extended and bent very slightly, the first finger stretched straight, and the second finger bent to the tip of the thumb and the thumb bent a little forwards. It is used to express the saying of "this or that," threatening, astonishment, explaining, rod, braid of hair, umbrella, beating the drum, life, solitude, lotus stalk, etc.

14. *CHANDRA KALA* (Digit of the Moon). The palm is raised facing outwards. The second, third and little fingers are bent forward parallel to the palm, and the first finger and thumb are stretched apart and extended straight. It is used to express the crescent moon, the face, the crown of Lord Shiva.

15. *PADMAKOSA* (Lotus Bud). The palm is hollowed and faces outwards. The four fingers are bent apart a little, and the thumb moved in towards the bent fingers. It is used to express the idea of frisking about, fruit, mango flowers, lotus bud, water lily, curve, bud, cluster of flowers, bell-shaped, brilliance, charm, coconut, blossoming of a bud.

16. *SARPA SIRSA* (Snake Head). The palm is hollowed slightly, raised and faces outwards. The fingers and thumb are close together, extended and bent a little at the top. It is used to express a snake, sandal paste, sprinkling, cherishing, giving water to the Gods, washing the face, short man, shoulders, image, water, very true.

17. *MRIGA SIRSA* (Deer Head). The palm is raised facing outwards. The little finger is extended straight, the three other fingers are bent parallel to the base of the palm, and the thumb tip touches the centre of the first finger. It is used to express fear, the face of a deer, discussion, drawing lines on the brow, cheek, patterns on the ground, calling the beloved, applying sandal paste, order.

18. *SIMHA MUKHA* (Lion Head). The palm is raised facing outwards. The first and little fingers are stretched straight; the second and third fingers are bent parallel to the palm, and the thumb touches their tips. It is used to express a lion's head, a lotus garland, stroking the hair, fragrance, a pearl, hare, elephant.

19. *LANGULA* (Tail). The palm is raised facing outwards, the third finger is extended straight, the first and second fingers are bent parallel to the palm, and the thumb is bent to touch the first joints of these fingers; and the little finger is bent to touch the first joint of the thumb. It is used to express water, water lily, little bells, partridge, grapes, seeds, blue lotus, coral, anything small.

20. *SOLA PADMA or ALA PADMA* (Full-blown Lotus). The palm is faced upwards and hollowed. All the fingers and thumb are spread out and bent to form a petalled circle. It is used to express the idea of a full-blown lotus, the hair knot, anger, praise, full moon, a round face, a ball, beauty, etc.

21. *CATURA* (Semi-circle). The palm is faced outwards and hollowed. The first, second and third fingers and the thumb are bent like a hooded snake, and the little finger is extended straight. It is used to express the sense of a little, sorrow, playful, converse, copper, sweetness, face, breaking.

22. *BHRAMARA* (The Bee). The palm is very slightly hollowed, and the third and little fingers are separated and bent a little. The second finger is bent parallel to the base of the palm, and the thumb bent to touch the tip of the second finger. The first finger is bent to touch the first joint of the thumb. It is used to express the bee, parrot, cuckoo, wing.

23. *HAMSASYA* (Swan Face). The palm is raised facing outwards and very slightly hollowed. The little finger is extended straight. The third finger is also extended but bent very slightly, and the first and second fingers are bent forward to touch the thumb at the tips. It is used to express swan's beak, tying the marriage thread, certainty, drop of water, carrying garlands, a jasmine.

24. *HAMSA PAKSHA* (Swan Feather). The palm is raised facing outwards and very slightly hollowed. The little finger is extended straight, and the other three fingers are bent a little forward, while the thumb bends over to touch the centre of the second finger underneath. It is used to express the number six, arranging things, a covering, feathers.

25. *SAMDAMSA* (Grasping). The palm is raised facing outwards. The first finger is bent down to touch the thumb at the tip, and the other three fingers are extended forward and very slightly bent at the joints. It is used to express generosity, sacrificial offerings, worship, the number five, small bud, gentle dances, sprout, firefly, blades of grass, eclipse, fly, garland, pointing, snow, etc.

26. *MUKULA* (Bud). The palm is raised facing outwards. The four fingers are bent forward together, and the thumb bent to touch the tips of the fingers. It is used to express water lily, eating, banana flower, prayer, lotus bud, life, self, worship, fruit.

27. *TAMRA CUDA* (Cock). The palm is raised facing outwards. The third and little fingers are bent into the palm. The first finger is bent and touches its own base, the second finger is bent forward, and the thumb goes to touch it at the first joint. It is used to express a cock, writing or drawing, camel, calf, the number three, Vedas, a leaf, etc.

28. *THRISULA* (Trident). The palm is raised facing outwards. The first, second and third fingers are extended straight, and the little finger is bent into the

1. Pataka   2. Tri-pataka   3. Ardha-pataka   4. Kartari Mukha   5. Mayura

6. Ardha-chandra   7. Arala   8. Sukutanda   9. Mushti

10. Sikhara   11. Kapiddha   12. Kataka Mukha   12A. Ardha-mukha

13. Suci   14. Chandra Kala   15. Padmakosa   16. Sarpa Sirsa

ALPHABET OF SINGLE HAND GESTURES. CLASSICAL SANSKRIT TREATISES

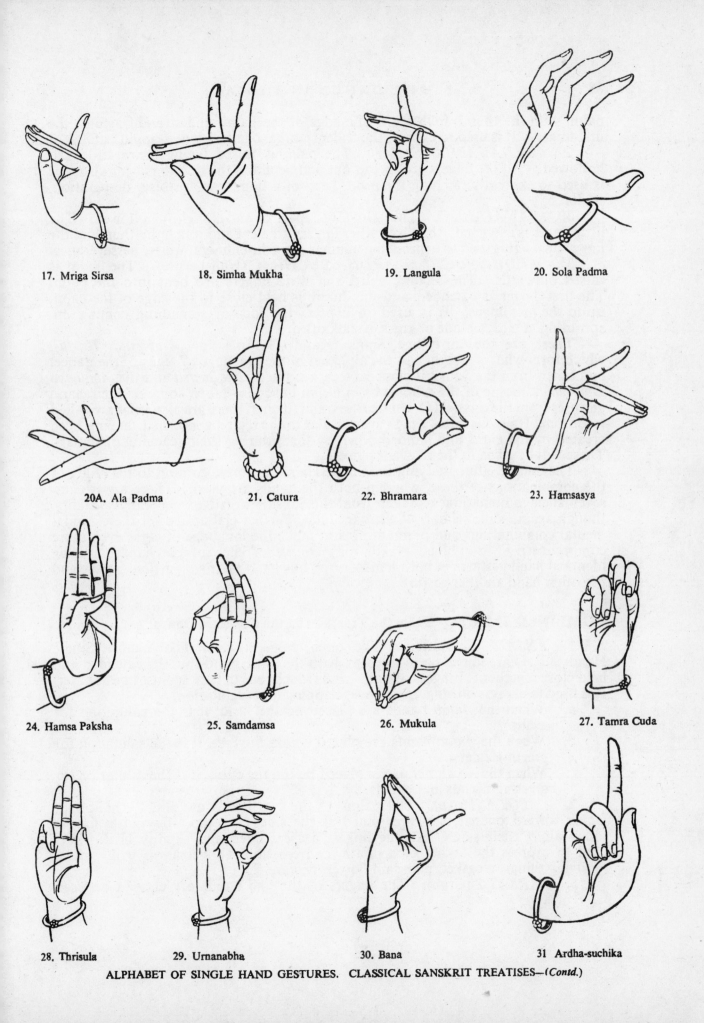

17. Mriga Sirsa

18. Simha Mukha

19. Langula

20. Sola Padma

20A. Ala Padma

21. Catura

22. Bhramara

23. Hamsasya

24. Hamsa Paksha

25. Samdamsa

26. Mukula

27. Tamra Cuda

28. Thrisula

29. Urnanabha

30. Bana

31 Ardha-suchika

ALPHABET OF SINGLE HAND GESTURES. CLASSICAL SANSKRIT TREATISES—*(Contd.)*

palm, with the thumb folded into the edge of the palm, and straight against the first finger.   It is used to express the trident, three together, wood-apple leaf.

29.   *URNANABHA* (Spider).   The palm is raised facing downwards and hollowed.   All the fingers are spread out and bent and the thumb is bent also.   It is used to express scratching the head, head of a lion, fear, tortoise, desperation, spider.

30.   *BANA* (Arrow).   The palm faces upwards and is slightly hollowed.   The little finger is extended; the three other fingers are bent and touch the thumb at the finger tips.   It is used to express the number six, contentment, quiet, perseverance.

31.   *ARDHA-SUCHI or ARDHA-SUCHIKA* (Half-needle).   The palm is raised outwards.   The second, third and little fingers are bent into the palm. The first finger is extended and the thumb is held close to the edge of the palm, up to the first finger.   It is used to express the idea of something coming up, sprouting, a bird, a blade of grass, a stalk of corn.

These are the thirty-one Single Hand Gestures or *Asamyuta Hastas*, which form what we might call the alphabet of the language of signs of the dance, and taken from the Sanskrit classical treatises the *Natya Sastra* and the *Abhinaya Dharpana*.   Some of the schools as in Orissi have also taken some of their hand gestures from the classical Orissi treatises, and further, there are also what are called traditional Hand Gestures which are peculiar to the region concerned, having been created by the *gurus* and handed down by them during their teaching of the art. These will be given in the relevant places.

The dancer, after studying the Single Hand Gestures, goes on to the study of the combinations of these, wherein both the hands are used.   There are twenty-seven such combinations as taken from the Sanskrit treatises, generally speaking, though again, some schools of the dance have further elaborated on these fundamental combinations and permutations to make the language of signs even more comprehensive.   Combined Hands may consist of each of the hands utilizing identical hand gestures in both hands, or by one hand taking a particular pose and the other hand another gesture.

COMBINED HANDS.   From the Treatises on the Classical Dance

1.   *ANJALI* (Salutation).   The open palms (two *Pataka* hands, Single Hands No. 1) are joined palm to palm, with the fingers and thumbs extended and held close together.   Fingers of both hands touch face to face against one another. It is used to express bowing, obedience, clapping time, salutation.

  a.   When the *Anjali* hands are placed on the head, it is the salutation for deities.

  b.   When the *Anjali* hands are placed before the face, it is the salutation for greeting elders.

  c.   When the *Anjali* hands are placed before the chest, it is the salutation for greeting friends and equals.

2.   *KAPOTA* (Dove).   The palms of the two hands are slightly hollowed, facing toward oneself, and are joined at the sides and top.   The little fingers touch along their sides.   All the fingers are extended and slightly bent.   It is used to express the taking of an oath, conversation, conversation with elders, receiving things, a casket, plaintain flower, nectar.

3.   *KARKATA* (Crab).   The fingers of the two hands are clasped between

one another and the hands are kept with the knuckles facing outwards. It is used to express the blowing of the conch shell, a crab, bending the bough of a tree.

4. *SVASTIKA* (Crossed). Two *Pataka* hands (Single Hands No. 1), are crossed at the wrists, where the bases of the palms touch, and the left hand is placed above the right. That is, the right hand with fingers and thumbs stretched and held close together pointing downwards; and the left hand with fingers and thumb in the same way, also pointing down, and crossed at the wrists, with the left hand on the right hand. It is used to express praise, timid speech, order, direction, swastika, crossed.

5. *DOLA* (Swing). Two *Pataka* hands (Single Hands No. 1) are used in this. That is, the hands with the fingers and thumbs stretched are placed with the palms resting on the thighs, the right hand on the right thigh and the left hand on the left high. It is used to express the beginning of the dance, welcome, fainting.

6. *PUSHPAPUTA* (Flower Casket). The *Sarpa Sirsa* hands are combined (Single Hands No. 16). That is, the palms of the hands are hollowed slightly and face one another, fingers and thumb close together and slightly bent at the tops. The finger tips and bases of the palms of each hand are placed to touch each other. It is used to express the offering of lights, water, receiving fruit, giving and taking flowers.

7. *UTSANGA* (Embrace). Here, the *Mriga Sirsa* hands (Single Hands No. 17) are combined. That is, the palm is raised facing outwards, the three fingers are bent towards the palms, and the thumb is bent to touch the centre of the first finger. In this case, the hands are held to touch opposite arm-pits at the finger tips. The little fingers are extended in both hands. It is used to express modesty, embracing, armlet.

8. *SHIVA LINGA* (The symbolic representation of Lord Shiva). Here is a combination of the *Ardha-chandra* (Single Hands No. 6) with the left hand and *Sikhara* (Single Hands No. 10), with the right hand. That is, the left hand is placed with the palm facing upwards, the four fingers are stretched together and slightly bent, and the thumb is stretched to its fullest away from the rest of the fingers. With the right hand, the four fingers are bent into the palm, and the thumb is extended straight out. The right hand is placed in the centre of the palm of the left hand, and the thumb of the right hand stands vertically straight up. It is used to express the Shiva Lingam, the symbolic representation of Lord Shiva.

9. *KATAKA VARDHANA* (Link of Increase). Here, there is the combined use of the *Kataka Mukha* (Single Hands No. 12). That is, the palms are raised outwards. The third and little fingers of both hands are extended and bent very slightly; the first fingers and thumbs are curved forwards to touch at the tips; and the second and third fingers are bent to touch at the base of the thumb. The hands are crossed at the wrists, with the hands slightly thrown back and facing in opposite directions. It is used to express marriage, ritual, blessing, certain flowers, garlands.

10. *KARTARI SVASTIKA* (Crossed Arrow Shafts). In this, there is the combined use of the *Kartari Mukha* (Single Hands No. 4) hands. The hands are raised, palms facing outwards. The first, second and little fingers of both hands are extended straight up, the third finger is bent into the palm, and the thumb is placed to touch the tip of the third finger. The hands are crossed at the wrists, with the palms facing outwards, the right hand over the left. It is used to express trees, the summit of a hill, branches.

11. *SAKATA or SHAKATA* (Car). In this, there is an adaptation of the *Arala* hand (Single Hands No. 7). The palms are raised, the second, third and little fingers are stretched straight, and the first fingers are curved and bent in half; but in this case, instead of the thumb being bent beside it as in the *Arala* it is extended apart. The hands are crossed at the wrists, the palms facing in opposite directions. It is used to express gestures describing demons.

12. *SANKHA or SHANKHA* (Conch). In this there is the combined use of the *Sikhara* hand (Single Hands No. 10). The palms are raised, but instead of the four fingers being bent into the palms as in the *Sikhara*, only the second, third and little fingers are bent into the palm, and the first finger is extended straight. Again, the thumb is not stretched apart as in the *Sikhara*, but extended straight beside the first finger. The palms of the hands face each other, and the tips of the knuckles of the bent fingers and the tips of the first fingers and thumbs in each hand touch. The two hands are kept close at the bases of the palms. This represents the conch shell.

13. *CAKRA* (Discus). Here, there is the combined use of the *Pataka* hand (Single Hands No. 1), slightly modified. The hands are clasped together, palms touching; the first, second and third fingers are stretched instead of all the fingers being stretched as in the *Pataka*; the thumbs and little fingers of each hand are bent over the hand. The stretched fingers form an X. It is used to express discussion, argument.

14. *SAMPUTA* (Casket). Here, there is a slight deviation and modification of the *Cakra* hands (Combined Hands No. 13). It is absolutely the same as *Cakra*, except that the first, second and third fingers are slightly bent instead of being stretched straight. It is used to express a casket, concealing things, closing something.

15. *PASA* (Noose). In this, there is an adaptation of the *Ardha-suci* hand (Single Hands No. 31). Instead of the second, third and little fingers being bent into the palm, only the third and little fingers and thumbs of each hand are bent into the palms, and the second fingers and thumbs of each hand touch at the tips. The hands are then crossed about the centre of the forearms, with the hands facing in opposite directions, and the first fingers of each hand interlaced. It is used to express a noose, manacles, enmity, a chain.

16. *KILAKA* (Bond). Here is used the combined hands of *Mriga Sirsa* (Single Hands No. 17). The palms are raised, the little fingers are extended straight with the first, second and third fingers of each hand bent parallel to the base of the palms, while the thumb tips touch the centre of the first fingers. These hands are crossed at the wrists, facing in opposite directions, and the extended little fingers are interlocked. It is used to express affection, lover's talk, fondness, love.

17. *MATSYA* (Fish). In this, the combined use of *Pataka* hands (Single Hands No. 1) is slightly modified. The open palm of the right hand faces down and the four fingers and thumb are extended, but the thumb instead of being placed beside the other fingers as in *Pataka*, is spread apart. The left hand with the palm facing down is placed over the right hand so that the fingers of each hand point in the same direction. This is used to denote a fish.

18. *KURMA* (Tortoise). In this, there is the modification of the combined *Cakra* hand (Combined Hands No. 13). The hands are clasped together with the palms touching, and the first, second and third fingers of each hand are bent

over to touch the back of the other hand, instead of being just stretched as in the *Cakra* hands. The thumbs and little fingers are stretched. It is used to denote the tortoise.

19. *GARUDA* (Garuda, bird of mythology). Here, the combined use of the *Ardha-chandra* hand (Single Hands No. 6) is used. The hands are raised, palms facing outwards, the four fingers are stretched and the thumbs are extended away from the rest of the fingers. The hands are then crossed at the wrists and the thumbs are interlocked. The palms of the hands face inwards. It is used to express the Garuda bird, the sacred vehicle of Vishnu.

20. *NAGA-BANDHA* (Serpent-tie). In this, there is the combined use of the *Sarpa Sirsa* hand (Single Hands No. 16). The palms are slightly hollowed and face outwards. The four fingers and thumb are extended close together and bent a little at the tips. These hands are crossed at the wrists. It is used to express pairs of hands, spells, coil of a snake.

21. *AVAHRITTHA* (Eagerness). In this, the combined hands of *Sukutanda* (Single Hands No. 8) is used. The palm is raised. The second and little fingers are stretched; the third and first fingers are curved forwards and the thumbs are bent gently against the heart. It is used to express eagerness, interest, keenness.

22. *SVASTIKA* (Crossed). Here, there is the combined use of the *Tri-pataka* hand (Single Hands No. 2). The palms face outwards. The thumb and first, second and little fingers are stretched straight; and the third finger is bent into the palm. The hands are crossed at the wrists and held at the left side, with the hands facing in opposite directions and slightly thrown back. It is used to express the swastika.

23. *AVIDDHA VARRA* (Swinging Curve). In this, there is the combined use of the *Pataka* hand (Single Hands No. 1). The open palms are held facing outwards, the four fingers and thumb held closely together. The hands are gently waved to and fro with grace, at the elbows. It is used to express slenderness in general, slenderness of the waist, slim.

24. *PAKSHA VANCITA* (Bent Wing). Here, there is the combined use of the *Tri-pataka* hand (Single Hands No. 2). The palms are open; the thumb, first, second and little fingers are stretched straight, and the third finger is bent into the palm. The hands are placed on the hips. It is used to express difference, comparison.

25. *NISEDHA* (Defence). In this, there is the combined use of *Mukula* hand (Single Hands No. 26), and *Kapitha* hand (Single Hands No. 11). In the left hand *Mukula*, the palm is raised, the four fingers are bent together and the thumb goes to touch the tips of the fingers. In the right hand, *Kapitha*, the second, third and little fingers are bent into the palm, and the first finger is bent forward, while the thumb goes to touch the tip of the first finger. In this combined gesture, the finger tips of the left hand are enclosed by the bent fingers of the right hand at the side of the palm of the right hand. It is used to express truth, honour, justice, faith.

26. *ARALA KATAKA MUKHA* (Bent Opening in a Link). In this, the two gestures *Arala* (Single Hands No. 7) and *Kataka Mukha* (Single Hands No. 12) are used. In the right hand, *Arala*, the palm is raised outwards, the second, third and little fingers are stretched straight; the first finger is curved and the thumb almost touches its tip. In the left hand, *Kataka Mukha*, the palm is raised outwards, the third and little fingers are extended and bent to touch the tips, and the

second finger is bent to touch the base of the thumb.   Then the right hand is crossed over the left at the wrists, with the hands facing in opposite directions.   It is used to express anxiety, dismay, giving betel leaf, apprehension, etc.

27. *SUCYAS YA* (Needle Face).   In this, there is the combined use of the *Suci* hand (Single Hands No. 13).   The palms are raised outwards.   The third and little fingers are extended and bent very slightly.   The first fingers are stretched straight and the second fingers are bent to touch the tips of the thumbs.   The hands are moved from right to left in front together in one sweeping gesture.   It is used to express "everything," all comprehensive, wide and open, etc.

These are the twenty-seven Combined Hand Gestures or *Hastas* which further develop the Alphabet of Single Hands.   It will be significant to see now, just how the various schools of the classical dance utilize these various basic gestures in developing their language of signs to express various parts of speech.

It should be noted here, however, that hereinafter in the following chapters dealing with representative examples of the various parts of speech used in the main schools of the dance, when the expression "Single Hands" or "Combined Hands" is used in brackets in explanation for its basis, they refer to the Alphabet of Hand Gestures from the classical treatises.   Otherwise, the name of any other source or particular region will be mentioned, such as, "Single Hands Orissi," or "Single Hands Kathakali" or "Single Hands Manipuri," and so on.

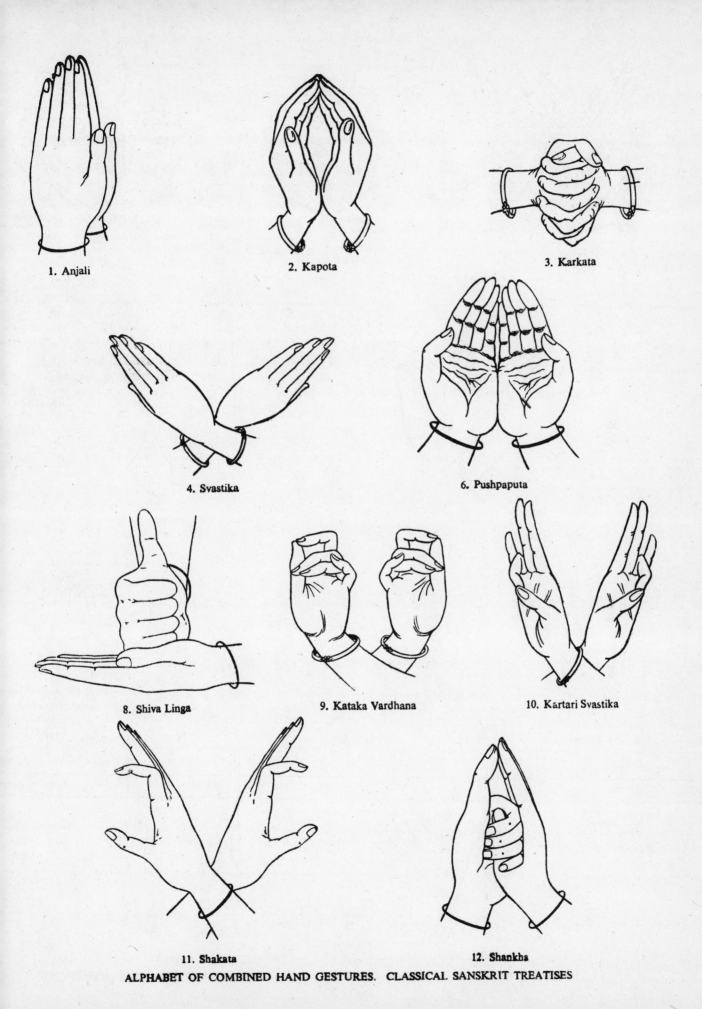

1. Anjali

2. Kapota

3. Karkata

4. Svastika

6. Pushpaputa

8. Shiva Linga

9. Kataka Vardhana

10. Kartari Svastika

11. Shakata

12. Shankha

ALPHABET OF COMBINED HAND GESTURES. CLASSICAL SANSKRIT TREATISES

13. Cakra

14. Samputa

15. Pasa

16. Kilaka

17. Matsya

18. Kurma

19. Garuda

25. Nisedha

26. Arala Kataka Mukha

27. Sucyas Ya

ALPHABET OF COMBINED HANDS GESTURES. CLASSICAL SANSKRIT TREATISES—(Contd.)

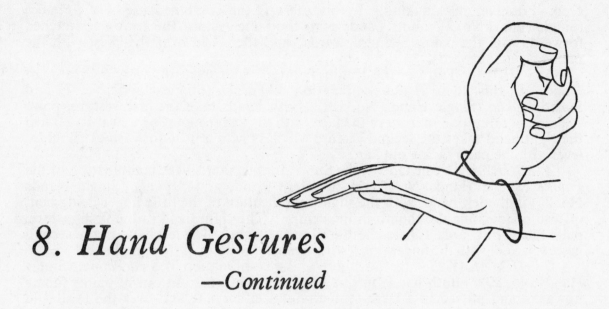

8. Hand Gestures

—Continued

HAVING CONSIDERED the Alphabet of Hand Gestures or language signs of the classical treatises, and further seen how these alphabets used in the Single Hands carrying certain meanings are again developed into fuller meanings by the combinations of these alphabets using both hands, we now turn to the slightly different aspect and use of them as "word signs," in the actual dance.

When a dance performance or dance drama is taking place, certain persons, subjects, objects and ideas are constantly being interpreted in the enactment of the story or lyric being told or sung. Each school has its own selection of these basic hand gestures for appropriately interpreting its own emotional content.

I propose to give some examples of various persons, objects and other parts of speech, as they are used in the different classical schools of the dance. It has to be understood, however, that the gestures by themselves are only a part of the method used for interpretation, and they must at all times be accompanied by the relevant postures, use of arms and hand positions, and mobile facial expressions. Then alone do they come to life and convey their true meaning.

USE OF HAND GESTURES IN BHARATA NATYAM. Based on the Classical Sanskrit Treatises

Proper Nouns

1. *BRAHMA*. The First of the Hindu Trinity and Creator of Mankind. In this, there is the combination of the *Samdamsa* (Single Hands No. 25) in the right hand, and *Mriga Sirsa* (Single Hands No. 17) in the left hand. The right

hand with the palm facing outwards is held in front, shoulder level, and the left hand is held at the same level, with the finger tips pointing outwards.

2. *VISNU*.   The Second of the Hindu Trinity and the Merciful Aspect of God —Preserver of Mankind.   In this, there is the combined use of *Tri-Pataka* (Single Hands No. 2).   Both hands using the same gesture, the arms are stretched forwards with the palms facing upwards; and then held near the chest with the palms facing outwards.

3. *SHIVA*.   Third of the Hindu Trinity.   Destroyer of Evil and Creator of Good.   In this, there is the combination of *Pataka* (Single Hands No. 1) and *Simha Mukha* (Single Hands No. 18).   Both hands take the first gesture, palm to palm, in salutation in front of the face, with the fingers pointing upwards.   Then the right hand takes the second gesture which is held a little forward at shoulder level with the palm facing outwards.

4. *SURYA*.   Vedic God of the Sun.   In this, there is the combination of the *Pataka* (Single Hands No. 1) in the right hand, and *Mukula* (Single Hands No. 26) in the left hand, with the slight modification of the little finger being bent instead of touching the thumb in the centre.   The right hand in the first gesture, palm facing outwards, is held chest level to the right.   The left hand in the second gesture is kept with the finger tips resting against the palm of the right hand.

5. *HIMALAYAS*.   In this, there is the combination of *Sola Padma* (Single Hands No. 20).   Both hands in this gesture are taken from down, palms facing upwards, and moved in a large semi-circle at either side and over the head and crossed at the wrists overhead.   The right hand over the left, the palms face inwards.

Nouns

1. *TREES*.   In this, *Kartari Mukha* (Single Hands No. 4) is used with the right hand only.   The hand is taken upwards on the right side and held with the palm facing outwards.

2. *WOMAN*.   In this, *Sarpa Sirsa* (Single Hands No. 16) is used with the right hand only.   It is held near the shoulder, palm facing outwards, and then brought a little forward with the palm facing down.

3. *WORLD*.   In this, *Ardha-suchika* (Single Hands No. 31) is used in both hands.   The two hands in this gesture are held at chest level, palms facing inwards.   Then they are taken in a little circle from one side to the other at shoulder level and brought back in front near the chest.

4. *BIRD*.   A created gesture.   The thumb is straight.   The first, second and third fingers are bent over it and the little finger is bent forward.   This can be used in either the right or the left hand.   One of the hands in this gesture is held near the shoulder with the side of the hand where the thumb is facing outwards.

5. *PEACOCK*.   In this, there is the combination of *Kapitha* (Single Hands No. 11), slightly modified, in that the first finger and thumb instead of touching at the tips are bent without touching, in the left hand; and *Sola Padma* (Single Hands No. 20) in the right hand.   The left hand in the first gesture is held shoulder level with the palm facing outwards.   The right hand in the second gesture is placed behind it on the wrist: the palm of the right hand faces the back of the left hand like the fan-tail of a bird.

6. *STAR and MOON*.   For the star, the gesture *Sarpa Sirsa* (Single Hands

No. 16) is used. For the moon, *Ardha-mukha* (an extra gesture in Bharata Natyam, in which the first, second and third fingers are bent slightly, the thumb is stretched apart and the little finger is bent in towards the palm). The right hand in the first gesture is held at chest level in front, palm facing upwards and fingers pointing towards the left hand, indicating the star. The left hand in the second gesture is raised to the left a little forward about chin level, palm facing upwards, the fingers pointing outwards, indicating the moon.

Verbs, Adverbs, Prepositions, Conjunctions

1. *IS, AM, ARE*. In this, there is a combination of the *Sarpa Sirsa* (Single Hands No. 16) in both hands, which in this gesture are held side by side at a slight slant at chest level, palms facing outwards and the fingers pointing outwards. The hands are moved together a little forwards.

2. *THAT*. In this, the *Ardha-suchika* (Single Hands No. 31) is used a little modified in the right hand. The thumb instead of being stretched straight is set over the second, third and little fingers, which are bent into the palm. The right hand in this gesture is taken from near the chest level forwards. The arm is stretched in a straight line, the first finger pointing up and the thumb side of the palm faced outwards.

3. *TOUCH*. In this, there is the use of *Pataka* (Single Hands No. 1) in the right hand, which in this gesture is held at chest level, palm facing down, the fingers pointing to the left. Then it is moved forwards as if touching an object.

4. *THERE*. In this, *Chandra Kala* (Single Hands No. 14) is used in the right hand, which hand in this gesture is held at the chest with the palm facing outwards and the first finger pointing up. The hand is taken forward and upwards, the first finger indicating an object or place.

5. *SEEING*. In this, there is the combination of *Kapitha* (Single Hands No. 11) and *Chandra Kala* (Single Hands No. 14), both gestures done with the right hand. The right hand in the first gesture is held near the right eye, palm facing outwards. Then changed to the second gesture, holding the hand in the same place, the finger pointing to the right eye obliquely. The palm faces inwards.

6. *NO*. In this, *Hamsa Paksha* (Single Hands No. 24) is used in the right hand, which in this gesture is held at shoulder level, the palm facing outwards, the fingers pointing up. Move the hand a little from right to left indicating "No."

7. *HERE*. In this, the *Hamsa Paksha* (Single Hands No. 24) is used with the right hand, which in this gesture is held at chest level with the fingers pointing to the chin, the palm facing outwards. The hand is now moved to the front, keeping the same gesture and taken down, the arm at an angle. The palm now faces left, with the fingers pointing down.

8. *WITH, TOGETHER*. In this, *Ardha-pataka* (Single Hands No. 3) is used in both hands, which in this gesture are held at chest level, a little forward, the palms of each hand facing each other. The hands are brought a little down in front, with the stretched finger tips of the hands touching and the palms facing inwards.

9. *WALKING*. In this, *Hamsa Paksha* (Single Hands No. 24) is used with both hands, which in this gesture are held at the chest, palms facing outwards. Then the hands are moved downwards, palms facing outwards, one hand being

placed before the other alternately as the feet move in walking.

10. *SAY or SPEAK*. In this, there is the combination of *Mukula* (Single Hands No. 26) in the right hand, and *Sola Padma* (Single Hands No. 20) also with the right hand. The right hand in the first gesture is held at the lips, palm facing to the left. Then the hand is changed into the second gesture and brought a little forward, palms facing upwards.

11. *GIVE ME*. In this, the *Sarpa Sirsa* (Single Hands No. 16) is used with both hands, which in this gesture are held at chest level, palms up, and the hands are joined on the sides of the little fingers. They are taken forward in this position, as though asking for something.

12. *LIVING, STAYING, SITTING*. In this, the *Sarpa Sirsa* (Single Hands No. 16) are used with both hands, which in this gesture are held side by side at a slant at chest level, palms facing outwards, and the fingers pointing upwards. The hands are then moved a little forwards.

Adjectives, Abstract Nouns

1. *GOLD, RICHES*. In this, there is a combination of *Pataka* (Single Hands No. 1) with the left hand and *Samdamsa* (Single Hands No. 25) with the right hand. The left hand in the first gesture, palm facing to the right, is held at chest level a little forward. The right hand in the second gesture has the thumb and first finger touching, held against the palm of the left hand at the base. They are then moved to the base of the fingers of the left palm as if writing.

2. *BREEZE*. In this, *Tri-pataka* (Single Hands No. 2) is used with both hands, which in this gesture are held raised forward above head level on the left, palms facing outwards. Then the right hand in the same gesture, palm facing down, is placed with the finger tips touching the left palm near the thumb base. Finally, the right hand is brought down in a sweep with a slight trembling of the hand.

3. *COLOUR*. In this, *Hamsa Paksha* (Single Hands No. 24) is used with both hands, which in this gesture are held a little forward chest level, palms facing upwards. They are then moved a little forward with the fingers pointing down at an angle.

4. *INNOCENT*. In this, there is the combination of *Pataka* (Single Hands No. 1) and *Samdamsa* (Single Hands No. 25) with the right hand only. The right hand in the first gesture, palm facing outwards and the fingers pointing upwards, is held a little forward at chest level. Then the hand is changed into the second gesture in the same position.

5. *MUSICAL NOTES, SONG, WRITING*. In this, there is the combination of *Mukula* (Single Hands No. 26) and *Sola Padma* (Single Hands No. 20) with the right hand only. The right hand in the first gesture is held at the lips, palm facing to the left. Then the hand changes into the second gesture and comes a little forward, palm facing upwards.

6. *GOOD, BEAUTIFUL*. In this, *Padmakosa* (Single Hands No. 15) is used with the right hand only. The right hand in this gesture, palm facing to the left, is held at chest level and then moved forward.

This is a representative set of examples of word signs in Bharata Natyam, and emphasises the dramatic value of the Indian classical dance in one of its various forms.

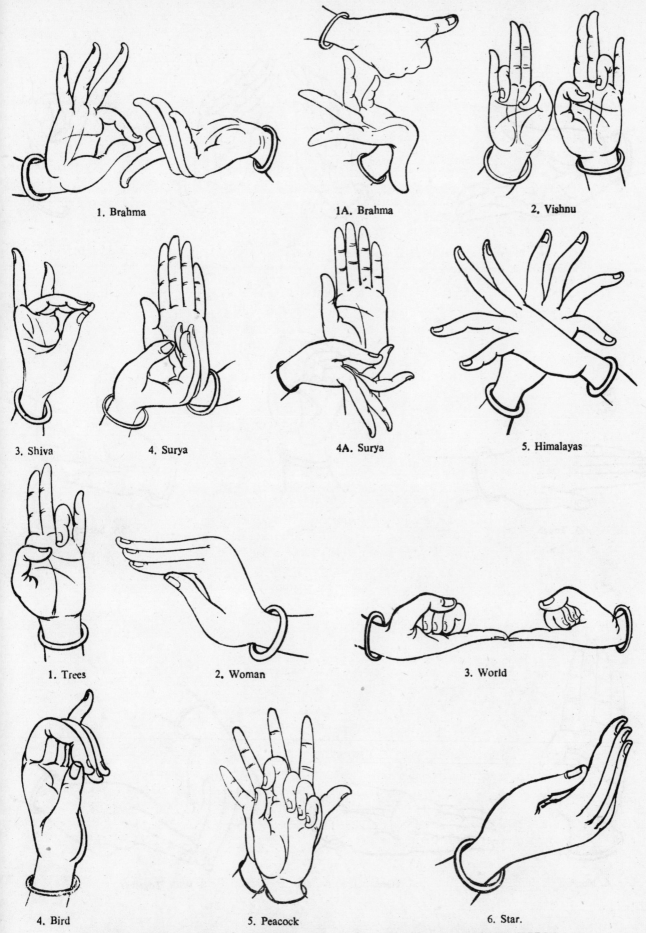

1. Brahma   1A. Brahma   2. Vishnu

3. Shiva   4. Surya   4A. Surya   5. Himalayas

1. Trees   2. Woman   3. World

4. Bird   5. Peacock   6. Star.

BHARATA NATYAM—HAND GESTURES USED WHEN EXPRESSING PARTS OF SPEECH

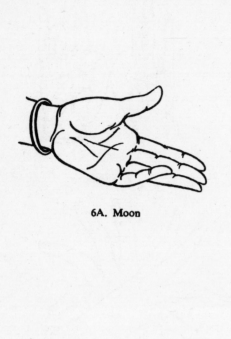

6A. Moon

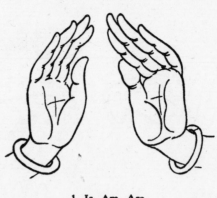

1. Is, Am, Are

2. That

3. Touch

5. Seeing

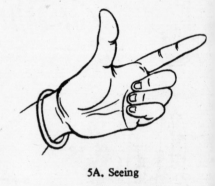

5A. Seeing

6. No

7. Here

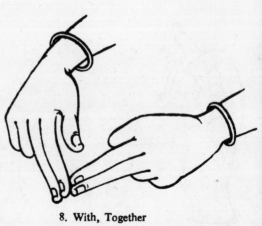

8. With, Together

BHARATA NATYAM—HAND GESTURES USED WHEN EXPRESSING PARTS OF SPEECH—(Contd.)

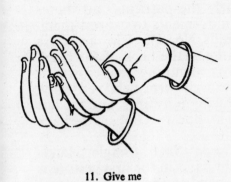

11. Give me

1. Gold, Riches

2. Breeze

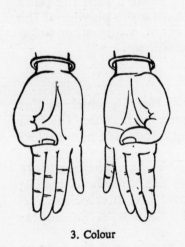

3. Colour

4. Innocent

6. Good, Beautiful

BHARATA NATYAM—28 EXAMPLES OF SOME OF THE HAND GESTURES USED WHEN EXPRESSING VARIOUS PARTS OF SPEECH.
BASED ON THE ALPHABETS (SINGLE AND COMBINED HAND GESTURES) OF THE CLASSICAL SANSKRIT TREATISES

USE OF HAND GESTURES IN KATHAK, The North Indian School of Classical Dancing

Proper Nouns

1. *VISHNU*. In Kathak, gestures indicate clearly the particular attributes of the subject being described, and there are several movements to express them. In this, both hands are used in the *Pataka* (Single Hands No. 1). The arms are raised to the head, with the hands in this gesture resting on the back of the head, palms facing outwards and fingers pointing upwards, denoting the crown of Vishnu. The same hands may also be used with the right arm held vertically, bent at the elbow, the right hand in *Pataka*, palm facing outwards, and the left hand held horizontally in the same gesture with the right elbow resting on the back of the left hand.

2. *SHIVA*. In this, there is the use of *Sarpa Sirsa* (Single Hands No. 16), and *Mushti* (Single Hands No. 9). The right hand in the first gesture is held on the head, palm facing outwards, and the left hand in the second gesture makes the movement of tying the hair of Lord Shiva in a knot on the head, and then held there. This is only one of the modes of expressing this subject.

3. *SRI KRISHNA*. In this there is a special gesture, in which the first, second and third fingers are slightly bent towards the palm, with the little finger bent slightly backwards. The thumb is bent into the palm to touch the middle finger in the centre. The right hand in this gesture is held with the palm facing outwards at about chin level, and the left hand in the same gesture with the palm facing inwards is held a little apart at the same level, indicating the playing of the flute. The same hands may also be held forwards one in front of the other to indicate the playing of another type of flute and in another position.

Nouns

1. *TREES*. Both hands in the *Pataka* (Single Hands No. 1), which in this gesture are held in front of the chest, palms facing towards each other, the first fingers slightly back, fingers pointing upwards. Then the hands are moved forwards, crossing each other two or three times.

2. *BIRDS*. Both hands in the *Pataka* (Single Hands No. 1). The hands are held with the palms facing inwards, and the four fingers are stretched straight pointing in opposite directions. The thumbs of each hand are interlocked and the hands are moved in a circular movement round and round with the fingers fluttering.

3. *WOMAN*. This gesture is indicated by pulling the veil over the face or slightly lifting it off, and it may be done with either one of the hands or with both hands. Here, there is the use of *Kapiddha* (Single Hands No. 11). The hand is held just a little above the right side of the forehead, and as if holding the tip of the veil, brought down a little towards the right eye; and then the hand is again lifted into the first position.

4. *FLOWER*. In this, there is the combination of *Mukula* (Single Hands No. 26) and *Padmakosa* (Single Hands No. 15), with the right hand only. The right hand in the first gesture is held forward to the right at chest level, palm up; and from this position, changed to the second gesture.

5. *PEACOCK*. In this, there is the use of *Samdamsa* (Single Hands

No. 25) with both hands. With the palms of the hands facing outwards, the hands are taken from one side to the other in a large circle over the head. At the top, the wrists touching, the palms facing outwards, the fingers pointing upwards, the hands are held side by side. It indicates actually the big tail of this famous bird.

6. *HALF-MOON*. In this, there is the use of the *Ardha-chandra* (Single Hands No. 6) with the right hand. The hand is raised slightly up to face level to the right.

7. *FULL MOON*. In this, there is the use of *Ardha-suchika* (Single Hands No. 31) with both hands. Both hands in this gesture are held forward at head level with the first fingers almost touching and pointing upwards. A full circle is made with the hands from the top, down to either side.

8. *FACE*. In this, there is the use of *Ardha-chandra* (Single Hands No. 6) with the right hand only, which in this gesture is held to the left of the face with the base of the palm at eye level. It is then brought slowly round the face under the chin to the right side of the face, so that the fingers point at the level of the right eye. All the time the thumb points upwards.

Verbs

1. *IS*. In this, there is the use of *Sarpa Sirsa* (Single Hands No. 16) with the right hand. It is slightly modified, in that instead of the little finger being held close to the extended fingers, it is a little bit out and apart. The right hand in this gesture is placed near the chest, with the palm facing outwards. It is then taken gently forward about a foot from the chest.

2. *TOUCH*. Here, there is the use of *Pataka* (Single Hands No. 1) with the right hand only. The right hand in this gesture is placed near the chest and moved forwards in a downward action, as if touching an object.

3. *SEEING, EYES*. Here, the verb and noun are shown by the same gesture. There is the use of *Mushti* (Single Hands No. 9) with the right hand, but slightly modified, in that the little finger instead of being bent into the palm, is stretched out straight. The right hand in this gesture is held near the right eye with the little finger pointing to the eye.

4. *HEARING*. In this, there is the use of *Simha Mukha* (Single Hands No. 18) with the right hand but slightly modified, in that the little finger instead of being stretched straight is bent a little. The right hand in this gesture, with the palm facing outwards, is placed at ear level; the first finger points to the right ear and then the hand is moved sideways with the finger pointing outwards.

5. *SPEAK, SONG*. Here, a verb and abstract noun are shown by the same gesture. There is the use of *Kapiddha* (Single Hands No. 11) with the right hand only. The right hand in this gesture is raised to the lips, with the palm facing up. From there, the hand is brought forward a little distance away from the lips.

6. *GIVE*. In this, there is a combination of the *Mushti* (Single Hands No. 9) and the *Pataka* (Single Hands No. 1), both gestures with the right hand. The right hand in the first gesture is held at the chest with the back of the hand facing outwards. Then, it changes to the second gesture, and the hand is moved forward with the palm up. Finally, the hand is moved downwards at a slant with the fingers pointing down and the open palm still facing upwards.

Pronouns, Adverbs, Adjectives

1. *THAT*. In this, there is the use of *Simha Mukha* (Single Hands No. 18) with the right hand but slightly modified, in that instead of the little finger being straight, it is bent a little. The right hand in this gesture is raised to chest level, palm facing inwards, and the first finger points to the left. The hand is moved forward as if pointing out something.

2. *NO*. In this, there is the use of *Pataka* (Single Hands No. 1) with the right hand only. The right hand in this gesture is raised with the palm facing outwards and the fingers pointing upwards. The hand is moved to and fro slightly at the wrist, indicating "No."

3. *HERE*. In this, there is the use of *Pataka* (Single Hands No. 1) with the right hand only. The right hand in this gesture is first held near the chest palm up, and then moved downwards straight in front, with the fingers pointing down.

4. *BEAUTIFUL*. Here, there is the use of *Kapiddha* (Single Hands No. 11) with the right hand only. The right hand in this gesture is held near the lips with the palm facing outwards, and it is moved to and fro in a horizontal action from the lips to the side and back again gently.

5. *PEACE*. Here, there is the use of *Pataka* (Single Hands No. 1) with the right hand only. The right hand in this gesture is held a little in front of the shoulder, with the palm facing outwards, and the fingers pointing upwards. The hand is held still to indicate peace or quiet.

6. *SORROW*. In this, there is the use of *Kartari Mukha* (Single Hands No. 4) with the right hand, but there is a slight modification, in that instead of the first, second and little fingers being stretched straight, they are slightly bent. The right hand in this gesture is raised to the right eye with the palm facing upwards, and with the third finger and thumb touching at the tips. They hold a tear drop and bring it down from the eye; at the same time, the hand is lowered and the tear drop released by flicking the tips of the third finger and the thumb.

In observing these few representative examples of the word signs from the Kathak school of the dance, it can readily be seen how differently Bharata Natyam and Kathak have utilized the basic Alphabet of Hand Gestures as detailed in the classical Sanskrit treatises for similar words. This gives each school its own unique code of "dance speech," that each one uses to the greatest effect in the interpretive part of the dance.

In the Kathakali school, for instance, they have an alphabet of twenty-four gestures for the single hands and the same number for the combined hands, built upon their text, the *Hastala Kshana Dipika*. This alphabet is based on the classical treatises with slight modifications but with different meanings.

ALPHABET OF SINGLE HANDS USED IN KATHAKALI and Their Combinations

1. *PATAKA*. Same gesture as the *Tri-pataka* (Single Hands No. 2). The palm faces outwards, the thumb, first, second and little fingers are kept straight; the third finger is bent parallel to the palm. It is used to express day, walk, tongue, forehead, body, "like" or "as," messenger, etc.

Combined. The same gesture used with both hands. It is used to express the sun, king, elephant, lion, bull, crocodile, arch, vessel, palace, creeper, flag,

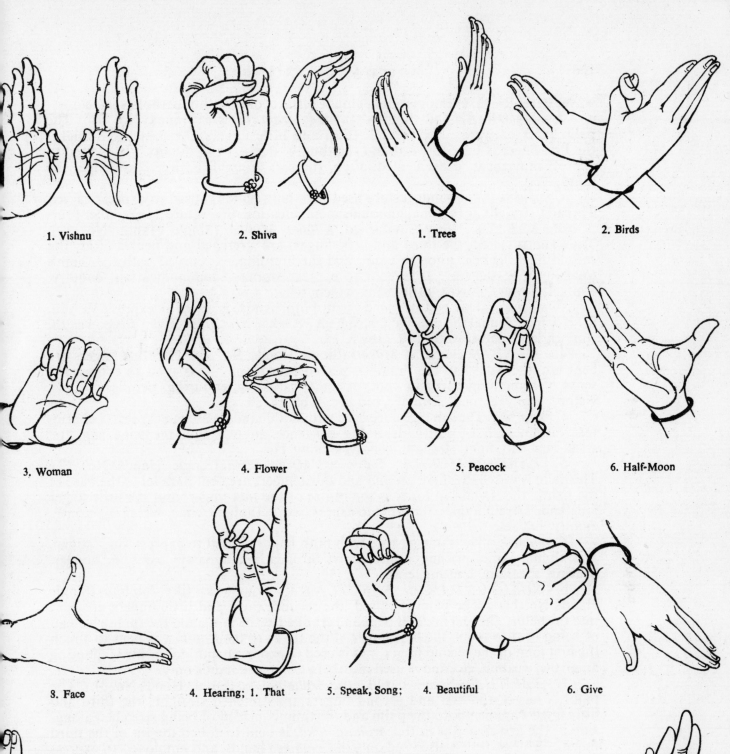

1. Vishnu   2. Shiva   1. Trees   2. Birds

3. Woman   4. Flower   5. Peacock   6. Half-Moon

8. Face   4. Hearing; 1. That   5. Speak, Song;   4. Beautiful   6. Give

6. Sorrow

KATHAK—20 EXAMPLES OF SOME OF THE HAND GESTURES USED
WHEN EXPRESSING VARIOUS PARTS OF SPEECH

BASED ON THE ALPHABETS (SINGLE AND COMBINED
HAND GESTURES) OF THE CLASSICAL SANSKRIT TREATISES

2. Touch   3. Here

wave, street, earth, evening, moon, cloud, surface, pillow, thunderbolt, seat, etc.

2. *MUDRAKHYA*. Somewhat like *Arala* (Single Hands No. 7). The palm faces outwards, the second, third and little fingers are stretched straight; the first finger is bent forward and the thumb touches it at the tip. It is used to express movement, heaven, meditation, the sea, thought, desire, knowledge, the mind, etc.

Combined. The same gesture used with both hands is used to express sacred Threads, straight, forgetting, announcement, creation, life, future, the number four.

3. *KATAKA*. Very similar to *Kataka Mukha* (Single Hands No. 12). The palm is raised, the third and little fingers are stretched and bent a little; the second finger is bent into the palm, and the first finger is curved with the thumb touching it at the tip. It is used to express woman, communication, enquiry, contact, flowers, mirror, little, who, whicn, what.

Combined. This gesture, made with both hands, is used to express Vishnu, Sri Krishna, Rama, the musical instrument *Veena*, arrow, gold, silver, sleep, wealth, star, garland, lotus, water lily, crown, etc.

4. *MUSHTI*. Same as *Mushti* (Single Hands No. 9). The four fingers are bent into the palm and the thumb is placed over them. It is used to express the sense of something being in vain, extreme, excessive, enduring, permission, gift, victory, bow, we, food, sentence, old age, robbing, etc.

Combined. The same gesture used with both hands is used to express a charioteer, loveliness, holy, purity, deserving, existence, ankle, Yama, medicine, sun, fire, stick, bow, gift, fight, strength, beauty, singing, etc.

5. *KARTARI MUKHA*. Same as *Mriga Sirsa* (Single Hands No. 17). The palm is raised, the first, second and third fingers are bent parallel to the base of the palm; the thumb tip touches the centre of the first finger, and the little finger is extended straight up. It is used to express word, thought, time, we, man, month, enmity, boy, etc.

Combined. The same gesture with both hands is used to express sin, fatigue, a Brahmin, fame, pitcher, house, now, purification, dynasty, bamboo, hunger, hearing, speaking, hunting, end.

6. *SUKUTUNDAM* or *SUKUTUNDA*. Somewhat like *Kapitha* (Single Hands No. 11). The palm is raised, the second, third and little fingers are bent into the palm; the first finger is bent and crooked at the joint, and the thumb instead of being bent to touch the first finger at the tip as in the *Kapitha*, is bent to touch the first joint of the second finger. It is used to express hand, good, bird, shooting an arrow, weapon, etc, and is used mostly in *Combined* hands only.

7. *KAPITHA*. Somewhat like the *Ardha-pataka* (Single Hands No. 3). The palm is raised, the first and second fingers are stretched straight; the third and little fingers are bent into the palm and the thumb instead of being stretched alongside of the first finger as in the *Ardha-pataka*, is bent to touch the tip of the third finger. This gesture is also used only in *Combined* hands, and employed to express a trap, reins, doubt, feather of a peacock, drink, touch, going back, outside, descending, footstep.

8. *HAMSAPAKSHA*. It is like the *Pataka* (Single Hands No. 1). The palm is open and facing outwards. The four fingers and the thumb are all stretched and held closely together. It is used to express you, sword, wrath, now, I, in front, axe, flame, call, prevent, etc.

Combined. When this gesture is used in both hands, it is employed to express the moon, cupid, wind, God, mountain, summit, everlasting, relation, rock, enjoyment, breast, cloth, conveyance, falsehood, lying down, fall, people, bowing, coming, covering, spreading, hauling, embracing, following, protecting, cheek, shoulder, obedient, worship, blessing, this, flesh, tortoise.

9. *SHIKARAM or SHIKARA*. Very much like *Kapitha* (Single Hands No. 11). The palm is raised, the first and second fingers instead of being stretched straight together, as in the *Kapitha*, are stretched straight with the first finger bent back a little behind the second finger; the third and little fingers are bent to touch the tip of the thumb. This gesture is generally used only in the *Combined* hands, and employed to express roaming, legs eyes, the number eight, way, search, ears, drink, hands, wonder, time, wheels, etc.

10. *HAMSASYAM or HAMSASYA*. Peculiar to Kathakali. The palm is raised, the third and little fingers held a little forward at a slant; the first and second fingers are bent parallel to the base of the palm and the thumb goes to touch them at the tips. It is used to express the first rain, hair, dew, etc.

Combined. When this gesture is used with both hands, it is employed to express the eyeball, soft, dust, pale, white, blue, red, mercy, etc.

11. *ANJALI*. Somewhat like the *Ardha-chandra* (Single Hands No. 6). The palm is raised facing outwards. The four fingers are stretched together and slightly bent, but instead of the thumb being stretched to its fullest away from the rest of the fingers as in the *Ardha-chandra*, it is held slightly bent close along the first finger. It is used to express the conch shell, anger, disquietude, hesitation, etc.

Combined. When used with both hands, this gesture is employed to express heavy rain, fire, stream, vibration, brightness, hair, earring, heat, sorrow, confusion, always, river, bathing, drinking, flowing, etc.

12. *ARDHA-CHANDRA or ARDHA-CANDRA*. Peculiar to Kathakali. The palm is raised. The second, third and little fingers are bent into the palm; the first finger is stretched, and the thumb too is stretched straight back a little. It is used to express the idea of starting, smiling, what, self-praise, half-moon, crescent, etc.

Combined. When used with both hands, it is employed to express what, if, sky, helplessness, luck, God, grass, hair, remembrance, etc.

13. *MUKURAM*. Peculiar to Kathakali. The palm is raised; the second and third fingers are bent parallel to the palm. The first and little fingers are stretched and bent forwards, and the thumb is bent to come near the second joint of the second finger. It is used to express an enemy, beetle, ray, anger, neck, excellent, bangle, armlet, negative (No), etc.

Combined. Used with both hands, it is employed to express elephant tusks, a fang, separation, Veda, brother, pillar, mortar, rapid, violent, devil, growth, nourishment, etc.

14. *BHRAMARA*. Somewhat like the *Arala* (Single Hands No. 7). The palm is raised. The second, third and little fingers are stretched straight together; the first finger is bent, and the thumb instead of being bent beside the first finger, is stretched apart. It is used to express a Gandharva (a heavenly musician), bee, birth, fear, weeping, etc.

Combined. Used with both hands, it is used to express a feather, song, water, umbrella, ear of the elephant, bee, etc.

15. *SUCHI*. Somewhat like the *Ardha-suchika* (Single Hands No. 31). The

palm is raised outwards. The second, third and little fingers are bent into the palm; the first finger is stretched straight; and the thumb instead of being held close to the palm as in *Ardha-suchika*, is bent to touch the top of the first joint of the second finger. It is used to express the idea of single, alas, dull, another, plural, hearing, a digit of the moon, ancient, this, one, kindness, kingdom, little, witness, giving, up, come, go, fight, etc.

Combined. Used with both hands, it is employed to express jumping, fall, upwards, wood, Lakshman (brother of Rama), month, elsewhere, eyebrow, loose, tail, etc.

16. *PALLAVA.* Peculiar to Kathakali. The palm is faced outwards. All the four fingers are stretched straight together, but the third finger is very slightly brought forward, and the thumb touches it at the base. It is used to express the idea of distance, leaf, smoke, tail, rice, etc.

Combined. When this gesture is used with both hands, it is employed to express the top of a mountain, ears of a cow, length of an eye, buffalo, spear, horn, etc.

17. *TRI-PATAKA.* The same as *Pataka* (Single Hands No. 1). The open palm is held facing outwards. The four fingers and the thumb are stretched and held closely together. Sometimes, the thumb is also bent a little when placed close to the first finger. It is used usually in the *Combined* Hands only, and is employed to express a sunset, greeting, commencement, drink, body, begging, etc.

18. *MRIGA SIRSA.* Same as the *Simha Mukha* (Single Hands No. 18). The palm is raised outwards. The first and little fingers are stretched straight. The second and third fingers are bent forward parallel to the base of the palm, and the thumb touches the tips. It is invariably used in the *Single* hands only, and is used to express a deer, a supreme Being, etc.

19. *SARPA SIRSA.* Same as *Sarpa Sirsa* (Single Hands No. 16). The palm is raised and hollowed slightly, and faced outwards. All the fingers and the thumb held close together are extended and bent slightly at the tips. When used either *Singly* or *Combined*, it is employed to express sandal paste, a snake, slowness, sprinkle, cherishing, flapping of an elephant's ears, message, saint, sage, giving water to the deities in worship.

20. *VARDHAMANA.* Peculiar to Kathakali. The palm is raised and faced upwards. The four fingers are bent into the palm near the bases of the fingers, but not actually touching the palm, and the thumb is stretched straight and bent a little backwards. It is used to express a well, a whirlpool, etc.

Combined. Used with both hands, this gesture is employed to express a earring, a jewelled garland, knee, drum, mahout (an elephant driver).

21. *ARALA.* Peculiar to Kathakali. The palm is raised outwards. The second, third and little fingers are slightly bent at the top joints; the first finger at the first joint. It is used generally with the *Combined* hands only, and is employed to express a tree, dull, wedge, bud, sprout, etc.

22. *URNANABHA.* Same as *Urnanabha* (Single Hands No. 29). The palm is faced downwards. The fingers and thumb are all bent apart and separated. This gesture is usually used only in the *Combined* hands, and is employed to express a spider, a full blown lotus, a horse, fruit, leopard, butter, ice, abundance, etc.

23. *MUKULA.* Same as *Mukula* (Single Hands No. 26). The palm is raised facing outwards. The four fingers and thumbs are all bent together and the

  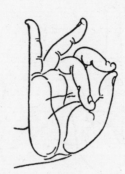 

1. Pataka   2. Mudrakhya   3. Kataka   4. Mushti

5. Kartari Mukha   6. Sukutundam

   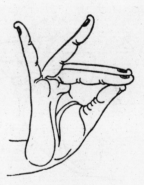

7. Kapitha   8. Hamsapaksha   9. Sikharam   10. Hamsasyam

11. Anjali   12. Ardha-chandra

ALPHABET OF SINGLE HAND GESTURES, KATHAKALI
SCHOOL. BASED ON THE CLASSICAL SANSKRIT AND
KATHAKALI TREATISES

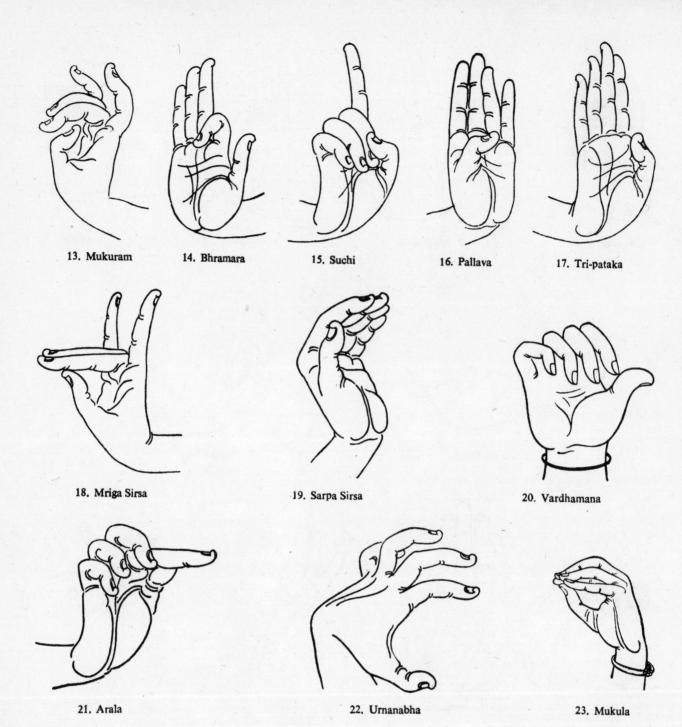

13. Mukuram   14. Bhramara   15. Suchi   16. Pallava   17. Tri-pataka

18. Mriga Sirsa   19. Sarpa Sirsa   20. Vardhamana

21. Arala   22. Urnanabha   23. Mukula

ALPHABET OF SINGLE HAND GESTURES, KATHAKALI SCHOOL—(*Contd.*)

24. Kataka Mukha

tips of the fingers as well as the tip of the thumbs all touch.   In both hands, the *Single* and *Combined*, it is used to express a bud, the number five, a jackal, a monkey, forgetting, etc.

24. *KATAKA MUKHA*. Peculiar to Kathakali.   The palm is raised sideways.   The four fingers are bent into the palm, and the thumbs are bent and slipped between the second and the third bent fingers.   It is generally used in the *Combined* hands, and is employed to express a hero, a servant, coating, arrow, wrestler, shooting, forest, space.

As mentioned previously, each gesture may be used to express several very different words, and the meaning can always be changed to suit the context, by the angle at which the hands are held, the positions of the arms and body, the expression on the face and the theme—in the same manner in which the meaning of the spoken word may change with the context, a change of accent or inflection of the voice, or a little variation in the spelling.

We must see next just how Kathakali dance dramas utilize these basic Single and Combined Hand Gestures in actual usage as a word language in the dramatic conversational parts of their plays, which are as realistic and impressive as actual beautiful diction.

USE OF HAND GESTURES IN KATHAKALI, THE DANCE DRAMAS OF KERALA. Taken from Their Own Alphabet of Gestures Based on the Classical Sanskrit Treatises, and Their Text the Hastala Kshana Dipika

Proper Nouns

1. *BRAHMA*.   This is expressed by the combination of *Pataka* (Kathakali Single Hands No. 1) with the right hand and *Kapitha* (Kathakali Single Hands No. 7) with the left hand.   From the position of the palms held face to face (denoting salutation), and held in front of the face, the hands are moved to either side of the face just in front of the shoulders, palms facing outwards.   At the same time, the right hand takes the first gesture and the left hand the second gesture.

2. *VISHNU*.   This is represented by a combination of *Kataka* (Kathakali Single Hands No. 3) with both hands.   From the position of the palms held face to face in front of the face (denoting salutation), the hands are moved to either side of the face, just in front of the shoulders, palms facing outwards.   At the same time, both hands take the gesture of *Kataka*.

3. *SHIVA*.   In this is used the combination of *Tri-pataka* (Kathakali Single Hands No. 17) with the right hand and *Mriga Sirsa* (Kathakali Single Hands No. 18) with the left hand.   From the gesture of salutation with the palms folded together in front of the face, the hands are moved to either side of the face, near the shoulders.   The right hand takes the first gesture and the left hand takes the second gesture.

Nouns

1. *TREES*.   In this, there is the combination of *Mudrakhya* (Kathakali Single Hands No. 2) and *Suchi* (Kathakali Single Hands No. 15).   At first, both hands are in the first gesture; from in front of the chest with the palms facing inwards, they are raised in a straight line a little above head level.   The hands are

then moved a little forwards with the three stretched fingers fluttering. As the hands reach the head level, they change into the second gesture with a jerk, the first fingers pointing upwards.

2. *WOMAN*. In this is used the combination of *Kataka* (Kathakali Single Hands No. 3) with the left hand and *Mudrakhya* (Kathakali Single Hands No. 2) with the right hand. The left hand is first kept in the first gesture with the palm facing down, near the chest. The right hand in the second gesture is taken near the left hand and the three straight fingers of the right hand are fluttered over the left hand. Finally, the tips of the fingers rest on the left hand.

3. *WORLD*. This is *Suchi* (Kathakali Single Hands No. 15) used with both hands. The hands in this gesture are placed so that the palms face inwards, and the first fingers of each hand are tip to tip. As the hands are moved forwards, the first fingers are circled one around the other. Finally, the hands are kept still, with the first fingers parallel to one another, pointing straight forwards.

4. *BIRD*. In this, there is the combination of *Kataka Mukha* (Kathakali Single Hands No. 24) with the left hand and *Sukutundam* (Kathakali Single Hands No. 6) with the right hand. The left hand in the first gesture is held a little forward with the side of the palm facing downwards. The right hand in the second gesture is placed over the left fist with the crooked finger of the right hand at the top.

5. *PEACOCK*. In this, the *Hamsasya* (Kathakali Single Hands No. 10) is used with both hands. The hands are held a little forward at chest level, and the third and little fingers of the right hand are placed over the third and little fingers of the left hand; the first and second fingers of each hand are placed against one another, face to face, and the thumbs touch along their entire length. In this position, the first and second fingers have their tips pointing outwards and the hands together form the shape of a beak. The same gesture is used to express a swan.

6. *STAR*. For this, *Kataka* (Kathakali Single Hands No. 3) is used with the right hand only. The right hand in this gesture is held a little forward, wrist raised and palm facing outwards.

7. *MOON*. In this, *Pataka* (Kathakali Single Hands No. 1) is used with both hands. The right and left hands in this gesture are held parallel to one another. Then, the left hand is quivered at the wrist and moved forwards in a straight line.

Verbs, Adverbs, Prepositions

1. *IS, AM, ARE*. For these three words, there is the combination of *Tri-pataka* (Kathakali Single Hands No. 17) and *Pataka* (Kathakali Single Hands No. 1) used with the right hand only. The right hand in the first gesture is placed with the palm facing down and the thumbs pointing at and touching the chest. Then the hand changes into the second gesture, and is moved forward with the palm still facing down. The arm is stretched forward, and the tip of the third finger points down.

2. *THAT*. In this, the *Suchi* (Kathakali Single Hands No. 15) is used with the right hand only. The right hand in this gesture is taken with the palm facing down, from near the chest and held forward with the first finger pointing to something, indicating "that one."

3. *THERE*.   In this, there is the use of *Suchi* (Kathakali Single Hands No. 15) with both hands which in this gesture are placed on the left side, chest level, with the first fingers pointing upwards and are then moved over in a semi-circle to the right side, to point at some object "over there."

4. *TOUCH*.   In this, there is the combination of *Mushti* (Kathakali Single Hands No. 4) with the left hand and *Tri-pataka* (Kathakali Single Hands No. 17) with the right hand.   The left hand in the first gesture is held forwards; and the right hand in the second gesture with the palm facing the left hand is moved a little outwards and then changed into the first gesture.   The movement is repeated twice.

5. *SEEING*.   In this, there is the combination of *Pallava* (Kathakali Single Hands No. 16) with both hands and *Sikhara* (Kathakali Single Hands No. 9) with both hands.   At first, both hands in the first gesture are held with the palms towards the face.   They are then moved in a semi-circle from left to right and are finally held, one hand on either side of the nose, palms towards the face, and the two fingers parallel to the eyes, in the second gesture; so that the eyes can look through the spaces formed between the first and second fingers of each hand.

6. *NO*.   In this, there is a combination of *Mushti* (Kathakali Single Hands No. 4) and *Pataka* (Kathakali Single Hands No. 1).   Both the gestures are used with the left hand only.   The left hand in the first gesture is placed at the left shoulder level, a little forward, with the palm facing outwards.   Then it is moved a little outwards to the extreme left into the second gesture, with the palm facing in front.

7. *HERE*.   In this, *Pallava* (Kathakali Single Hands No. 16) is used with the left hand only.   The left hand in this gesture is taken forward from chest level, palm facing outwards and placed with the fingers pointing down, indicating "this place" or "here."

8. *WITH, TOGETHER*.   Doing this gesture, there is the combination of *Tri-pataka* (Kathakali Single Hands No. 17) with both hands in two positions. Both hands in this gesture are first held in front of the chest with the finger tips touching.   Then the hands in the same gesture are moved round together in a small circle, from right to left, the palms facing down.

9. *WALKING*.   In this, *Sikhara* (Kathakali Single Hands No. 9) is used with both hands.   Both hands in this gesture are held parallel to each other a little forward, palms facing.   The hands are moved forward alternately, as if demonstrating the act of walking; and the fingers point down.

10. *SAY, SPEAK*.   In this, *Kartari Mukha* (Kathakali Single Hands No. 5) is used with the right hand only.   The right hand in this gesture is held near the lips with the fingers parallel to the line of the lips.   The hand is then moved with the palm down, a little forward.   As the hand is moved, the thumb is stretched and brought to touch the fingers again.

11. *GIVE ME*.   In this, there is a combination of *Mushti* (Kathakali Single Hands No. 4) with the left hand and *Tri-pataka* (Kathakali Single Hands No. 17) with the right hand.   The right hand in the second gesture, palm facing upwards, is placed on the left hand which is in the first gesture.   The back of the right hand rests on the left and the fingers of the right hand point downwards.   The fingers of the right hand are then closed, taking the first gesture, as though closing something within the palm.

12. *TO KNOW or UNDERSTAND*.   In this, there is a combination of

Tri-pataka (Kathakali Single Hands No. 17) and *Mudrakhya* (Kathakali Single Hands No. 2). The left hand is used for both gestures. The left hand in the first gesture, palm facing upwards, the side of the palm parallel to the chest, with the thumb on the outside. From this position, the hand is moved in a small circle forwards from right to left, and then brought back to its original position in the second gesture.

13.   *LIVING, SITTING, STAYING.*   For these three words the same gestures hold. There is a combination of *Tri-pataka* (Kathakali Single Hands No. 17) and *Mushti* (Kathakali Single Hands No. 4). Both gestures are done with both hands. Both hands in the first gesture, with the palms facing outwards chin level and held a little forward. The palm of the right hand is crossed over the back of the left hand with the thumbs overlapping and crossed below. From this, the hands are moved into the second gesture, one hand taken on each side at the same level and the fingers are closed with the palms facing outwards.

14.   *LOVE.*   In this, *Mudrakhya* (Kathakali Single Hands No. 2) is used with the left hand only. The left hand in this gesture is held at the heart, the first finger and thumb touching the heart. Then the hand is moved in a small circle from right to left and brought back to its position with the palm facing to the right all the time. During the movement, the three stretched fingers are trembled and fluttered.

Adjectives, Nouns, Abstract Nouns

1. *GOLD, RICHES.*   In this, there is a combination of *Tri-pataka* (Kathakali Single Hands No. 17) and *Kataka* (Kathakali Single Hands No. 3) with both hands. Both hands in the first gesture, palms facing down and one hand on each side of the chest, but a little forward, are then changed into the second gesture with the palms facing upwards. The hands are moved forward and back and forward again.

2. *BREEZE.*   In this, *Tri-pataka* (Kathakali Single Hands No. 17) is used with both hands. The two hands are held in this gesture with the palms forward and facing down, held close to each other at chest level. They are gently rocked with a swinging movement at the wrists, from right to left. The hands are kept close together all the time.

3. *COLOUR.*   In this, *Hamsasyam* (Kathakali Single Hands No. 10) is used with both hands. The two hands in this gesture are moved together in a wide circle from right to left, moving above the head and back to position. All the time the tips of the first and second fingers and the thumbs are rubbed against one another as if investigating the feel or texture of something.

4. *INNOCENT.*   In this, *Mudrakhya* (Kathakali Single Hands No. 2) is used with both hands. The two hands in this gesture are combined so that they are crossed at the centre of the forearms, with the right palm facing upwards and the left palm facing downwards. The right hand is then raised above the left to the level of the face, and keeping the arms parallel to the body, the three stretched fingers are trembled and fluttered all the time.

5. *NIGHT.*   In this, there is the combination of *Tri-pataka* (Kathakali Single Hands No. 17) and *Pataka* (Kathakali Single Hands No. 1) with both hands. The two hands in the first gesture are held side by side a little forward, chest level, with the palms facing down. The left hand is then changed into the second gesture

near the chest, palm facing the chest, and held there. Finally, the right hand is changed into the second gesture and held first to the right and then to the left of the left hand, palm facing outwards. The right hand is then brought to rest just below the wrist of the left hand and in front of it.

6. *MUSICAL NOTES*. In this, *Ardha-chandra* (Kathakali Single Hands No. 12) is used with the right hand only. The right hand in this gesture is raised to the cheek with the first finger pointing to it, palm facing outwards; and the second and third fingers are trembled slightly.

7. *SONG, WRITING*. This has the same gesture for both words. In this, *Sukutunda* (Kathakali Single Hands No. 6) is used with both hands. Both hands in this gesture with the palms facing each other, held side by side a little forward at chest level, are circled round and round each other at the point where the first fingers meet the thumbs at the tips.

8. *HEART*. In this, there is a combination of *Tri-pataka* (Kathakali Single Hands No. 17) and *Mudrakhya* (Kathakali Single Hands No. 2) with the left and right hands respectively. The left hand in the first gesture is held with the palm upwards, fingers pointing to the right, chest level and near the chest. The hand is then changed into the second gesture at the same place with the palm facing down. The right hand meanwhile is held hanging down all the time, a little way from the body at a slant, and is in the first gesture with the fingers pointing down.

9. *THOUGHT*. In this, there is a combination of *Tri-pataka* (Kathakali Single Hands No. 17) with the left hand and *Mudrakhya* (Kathakali Single Hands No. 2) with the right hand. The left hand in the first gesture is held with the palm facing upwards, fingers pointing to the right, chest level and near the chest. It is then changed into the second gesture at the same place with the palm facing down. The right hand in the second gesture, fingers pointing upwards, palms facing outwards, is moved forward in a straight line to the full length of the arm. At the same time, the left hand is changed into the first gesture and moved into the position of the arm hanging down a little way from the body at a slant, the fingers pointing down.

10. *HAPPY, GLADNESS, JOY*. Same gesture for all three words. In this, there is a combination of *Mushti* (Kathakali Single Hands No. 4) and *Mudrakhya* (Kathakali Single Hands No. 2) with both hands. Both hands in the first gesture are held with the right hand above the left, the palms facing inwards, chest level and a little forward. Then they are reversed, with the left hand held above the right, and the hands are changed into the second gesture. Finally, the extended fingers of both hands are trembled gently.

11. *GOOD, BEAUTIFUL*. Same gesture for both words. In this, there is a combination of *Suchi* (Kathakali Single Hands No. 15) with the left hand and *Urnanabha* (Kathakali Single Hands No. 22) with the right hand. The left hand in the first gesture is held near the chest with the palm facing it and the first finger pointing to the right. The right hand is in the second gesture with the finger tips facing the tip of the first finger of the left hand. The right hand is gently turned to and fro in a quick movement.

12. *PEACE*. In this, there is a combination of *Mushti* (Kathakali Single Hands No. 4) with the left hand and *Tri-pataka* (Kathakali Single Hands No. 17) with the right hand. The left hand in the first gesture is held with the palm facing the chest and near it. The right hand in the second gesture with the palm facing

down and the fingers pointing to the left side, is passed over the left hand and brought beside it in the same position as the left hand.

In the Kathakali school of the dance, one is able to see that the Alphabet of Single Hands and the evolved Combined Hands as given in the classical treatises have been used to form an Alphabet of Single and Combined Hands peculiar to this school.   From these created symbols, it has made its own dance speech. The regional differences of the word signs have added tremendously to the richness of the interpretive aspect of the classical dance in general and given it a variety and beauty that accentuate the importance of the use of the hands in human expression.

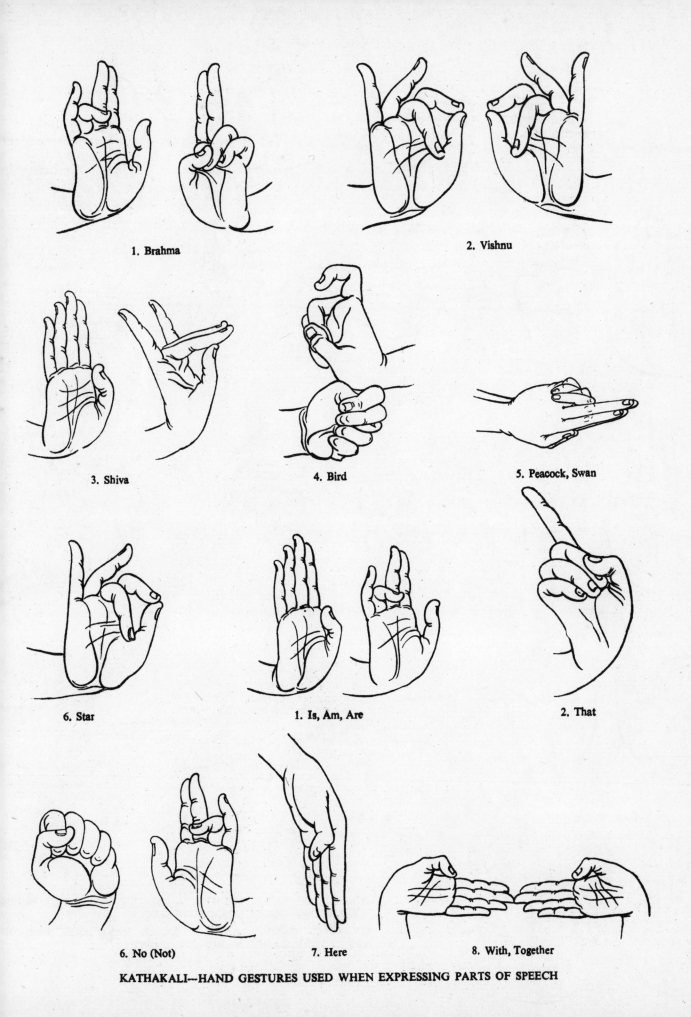

1. Brahma

2. Vishnu

3. Shiva

4. Bird

5. Peacock, Swan

6. Star

1. Is, Am, Are

2. That

6. No (Not)

7. Here

8. With, Together

KATHAKALI—HAND GESTURES USED WHEN EXPRESSING PARTS OF SPEECH

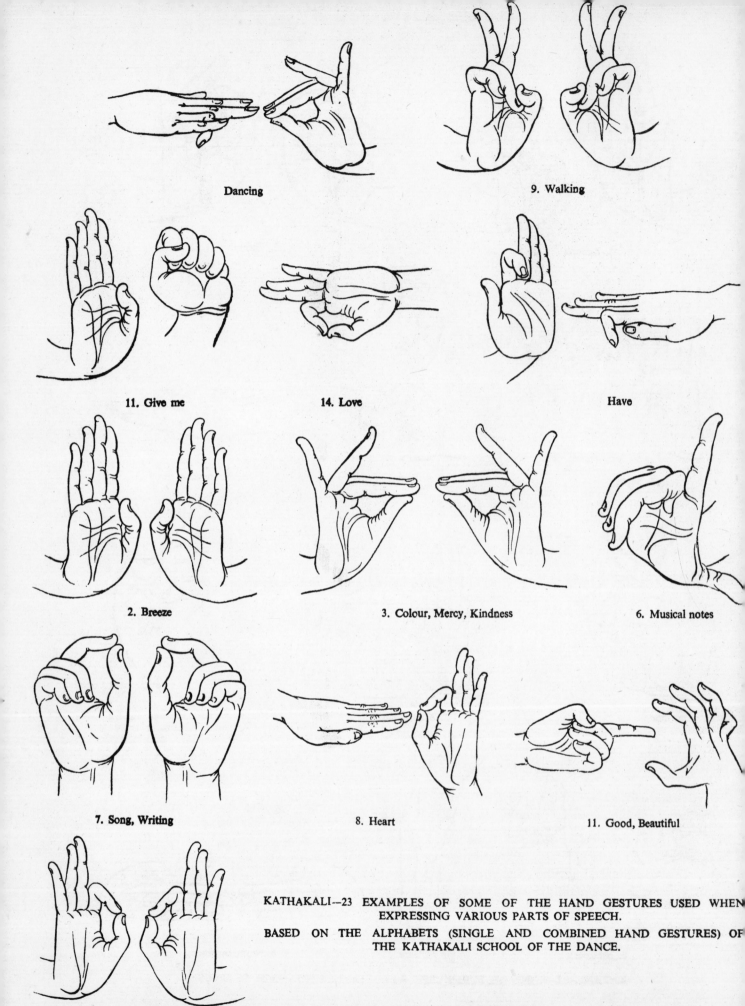

Dancing

9. Walking

11. Give me

14. Love

Have

2. Breeze

3. Colour, Mercy, Kindness

6. Musical notes

7. Song, Writing

8. Heart

11. Good, Beautiful

KATHAKALI—23 EXAMPLES OF SOME OF THE HAND GESTURES USED WHEN EXPRESSING VARIOUS PARTS OF SPEECH.

BASED ON THE ALPHABETS (SINGLE AND COMBINED HAND GESTURES) OF THE KATHAKALI SCHOOL OF THE DANCE.

The Same (Equal)

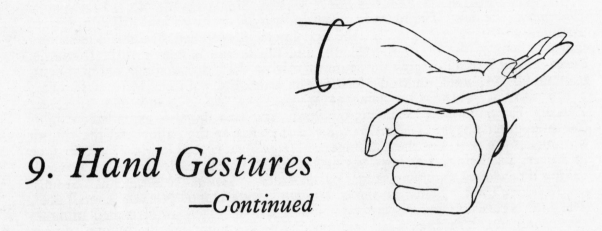

9. Hand Gestures
—Continued

In the Orissi school of the classical dance, the hand gestures follow the textual Hand Gestures as described in the Sanskrit treatises, the *Natya Sastra* by Bharata Muni and the *Abhinaya Dharpana* by Nandikeshwara, and the 12th century A.D. Orissi language treatise the *Abhinaya Chandrika*. Besides these, the Orissi dance uses certain traditional hand gestures of its own as taught by the *gurus* and handed down through the generations. In all, therefore, there are the Single Hand Gestures following the Sanskrit and Orissi texts, as well as the traditional hand gestures as taught by the *gurus*. And from these, a code of Combined Hand Gestures have been evolved. These Single Traditional and Combined Hands are the basis for the word symbols used in the actual dance.

ALPHABET OF IMPORTANT SINGLE HANDS IN ORISSI DANCE

1. *DHWAJA.* This is the same as *Pataka*, Single Hands No. 1 (The Flag). The open palm is held facing outwards, the four fingers and thumb all close together. *Pataka* is used to show the beginning of the dance, clouds, a forest, things, bosom, might, peace, a river, heaven, prowess, favour, moonlight, strong, sunlight, wave, entering, silence, an oath, the sea, sword, a palmyra leaf.

2. *DHAYANA.* Same as *Arala*, Single Hands No. 7 (Bent). The palm is raised and facing outwards, the second, third and little fingers are stretched straight; the first finger is crooked or curved and the thumb is a little bent beside it and almost touching the tip of the thumb. *Arala* is used to show nectar, drinking, poison, benediction, dressing the hair, decorating the face, etc.

3. *ANUKUSHA.* Same as *Kapitha*, Single Hands No. 11 (Elephant Apple). The palm is raised outwards, the second, third and little fingers are bent into the palm, and the first finger is bent forwards; the thumb goes to touch the tip of the first finger. *Kapitha* is used to show the sense of holding cymbals, flowers, or a rope, offering incense of gifts or lights, Lakshmi (Goddess of Wealth), Saraswati (Goddess of Learning), milk, showing a dance, pounding seed, winding.

119

4. *BAYA*.   Same as *Mukula*, Single Hands No. 26 (Bud).   The palm is raised facing outwards; the four fingers are bent forward together, and the thumb goes to touch the tips of the fingers.   *Mukula* is used to show a water lily, eating, banana flower, prayer, lotus bud, life, self, worship, fruit.

5. *NIRDESHIKA*.   Same as *Suchi Mukha*, Single Hands No. 13 (*Abhinaya Dharpana*, Needle).   The palm is raised outwards, the third and little fingers are extended and bent very slightly; the first finger is stretched straight; the second finger is bent to the tip of the thumb, and the thumb is bent a little forwards. *Suchi Mukha* is used to show the sense of this or that, threatening, astonishment, explaining, rod, braid, umbrella, beating the drum, life, solitude, lotus stalk, etc.

6. *HANSH PAKSHA*.   Same as *Mriga Sirsa*, Single Hands No. 17 (Deer Head).   The palm is raised facing outwards, the little finger is extended straight, the three other fingers are bent parallel to the base of the palm; and the thumb tip touches the centre of the first finger.   *Mriga Sirsa* is used to show fear, the face of a deer, discussion, drawing lines on the brow, cheek, patterns on the ground, calling the beloved, applying sandal paste, order.   *Hansh Paksha* means "Swan."

7. *GOMUKA*.   Same as *Simha Mukha*, Single Hands No. 18 (Lion Face). The palm is raised facing outwards, the first and little fingers are stretched straight; the second and third fingers are bent parallel to the palm, and the thumb touches their tips.   *Simha Mukha* is used to show lion's head, a lotus garland, stroking the hair, goodness, fragrance, a pearl, hare, elephant.

8. *MRUGAKSHYA*.   Same as *Hamsasya*, Single Hands No. 23 (Swan Face). The palm is raised facing outwards and very slightly hollowed.   The little finger is extended straight ; the third finger is also extended but bent very slightly; and the first finger and second finger are bent forward to touch the thumb at the tips. *Hamsasya* is used to show a swan's beak, tying the marriage thread, certainty, drop of water, carrying garlands, a jasmine.   *Mrugakshya* means "Deer Eye."

9. *ARDHA-CHANDRA*.   Same as *Ardha-chandra*, Single Hands No. 6 (Half-moon).   The palm is faced upwards slightly, the four fingers are stretched together and slightly bent; and the thumb is stretched to its fullest away from the rest of the fingers.   *Ardha-chandra* is used to show the moon on the eighth day, anxiety, prayer, greeting, meditation, bangle, wrist, mirror, ear of an elephant, moon, eyebrow, bow.

10. *ARATRIKA*.   Same as *Sikhara*, Single Hands No. 10 (Spire).   The palm is raised outwards, the four fingers are bent into the palm, and the thumb is extended straight out.   *Sikhara* is used to show silence, questioning, hero, steadfastness, friend, the number four, a sapphire, intensity.

11. *KSHIPTA*.   Same as *Ala Padma* or *Sola Padma*, Single Hands No. 20 (Full blown lotus).   The palm is faced upwards and hollowed.   All the fingers and the thumb are spread out and bent to form a petalled circlet.   *Ala Padma* is used to show a full blown lotus, the hair knot, anger, praise, full moon, a round face, a ball, beauty, etc.

12. *DANDA*.   Same as *Kapitha* of the Kathakali Single Hands No. 7, and somewhat like the *Ardha-pataka*, Single Hands No. 3 (Half Flag).   The palm is raised, the first and second fingers are stretched straight; the third and little fingers are bent into the palm and the thumb instead of being stretched alongside of the first finger as in the *Ardha-pataka*, is bent to touch the tip of the third finger.   This gesture is taken from the Orissi treatise the *Abhinaya Chandrika*.   It may be used to express the same meanings, namely, saying two or both, horn, tower, knife, etc.

13. *SARPA SIRSA.* Very different to the gesture of the same name as mentioned in the Single Hands of the Sanskrit treatises. This gesture is peculiar to Orissi usage and resembles *Mukuram*, Kathakali Single Hands No. 13. This is again taken from the Orissi treatise the *Abhinaya Chandrika.* As the name denotes, it means Snake Head, and is used to express in all probability the same meanings, namely, a snake, sandal paste, sprinkling, cherishing, giving water to the Gods, washing the face, image, etc.

14. *BALAYA.* This is the same as *Kapitha* or *Kapiddha* (Single Hands No. 11) and practically the same as *Anukusha* (Orissi Single Hands No. 3) being found both in the Sanskrit treatises and the Orissi *Abhinaya Chandrika.* Usage is very similar.

15. *CHATURA.* This is the same as *Catura*, Single Hands No. 21 (Semi-circle). The palm is faced outwards and hollowed. The first, second and third fingers and the thumb are bent like a hooded snake, and the little finger is extended straight. *Catura* is used to show the sense of little, sorrow, playful, converse, copper, sweetness, face, breaking.

The following Single Gestures are peculiar to the Orissi school of the dance and are taken from the Orissi treatise the *Abhinaya Chandrika.* The usage of these hand gestures with their meanings will be given when describing words of speech as illustrated in the dance.

16. *PRABODHIKA.* Taken from the *Abhinaya Chandrika*, it is somewhat like the *Ardha-suchika*, Single Hands No. 31. Only, instead of the three bent fingers being bent into the palm, they are bent in towards the palm but not actually touching it. Also, the three fingers are kept a little apart instead of touching close together. The thumb is kept straight and a little apart instead of being close to the side of the stretched first finger.

17. *SHAKU CHANCHU.* Peculiar to Orissi, this gesture is taken from the *Abhinaya Chandrika.* In it, the first, third and little fingers are bent and held a little separated from one another; and the second finger is bent to touch the thumb at the first joint.

18. *BIRODHA.* Though this gesture resembles the *Mushti* (Single Hands No. 9) and the *Kataka Mukha* (Kathakali Single Hands No. 24), it is different and taken from the *Abhinaya Chandrika.* In this gesture, the four fingers are bent into the palm and the thumb is bent over them. It is peculiar to Orissi.

19. *LULITA.* Taken from the *Abhinaya Chandrika*, this gesture is peculiar to Orissi. In it, the hand is held with the fingers pointing downwards, bent at the wrist, and all four fingers and thumb are stretched straight close together.

20. *TAMBULA.* Once again, although this gesture resembles *Kapitha* or *Kapiddha* (Single Hands No. 11), it is different and peculiar to Orissi, being taken from the *Abhinaya Chandrika.* In it, the palm is raised outwards, the second, third and little fingers are bent into the palm and the first finger is bent forward; the thumb touches the first finger at the first joint.

21. *BASTRA.* Taken from the *Abhinaya Chandrika*, this gesture is peculiar to Orissi. In it, the thumb, first and third and little fingers are stretched straight, and the second finger is bent into the palm.

22. *CHATUR MUKHA.* This is yet another gesture peculiar to Orissi, and taken from the *Abhinaya Chandrika.* In this, the thumb and first finger touch at the tips and the other three fingers are bent close together at their first joints.

The following eight Hand Gestures are peculiar to Orissi and have been taught by tradition by the *gurus* through the generations. The usage of these gestures with their meanings will be given when describing words of speech as illustrated in the dance.

23. *KARTARI MUKHA*. This is a traditional gesture taught by the *gurus*, and is peculiar to Orissi, bearing no likeness to the gesture of the same name in the Alphabet of Single Hands from the Sanskrit treatises (Single Hands No. 4).

24. *BHRAMARA*. This gesture again, although having the same name as Single Hand Gesture No. 22, is quite different and peculiar to Orissi, being taught traditionally by the *gurus*.

25. *PUSHPA*. Peculiar to Orissi, being a traditional gesture as taught by the *gurus*. In this gesture, the thumb touches the second finger at its first joint, and the third and little fingers are bent into the palm. The first finger is bent forwards straight.

26. *DANSA*. A traditional hand gesture, taught by the *gurus*, and so, peculiar to Orissi.

27. *DHANU*. Another traditional gesture taught by the *gurus*, and so, peculiar to Orissi. In it, the first, second and third fingers are bent into the palm; and the little finger is stretched straight, while the thumb is stretched straight outwards.

28. *PECHKA MUKHA*. Yet another traditional gesture in the Orissi dance, taught by the *gurus*. In it, the third and little fingers are bent towards the palm, and the first finger is bent similarly, but a little less forward. The thumb touches the second finger just above the finger nail at its joint.

29. *BARDHAMANAKA*. This gesture though traditional and taught by the *gurus*, is peculiar to Orissi, but at the same time it is the same as *Vardhamana* (Kathakali Single Hands No. 20). In it, the palm is raised, the four fingers are bent near the bases of the fingers, but not actually touching the palm. The thumb is stretched straight and bent a little backwards.

30. *HANSAYA*. Traditionally taught by the *gurus*, this gesture is again peculiar to Orissi.

SOME IMPORTANT COMBINED HANDS IN THE ORISSI SCHOOL

The following important Combined Hands follow the Sanskrit classical treatises, as detailed in Chapter 7 of this book.

1. *ANJALI*.   Same as *Anjali*, Combined Hands No. 1 (Salutation).
2. *PUSHPAPUTA*. Same as *Pushpaputa* or *Puspaputa*, Combined Hands No. 6 (Flower Casket).
3. *KARAKATIKA*. Same as *Karkata*, Combined Hands No. 3 (The Crab).
4. *KAPOTA*.   Same as *Kapota*, Combined Hands No. 2 (The Dove).
5. *SAMPUTA*.   Same as *Samputa*, Combined Hands No. 14 (Casket).
6. *PASHA*.   Same as *Pasa*, Combined Hands No. 15 (The Noose).
7. *MATSHYA*.   Same as *Matysa*, Combined Hands No. 17 (Fish).
8. *KURMA*.   Same as *Kurma*, Combined Hands No. 18 (Tortoise).
9. *GARUDA*.   Same as *Garuda*, Combined Hands No. 19 (The Garuda Bird).
10. *SHIBA LINGA*. Same as *Shiva Linga*, Combined Hands No. 8 (The symbolic representation of Lord Shiva).
11. *UTSANGA*.   Same as *Utsanga*, Combined Hands No. 7 (Embrace).

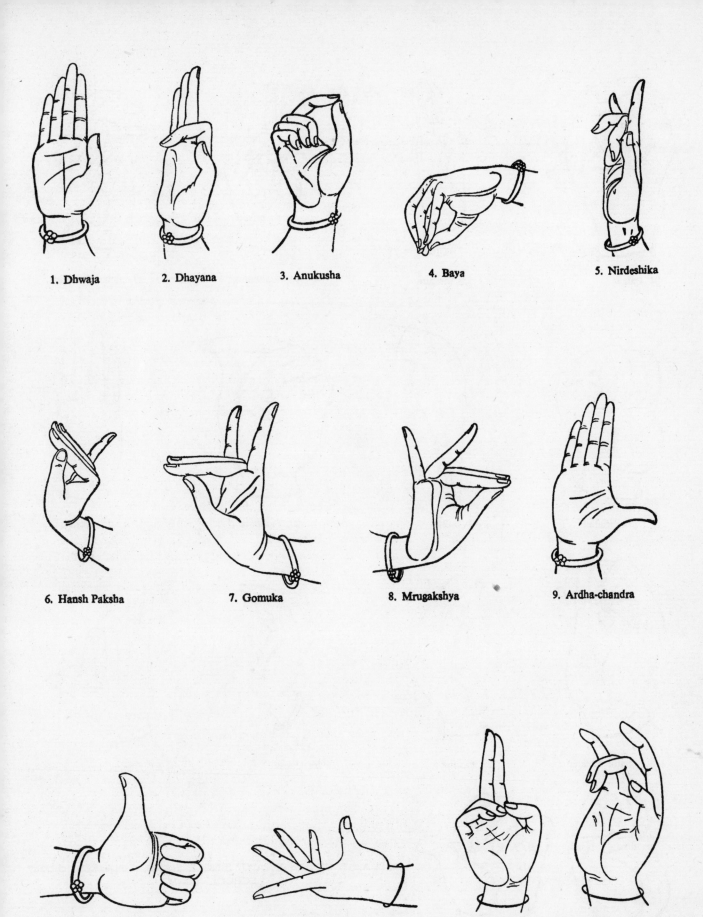

1. Dhwaja   2. Dhayana   3. Anukusha   4. Baya   5. Nirdeshika

6. Hansh Paksha   7. Gomuka   8. Mrugakshya   9. Ardha-chandra

10. Aratrika   11. Kshipta   12. Danda   13. Sarpa Sirsa

ALPHABET OF IMPORTANT SINGLE HAND GESTURES, ORISSI OR ODISSI SCHOOL. BASED ON THE
CLASSICAL SANSKRIT AND ORISSI TREATISES

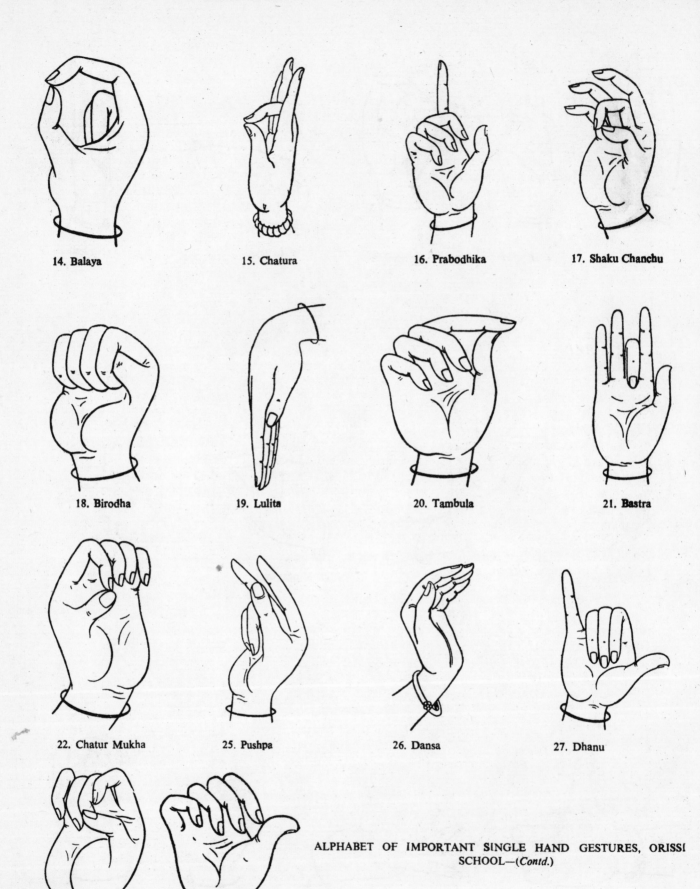

14. Balaya 15. Chatura 16. Prabodhika 17. Shaku Chanchu

18. Birodha 19. Lulita 20. Tambula 21. Bastra

22. Chatur Mukha 25. Pushpa 26. Dansa 27. Dhanu

28. Pechka Muka 29. Bardhamanaka

ALPHABET OF IMPORTANT SINGLE HAND GESTURES, ORISSI
SCHOOL—(*Contd.*)

12. *DOLA HASTA.* Same as *Dola*, Combined Hands No. 5 (Swing).
13. *SANKHA.* Same as *Sankha*, Combined Hands No. 12 (Conch).
14. *CHAKRA.* Same as *Cakra*, Combined Hands No. 13 (Discus).

There are about twelve other Combined Hand Gestures used in Orissi, which have been adapted and somewhat akin to the other Combined Hands of the Sanskrit classical treatises. These include some which have become traditional and are all peculiar to this school. The usage of these gestures with their meanings will be given when describing representative words of speech as illustrated in the actual dance in which they may be used.

15. *UBHAYA KARTARI.* Somewhat akin to *Kartari Svastika*, Combined Hands No. 10 of the classical treatises (Crossed Arrow Shafts).

16. *BADDHA MUSTI.* A traditional hand gesture of Orissi, somewhat like *Mushti* (Single Hands No. 9), but instead of the thumb being held over the four fingers that are closed into the palm, the thumb is held beside the closed first finger. In this gesture of Combined Hands, both hands use the same gesture.

17. *BARADA.* Another traditional hand gesture of Orissi, somewhat like *Pataka* (Single Hands No. 1), in that all the fingers and the thumb are stretched straight close together. But it is mainly in the position that this gesture differs. In the Combined use, both hands use the same gesture, are held slightly at a slant, with an almost imperceptible bend in the fingers.

18. *ASHRITA.* Here, the combined use of *Samdamsa* (Single Hands No. 25 of the Classical Sanskrit treatises) and *Sambhaba* of Orissi, in which the four fingers are close together and very slightly bent; the thumb is a little apart with a slight bend at the wrist. In the Combined Hands, therefore, the left hand is held in the second gesture of *Sambhaba* with the fingers pointing downwards, and the right hand in the first gesture of *Samdamsa* is held under it at the wrists. The right hand faces outwards with the fingers pointing upwards.

19. *ARCHEKA.* 20. *MESHA JUDDA.* 21. *POTALA.* 22. *SHIBAKARA.* 23. *KHATWA.* 24. *PRADIPA.* These six Combined Hand Gestures have been taken from the Sanskrit classical treatises and adapted to Orissi.

These are in the main the important hand gestures or the alphabet of language signs on which the Orissi classical dance forms its language of gestures for its actual performance. It will be interesting to study a few representative examples from this school too of some of the parts of speech as has been shown in the other schools of the dance.

USE OF HAND GESTURES IN ORISSI. Based on the Single and Combined Hands as Evolved in Their Alphabet of Language Signs

Proper Nouns

1. *BRAHMA.* In this, there is the combination of *Chatura* (Orissi Single Hands No. 15) and *Hamsasya* (Single Hands No. 23). The right hand in the second gesture, and the left hand in the first gesture, are held chest level, a little forward, palms facing outwards.

2. *VISHNU.* In this, both hands use the *Tri-pataka* (Single Hands No. 2). Both hands in this gesture are held at chest level, a little forward, with the palms facing outwards.

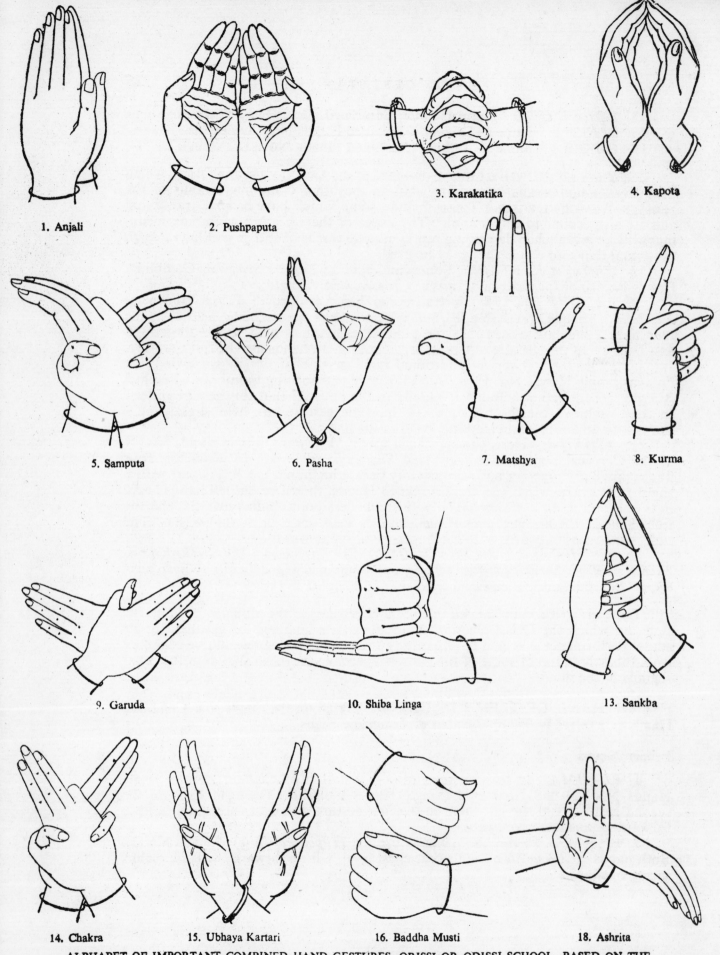

1. Anjali
2. Pushpaputa
3. Karakatika
4. Kapota
5. Samputa
6. Pasha
7. Matshya
8. Kurma
9. Garuda
10. Shiba Linga
13. Sankba
14. Chakra
15. Ubhaya Kartari
16. Baddha Musti
18. Ashrita

ALPHABET OF IMPORTANT COMBINED HAND GESTURES, ORISSI OR ODISSI SCHOOL. BASED ON THE
CLASSICAL SANSKRIT AND ORISSI TREATISES

3. *SHIVA*. In this, there is the combination of *Thrisula* or *Tri-pataka* (Single Hands No. 28 and No. 2 respectively) and *Mriga Sirsa* (Single Hands No. 17). The right hand in one of the first two gestures and the left hand in the third gesture are held chest level, a little forward, palms facing outwards.

4. *HIMALAYAS*. In this, both hands use the *Pataka* (Single Hands No. 1), corresponding to *Dhwaja* (Orissi Single Hands No. 1). The hands in this gesture are raised from the waist upwards to paint a mountain shape.

Nouns

1. *TREES*. In this, both hands use *Pataka* (Single Hands No. 1), corresponding to *Dhwaja* (Orissi Single Hands No. 1). Both hands in this gesture have the palms facing outwards; the hands are raised up in front and then separated.

2. *WOMAN*. In this, there is the combination of *Catura* (Single Hands No. 21), corresponding to *Chatura* (Orissi Single Hands No. 15) and *Hamsapaksha* (Single Hands No. 24). The right hand in the first gesture is held at chest level, a little forward, and the left hand in the second gesture is placed erect over the right hand, so that the edge of the left hand touches the edge of the palm of the right hand at the wrists.

3. *WORLD*. In this, there is the use of *Ardha-suchika* or *Ardha-suchi* (Single Hands No. 31). Only the right hand is used in this gesture, The palm is raised outwards and moved in a circle before the face.

4. *BIRD*. In this, there is the combination of *Ardha-chandra* (Single Hands No. 6), corresponding to *Ardha-chandra* (Orissi Single Hands No. 9) and *Kapitha* (Single Hands No. 11), corresponding to *Anukusha* (Orissi Single Hands No. 3). The right hand is in the first gesture, palm facing down; and the left hand is in the second gesture, placed erect on the right hand, wrists of both hands touching.

5. *PEACOCK*. In this, there is the combination of *Kapitha* (Single Hands No. 11), corresponding to *Anukusha* (Orissi Single Hands No. 3) and *Ala Padma* (Single Hands No. 20), corresponding to *Kshipta* (Orissi Single Hands No. 11). The left hand in the first gesture is held forwards, palm facing outwards. The right hand in the second gesture, is placed behind it, on the wrist. The palm of the right hand faces the back of the left hand, like a fantail of the bird.

6. *MOON* and *SUN*. In this, there is the combination of *Pataka* (Single Hands No. 1), corresponding to *Dhwaja* (Orissi Single Hands No. 1) and *Ardha-suchika* (Single Hands No. 31) for both words. The left hand in the first gesture is held forwards, palm facing upwards, and the right hand in the second gesture is held under it, so that the first finger points at the back of the left hand—this is for the moon. For the sun, the gesture is the same, except that the left hand is held palm facing downwards.

7. *LAMP*. In this, there is the combination of *Sarpa Sirsa* (Single Hands No. 16) and *Mushti* (Single Hands No. 9). The right hand in the first gesture is held with the palm facing upwards, resting on the top of the left hand, which is in the second gesture, the back of its fingers facing outwards.

Verbs

1. *IS*. In this, there is the use of *Ardha-suchi* (Single Hands No. 31). The right hand in this gesture is held with the palm facing outwards, and then taken forwards.

2. *AM, ARE.* In this, there is the use of *Pataka* (Single Hands No. 1), corresponding to *Dhwaja* (Orissi Single Hands No. 1). The right hand in this gesture is taken forward.

3. *SEEING.* In this, there is the use of *Kartari Mukha* (Single Hands No. 4). The right hand in this gesture is placed near the right eye, fingers pointing to it.

4. *NO.* In this, there is the use of *Pataka* (Single Hands No. 1), corresponding to *Dhwaja* (Orissi Single Hands No. 1). The right hand in this gesture, palm facing outwards, is trembled to indicate "No."

5. *HERE.* In this, there is the combination of *Ala Padma* (Single Hands No. 20), corresponding to *Kshipta* (Orissi Single Hands No. 11) and *Pataka* (Single Hands No. 1), corresponding to *Dhwaja* (Orissi Single Hands No. 1). The right hand in the second gesture and the left hand in the first gesture are held at chest level, a little forward, palms facing outwards.

6. *WITH, TOGETHER.* In this, there is the use of *Hamsa Paksha* (Single Hands No. 24). Both hands in this gesture are held at chest level, a little forward, facing each other.

7. *WALKING.* In this, there is the use of *Sarpa Sirsa* (Single Hands No. 16). Both hands in this gesture, palms facing slightly downwards, are moved forwards to indicate movement.

8. *LIVING, STAYING.* In this, there is the use of *Pataka* (Single Hands No. 1), corresponding to *Dhwaja* (Orissi Single Hands No. 1). Both hands in this gesture, palms facing down, are moved a little forward to indicate the act of staying or living.

Adjectives, Abstract Nouns

1. *BREEZE.* In this, there is the use of *Pataka* (Single Hands No. 1), corresponding to *Dhwaja* (Orissi Single Hands No. 1). Both hands in this gesture, in a trembling movement, are taken from behind to the front.

2. *COLOUR.* In this, there is the use of *Hamsa Paksha* (Single Hands No. 24) and *Sarpa Sirsa* (Single Hands No. 16). The right hand in the first gesture, and the left hand in the second gesture are held forwards, the palms facing outwards.

3. *INNOCENCE.* In this, there is the use of a combined gesture; either *Baddha Mushti* (Orissi Combined Hands No. 16) or *Samputa* (Combined Hands No. 14), corresponding to *Samputa* (Orissi Combined Hands No. 5). The hands in the first gesture are held in front, one below the other, with the back of the hands facing outwards. If the second gesture is used, then the hands are clasped and held at chest level, a little forward.

4. *GOOD, BEAUTIFUL.* In this, there is the use of *Hamsasya* (Single Hands No. 23), corresponding to *Mrugakshya* (Orissi Single Hands No. 8). The right hand in this gesture is held forwards to the right.

This is a representative set of examples of word signs from the Orissi or Odissi School of the dance, and emphasises the dramatic value in the *Abhinaya*. It will be seen that in forming these words, hand gestures as detailed basically in the Alphabet of Gestures in the classical treatises have been followed, as well as the alphabet as evolved by the Orissi *gurus*. In spite of the close adherence to the code of the classical treatises, it can be readily seen that in the formation of the words there are subtle differences between how they are formed and the

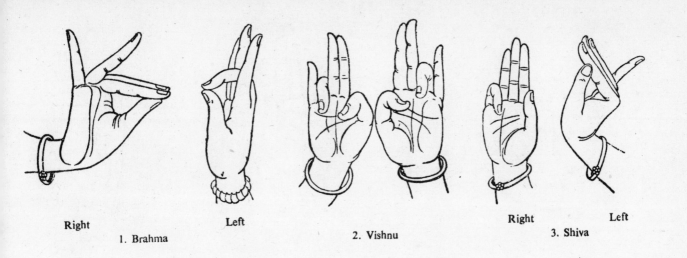

Right   Left

1. Brahma

2. Vishnu

Right   Left

3. Shiva

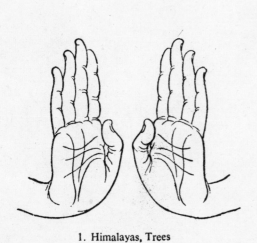

1. Himalayas, Trees

2. Woman

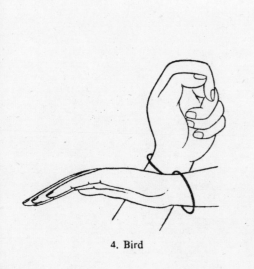

4. Bird

5. Peacock

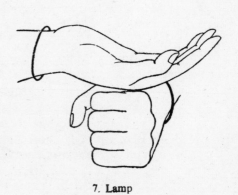

7. Lamp

ORISSI OR ODISSI—SOME EXAMPLES OF THE HAND GESTURES USED WHEN EXPRESSING VARIOUS PARTS OF SPEECH BASED ON THE ALPHABETS (SINGLE AND COMBINED) OF THE ORISSI SCHOOL

1. Is

2. Am, Are, No

Seeing

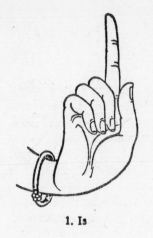

Right

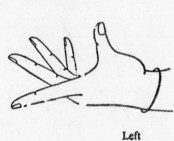

5. Here

Left

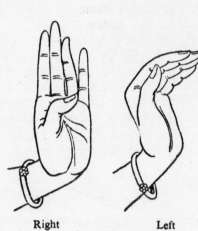

Right

2. Colour

Left

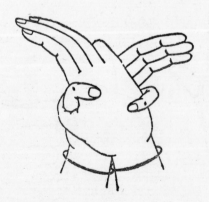

3. Innocence

4. Good, Beautiful

ORISSI OR ODISSI—SOME MORE EXAMPLES OF THE HAND GESTURES USED WHEN EXPRESSING
VARIOUS PARTS OF SPEECH

usage as adapted in the word formation of the other classical schools. This variety in evolving a language word code from the basic Alphabet of Hand Gestures of the classical treatises by each style of the dance, gives both richness and a diversity of character to the art of the dance in India as a whole.

In the Kuchipudi school of the classical dance, the basic Alphabet of Hand Gestures utilized for evolving its own language of signs, is taken from the *Natya Sastra* by Bharata Muni, the *Abhinaya Dharpana* by Nandikeshwara, and the famous 13th century A.D. treatise written on palm leaves, the *Nritta Ratnavali* by Jayapa Senani. In addition, traditional hand gestures have been evolved by the *gurus* to suit particular needs and handed down to their pupils through the generations. Therefore, the sources from which the hand gestures of the Kuchipudi school have been evolved provide detailed and comprehensive material for the highly dramatic interpretation of the dance dramas.

In this context, it will be noticed here again, that with the additional and different material from which the hand gestures have been evolved, in this school of the dance, the gestures denoting various proper names, nouns and other parts of speech necessarily differ from the grammar of word signs as used in Bharata Natyam of Tamil Nad and the other classical schools. It will be interesting to note some representative examples of various words as used in Kuchipudi, for their language of gesture.

KUCHIPUDI USE OF HAND GESTURES FOR ITS LANGUAGE SIGNS

Proper Nouns

1. *BRAHMA*. In this, there is a combination of *Hamsasya* (Swan Face, Single Hands No. 23) and *Catura* (Semi-circle, Single Hands No. 21). The right hand in the first gesture with the palm facing outwards is held in front at chest level, and the left hand in the second gesture is held close beside it.
2. *VISHNU*. In this, there is the use of *Tri-pataka* (Single Hands No. 2) with both hands. Both hands in this gesture are held forwards with the palms facing outwards.
3. *SHIVA*. In this there is the combined use of *Tri-pataka* (Single Hands No. 2) and *Mriga Sirsa* (Deer Head, Single Hands No. 17). The right hand in the first gesture and the left hand in the second gesture are held forwards with the palms facing outwards.
4. *SURYA*. In this, there is the combination of *Kapitha* (Elephant Apple, Single Hands No. 11) and *Sola Padma* (Full Blown Lotus, Single Hands No. 20). The right hand in the first gesture and the left hand in the second gesture are held forwards.
5. *HIMALAYAS*. In this, there is the use of *ALA PADAMA* (Single Hands No. 20) with both hands. Both hands in this gesture are crossed and raised in front.

Nouns

1. *TREES*. In this, there is the use of *Pataka* (The Flag, Single Hands No. 1) with both hands. Both hands in this gesture are raised crossing one another.
2. *WOMAN*. In this, *Mriga Sirsa* (Deer Head, Single Hands No. 17) is

used in the right hand only. The right hand in this gesture is held shoulder level, palm facing sideways, and then brought forwards.

3. *PEACOCK*. In this, there is the use of *Mayura* (Peacock, Single Hands No. 5). The left hand in this gesture is held forwards to indicate the head and beak of the bird.

4. *STAR*. In this, there is the use of *Tri-pataka* (Three Parts of the Flag, Single Hands No. 2) with one hand only. The left hand in this gesture is held a little forward and raised, and then moved from the front to the side.

5. *MOON*. In this, there is the use of *Chandrakala* (Digit of the Moon, Single Hands No. 14) with one hand only. The left hand in this gesture is held raised slightly at a slant to the left, indicating the shape of the half moon.

Verbs, Adverbs and Other Parts of Speech

1. *IS*. In this, there is the use of *Hamsasya* (Swan Face, Single Hands No. 23) with one hand only. The right hand in this gesture is held slightly at a slant at chest level and forwards, with the fingers pointing outwards.

2. *AM, ARE*. In this, there is the use of *Hamsa Paksha* (Swan Feather, Single Hands No. 24) with one hand only. The left hand in this gesture is held forwards at a slant.

3. *THAT*. In this, there is the use of *Pataka* (The Flag, Single Hands No. 1) with one hand only. The right hand in this gesture is taken forwards from in front at chest level, with the palm facing downwards.

4. *THERE*. In this, there is the use of *Ardha-chandra* (Half Moon, Single Hands No. 6) with one hand only. The left hand in this gesture is held at chest level, palm facing outwards, and as though indicating "there."

5. *SEEING*. In this, there is the use of *Kartari Mukha* (Face of the Arrow Shaft, Single Hands No. 4) with both hands, which in this gesture are placed side by side, palms facing downwards, and are taken forwards to eye level.

6. *NO*. In this, there is the use of *Pataka* (The Flag, Single Hands No. 1) with both hands, which in this gesture are moved to and fro from side to side indicating "No."

7. *HERE*. In this, there is the use of *Catura* (Semi-circle, Single Hands No. 21) with one hand only. The left hand in this gesture is moved forwards with the palm facing downwards at a slant.

8. *WITH, TOGETHER*. In this, there is the use of *Kartari Mukha* (Face of the Arrow Shaft, Single Hands No. 4) with both hands, which in this gesture are held forwards facing each other.

9. *WALKING*. In this, there is the use of *Catura* (Semi-circle, Single Hands No. 21) with both hands, which in this gesture are held a little forward, and then the right hand is moved a little further forwards, to indicate "movement."

10. *GIVE ME*. In this, there is the use of *Mukula* (Bud, Single Hands No. 26) with one hand only. The right hand in this gesture, with the finger tips pointing upwards, is taken from forward towards the chest.

Abstract Nouns, Nouns

1. *GOLD, RICHES*. In this, there is the combined use of *Pataka* (The Flag, Single Hands No. 1) and *Kapitha* (Elephant Apple, Single Hands No. 11). The right hand in the first gesture is held with the palm facing outwards, and the

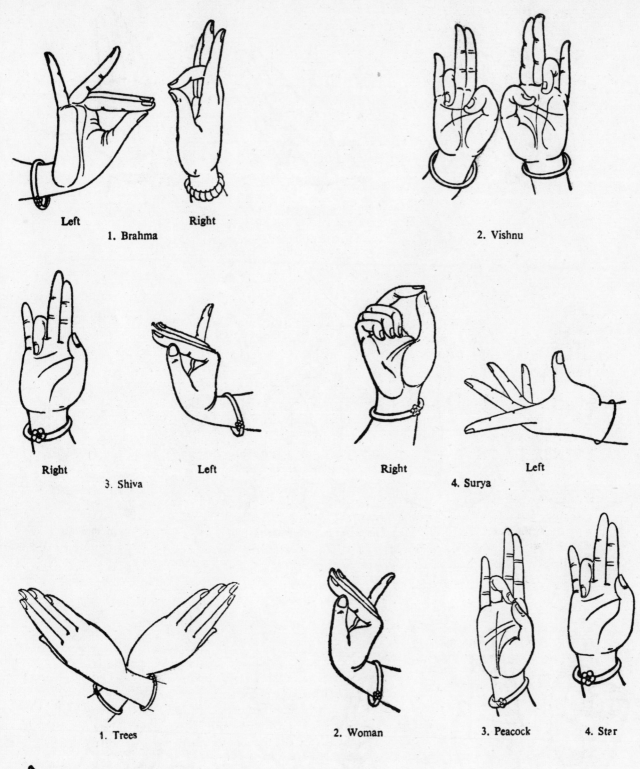

Left   Right

1. Brahma

2. Vishnu

Right   Left

3. Shiva

Right   Left

4. Surya

1. Trees

2. Woman

3. Peacock

4. Star

5. Moon

KUCHIPUDI—SOME EXAMPLES OF THE HAND GESTURES USED WHEN EXPRESSING VARIOUS PARTS OF SPEECH. BASED ON THE ALPHABETS (SINGLE AND COMBINED) OF THE CLASSICAL TREATISES

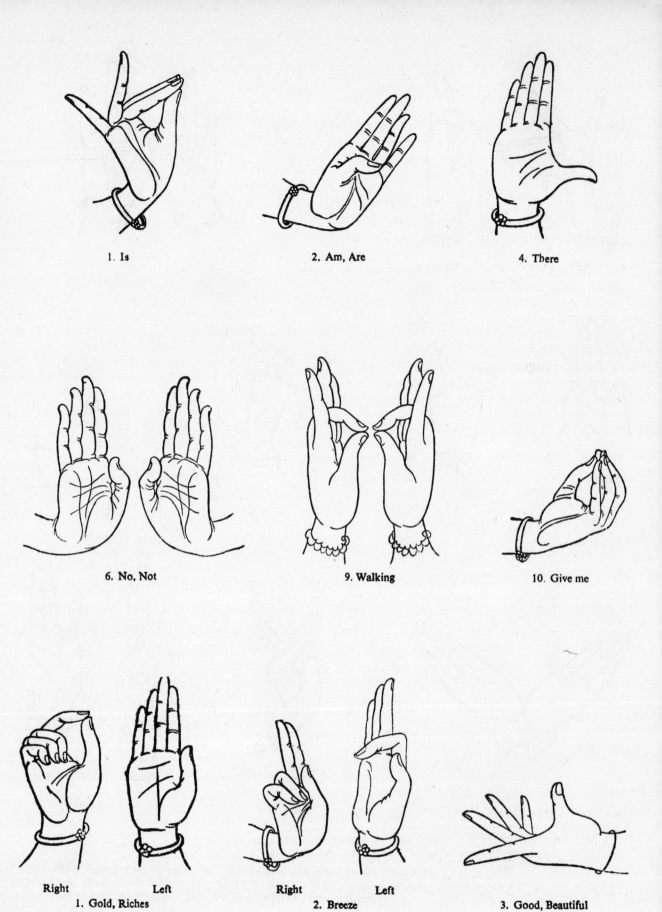

1. Is   2. Am, Are   4. There

6. No, Not   9. Walking   10. Give me

Right   Left   Right   Left

1. Gold, Riches   2. Breeze   3. Good, Beautiful

KUCHIPUDI—SOME MORE EXAMPLES OF THE HAND GESTURES USED WHEN EXPRESSING VARIOUS PARTS OF SPEECH.—(Contd.)

left hand in the second gesture is moved from beside it a little forwards.

2. *BREEZE.*   In this, there is the combined use of *Arala* (Bent, Single Hands No. 7) and *Ardha-pataka* (Half Flag, Single Hands No. 3).   The right hand in the first gesture is held forwards, and the left hand in the second gesture is held beside it.

3. *GOOD, BEAUTIFUL.*   In this, there is the use of *Ala Padma* (Lotus, Single Hands No. 20) with one hand only.   The right hand in this gesture, with the palm facing upwards, is taken forwards.

The Kuchipudi school of the dance as has been explained is a highly dramatic style, and therefore these hand gestures vividly express with posture, arm and bodily movements and facial expression all that they wish to expound in their *Abhinayam.*   In describing the grammar of gestures used in the various schools, it must be emphasised here once again, that just the actual basic gestures used have been explained, mainly to show how differently each school has evolved its own mode of language signs.   It must at all times be remembered that these gestures only take on full meaning when accompanied by the correct arm and bodily movements, posture and facial expressions.   The gestures in themselves are like mere words in a language, but when the arms are moved or cast about, the whole body takes its postures and mobility, and the face is illuminated with the relevant expressions, then alone do the gestures become lucid and meaningful. Just as when words are meaningfully placed in a sentence and supported by significant expression of tone and features, they carry a world of comprehension.

In the dance of Manipur, they have followed the important treatise of Manipur the *Govinda Sangeeta Leelavilasa,* believed to have been written by Maharaja Bhagyachandra of Manipur.   I shall give here the gestures forming the alphabet of language signs totalling twenty-five in number as given in the above manuscript.   And show some of the differences and varied meanings found in this school, adding yet another distinctive attraction to the language of gestures.

ALPHABET OF SINGLE HANDS IN THE MANIPUR DANCE

1. *PATAKA.*   Similar to *Pataka* (Single Hands No. 1).   It is used to express to strike, deny, to smother, letter, to defend, playing the drum, to roll, long hair, wall, fan, scripture, peacock feathered crown, to level.

2. *TRI-PATAKA.*   Similar to *Kartari Mukha* (Single Hands No. 4).   It is used to express flame, to put a mark on the forehead, to comb the hair, tears, to close the ears.

3. *ARDHA-PATAKA.*   Similar to *Ardha-pataka* (Single Hands No. 3).   It is used to express similar, axe, mountain top.

4. *KHATAKA MUKHA.*   Peculiar to Manipur dance.   The little finger is stretched, the third finger is bent forwards, the middle finger is bent into the palm, and the first finger and thumb touch at the tips.   It is used to express arrow, to show a diamond, to churn butter, earrings, to tie something, garland, to thresh, to weave.

5. *SAMDANSHA.*   Peculiar to Manipur dance.   The second, third and little fingers are stretched straight apart, and the first finger touches the thumb at the tip.   It is used to express Soul, to paint, beautiful, to pluck, to indicate the colour of any part of the body, necklace, to play the flute.

6. *MRIGA SHIRSA*. Similar to *Simha Mukha* (Single Hands No. 18). It is used to express deer, head of an elephant, an animal.

7. *HANSASYA*. Similar to *Hamsasya*, (Single Hands No. 23), except that the third finger is stretched straight. It is used to express to spin, to speak, soft, to sprinkle, head of a swan, to gather flowers.

8. *ALAPALLAVA*. Similar to *Ala Padma* (Single Hands No. 20). It is used to express full blown lotus, to denote a beautiful person, to ask.

9. *BHRUNGA*. Similar to *Bhramara* (Single Hands No. 22), except that the third and little fingers are stretched straight and a little apart. It is used to express the bee, to hold a flower by the stem, earrings.

10. *ANKUSHA*. Similar to *Arala* (Single Hands No. 7), except that the first finger and thumb touch at the tips. It is used to express a musical instrument, nectar, to control an elephant, blessings.

11. *ARDHA-CHANDRA*. Similar to *Ardha-chandra* (Single Hands No. 6). It is used to express half moon, neck, to show different parts of the human body, the sun's rays, to make a hair knot, flow of a river, to hold a child.

12. *KORAKA*. Similar to *Mukula* (Single Hands No. 26). It is used to express bud, kiss, mouthful, woman, offering, banana flower.

13. *MUSHTHI*. Similar to *Mushti* (Single Hands No. 9). It is used to express holding a spear, a stick, a sword, hair, to show pain, to hit, to squeeze, fate, destiny.

14. *ANKURA*. Similar to *Ardha-suchi* (Single Hands No. 31), except that the thumb touches the first finger at the first joint. It is used to express playing the *Veena*, little, pen, sprout, to milk the cow, to play cymbals, to swing.

15. *SHARDULASHAYA*. Similar to *Urnanabha* (Single Hands No. 29). It is used to express a ball, claws of a tiger, to tear.

16. *KANGULA*. Similar to *Langula* (Single Hands No. 19). It is used to express to eat a small fruit, to hold a child at the chin, fireplace.

17. *THRISHULA*. Peculiar to Manipur dance. The first, second and third fingers are stretched straight and apart, and the thumb tip is held over the nail of the little finger. It is used to express the trident, the Three Worlds, Shiva.

18. *KARTARI MUKHA*. Peculiar to Manipur dance. The first and second fingers are stretched straight together, and the thumb tip is placed over the first joints of the third and little fingers which are bent to almost touch the palm of the hand. It is used to express the eyes, the mark (*tilak*) on the forehead, to point out an object, winding path, lightning, go away, a cot, love, to apply the henna on the feet.

19. *SUCHI MUKHA*. Peculiar to Manipur dance. The second, third and little fingers are bent towards the palm of the hand, the first finger is stretched straight, and the thumb touches the second finger at the tip. It is used to express a stick, bracelet, smile, pillar, a budding plant, to apply eye shadow, thin, similar, to think, to mark a spot.

20. *PADMAKOSHA*. Similar to *Padmakosa* (Single Hands No. 15). It is used to express a semi-blossomed flower, a bunch of flowers, a branch bending with flowers.

21. *SHIKHARA*. Similar to *Sikhara* (Single Hands No. 10). It is used to express steadfast, to hold a bow, to drink, Shivalinga (the symbolic emblem of Lord Shiva), to churn, a bell, the teeth of an asura (demon).

22. *HANSA PAKSHA*. Similar to *Mriga Sirsa* (Single Hands No. 17). It

is used to express the forehead, wings, height, to look, to wait, to hear, far away, bashfulness, to apply an armlet, to embrace.

23. *AHITUNDA.* Similar to *Sarpa Sirsa* (Single Hands No. 16). It is used to express holding water, making an offering, a snake, a person of very small stature.

24. *CHATURA.* Peculiar to Manipur dance. The four fingers are stretched straight together, and the thumb touches the third finger at the base. It is used to express a measure to receive, a ceremonial lamp, to surrender.

25. *DHENU.* Peculiar to Manipur dance. The first, second and third fingers are bent parallel to the palm of the hand, and the thumb and little finger are stretched straight. It is used to express a cow, nearness, to play dice, to play the *Veena*, to speak softly, to walk.

From these 25 Single Hands or *Hastas*, 12 important Combined Hands are formed for use and adaptation in the dance of Manipur.

ALPHABET OF COMBINED HANDS IN THE MANIPUR DANCE

1. *SHANKHA.* The thumb of the right hand is held under the four fingers of the left hand, the three fingers of the right hand are stretched straight and the tips touch the stretched thumb of the left hand. It is used to express the conch shell, the throat.

2. *CHAKRA.* All the fingers and thumbs of both hands are stretched straight and apart, and the palms are held against each other, with the little finger of the right hand crossing the first finger of the left hand and the thumb touching at the wrist. It is used to express a wheel.

3. *ANJALI.* Similar to *Anjali* (Combined Hands No. 1). It is used to express greeting, salutation.

4. *TARKSHYA.* The *Dhenu* (Manipur Single Hands No. 25) in both hands. The hands are crossed and the little fingers are entwined. It is used to express the Garuda or eagle, love.

5. *PASHA.* Similar to *Pasa* (Combined Hands No. 15), except that the hands are not crossed at the wrists. It is used to express a quarrel, love, a chain, bondage, betrayed.

6. *KARKATA.* The two hands are clasped, so that the fingers of each hand overlap on the back of the other, and the thumbs cross each other as they overlap. It is used to express sorrow, sadness, anxiety, a hut.

7. *SAMPUTA.* Similar to *Karkata* (Combined Hands No. 3). It is used to express sorrow, to close something, to squeeze.

8. *RAMBHASUMA.* Similar to *Pushpaputa* (Combined Hands No. 6). It is used to express the spire of the temple, to accept graciously something covered.

9. *PUSHPAPUTA.* Similar to *Kapota* (Combined Hands No. 2). It is used to express to hold flowers, and offering, to beg, to invoke.

10. *KOKILA.* Similar to *Garuda* (Combined Hands No. 19). It is used to express the cuckoo, trembling heart.

11. *SWASTIKA,* Similar to *Svastika* (Combined Hands No. 4). It is used to express symbol over the Forest Deity's temple, feeling cold, feeling shy.

12. *SHUKA.* The right hand is in *Dhenu* (Manipur Single Hands No. 25), and the left hand has the second, third and little fingers bent, with the thumb

touching the tip of the second finger, and the first finger is crooked. The hands are crossed at the wrists. It is used to express a bird.

These are the elements of the basic Alphabet of Hand Gestures or language signs on which the dance of Manipur forms its own language of gestures as used in the dance. Single and Combined alphabets are utilized to the fullest degree for expression and in the dance itself.

USE OF HAND GESTURES IN THE MANIPUR DANCE. Taken from Their Own Alphabet of Gestures

Nouns

1. *EARRINGS.* In this, both the hands are used in *Khataka Mukha* (Manipur Single Hands No. 4). Both the hands in this gesture are held near the lobe of the ear, with the right hand palm facing left and the left hand palm facing right, the left hand a little below the right.

2. *LOTUS.* The right hand in the gesture of *Alapallava* (Manipur Single Hands No. 8) is held a little forward, chest level, with the palm facing upwards.

3. *CONCH-SHELL.* Use is made of *Shankha* (Manipur Combined Hands No. 1).

4. *SRI KRISHNA.* In this, both the hands are used in *Samdansha* (Manipur Single Hands No. 5). The left hand in this gesture, with the palm facing right, is held near the lips; and the right hand in the same gesture, the palm facing outwards, is held at shoulder level. Both hands have the fingers pointing upwards. It indicates the playing of the flute.

5. *BEE COMING TO THE BUD.* In this, there is the combined use of *Koraka* (Manipur Single Hands No. 12) and *Bhrunga* (Manipur Single Hands No. 9). The left hand in the first gesture is held at chest level, a little forward, with the finger tips facing right; and the right hand in the second gesture is held a little above it, the finger tips towards the finger tips of the left hand.

6. *FLOWERS FOR THE HAIR.* In this, both hands are used in *Samdansha* (Manipur Single Hands No. 5) The hands are held near the side of the knot of the hair, the palms of the hands facing each other.

7. *BIRD.* Use is made of the *Kokila* (Manipur Combined Hands No. 10).

8. *WHEEL.* Use is made of *Chakra* (Manipur Combined Hands No. 2).

Parts of Speech

1. *WHY.* In this, there is the use of *Alapallava* (Manipur Single Hands No. 8). The right hand in this gesture is held at chest level, a little forward, with the palm facing upwards, to indicate asking a question.

2. *OFFERING.* Use is made of *Pushpaputa* (Manipur Combined Hands No. 9).

3. *JOY.* Both hands in this are used in *Alapallava* (Manipur Single Hands No. 8). Both hands in this gesture are held at forehead level, the palms facing the forehead, about a foot apart.

4. *LITTLE.* In this, there is the use of *Ankura* (Manipur Single Hands No. 14). The right hand in this gesture is held with the palm up, a little forward, fingers pointing at a slant.

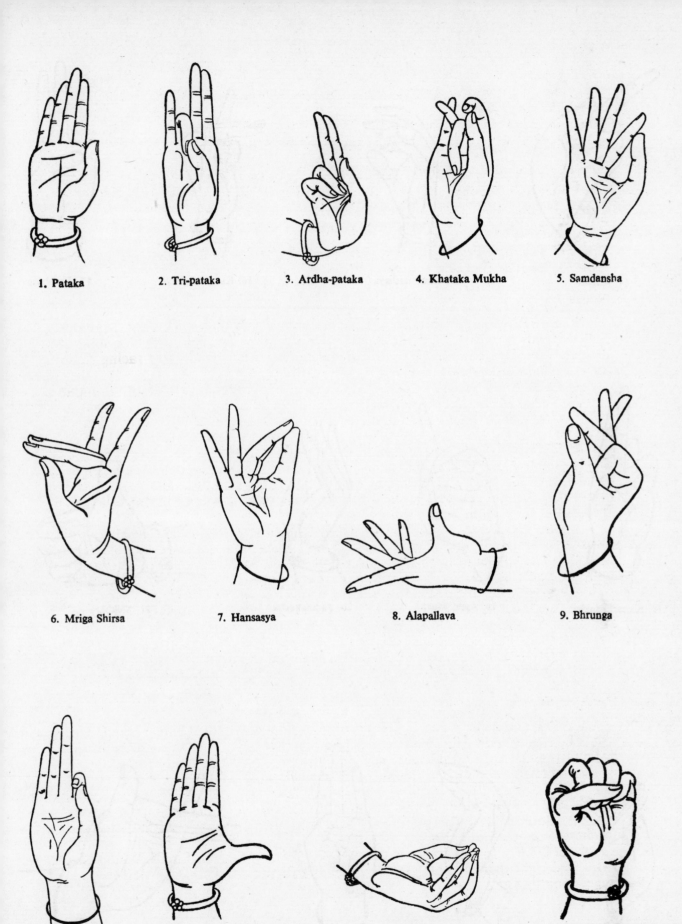

1. Pataka   2. Tri-pataka   3. Ardha-pataka   4. Khataka Mukha   5. Samdansha

6. Mriga Shirsa   7. Hansasya   8. Alapallava   9. Bhrunga

10. Ankusha   11. Ardha-chandra   12. Koraka   13. Mushthi

ALPHABET OF SINGLE HAND GESTURES, MANIPURI SCHOOL. BASED ON THE IMPORTANT TREATISE OF
MANIPUR, *THE GOVINDA SANGEETA LEELAVILASA*

14. Ankura

15. Shardulashaya

16. Kangula

17. Thrishula

18. Kartari Mukha

19. Suchi Mukha

20. Padmakosha

21. Shikhara

22. Hansa Paksha

23. Ahitunda

24. Chatura

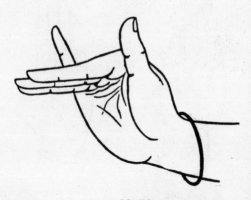

25. Dhenu

ALPHABET OF SINGLE HAND GESTURES, MANIPURI SCHOOL—(*Contd.*)

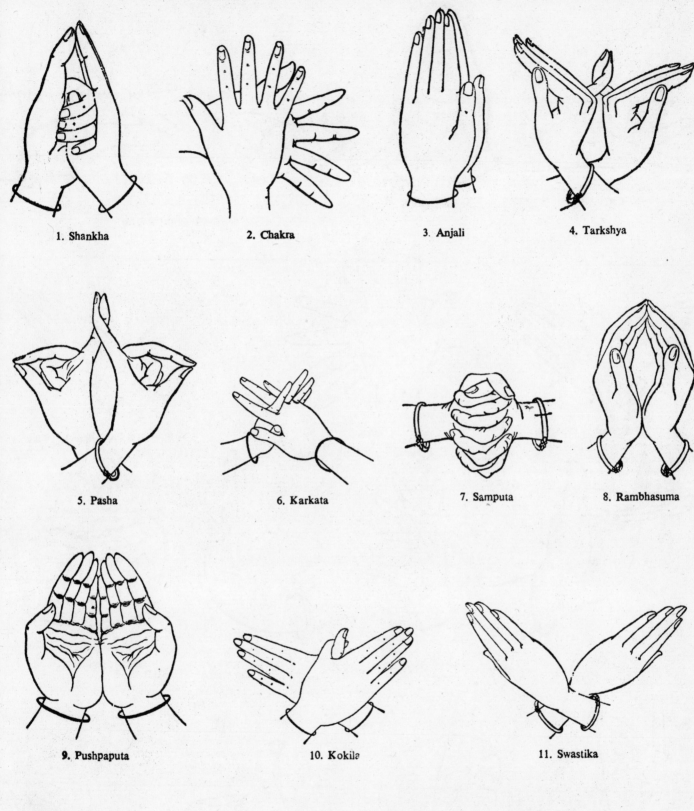

1. Shankha   2. Chakra   3. Anjali   4. Tarkshya

5. Pasha   6. Karkata   7. Samputa   8. Rambhasuma

9. Pushpaputa   10. Kokila   11. Swastika

12. Shuka

ALPHABET OF COMBINED HAND GESTURES, MANIPURI SCHOOL. BASED ON THE IMPORTANT TREATISE OF MANIPUR, *THE GOVINDA SANGEETA LEELAVILASA*

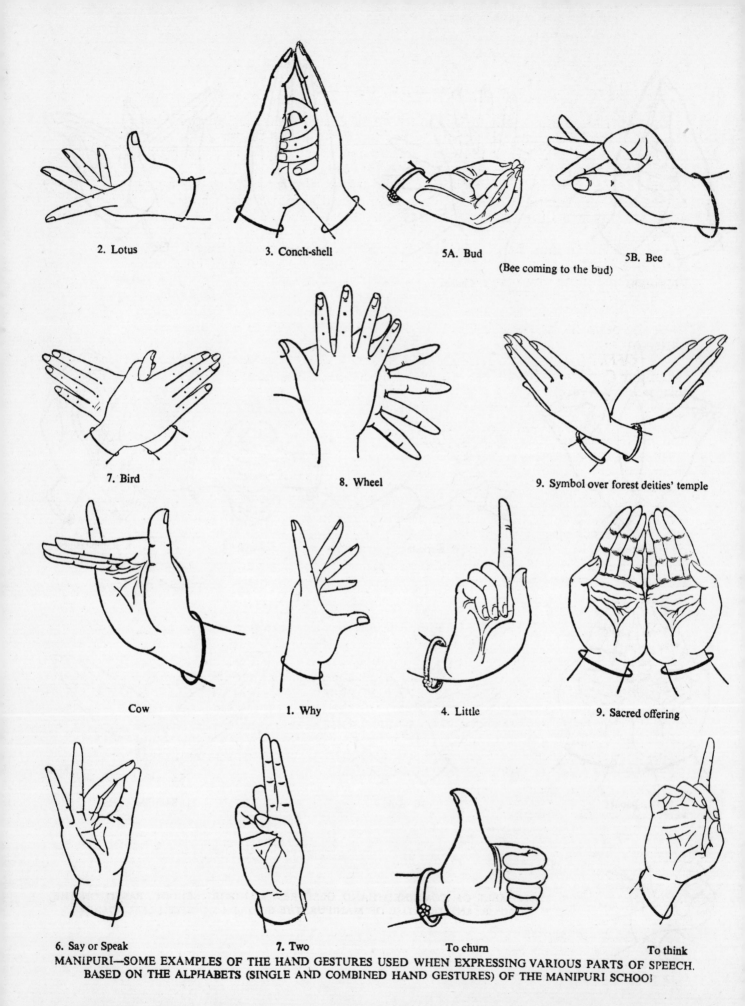

2. Lotus

3. Conch-shell

5A. Bud

5B. Bee

(Bee coming to the bud)

7. Bird

8. Wheel

9. Symbol over forest deities' temple

Cow

1. Why

4. Little

9. Sacred offering

6. Say or Speak

7. Two

To churn

To think

MANIPURI—SOME EXAMPLES OF THE HAND GESTURES USED WHEN EXPRESSING VARIOUS PARTS OF SPEECH. BASED ON THE ALPHABETS (SINGLE AND COMBINED HAND GESTURES) OF THE MANIPURI SCHOOI!

5. *WALK*. Both hands in this are used in *Dhenu* (Manipur Single Hands No. 25). The left hand in this gesture is held at chest level, with the palm facing down; and the right hand in the same gesture and in the same position is held a little forward, to indicate the action of going forwards.

6. *SAY or SPEAK*. In this, there is the use of *Hansasya* (Manipur Single Hands No. 7). The right hand in this gesture is held at mouth level, a little forward and taken a little further forwards, to indicate words coming out of the mouth.

7. *TWO*. In this, there is the use of *Kartari Mukha* (Manipur Single Hands No. 19). The right hand in this gesture is held a little forward, chest level, with the fingers pointing upwards.

8. *BEAUTIFUL AS THE MOON*. In this, there is the use of *Ardha-chandra* (Manipur Single Hands No. 11). The right hand in this gesture is held at chest level, the palm facing the chest, and slightly moved forwards to indicate a comparison.

9. *OFFERING SOMETHING*. Use is made of the gesture *Rambhasuma* (Manipur Combined Hands No. 8), with the hands in this gesture held a little forward, chest level.

These are some examples of how hand gestures are utilised in the actual dance and the *Abhinaya* in the Manipur school of the classical dance. Manipur incorporates these hand gestures into the fine soft undulating movements, weaving them beautifully into a pattern of gentle sway of the body and arms, and with explicit facial expressions. There is a gracious flow of the entire body, and limbs, head, and use of arms with these hand gestures, expressing between them the mood, the sentiment and the theme to be interpreted.

We can see these hand gestures shown to their fullest expression in the *Abhisars* of the various Ras Lilas, where there is the portrayal of emotional interpretation. The Radha-Krishna Idylls, with their parable stories, are indeed perfect themes for the use of these hand gestures that so aptly explain each phase of the dance dramas.

Previously I have mentioned that *Abhinaya* or emotional interpretation is fourfold, namely, *Angika*, *Sattvika*, *Vachika* and *Aharya*. As the dancer does her *Abhinaya*, translating the text of the song or lyric or dramatic passages into dance expression, she walks gracefully in certain prescribed modes as directed by a simple rhythm. She uses her arms in the manner to confirm with the style of the dance and as taught by the *gurus*. For the facial expressions, there are certain fundamental technical aids that she must learn in order to help her achieve perfection of mood and aid the gestural language. Expressions of the face, and head, eyes, eyebrows, and neck movements, play their part in assisting this dramatic side of the dance to produce the maximum effect.

10. Face, Head, Eyes, Eyebrows and Neck

THE BEAUTY of the technique of the Indian Dance is enhanced by what may well be termed "The Technique of Mood." Expression is not left to the personal interpretation of the dancer alone; the ecstasy of joy, sorrow, anger, serenity, worship, and indeed the whole gamut of human emotions, has no doubt to be felt from within, but this alone is not sufficient. A certain recognised technique, equivalent to that studied for dramatic art, has to be cultivated and learned. In this way, natural emotional talent is assisted and given its best scope. The human features are trained no less than the eyes, the eyebrows, the head, and muscles, in order that they can take on immediately the relevant expression required for the particular mood. For this technical training of the emotional side of the dance, a method of certain facial expressions relating to various moods, head and neck movements, and play of the eyes and eyebrows, have been evolved and detailed in the great ancient treatises, particularly the *Natya Sastra* by Bharata Muni and the *Abhinaya Dharpana* by Nandikeshwara.

This art of expression is known as *Abhinaya* and is fourfold as mentioned previously, namely:

ANGIKA: Expression through the limbs and body.
SATTVIKA: Mental expression of feeling and emotion by facial expression and the use of the eyes.
VACHIKA: Expression through the voice.
AHARYA: Expression through dress, ornaments and other aids.

In the Kathakali dance dramas of Kerala, this detail of emotional exhibition is raised to a fine art. Every muscle of the face is trained to move at will. The cheeks sag and become hollow at the feeling of sorrow; the lips curl up and down according to the mood expressed; the cheek muscles literally dance with varying

144

emotions; while with anger, the whole face seems to quiver with agitation, just as it does with laughter.   The eyebrows are moved at a maddening speed, reaching a high degree of mobility or can just quiver as gently as a butterfly's wing, and they can be made to tremble as the dancer expresses any emotion.   The eyes can roll and twinkle and blaze at a moment's notice.   And all the time, these technical aids to expression help the dancer keep even the muscles and eyes and eyebrows, the neck and head, moving in perfect harmony with the rhythmic timing of the other bodily movements and the time beats.

In the other classical schools of the dance too, there has to be this meticulous training for expression, though not to such a great extent as in Kathakali.   From the few examples of face, head, eye and eyebrow and neck movements as described in the classical Sanskrit treatises explained here, it will be possible to realise the intricacies of the requirements for perfect *Abhinaya*.

FACIAL EXPRESSIONS

There are nine Facial Expressions that are taught by means of training of the muscles.

1.	SHRINGA	..	..	..	..	Love
2.	VIR	..	..	..	..	Valour
3.	KARUNA	..	..	..	..	Compassion
4.	HASYA	..	..	..	..	Contempt
5.	ALIRIDHA	..	..	..	..	Wonder
6.	BHAYANA	..	..	..	..	Fear
7.	BHIBHALSA	..	..	..	..	Repulsion
8.	DRYNDRA	..	..	..	..	Wrath
9.	SHANTA	..	..	..	..	Peace

HEAD MOVEMENTS.   There are Twenty-four Head Movements

1. *SAMA* (Level).   Not moving, not bent nor raised.   It is used for expressing the beginning of the dance, at prayer, when being authoritative, satisfied, showing anger, indifference.

2. *UDVAHITA* (Raised).   Raising the head and keeping it still, is used when expressing a flat object, the moon, the firmament, a mountain, flying things, anything tall.

3. *ADHOMUAKA* (Face inclined).   The head is bent, and is used when expressing modesty, sorrow, bowing, regarding anything, fainting, bathing.

4. *ALOLITA* (Rolling).   The head is moved in a circle, and is used when expressing sleeplessness, intoxication, faintness, hesitation, laughter.

5. *DHUTA* (Shaken).   The head is turned from right to left and left to right, to and fro.   It is used when expressing denial, looking repeatedly at things, astonishment, dismay, rejection, impatience.

6. *KAMPITA* (Nodded).   Shaking the head up and down   It is used when expressing indignation, enquiry, threatening, summoning, calling.

7. *PARAVRITTA* (Turned round).   The head is turned aside.   It is used when expressing "do this," aversion, modesty, disdain, quivering, trembling, dislike, refraining.

8. *UTKSIPTA* (Tossed).   Turning the head aside and upwards.   It is used

when expressing "take this," indication, cherishing, assent, some divine things, respect, awe, wonder, honour.

9. *PARIVAHITA* (Wagging). The head is moved from side to side like a fan. It is used when expressing being in love, yearning, yearning for the beloved, gratification, reflection, pleasure, happiness, contentment, anticipation, satisfaction.

10. *ANCITA* (Bending). Bending the head slowly to one side. It is used when expressing swooning, sorrow, pain, anguish, grief, pity, disappointment.

11. *NIHANCITA* (Elevating). Elevating the shoulder, the head slightly touching it, the eyebrows arched. It is used when expressing affectation, affection, self-restraint, dignity, tenderness, pride.

12. *VIDHUTA* (Moving quickly). Moving the head quickly to and fro. It is used when expressing cold, heat, fear, distant, keeping aloof.

13. *ADHUTA* (Slightly raising). The head is raised slightly and turned sharply. It is used when expressing dignity, utility, looking at oneself, studying, impressing pride.

14. *AVADHUTA* (Inclining). The head is inclined sharply. It is used when expressing "stay here," asking a question, stop, listen, hark!

15. *AKAMPTA* (Raising). The head is raised high and shaken slowly. It is used when expressing enquiry, instructions, narration, telling, explaining, verifying.

16. *LOLITA* (Head moved round). The head is moved round freely. It is used when expressing the offering of flowers, devotion, gift giving.

17. *TIRYONNATANNATA* (Up and down). The head is moved up and down. It is used when expressing indifference, solitude, independence.

18. *SKANDHANTA* (Resting). The head is rested on the shoulder. It is used when expressing sleep, anxiety, fainting, rest, tiredness.

19. *ARATRIKA* (Turning). Turning the head towards both sides and just touching the shoulders. It is used when expressing astonishment, amazement, wonder, justice, straight-forwardness.

20. *PARSVABHIMUKA* (Turned aside). The head is turned aside. It is used when expressing looking at persons from one side, glancing sideways, shyness.

21. *SAUMYA* (Motionless). The head is held motionless. It is used when expressing the beginning of the dance.

22. *TIRASCINA* (Looking up). Looking up on both sides. It is used when expressing the showing of modesty when dancing and in dances.

23. *PRAKAMPITA* (Moving all sides). The head is waved about and repeatedly moved forward and to and fro, to both sides. It is used when expressing a song, something marvellous, a theme, wonderful.

24. *SAMDARYA* (Elegance). Moving the head so as to look up and down with the trunk of the body bent. It is used when expressing a cause, a reason, understanding, answer.

Simultaneously with the study of these twenty-four Head Movements and their use in the dance, the dancer learns the corresponding Eye Movements. There are in all twenty-six eye glances.

EYE MOVEMENTS. There are Twenty-six Eye Movements

1. *SAMA* (Level). Gazing without winking. It is used when expressing surprise, or is the expression shown at the beginning of a dance.

2. *ALOKITA* (Inspecting). Swiftly turning with keen glances. It is used when expressing the emotion of strong desires.

3. *SUCI or SUCHI* (Side-long). Looking out of the corners of the eyes and not moving the head. It is used when expressing a secret purpose.

4. *PRALOKITA* (Swiftness). Turning the eyes from side to side. It is used when expressing looking at things on both sides, making signs.

5. *NIMILITA* (Closed). The eyes are half closed. It is used when expressing prayer, meditation, greeting.

6. *ULOKITA* (Looking up). Directing the glances keenly up and then aside. It is used when expressing moonlight, heights, the mountains, anything high above.

7. *ANUVRITTA* (Following). Darting the glance quickly up and down. It is used when expressing anger, friendly invitation.

8. *AVALOKITA* (Looking down). The glances are cast down. It is used when expressing a shadow, reflection, study.

9. *SNIGDHA* (Tender). A sweet and tender glance. It is used when expressing affection, joy, pleasure, anticipation, love.

10. *SRINGARA* (Love). Raising the eyebrows and looking out of the corners of the eyes. It is used when expressing mutual love.

11. *ADBHUTA* (Ecstasy). The ends of the eyelids are delicately curved, the eyes glistening and the eyebrows raised in wonderment. It is used when expressing wonder, ecstasy, the marvellous.

12. *KARUNA* (Compassion). A downcast glance, the pupil of the eye moving slowly. It is used when expressing compassion, pathetic, helplessness, weakness.

13. *VISMAYA* (Astonishment). The eyes are quickly moved and brought to the position of staring straight ahead. It is used when expressing astonishment, being taken aback, great surprise.

14. *TRIPTA* (Satisfaction). Steady pupil of the eyes with the eyes wide open. It is used when expressing resolution, realisation, experience in expression of the will, control.

15. *VISANNA* (Staring). The eyes are fixed and wide open. It is used when expressing dismay, fear, doubt, chagrin.

16. *DRUTA* (Darting). Both the pupils of the eyes are moved in a darting manner. It is used when expressing thrill, excitement, exuberance, pleasurable anticipation.

17. *VIRA* (Heroic). The eye glances are radiant and direct. It is used when expressing the heroic.

18. *RUDRA* (Cruel). Unfriendly eyes. The eyebrows are raised and contracted. It is used when expressing cruelty, unrelenting, determined, anger.

19. *VILOKITA* (Looking back). Looking back and seeing things behind. It is used when expressing seeing things that are behind one, at the back, rear.

20. *VITARKITA* (Deliberate). The eyes are direct and wide open. It is used when expressing consideration, deliberation, thoughtfulness, seriousness.

21. *SANKITA* (Apprehension). The eyes are moved a little, held a little at rest, slightly raised and then moved to and fro; the pupils of the eyes are partially hidden by the lids. It is used when expressing hesitation, doubt, not being sure of a thing.

22. *VIBHRANTA* (Wandering). The pupils of the eyes are moved and rolled. It is used when expressing laughter and tears, great excitement, happy anticipation, gratitude.

23. *HRISTA* (Merry). The eyes are fluttered, trembled and pleasantly twinkled. It is used when expressing laughter, merriment, happiness.

24. *LAJJITA* (Coy). The upper lids are dropped and the pupils of the eyes are lowered bashfully, so that the eye-lashes meet. It is used when expressing modesty, shyness, coyness, tremulousness.

25. *MUKULA* (Bliss). The lashes are made to tremble and touch each other and the upper lids are lowered. It is used when expressing bliss, supreme content, thankfulness.

26. *SHANTA* (Peace). Gradually closing the lids, the eyes moving very slightly. It is used when expressing peace, calm, quiet.

With the study of these Eye Movements, the eyebrows are also trained to work in harmony and mood. Six Eyebrow Movements are recognised by the Sanskrit classical treatises.

EYEBROWS. The Six Eyebrow Movements

1. *SAHAJA or SAHIJA.* The eyebrow is kept still. It is used when expressing the natural condition, undisturbed, calm.

2. *PATITA.* The eyebrows are drawn in a frown. It is used when expressing distaste, astonishment, jealousy, anger, disapproval.

3. *UTKSIPTA.* Either or both eyebrows are raised. It is used when expressing anger, telling the truth, assurance, a definite statement, certainty.

4. *CATURA.* The eyebrows meet and are made to quiver faintly. It is used when expressing bliss, excitement, great emotion, happiness.

5. *RECITA.* One eyebrow is contracted with great charm and sweetness. It is used when expressing the action of listening to a secret.

6. *KUNCITA.* One or both eyebrows are arched. It is used when expressing pleasure, happiness, remembrance, recollection, longing.

Neck Movements are used to add to the other modes of expression that have been described above. These are unique to the Indian dance and are introduced as much for added expression as for beauty. These movements too have to be in perfect harmony with the timing and mood. There are four recognised Neck Movements according to the authoritative treatises on the dance.

NECK MOVEMENTS. The Four Neck Movements

1. *SUNDARI* (Beautiful). Moving the neck to and fro horizontally, so typical of the classical schools, except Manipur. It is used when expressing pleasure, affection, bandinage, happy talk.

2. *TIRASCINA.* An upward movement on both sides like the gliding of a serpent. It is used when expressing the movements of a snake.

3. *PARAVARTITA.* Moving the neck to the right and left like a half-moon, in a lilting manner. It is used when expressing kissing, love, tenderness.

4. *PRAKAMPITA.* Moving the neck with the head going backwards and forwards like a pigeon. It is used when expressing you and I, swinging, talking, explaining.

These various facial expressions and movements of the head, eyes, eyebrows and neck take meaning when they support the relevant hand gestures. The great teachers, in evolving their *Abhinaya* in each school of the dance, have envisaged just how perfectly all this can be shown to the maximum effect, in their particular style of performance and technique. They have established certain appropriate prescribed modes of posture (sitting or standing), and rhythmic walk and stepping, set to a simple rhythm that would best suit each sentiment being portrayed. Fast, intricate stepping is usually confined to the technique of pure dance movement; and in order not to disturb the mood, grace, dignity and poise of interpretation, moderate speed marks the movements for the *Abhinaya*. The stress is on the emotional interpretation, song and lyrics.

In fact, the dancer must learn the lyrics and songs that are so important a part of the dance, so that she can interpret them correctly and in proper mood. Traditionally, an accomplished dancer was expected to sing the lyrics and songs when the occasion demanded during the course of her *Abhinaya*. For this adds emotional expression dramatically, and introduces a feeling of vitality to the acting. Even today, the dancer frequently sings while portraying her *Abhinaya* if she is gifted with a sweet voice and has mastered her *Sahitya*—the text.

When these particular postures of walk, with hand gestures (*Angika*, or the expression through the limbs and body); ability to sing (*Vachika*, or the expression through the voice); mastery of the facial expressions, including those of the head, eyes, eyebrows and neck (*Sattvika*), and the correct dress (*Aharya*, or the expression through dress, ornament and other aids) are all in perfect harmony, then *Abhinaya*, the dramatic side and half of the Indian dance is truly complete. The other half is the technique of pure dance.

The general idea to be followed, after making a study of these various movements of the features, is to use them pertinently as described below, together with the corresponding postures of limbs and relevant hand gestures. Through guidance of the teacher who has mastered the methods peculiar to each school of the combinations of the different modes of expression, the dancer learns accurately each specific type of *Abhinaya* and is able to interpret any song or lyric so required.

1. *TO EXPRESS THE BEGINNING OF THE DANCE.* The dancer has a calm, beautiful expression in perfect repose, her head in *Sama* (Level) (Head Movements No. 1).

The eyes are in *Sama* (Level) (Eye Movements No. 1), gazing without winking. No neck movement.

The eyebrows are in the natural state with smooth features, *Sahaja* (Eyebrow Movements No. 1).

2. *PLEASURE, JOY, LOVE, HAPPINESS.* The shoulder is raised and is touched with the head, *Nihancita* (Elevating) (Head Movements No. 11).

The eye expression in *Snigdha* (Tender) (Eye Movements No. 9), expressing affection, joy, pleasure.

The brows in *Kuncita* (Eyebrow Movements No. 6); one or both brows arched.

The neck in *Sundari* (Beautiful) (Neck Movements No. 1); moving it to and fro horizontally.

3. *THE MOON, ANYTHING TALL, THE MOUNTAINS, THE CLOUDS* The head is in *Udvahita* (Raised) (Head Movements No. 2); raising the head and keeping it still.

The eye expressions are in *Ulokita* (Looking up) (Eye Movements No. 6), directing the glances keenly up and aside.

No brow movements, just kept calm and natural.

No neck movement.

4. *BEING IN LOVE, YEARNING FOR THE BELOVED.* The head is in *Parivahita* (Wagging) (Head Movements No. 9); the head is moved from side to side like a fan.

The eye expressions are in *Sringara* (Love) (Eye Movements No. 10), showing love.

The brows are in *Kuncita* (Eyebrow Movements No. 6); one or both eyebrows are arched.

The neck is in *Paravartita* (Neck Movements No. 3); moving the neck to the right and left like a half-moon.

5. *ENQUIRY, INSTRUCTION, NARRATION.* The head is in *Akampta* (Raising) (Head Movements No. 15); raising the head high and shaking it slowly.

The eye expressions are in *Vitarkita* (Deliberate) (Eye Movements No. 20), direct and wide open.

The brows are in *Utksipta* (Eyebrow Movements No. 3); either one or both brows are raised.

No neck movement.

6. *LAUGHTER.* The head is in *Alolita* (Rolling) (Head Movements No. 4); the head is moved in a circle.

The eye expressions are in *Hrista* (Merry) (Eye Movements No. 23), fluttering, pleasant and twinkling.

The brows are in *Kuncita* (Eyebrow Movements No. 6); one or both brows arched.

7. *THE MARVELLOUS, WONDER, ECSTASY.* The head is in *Prakampita* (Moving all sides) (Head Movements No. 23); the head is waved about repeatedly, moving the head forward and to and fro to both sides.

The eye expressions are in *Adbhuta* (Ecstasy) (Eye Movements No. 11), the ends of the eyelids slightly curved, the eyebrows shiningly raised in wonder, the eyes shining. The brows are in *Kuncita* (Eyebrow Movements No. 6); the brows are arched.

The neck is in *Sundari* (Beautiful) (Neck Movements No. 1), moving it horizontally to and fro.

8. *MODESTY, SHYNESS, COYNESS.* The head is in *Adhomuaka* (Face inclined) (Head Movements No. 3); the head is bent.

The eye expressions are in *Lajjita* (Coy) (Eye Movements No. 24); the upper eyelids dropped, the pupils of the eyes lowered bashfully, the lashes meeting.

The brows are at rest.

No neck movement.

9. *SORROW, PATHETIC, FAINTING.* The head is in *Adhomuaka* (Face inclined) (Head Movements No. 3); the face is inclined and the head is bent.

The eye expressions are in *Karuna* (Compassion) (Eye Movements No. 12); a downcast glance, the pupils of the eyes moving slowly.

The brows are in *Catura* (Eyebrow Movements No. 4); the brows meet and are made to quiver faintly.

No neck movement.

10. *PRAYER, MEDITATION, GREETING.* The head is in *Sama* (Level)

Plate 73

Balasaraswati in *Abhinayam* in Bharata Natyam, showing (1) Krishna playing the flute ; (2) Birds mating ; (3) Krishna holding the flute and waiting for the Gopis (Photos, Dr. Robert E. Brown); (4) Appealing to God to protect and give salvation from the sufferings of this world. (Photo, Fumio Koisumi, Japan. Courtesy. T. Viswanathan.)

Plate 74

1

3

(1) Indrani in *Abhinayam* in Orissi showing the "lotus flower" (2) Indrani in *Abhinayam* in Bharat Natyam showing "the deer." (Photos, H. Rahman.) (3) Kumari Kamala in *Abhinayam* in Bharat Natyam showing "Sorrow", holding *Hamsasya Mudra* for depicting tears flowing from the eyes. (Courtesy, Kumari Kamala.)

2

Plate 75

1   2

Cita Pooviah in *Abhinaya* in Kathak showing (1) "Love" and (2) "Why". (Courtesy, Cita Pooviah.)

Rita Devi in Kuchipudi *Abhinaya*, (3) "Struck by Kamadeva's arrows". (4) Playing ball. (Courtesy, Ritha Devi. Photos, S. Santhanam.)

3   4

Plate 76

1. *"Here come the arrows of love that make me shudder. Oh ! how painful is this suffering."*

2. *"My deeply disturbed soul boils in turmoil."*

Sudha Doraiswamy (now Sudha Sekhar) in *Abhinayam* postures in the famous *Padam*, "Padari Varugudu", *Rag* Kambodhi, *Tala* Rupakam. (Courtesy, Sudha Sekhar.)

5. *"Can't you wait?"*

6. *"Your heart seems to be .."*

Plate 77

3. *"Speak to Him of all this."*

4. *"Just a short while."*

Abhinayam postures in the Padam
"Padari Varugudu"—*Continued.*

7. *"....as hard as stone."*

8. *"Come, Come..."*

Plate 78

9. "....*enough of all this coquetry.*"

10. "*Go away, please, and bring Him unto me.*"

Padam "Padari Varugudu": A love-lorn maiden, long separated from her beloved Lord Muruga (Subrahmanya), speaks of her longing to see Him, to her maid companion. "Is thy heart made of stone, that you won't even hear me. Please go and bring my Lord here after explaining to Him of my sufferings." (Courtesy, Sudha Sekhar.)

11. "*The God of Love (Manmatha) launches his attack with flowery arrows.*"

Plate 79

12. *"How unbearable is this separation* (Viraha)."

13. *"Come, O dearest."*

14. *"Please do come here."*

15. *A statuesque pose depicting Lord Muruga* (Subrahmanya).

Plate 80

1

2

3

4

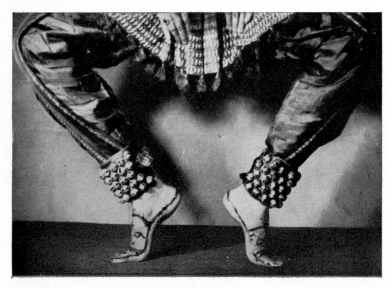

5

The five main positions of the feet in Bharata Natyam. (Photos copyright, Mohan Khokar.)

(Head Movements No. 1); not moving, not bent nor raised, just straight.

The eye expressions are in *Nimilita* (Closed) (Eye Movements No. 5); the eyes are half closed and half open.

The brows are in *Sahaja* (Eyebrow Movements No. 1); the natural brow in a calm face.

The neck is steady.

From these ten examples, it will be noted how the *Abhinaya* is built up, and the dancer trained to use her head, eyes, eyebrows and neck in accordance with the rules of the classical treatises. In actual practice, however, in each school of the dance, tradition, adaptation by the *gurus* and experts, and regional development of style, have all left their impress and influence on textual formulas.

The following quotation, poetically describes woman. It provides apt material for the illustration of *Abhinaya*, wherein phrasing and expression play together a pleasing part.

"(In the beginning, says Hindu legend, when Twashtri, the Divine Artificer, came to the creation of woman he found that he had exhausted his materials in the making of man and had no solid elements left. In this dilemma, he fashioned her eclectically out of the odds and ends of creation).

"He took the rotundity of the moon, and the curves of creepers, and the clinging tendrils, and the trembling of grass, and the slenderness of the reed, and the bloom of flowers and the lightness of leaves, and the tapering of the elephant's trunk, and the glances of the deer, and the clustering of rows of bees, and the joyous gaiety of sunbeams, and the weeping of clouds, and the fickleness of the winds, and the timidity of the hare, and the vanity of the peacock, and the softness of the parrot's bosom, and the hardness of adamant, and the sweetness of honey, and the cruelty of the tiger, and the warm flow of fire, and the coldness of snow, and the chattering of jays, and the cooing of the kokila, and the hypocrisy of the crane, and the fidelity of the chakravaka; and the compounding of all these together he made woman, and gave her to man."[1]

Example of a Padam, "Padari Varugudu" in *Rag Kambodhi—Tala Rupakam* from Bharata Natyam, in the *Sringara Bhava* or mood of love.

"A love-lorn maiden, long separated from her beloved Lord Murugu (Subhramanya) speaks of her longing to see Him to her maid-companion. 'Is thy heart made of stone, that you won't even hear me. Please go and bring my Lord here after explaining to Him of my sufferings.'"

Example of a *Kirthana,* "Kalai Tooki" from Bharata, Natyam, a sacred song addressed to Lord Shiva.

In describing the beauty of the techniques and Mood of the various schools of the classical dance, emphasis must be laid once more on the importance of timing and rhythm. In the *Nrtta* or pure dance sequences, every single step must find its counterpart in the drum beats, and in the *Abhinaya* or emotional expression, the dancer must walk and move in certain prescribed modes as directed by a chosen timing and rhythm. To fully achieve this perfect harmony, there must be complete control of the feet and understanding of timing and rhythm by the dancer.

[1] F. W. Bain, *The Digit of the Moon*

11. The Feet, Timing and Rhythm

TIMING AND RHYTHM IN THE INDIAN DANCE

THE KEYNOTE of the Indian Dance is a perfect sense of harmony and rhythm. The first lessons learned by the creators of the art were without doubt taken from Nature, where harmony is self-evident within its tremendous variety and multiplicity, and where perfect co-ordination and systematic order gives a unity to the whole.

Rhythm and harmony are closely allied. According to the ideals of the Indian Dance, perfect rhythm is achieved when a true unison of the inner self and the physical being is immersed in the Divine Law. That is, becoming one with the world harmonies and attaining an exquisite attunement with the one supreme circle of movement and balance existing in the Universe. When we speak of rhythm in the dance, we mean that essential co-ordination of footwork, bodily movement, hand gestures, placement of arms and movements of the head, eyes, eyebrows, and neck, with the time beats of the drum. For this absolute co-ordination between sound and footwork, the creators of the Indian Dance ordained that there be a symmetry of count and metre between the finely intricate beats of time and every unit of the dance step and bodily movement. This can only come about when there is a sympathetic unison of spirit and physical being during the performance. Rhythm therefore became the factor which if present was taken for granted, and if absent caused disharmony and confusion. Nature's lessons constantly guided them with its own evidence of perfect rhythm and pattern, in the regular beats of the heart, in the cosmic waves that put matter into motion, in the grace of the strutting peacock, and even in the clumsy dance of the bear.

Therefore when the main timings were composed, they were broken up into counts of three, four, six, seven, eight, ten, twelve, fourteen and so on. This meant there were so many beats in the bar or sub-divisions of equal metrical length. But the Indian composer with his ingrained consciousness for pattern and love of infinite variety, which he had learnt so early from Nature, became ambitious. His freedom to express emotional content, his fervent flair for mathematics, and the permutations and combinations thereof, made him dissatisfied with the mere regular beats of the main counts.

He began weaving patterns and designs within these, showing lights and shades of sounds and delicate traceries of tone. Loud bits, soft bits, and quick punctuated bits, were created, that sped along within each systematised beat and the next. And yet he kept the main regular beats intact. These subtle fascinating hundreds of divisions and sub-divisions between the main intervals of time, and the multiplication of these into still smaller and more fractional measures, all working within the recognised beats, became characteristic.

As has already been explained in Chapter V, the intricate and harmonious balance of the main timing of regular beats or *Tala*, the patterned sounds of the drum (*Chollu* in Bharata Natyam, *Bol* in Kathak, *Bani* or *Ukuttas* in Orissi, and so on), and the great number of feet rhythms with their patterns (*Jatis* in Bharata Natyam, and so on), and the recitations of these word syllables by the musicians (*Sollu-kuttu* in Bharata Natyam, Kuchipudi, and so on), all work together to create one harmonious whole. With the transition of time and the influence of environment, these stylised patterns became slightly different in each of the classical dance schools, and the word syllables were naturally influenced by the differences in language.

Take one of the simplest examples of these wordings of the drum in an eight beat count or *Tala*. It goes like this:

Drum Beats:	DADEE	NAKA	NAKA	DINA
	1	2	3	4
	DADEE	NAKA	NAKA	DINA
	5	6	7	8

This is the main wording of the main beats of the drum in what is called *Kherwa* timing or *Tal*, with eight sub-divisions, in the North Indian or Hindustani School of Music. In this, the first beat carries the emphasis, with further emphasis on each of the following odd numbers, as for example, $\bar{1}$, 2, $\bar{3}$, 4, $\bar{5}$, 6, $\bar{7}$, 8.

When the dance ends or a complete verse of the *Sollu-kuttu* or *Thora* ends (usually each verse being repeated three times for one complete cycle), it has to complete the eight main beats, once, twice, three times or more according to its length, and come to rest on the last beat, ready to start the new verse of the next *Sollu-kuttu* or *Thora* on the first beat again. This point where the dancer ends on the last beat of the timing, is called *Sum*.

Perfect synchronization of timing, movement and stepping is achieved as the dancer ends each cycle or ensemble of *Sollu-kuttu* verse or *Thoras* on the exact dot of the last beat of the timing or *Sum*, ready to commence once again her next new *Thora* verse or *Sollu-kuttu* piece.

Thus in the *Kherwa Tal*, which has eight *Matras* or sub-divisions in its rhythm, the dancer starts on Beat 1, goes on doing the *Thora* verse, usually repeating it three times, and ends on Beat 8, without any hesitation, at the exact moment that the drummer is ready to start on Beat 1 again, and the musician reciting the verse words ends his ensemble.

Main Rhythm of Tala	1	2	3	4	5	6	7	8
Main Rhythm In Drum Beats	DADEE	NAKA	NAKA DINA		DADEE	NAKA	NAKA	DINA
Words Fitted and Played by Drummer, Danced and Recited	1, 2 TATA	3, 4 TATHOME	5, 6, 7 THOMETA		8 THOME	9, 10 THAKA	11, 12 DITA	13 THOME
	14, 15 THAKA	16, 17 THITA	18, 19, 20, 21 THIKA THATA		22, 23 TH-OME	24, 25 THAYA	26, 27 TH-OM	28, 29 THAKA
	30 DEE	31 THA	32, 33 THE THA		34, 35 THAKA	36, 37 KITA	38, 39 THATA	40 THOME

When the main *Tala* has played eight beats, the dancer's feet, the drum patterns and recitations of the musicians have done thirteen patterned word syllables. When the main *Tala* has played eight more beats, the pattern is twenty-nine; and with eight more beats of the main *Tala*, forty steps of the pattern have been completed, followed by the drum wordings and recited syllables. Thus forty "dance steps" are skilfully danced into twenty-four beats of the main *Tala*. Most often this one verse of *Thora* of dance word syllables is repeated three times and becomes one piece; and there are hundreds of such "verses" or *Thoras* or *Sollukuttu* pieces in each of the dance schools; some simple and short, and others longer and more complicated. A very simple example has been cited just to show the system, but as the timings become more complicated, such as in the case of fourteen or twelve or more *Matras* or sub-divisions in the main timing, the patterns become more and more intricate and patterned, adding great brilliance to the technique. The example given above is from the Kathak school of the dance.

Here is a different example from the Bharata Natyam school, and the main wordings of the main beats of the drum in the Southern School or Karnatic music, with eight sub-divisions or *Matras* in the main timing. The playing on the cymbals would keep the main *Tala* or timing with the *Mirdanga*, counting 1. 2. 3. 4. 5. 6. 7. 8; which translated into the drum beats would be THAKA, JUNA, THAKA, DIMI, THAKA, JUNA, THAKA, DIMI.

Main Rhythm in Tala	1	2	3	4	5	6	7	8
Main Rhythm In Drum Beats	THAKA	JUNA	THAKA	DIMI	THAKA	JUNA	THAKA	DIMI
Words Fitted and Played by Drummer, Danced in Stepping and Recited	1, 2, 3,	4, 5, 6, 7,	8, 9, 10,	11, 12, 13, 14,	15, 16, 17,	18, 19, 20, 21, 22,	23, 24, 25, 26, 27,	28, 29, 30, 31, 32.
	THAM-THAKA	KITA-NAKA	JHUM-THARI	KITA-THAKA	DAL-ANG-KU	THARA-GIDA-THOME	THARA-GIDA-THOME	THARA-GIDA-THOME

Here again, when the main *Tala* has played eight beats, the dancer's feet, the drum patterns and recitations have done thirty-two patterned word syllables. The main timing is slightly slow, the foot stepping as it moves, sometimes taking three steps to a beat, sometimes four and sometimes five steps to a beat, followed closely by the recited word syllables of the corresponding drum word syllables.

The postures change as fast as the feet; as the dancer bends to right and left, forwards or backwards, the legs change from bent to straight or raised or crossed, and yet the hands might be posed on the hips or waist or crossed at the chest; be stretched at the sides or be cast backwards and forwards with beautiful and fast changing gestures. The arms may move at half the speed, one-fourth the speed or even at times as fast as the foot stepping, depending on the particular sequence of the dance that is being performed.

Sound and movement, like the colours on a print, may be far apart in places, close together in others, delicately grouped in still others, yet maintain one uniform whole in perfect harmony.

In this connection, it is important to note that there are Five Basic Elements that help towards that perfect harmony of rhythms by the dancer.

These are:

1. THE MANDALAS   ..   .. Posture
2. THE UTPALAVANAS   .. Jumping
3. THE BHRAMARIS   ..   .. Turning round fast
4. THE CARIS   ..   .. Gait or Walk
5. THE GATIS ..   ..   .. Steppings

When the hand gestures express the language of signs and whole conversations are made, or the lyrics and songs are interpreted between sequences of the technique of pure dance, then the feet play a part akin to the piano accompaniment to a song.

The hands may be said to speak, the eyes and facial expressions give the emotional tone, the bodily movements and postures cast the mantle of beauty and add *Rasa* or Flavour, while the feet which mark the timing and rhythm, support the whole performance.

For the perfection of jumps, turns, the gait or walk and steps, there are eighteen or more different kinds of what we might call "ways of holding the body" (*Mandalas*) that are dependent on the placement, firmness and practised technique of the feet.

PLACEMENT AND CONTROL OF THE FEET

1. The feet are first placed or kept together, flat on the ground, toes close together, perfect balance of the body on both feet equally distributed; the upper portion of the body slightly held forward and the hands on the hips with the four fingers resting on the hips, and the thumbs on the waist and pointing back.

This is for the beginning of the dance, and shows the figure in all its grace, shapeliness and erect position, with perfect symmetry of balance.

2. Feet about a foot apart, knees bent and turned outwards, toes also pointing outwards. The feet are placed flat with the heels together. The upper part of the body is straight and the head erect.

3. Feet are raised on the toes, crossed at the ankles and rested on the ball of the foot, the knees bent slightly. The top portion of the body is straight.

4. The peculiar emphasis in this is on the waist and hip. The left foot is placed flat, the right foot is behind it on the toes. The body is bent a little to the left. The waist is then pushed in at the right side and the left hip pushed out.

5. The left foot flat and still, the right foot forward on the heel, the sole raised and the toes pointing up. The body is bent slightly backwards, the waist bent to the right, and the left hip pushed out prominently.

6. The left foot flat, the right foot forward on the heel, the sole raised and the toes pointing up. The body is bent forwards, so that the right hand goes down, almost touching the right toes. The left hand is on the hip.

7. Standing on the left flat foot with even balance, the right foot is crossed over it and kept on the ball of the foot, the sole facing backwards, the toe tips forward. The body is erect. The hands are poised gracefully on the hips in the gesture of closed fists with the thumbs set on the fingers that are bent into the palm.

8. The left foot is on the flat, and the right foot is placed close beside it on the ball of the foot, the toes pointing outwards to the right, the sole of the foot touching the left ankle. The left hand is held lightly on the waist and the right hand hangs loosely at the right side about a foot away from the body.

9. Both the feet are close together, standing on the ball of each foot. The body erect, the legs straight.

10. Standing on the left flat foot, well balanced, the right foot is raised across the left leg, so that the toes point to the ground and the back of the foot touches the left knee. The right hand is held at the chest, with the palm facing outwards, the second, third and little fingers stretched and slightly bent, the first finger and thumb touching at the tips. The left arm is raised to shoulder level, straight, with the wrist dropped, so that the fingers point downwards.

11. Standing on the left flat foot, the right foot is raised and crossed at the back of the left foot, so that the sole faces back and the instep touches the back of the left knee. The body is erect, and the hands are poised gracefully on the waist.

12. The two feet are on the ball of each foot, close together, toes facing outwards and heels touching at the top. The soles of the feet face each other. The knees are bent and the top portion of the body is erect, with the arms crossed on the chest.

13. The left foot is on the flat with the toes pointing a little leftwards and out. The right foot is taken back at an angle on the left of the foot, with the body leaning back and resting on the right leg; the right palm is placed on the back of the head, and the left arm is held parallel to the left foot, with all the fingers and thumb stretched close together and pointing to the ground.

14. Standing on the left flat foot, the right foot is raised forward to the height of the left knee with the sole facing downwards, toes straight. The left hand is on the waist, and the right hand is stretched at a slight angle from the body, with the fingers and thumb stretched close together.

15. Both feet are placed on the heels, feet a little apart, and the body balance resting a little backwards. The arms are stretched forwards to each side, shoulder level, with the wrists dropped and the fingers and thumbs stretched close together and pointing to the ground. The feet may be reversed and the same done with

the right foot or left foot. When the right foot is changed to flat of foot, the left foot moves forward and back on the heel in four counts; and when the left foot is steady, the right foot is moved likewise.

16. Sitting down with the right foot flat and straight, the left foot is stretched at an angle, midway between the actual side and straight. It is held on the heel with the sole facing outwards and the toes pointing upwards. The body rests backwards to the right, and the right hand is on the hips. The left arm is stretched parallel to the left leg.

17. Sitting down and resting on the two flat feet, with the toes pointing outwards and the heels close together, the knees are spread apart. The body is erect, and the two arms are stretched straight on either side, with all the fingers and thumbs stretched close together.

18. The body is turned sideways, facing to the left, with the left knee bent and the left foot on the flat with the toes facing in the same direction. The right leg is stretched back and held on the ball of the foot. The body is bent forward in a lunging position, with the right arm stretched parallel to the right leg and the left hand placed at chest level, a little forward, palm facing upwards and all the fingers stretched and slightly bent.

These eighteen "ways of holding the body," combining the five Basic Elements of control and placement of the feet for the dance, are utilized for the actual mobile steppings to take form and shape.

SOME EXAMPLES OF BASIC FOOTWORK USED IN THE DANCE IN GENERAL

1. Advance with the right flat foot, beating the ground three times in one place, and take one step forward on the flat of foot with the right foot. Do the same with the left foot and continue so, using alternate feet, till an advance has been made for some distance, counting four beats alternately, first for the right foot and then for the left.

2. Right and left foot alternately, banging the ground in front with the heel, coming back to position on the flat of feet. Continue so, moving forwards slowly with each tap of the heel and flat of foot; and then do the same to return to starting point. One beat for each movement of each foot.

3. Right flat, left flat, right forward on the heel, left foot on the flat, and the right on the flat beside it. The beats are actually four—the counts for the feet are five steps. So that, it is done by counting right flat 1, left flat 2, right forward on heel 3, left flat and right flat beside it 4. This means that the last two steps are counted as 4, and are done in double time, half a beat each step, making one count. The same is done by reversing the process, and starting with the left foot flat, and done thus alternately, advancing forward.

4. The right foot is raised with a little jump, and is placed down on the flat, a little forward, and then the left foot is placed on the flat beside it. The jump is done by just raising the left foot up on the ball of the foot, and then coming down on the flat as the right foot is placed down on the flat forward. This movement is repeated, moving forwards each time.

5. Right foot forward on the flat, left foot on the flat beside it; right foot in the same place, left foot flat in the same place. Count four beats, one for each foot movement. Reverse this, starting once with the right foot and once

with the left foot, alternately in each set of four counts. Move forward, giving an emphasis each time on count 1; and return the same way, after having moved towards the front of the stage.

6. Left foot flat, cross the right foot on the toes behind the left foot; and jump to the right on the flat of the right foot. Place left foot on the toes behind the right flat foot and jump to the left on the flat left foot— the right foot being placed back on the toes behind the left foot. Then place right foot on the flat forward and take the left foot on the flat beside it. There are thus seven steps in all and should be repeated going forwards.

7. Take the position with both feet on the flat close together. Move forwards, alternate feet, to a count of four. Right foot forward on the ball of the foot and then flat; left foot forward on the ball of the foot and then flat. Each time, two counts are made for each foot as it advances (one count for the foot going up on the ball of the foot, and one count as it comes down flat). Advance forwards like this to the front of the stage and return the same way, turning the body sideways. In this stepping, the knees must be bent.

8. (a) jump to the side on the right foot flat, with the left foot raised in front near the right knee. (b) Jump the same way to the left, raising the right foot. (c, d, e) Right foot flat in front, left foot flat in front, rise on the toes and come down on both flat feet. (f, g, h) Jump, bringing the left foot almost to knee of the right foot and rising on the toes, come down on both feet. (i, j, k) Right foot on the heel forward, left foot on the flat at place, bring the right foot on the flat beside the left. This whole movement is to be repeated twice or four times.

Recounted above are but a few examples of the foot patterns possible in the dance. There are hundreds of these combinations in varying timings and rhythms.

Similarity of footwork can be traced in the various schools of the classical dance. The fast pirouetting (*Bhramaris*) which is common to all, but done sometimes slowly also, is usually accomplished by either raising the right foot a little and doing a quick turn on the ball of the left foot, going anti-clockwise; or by going round in one place on the flat of the left foot, with the right foot on the ball of the foot a little apart and a little behind, the dancer moving simultaneously with the left foot as it is moved round in the same spot, while the right foot makes the circle, working much as a pair of compasses drawing a circle. In the Kathak school, these pirouettes are characteristic and are done very fast, during the recitation and drum beats in the pattern of syllable wordings and this pirouetting is very beautiful, as it appears so frequently. The jumps (*Utpalavanas*) are common too and add beauty to the unique system of posture, varying in each school, and particularly stressed in Bharata Natyam, Orissi and Kuchipudi.

Most of the classical dances, and particularly the Bharata Natyam, employ elegant characteristic styles of walk or gait (*Caris*) between each series of pure dance movements, and each *Abhinaya* sequence, moving backwards, sideways or in a semi-circle. The special gestural and arm positions used with the various walks enhance the beauty of composition. Finally, the varied steppings (*Gatis*) with skilful use of the flat of foot, toes, ball of the foot and heel done to the different *Talas* or timings for the harmonious blending of the feet, timing and rhythm, are common to all schools.

Throughout the dance, however, in its technical aspects and its emotional content, it is the music that sustains its sheer beauty of rhythm and dramatic meaning. Timing, rhythm and pure dance are dependent on the drums and cymbals and the chant recitations of the word syllables by the musicians, just as the emotional interpretations are dependent on the *Raga* melodies, songs and lyrics. Indeed, it is the music that uplifts the dance into the realm of the sublime and the soulful.

12. Indian Music and Musical Instruments

THE INDIAN Dance being interpretive, it strives to portray in movement what the music and songs describe. In Sanskrit there is an old saying that "Music is the tree of Nature's symphonies and the dance is the blossom of all Music."

In the Indian Dance, there is the reflection of music (*Sangit*), together with poetry (*Sahitya*) and drama (*Natya*), beautifully balanced, and so in its expression, the body becomes the medium of thought, infinitely emotional, as vivid as sculpture and as descriptive as painting, yet more true, because it is imbued with pulsating life; and when it is in perfect accord and harmony with the rhythm of the universe, then indeed have we found the means for truly interpreting life's forces.

This merging of the physical being with the spirit within one and the Universal Spirit, achieves for us a proper perspective of our place in the scheme of things. Indian music seeks to create this perfect fusion between the spirit within us and life outside. As Ananda Coomaraswamy aptly describes it, "Indian music is essentially impersonal. It reflects an emotion and an experience, which are deeper and wider and older than the emotion or wisdom of any single individual. Its sorrow is without tears, its joy without exaltation, and it is passionate without any loss of serenity. It is in the deepest sense of the words all-human".[1]

Just as the dance is given a divine origin, so it is believed that Narada, the sage and Spiritual Son of Brahma the Creator, was the first Musician, even as Shiva was the first Dancer, and Vishnu the Originator of sovereign song. Narada is believed to have created the *Saraswati Veena*, India's oldest stringed instrument, and the favourite of Saraswati, Goddess of Learning, whose symbol it became. She is the Twin Aspect and Consort of Brahma.

Indian music is as old as time, and has come down since ages past, enriched en route by the various influences it encountered during the passage of time and history in our country. The indigenous music of the Indus Valley and the Dravi-

[1] Ananda Coomaraswamy, *Dance of Shiva and Fourteen Other Essays*

160

Plate 81

The feet in Kathak *Tatkar*, which comprises the simplest form and basic footwork of this school.

Drums, comprising the *Tablah* (*left*) and the *Bahya* (*right*) used primarily in the Hindusthani or North Indian school of music. (Photo, R. J. Chinwalla.)

Plate 82

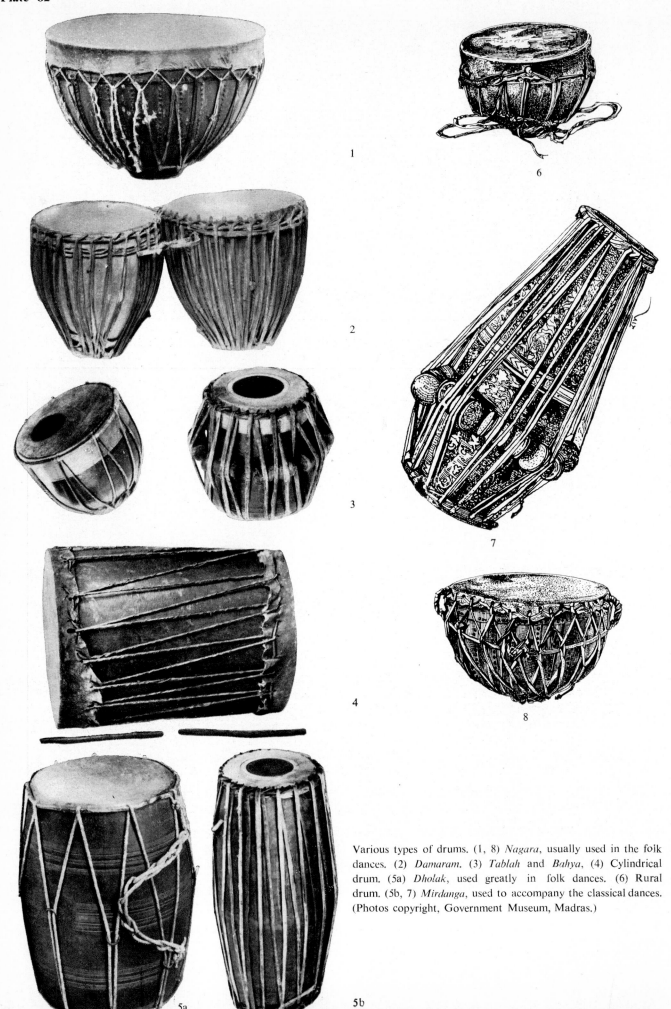

Various types of drums. (1, 8) *Nagara*, usually used in the folk dances. (2) *Damaram*. (3) *Tablah* and *Bahya*, (4) Cylindrical drum. (5a) *Dholak*, used greatly in folk dances. (6) Rural drum. (5b, 7) *Mirdanga*, used to accompany the classical dances. (Photos copyright, Government Museum, Madras.)

Plate 83

Temple sculptures depicting musicians and musical instruments. (1) From Khajuraho, 11th century A.D. (2) From the Ramappa temple, Palampet, Andhra Pradesh. (3, 4) From Belur, 12th century A.D. (5) From Hoysala temple, Halebid, 12th century A.D. (Copyright, Department of Archaeology, Government of India.)

Plate 84

Temple sculptures depicting musicians, musical instruments and dancers. (1, 2) From the Hoysala temple, Halebid, 12th century A.D. (3) From Sikar, Rajasthan. (Copyright, Department of Archaeology, Government of India.)

dian civilizations, Greek, Persian and Arabic contacts, have all left some imprint on this ancient art that can be traced as far back as the Aryan civilization in India. And though the beautiful melodic system has remained unimpaired, emotional trends have added to its unique qualities.

Indian musical composition is based on the *Raga*. *Raga* means colouring, literally, that which imparts colour in a psychological sense or emotion, and therefore indicates Mood. It expresses and awakens certain deep feelings in the human being and even affects Nature. A *Raga* has been defined as "the traditional melody into which the Indian musician has woven his improvisations, and it is a selection of five, six or seven notes distributed along the scale, each *Raga* symbolising in rhythmic form some emotion, elemental force or particular aspect of Nature when it may be appropriately sung or played." In other words, a *Raga* comprises a composition of tones or *Svara* which occur in succession to one another and create a musical effect or *Varna*. Each *Raga* not only has its own individual melodic pattern and structure, consisting of its particular musical notes or tones (*Svara*), but possesses an inner emotional character (*Bhava*). Both these aspects combine to give each *Raga* its intrinsic beauty and meaning. Thus, the *Svaras* or tones are the substance of the *Raga*, the composition of *Svara* in an order of succession is its structure, and the *Varna* or beauty of musical effect is its explicit form.

Theoretically, there are seven main *Svaras* or tones or notes in Indian music that follow one another in succession at regular musical intervals and form the scale, namely:

SHAGDA	..	Sa	— Do or Middle C in Western music.
RISHABA	..	Ri	— Re or D in Western music.
GANDHARA	..	Ga	— Mee or E in Western music.
MADHYAMA	..	Ma	— Fa or F in Western music.
PANCHAMA	..	Pa	— So or G in Western music.
DHAIVATA	..	Dha	— La or A in Western music.
NISHADA	..	Ni	— See or B in Western music.

In Indian music, however, it has been established that out of these seven main *Svaras* or tones, five of them, namely, Ri (D) Ga (E) Ma (F) Dha (A) and Ni (B) are *Chala Svaras* or *Svaras* capable of being moved in certain *Ragas*; while Sa (C) and Pa (G) are *Achala Svaras* or immovable *Svaras*, and remain static in all *Ragas*. Of the five movable *Svaras*, four of them, namely, Ri (D) Ga (E) Dha (A) and Ni (B), can be brought down to a lower degree of pitch or intensity in some *Ragas*, and become what is known as *Komal* or Flat; while Ma (F), the tonic note, can be raised to a higher degree of pitch or *Tivra* for some *Ragas*, as the use of the Sharp in Western music.

There are accordingly twelve *Svaras* or tones in Indian music as given below. There is however a slight difference in the names of the notes between the Hindustani or North Indian system and the Karnatic or Southern system. Nearly the same twelve semi-tones are used in the two schools.

HINDUSTANI			*KARNATIC*		
1. SHAGDA	..	Sa	1. SADJAMAM	..	Sa
2. KOMAL RISHABHA	..	Ri Komal	2. SUDHA RISHABAM	..	Ri
3. RISHABA	..	Ri	3. CHATSRUTI RISHABAM	..	Ri

HINDUSTANI			*KARNATIC*	
4. KOMAL GANDHARA	.. Ga Komal		4. SADHARANA GANDHARAM	.. Ga
5. GANDHARA	.. Ga		5. ANTARA GANDHARAM	.. Ga
6. MADHYAMA	.. Ma		6. SUDHA MADHYAMAM	.. Ma
7. TIRVA MADHYMA	.. Ma Tivra		7. PRADIT MADHYAMAM	.. Ma
8. PANCHAMA	.. Pa		8. PANCHAMAM	.. Pa
9. KOMAL DHAIVATA	.. Dha Komal		9. SUDHA DHAIVATAM	.. Dha
10. DHAIVATA	.. Dha		10. CHATUSRUTI DHAIVA-TAM	.. Dha
11. KOMAL NISHADA	.. Ni Komal		11. KAISHIK NISHADAM	.. Ni
12. NISHADA	.. Ni		12. KAKALI NISHADAM	.. Ni

Each *Svara* has approximately an interval of one semi-tone between it and the succeeding *Svara* above and below. In addition, Indian music makes use of quarter tones in between two consecutive *Svaras*, making for more minute degrees of pitch and thus creating in all twenty-two such degrees of pitch known as *Srutis*, all within one octave from lower Sa to top Sa. Twelve of these twenty-two *Srutis* having been retained for composing the *Ragas*; the remaining ten *Srutis* are used to add richness and delicate traceries of sound and embellishment to each of the *Ragas* as the composition comes into being. A *Raga* may have a selection of five, six, or seven of the twelve *Svaras* distributed along the scale of its composition. Further, numberless tonal created notes known as *Meend*[1] are achieved by the musician or singer carrying the sound from a particular *Svara* or *Sruti* to a created tone (as in the case of harmonics created on the violin in Western music), to further beautify the mode. In fact, the Indian musician or singer may invent any number of improvisations utilizing a fund of created grace notes within the allotted scale of the *Raga* to give it varying degrees of assonance and continuity of sweetness of sounds.

With the mode of what are known as the *Alap* (done in slow tempo) and the *Tana* (done in medium and fast tempo), the thematic melody is greatly intensified. The musician or singer in the *Alap* and the *Tana* can use within the allotted scale of the *Raga*, several original and novel combinations of tones utilizing pure vowels (Ah......) undisturbed by words while singing these, and utilizing pure sound for instrumental music, to prove his or her virtuosity, originality and accomplishment. In the Southern school this is known as *Alapanam* in *Chauka Kalam* and *Madhyama Kalam*. In this system improvisations are also achieved by using the actual words of the song known as *Neraval*, followed invariably by the *Manodharma Svarams* which are permutations and combinations of the actual notes or *Svaras* of the *Raga* being sung. This system of *Raga* composition necessarily gives Indian music its unmistakable character of being based on melody and therefore being essentially melodic as opposed to music which is based on harmony; having as it does its system of *Svaras* or tones occurring in an order of succession and not sounded simultaneously as is required in harmonised music. Harmony is achieved in the context of Indian music, when there is beauty of musical expression and composition of tones, excellent and pleasing combination of the smallest degrees of pitch (intensity) during the weaving of the improvisations, and perfect timing (*Tala*) and rhythm (*Laya*).

[1] *Gamagam* in the Southern school

Just as all Indian art has been influenced by Nature, it is believed by some sources that in its earliest conception, Indian music was also deeply influenced by Nature, being associated, as authorities actually tell us, with the cries of animals and birds, serving as concrete tests for the accuracy of reproduction. Suggesting its origin in Nature, the seven notes of the main tonic scale are classified as follows:

Middle C — Sa (Shagda) — The cry of the peacock.
D — Ri (Rishaba) — The sound made by the cow calling her calf.
E — Ga (Gandhara) — The bleat of the goat.
F — Ma (Madhyama) — The cry of the heron, and the tonic note of Nature.
G — Pa (Panchama) — The note of the cuckoo or Kokila, the Indian nightingale.
A — Dha (Dhaivata) — The neighing of the horse.
B — Ni (Nishada) — The trumpeting of the elephant.

RAGAS AND RAGINIS

Each *Raga* or Melody varies in Mood and Theme according to different sentiments called *Rasas*, such as *Sringara* (Love), *Hasya* (Mirth), *Karuna* (Tenderness), *Raudra* (Anger), *Vira* (Heroism), *Bhayanaka* (Terror), *Vighasta* (Disgust) and *Ashuta* (Surprise), just as we find in the moods of the dance. The *Ragini* is the feminine form of the *Raga*, and suggests a condensation of the main theme of the melody.

The origin of the *Ragas* we are told is various: "Some, like *Pahari*, are derived from local folk-song, others like *Jog*, from the songs of wandering ascetics, and still others are the creation of great musicians by whose names they are known. More than sixty are mentioned in a Sanskrit-Tibetan vocabulary of the seventh century, with names such as With-a-voice-like-a-thunder-cloud, Like-the-God-Indra, and Delighting-the-heart. Amongst the *Raga* names in modern use may be cited Spring, Evening-beauty, Honey-flower, The Swing, and Intoxication."[1]

According to some of the old classifications, there are six principal *Ragas*: *Hindole* (played to produce all the sweetness of springtime, sweet as honey and fragrant as flowers); *Sri Raga* (a melody to produce the calm and serenity of eventide, and fill the mind with gladness); *Megh* (so descriptive that it can produce rain and clouds); *Deepak* (can create fire); *Bhairava* (creates the feeling of the freshness of early dawn, with the song of birds and the beauty of breaking day); and *Malkaus* (relaxing and awareness of mind). Each of these are represented as a "demi-God," "married" to six *Raginis* or nymphs; and from each of these thirty-six, three more *Raginis* are created which give rise to the special qualities of their parents; and these again give rise to more *Raginis*, each one having a clear beauty and character of its own. With time, modes were added and every book on the subject varies in the details as to the *Ragas* and *Raginis* in their classifications, and in their number and importance. Sarngadeva, for instance, one of the greatest authorities (A.D. 1210 to 1247), mentions 664 *Ragas* and *Raginis* in his *Sangitaratnakara*. Legend says that there were once in ages past, 16,000 melodies that were so beautiful and varied that the Gods themselves took delight in the art of music.

[1] Ananda Coomaraswamy, *Dance of Shiva and Fourteen Other Essays*

The spiritual context behind each melody and composition and its background of Nature, makes Indian music as idealistic as the dance with its highly philosophical conception. "When Shiva expounds the technique of the Drama to Bharata—the famous author of *Natya Sastra*—he declares that human art must be subject to law, because in man the inner and outer life are still in conflict. Man has not yet found Himself, but all his activity proceeds from a laborious working of the mind, and all his virtue is self-conscious. What we call our life is uncoordinated, and far from the harmony of art, which rises above good and evil. It is otherwise with the Gods, whose every gesture immediately reflects the affections of the inner life. Art is an imitation of that perfect spontaneity —the identity of intuition and expression in those who are of the kingdom of heaven, which is within us."[1] Indeed, Indian music is said to possess great psychological and elemental power, and there is a belief that the *Ragas* can stir the elements and even cure illnesses by their vibrations if played in the correct season, at the appropriate time, and follow the correct form laid down in the classical treatises. *Sri Raga*, for instance, one of the sweetest of melodies, soft and plaintive, if sung at close of day in winter, about six o'clock in the evening, during January-February, is supposed to ease tension in the human heart and mind. *Bhairava Raga*, when played at five o'clock in the morning during September-October, has the power to cure diseases of the liver, cough, and to regulate the action of the heart. *Megh Raga*, as the name indicates, means a "cloud", and is mentioned historically as having the power to bring rain. While *Deepak* can create fire. *Bahaar*, the melody of springtime, is gay and lively, and induces happiness and light-heartedness. *Darbari* again is contemplative, grave and dignified and if sung at midnight till about three o'clock in the morning, creates a meditative mood; while *Bageshwari* is romantic and passionate and when sung at midnight, fills the heart with tender emotions.

INDIAN MUSICAL INSTRUMENTS

Turning to Indian musical instruments, according to the old classical treatises like *Sangitaratnakara*, the musical instruments have been classified into four main groups: the *Tat* and *Betat*, which are stringed instruments; *Sushir* or wind instruments; *Avanagh* or drums; and the *Ghan* or cymbals; and there are a variety in each group.

The *Tat* instruments are those that are played with a bow, examples of which are the *Sarangi* and the *Dilruba*.

The *Betat* instruments are those in which the strings are plucked with the fingers, examples of which are the *Thanpura, Sitar, Veena, Been and Sarode*.

In the *Tat* and *Betat* instruments again, there are those played on the open strings, while others are arranged with movable frets placed at measured distances on the body of the instrument against which the strings press when played upon.

The *Tat* instruments are considered the nearest in tone to the human voice in so far as the subtle inflections and unbroken succession of tonal notes is concerned. The *Sarangi* and *Dilruba* are examples of this.

In the *Betat* type of instruments, the strings being plucked either by the fingers, the finger nails grown specially long, or by means of a plectrum or *Mizrab*, the notes are staccatto, with beautiful overtones that prolong the notes into sweetness, by the *Meend* or microtonal created notes achieved by legato movements,

[1]Ananda Coomaraswamy, *Dance of Shiva and Fourteen Other Essays*

Plate 85

Miniature paintings illustrating important *Ragas.* (1) Malkaus, Bundi school, mid-18th century A.D. (2) Deepak, Bundi school, mid-18th century A.D. (3) Vasanta, Pahari school, early 19th century A. D. (Courtesy, National Museum, New Delhi). (4) Hindole, (Courtesy, Prince of Wales Museum, Bombay.)

Plate 86

1

2

3

4

Miniature paintings illustrating one of the important *Ragas* and three *Raginis*. (1) The Megh Raga. (Courtesy, Prince of Wales Museum, Bombay.) (2) Todi Ragini, Mewar, 17th century A.D. (3) Bhairavi Ragini, Mewar, c. 1650 A.D. (4) Megh Malahar Ragini, Mewar, 17th century A.D. (Courtesy, National Museum, New Delhi.)

Plate 87

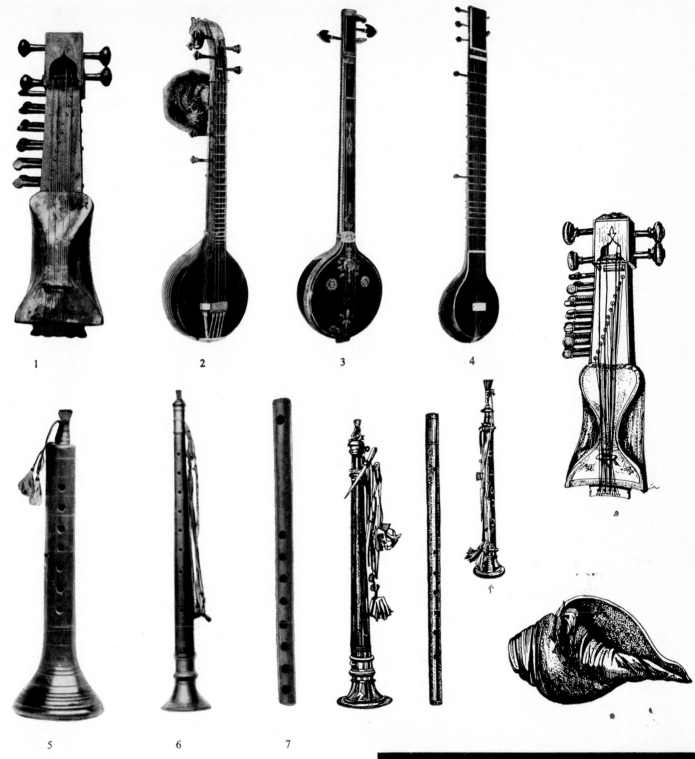

Various types of string and wind instruments. (1) *Sarangi*. (2) *Veena* (Tanjore model). (3) *Thanpura* (Tanjore model). (4) *Sitar*. (5) *Shanai*. (6) *Nagasvaram*. (7) Flute. (8) Conch. (Photos copyright, Government Museum, Madras.)

Plate 88

(1) The *Sitar* (Punjab). (Photo, A. L. Syed.) (2) *Veena* (Photo, E.S. Mahalingham.)

1

2

whereby sound is carried from note to note. In the Hindustani or North Indian style of classical music, the well-known instruments are the *Sarangi*, the *Dilruba* (mostly used in Bengal), the *Sitar* and the *Been*. In the Karnatic or Southern style of classical music, the *Veena* is the best known and most popular.

The *Thanpura*, drums, *Shanai* or *Nagasvaram* and *cymbals* are common to both schools of music. The *Thanpura* belongs to the lute family. It has no frets and only four long strings, which are tuned to the sound of the key note, the upper key note twice and the octave below, notes which are common to all *Raga* melodies. The pitch is adjusted to the singer's voice, and the strings are played continuously one after the other; as they vibrate, they lend the background accompaniment to the song and help the singer keep in tune. Expert singers use only the *Thanpura* for their accompaniment which supports the beauty of pattern of the melody and voice.

In the *Sarangi* there are four main open strings for creating notes with the fingers of the left hand pressing on the correct spots. It has also about thirty-two open *Tarabs* or resonance wires that vibrate in harmony as the melody is played. In the *Dilruba*, there are movable frets placed at measured distances against which the strings press and specific notes are produced. The bow gives the notes a long and sweet tone.

The *Sitar* has seven main strings and twenty sympathetic strings for resonance. Its frets are adjustable and are arranged according to the *Raga* being played.

The *Veena* again has frets and is India's most famous sweet-sounding stringed instrument. The strings are plucked with the right hand, while the left hand plays on the seven main strings that press on the twenty-four frets. Four strings passing over the body from the tuning pegs aid rhythm; and with one plucking of one of the strings, a series of tones can be created by the left hand passing over the string and pulling it outwards to prolong and embroider the sound. The compass of the *Veena* extends over three and a half octaves, lending it tremendous scope for many grace notes and an infinite variety of harmonics and even double-stopping as is achieved in the violin in Western music. Richness of sound is gained by its having two gourds, one at either end.

The *Been* of North India is somewhat like the *Veena* of the South, in that it has two gourds also. There are four main strings for playing the melody and three to give the rhythmic beats of time. As rhythm plays an important part in all Indian music, the instrumentalists help guide their melody by using their little fingers to flick the last string and mark the time. The frequent use of cross rhythms gives Indian music its stylised character and mode of the very expressive combination of tones and microtones. The rhythms being founded on accent and verse metre emphasise continuity of sound.

The *Mirdanga* is the long classical drum, played with both hands, one hand on each end. While being played, the instrument is placed with its body resting on the ground.

The *Shanai* (North India), and the *Nagasvaram* (South India) are types of clarionet, and when well played are very melodious; particularly the *Shanai*, which is softer and sweeter in tone than the *Nagasvaram*.

MUSIC AND THE DANCE

All classical dances are accompanied by orchestras comprising several musical instruments and one or more singers.

In the Bharata Natyam of Tamil Nad and the Kuchipudi of Andhra Pradesh, where the Karnatic or Southern school of music is followed, there is the recitation of the dance word syllables which are duplicated on the *Mirdanga*, and the rhythmic beat of the main timing by another *Mirdanga* and cymbals. The recitation is done in a sing-song fashion either with the mode of certain dance syllables or the actual names of the scale (Sa, ri, ga, ma, pa, dha, ni, sa) in the particular *Raga* melody being used. The *Mirdanga* keeps the main *Tala* that has been selected and another one is played with the dance word syllables that follow each step of the dancer. The singer recites the dance word syllables synchronising with this drum and the cymbals. Where the *Abhinayam* or emotional interpretation enters, the beautiful lyrics are sung in Telugu, Tamil, or Sanskrit, and accompanied by the soft melodious tones of the *Saraswati Veena* and the *Thanpura*, and often the violin also, which keep the singing in perfect tune and maintain the correct key. Often the flute is used, particularly in the Krishna themes; and the *Nagasvaram* is played when triumphant or marriage music is required.

In Kuchipudi, one of the unique instruments used is the *Thithi*, a wind-bag instrument with a reed mouth-piece to emphasise the *Sruti* or degrees of pitch and the embellishments displayed in the music.

In the Kathak and Orissi schools of the dance, there is the use of the Hindustani or North Indian school of music. The recitation of the dance word syllables are duplicated most popularly on the pair of drums called *Tablahs*, though quite frequently the *Pakahvaj* also is used, and the rhythmic beat of the *Manjiras* (cymbals). The *Sitar* is often played with conspicuous success in the pure dance sections, with its beauty of staccato and legato melodious tones in a harmony of support to the intricate rhythms. In the *Abhinaya* or emotional interpretation of Kathak, the songs are sung in the old *Brij Bhasha* or chaste Hindi or Urdu and accompanied most frequently by the *Sarangi*, soft, gentle, plaintive and sympathetic, giving subsistence and grace to the human voice. Here, too, the flute is popular in all the Krishna themes. In Orissi, the songs are sung in fine poetic Orissi language or in Sanskrit.

In the *Kathakali* dance dramas, one finds that the music accompaniment comes nearest to real opera, except for the fact that it is the musicians and not the actors who sing. The entire drama savours of a picturesque highly dramatic operatic pantomime, with highly skilled classical techniques and a marvellous gesture language, supported by facial expressions. One sees in this school a magic world of dance and acting unique in the world. There is the use of the *Madala* (type of *Mirdanga*) and the *Chenda*, a cylindrical drum peculiar to Kerala, the gong on which the chief singer keeps time while singing, cymbals for rhythmic beats and the deep sounding conch shell to intensify the dramatic effect of certain sequences. The music is used to support the whole drama, and the Karnatic or Southern school of classical music is employed, sung in Malayalam.

In Manipur, as has already been explained, the emphasis is on the *Mirdanga*, slightly different to that of the classical shape, in that it narrows more at either end, and a wonderful combination of sounds is produced when played, wherein one side emits bass sounds while the other side sounds in a higher key. The *Esraj*, a special stringed instrument, *Manjiras* (small cymbals) and the sweet-toned bamboo flute complete the instrumental accompaniment. The chanting of the beautiful lyrics is done in Sanskrit, Bengali, the old Meitheli language or in one of the Manipur dialects.

As the classical dance in India was the fore-runner of the Sanskrit drama, music and acting play an important part, and are complementary. The dance has in it all the elements to explain a story and interpret it fully. Music supports these, illuminating the dance movements and throwing them into focus. It is therefore that both instrumental and vocal music form such an essential part of all dance in India, whether it be the classical or folk forms. Traditionally, all the classical treatises tell us that dance and music must flow in one perfect pattern of visual and aural synthesis—acting and dramatic interpretation giving them lucid meaning.

With the conclusion of this chapter, the Dance in India, has been described in its many facets. Its early beginnings in Nature, its philosophical content, its foundations, its various classical interpretations in the different regions of India, its comprehensive language of gestures and its close relation with timing, rhythm, music and dramatic interpretation. Now we turn to the final phase, namely, costume and jewelry, two very vital factors that give the Indian Dance its distinctive character in the actual performance. Design creates beauty in both costume and jewelry, and these in turn beautify both dancer and the dance.

13. Design, Costume and Jewelry in the Dance

DESIGN, COSTUME and jewelry play a very important part in the dance, and in fact, to tradition in India. The classical dance treatise, the *Natya Sastra* by Bharata Muni, clearly tells us that *Aharya* or expression through dress, ornaments and other aids are an essential part of the *Abhinaya*, the other three being, *Angika* or expression through the limbs and body, *Vachika* or expression through the voice, and *Sattvika* or the mental expression of feeling and emotion through facial expressions and use of the eyes and eyebrows, neck, etc.

Indian design has taken the same course as the Indian Dance and the other arts in using Nature as the model, and by taking inspiration from the religious and philosophical ideals underlying Natural Creation—Nature mysteriously and subtly transformed by the symbolic. It is evident that the early Hindu artist let his mind dwell on the refreshing calm of Nature and he sought to invest in his designs a beautiful whole, the entire conception of which would be one of perfect content. His decorative sense was influenced by suitability of background, proportion and harmony. True beauty according to him was achieved when the mind was pleased equally with what the eye discerned. He followed the simple rules of Nature for his patterns, without the symmetry being too obvious. So he studied the lotus and the jasmine, the rose and the water-lily, the marigold and the temple flower, the mango and the cashew apple, stars and moon, fish and birds, trees and creepers, for his inspiration. And though he did not always copy their actual colours, he used tints that would in no wise destroy the suggestion underlying them. Then he used gold and silver to create richness and form a striking background to offset textiles and jewelry.

In order to substantiate the fineness of patterns and enhance mood, light and shade of colour were considered. Noting the rainbow as it arched against the sky, he used primary colours on small surfaces and in small quantities, balanced and contrasted by primary colours of the same intensity to harmonize with one

168

another. This was required so that in the variety of tones he used, there should be no encroachment of one shade of colour on the other.

With these strict ideals before him, it is no wonder that the Indian designer achieved so much interrelation of pattern, so much skill and thought, with the quality of delicacy in ornamentation and execution. Many times too, he invested his design with the figures of Gods and Goddesses and other mythological characters whose characteristics he had become familiar with and which had become firmly imprinted on his mind from his constant association with festival and religious ceremony, drama, dance and legend. Much of all these thoughts and concepts are traceable to the old beautiful designs of prints, weave and embroidery that have come to posterity; not to speak of the many other crafts in which we find these same ideals and motifs—ceramics, paintings and jewelry, to name just a few.

Indian dress throughout the ages is unthinkable without the added beauty of ornament. Hindu painters and sculptors from earliest times have shown vividly the charm and excellent workmanship of jewels worn through the ages. Our temples are profusely illustrated with sculptures that are repositories of the varied styles of jewelry and ornament. Gods and Goddesses were given unique and characteristic jewels, and part of the wonder and majesty of these deities was their resplendent apparel and jewelry.

Indian jewelry has been created to suit the ideals of Hindu design, dress and environment. Artists' ideals of floral pattern, figures, line, composition, geometrical design, birds and leaves, have been woven into it, so that Indian jewelry remains ageless, and even today, women the world over can wear it with the greatest effect, no matter what their national dress; whether their choice is of jewelry comprising necklaces of gold and silver, gem studded or enamelled in translucent colours, chaplets of pearls, armlets, earrings, bracelets, anklets or rings.

Turning to the costumes and ornaments worn in the various classical dances of India, one finds an emphasis on the decorative motif, with an eye to line and comfort in movement.

BHARATA NATYAM

The girls wear a rich blouse (*Cholie*) that is cut short about three inches above the waist, made of gold or of a bright hue, edged at the elbow length sleeves with a wide border of contrasting colour woven with gold. The drapery consists of a fine soft silk *Saree* of any bright shade such as red, peacock blue, orange, green or even rich ivory, either plain or designed, with gold motifs on the material, composed of thin lines or squares, or a sprinkling of dots and flowers, and bordered by a wide heavy embossed edging of brocaded gold in floral pattern.

In traditional style, one end of the nine yards long *Saree* is tucked between the legs and taken to the back and tucked into the waist to allow freedom of movement. The other end (the *Pallav*), which is very richly woven with gold and designs, is draped in front like an apron, so that as the dancer moves, it opens out like a great petal of gold.

Today, many dancers have the *Saree* stitched into this shape, instead of draping it, as it is easier to wear and falls into the required lines without effort.

The dancer also wears a gold waist belt decorated with minute bells, a neck choker of antique design called an *Addigay*, composed of a single row of large rubies, and a pendant of rubies and pearls. Also a large garland-necklace called a *Mānga-Mālay* (Mango garland) in gold, consisting of a number of small mango-shaped pieces studded with small rubies and strung together, with a splendid large pendant of precious stones and gold. The lotus-shaped ear-tops rest on the lobes of the ears, and have small bell-shaped jewels dangling from them. A matching head jewel of rubies outlines the forehead at the hair line, with a small pendant that rests in the centre of the forehead; this jewel has a narrow jewelled piece running along the centre parted hair, with two circular jewels fixed on either side of it. On the knot of hair at the back, a circular jewel is screwed on, and jasmine flowers are woven round the chignon. Often the dancer wears her hair in a long thick braid. In this case, the entire length of the plaited hair is thickly woven with flowers and she has the same flowers made into a sort of crown for her head. On the feet, tiny ankle bells, the number varying from fifty to many more for each foot, are fixed on a band. They tinkle musically and help the dancer in maintaining her rhythm.

ORISSI

Girl dancers today wear the saree to flow gracefully from the waist to the feet, with the loose end fixed to fall from the left hip instead of being draped across the chest and over the left shoulder. The decorative *cholie* is embellished at the neckline by a heavy jewelled necklace. An ornamental waist belt, armlets, bracelets, a head jewel with a pendant reaching to the centre of the forehead, flowers in the hair and ankle bells complete the ensemble.

KATHAK

Girls often wear a short glittering skirt, and it spreads out like an up-turned blue-bell as they pirouette. The skirt falls over a tight fitting, tapering, ankle-length satin trousers. A short top blouse (*Cholie*) in brocade or bright silk is enhanced by the use of a delicate gossamer length of gold-designed material which is draped over the head, across the chest and tucked into the waist at one side. Bracelets, necklaces, a head jewel, often similar to the one worn in the Bharata Natyam, bordering the hair line at the forehead with a pendant, or a beautifully designed fan-shaped jewel that is fixed to one half of the head, are both equally effective.

Today, however, this costume is less often seen, and dancers prefer either the conventional *Saree* or use a tight fitting tunic (*Kurta*) reaching to the knees, in place of the skirt.

KATHAKALI

The costume and jewelry of the dancers in these dance dramas of Kerala are most unique. According to tradition, these dances are performed exclusively by men and grown up boys taking the feminine roles, though today girls are playing their own roles in increasing numbers. The men wear a large jewelled crown studded with coloured stones, a pair of earrings to match the crown, fixed by means of a stick pushed over the top of the ears, so that the earring covers the entire ear. Bracelets and armlets are very ornamental. Three long scarves, called *Uttariya*, flow over the shoulders and fall in front on either side, where the ends of the material are formed into large rosettes. Into these rosettes, mirrors are fixed for the artistes to use.

A wide billowing skirt in white material flared with red and slightly padded to stand out, their chests covered with colourful breast plates set with stones; flowing hair made from fine strips of bark from an indigenous tree and falling long at the back up to the knees, and ankle bells, complete this striking costume.

There is a legend that the author of Kathakali went and lay down on the sea-shore to contemplate about the costume and make-up of the players. A vision passed before his eyes on the crest of the waves, and each character appeared fully dressed. But because they stood on the waves, he could only see their get-up from the knees upwards. He therefore copied each detail, and then gave all the actors the billowing white skirt to represent the foaming sea.

The female characters use a short, close fitting jacket covered by several necklaces, and long tapering sleeves. A splendid designed cloth is draped around the waist and falls like a sarong in straight lines. The head drapery tied closely around the head is made to protrude to the left, its ends falling at the back. Saints and ascetics wear long artificial hair tied on the top of their heads in a large knot.

MANIPUR

The girls wear bright coloured satin ankle-length skirts that are heavily embroidered and ornamented with sequins and tiny scintillating mirrors. The embroidery, which runs from the edge to half-way up the skirt, is so heavy that the garment stands out stiffly. Over this, a transparent silver striped over-skirt is worn, reaching to the knees, and this too on account of the very heavy silver- and mirror-worked border stands out in graceful folds all round. A velvet jacket and a diaphanous head handkerchief covering the face and slightly raised on the top of the head by means of a conical head jewel, complete the ensemble.

A waist belt of gilt and sequins and mirrors with a front piece ending in a square that is richly embroided and sparkles with a myriad facets, add more lustre to the costume. Rows of silver bracelets and a necklace are the only ornaments. Sometimes a garland is worn or flowers encircle the wrists. No dance bells are used.

The boy dancer who generally plays the role of Krishna in the group dances, wears a fine gold coloured waist cloth that falls to the ankles. Breast pieces crossed on the chest are worked with silver, beads and tinsel, and he uses a magnificent headdress which is topped with a fan-shaped plume of peacock feathers interspersed with red and tinsel. Jewelled pendants and necklaces add the finishing touches.

The men who take part in the Drum and Kartal dances are dressed more simply. They usually wear the long waist cloth with a plain jacket and a red and gold bordered white turban. Round their necks they wear a velvet garland.

KUCHIPUDI

In Andhra, as already explained in the chapter describing the classical dance dramas of the Bhagavata Mela Natakam of Kuchipudi, it was shown how these

Brahmin Bhagavatulus formed themselves into a group after the high standards and ideals of the dance of the Devadasis began to deteriorate. They used the old dance drama form of the Yakshagana which was formerly performed by the Brahmins in the temple *Mandapams* for the entertainment of worshippers. To this form of dance drama, they added fine classical dance techniques, *Daruvus*, *Padas*, and hand gestures, developing the art of the Bhagavata Mela Natakam dance dramas, the Parijata Apharanam, which developed into the Bhama Kalapam, being the most famous of their dance dramas. In these dance dramas, much of the old costumes and make-up seem to have been retained in Andhra, and so the dance dramas today graciously present that stylised old-world atmosphere and colourful characteristics that one finds in the Kathakali dance dramas of Kerala.

THE BHAGAVATA MELA NATAKAM OF KUCHIPUDI

Traditionally only men took part, and do so even now, Vedantam Satyanarayana Sharma being celebrated today for his wonderful, inspiring and realistic performance as Satyabhama in the dance drama, Bhama Kalapam. In all the dance dramas, the costumes are rich and full of colour; and usually the important characters and kings wear a bright waist cloth draped like a pair of trousers, with the ends folded and kept in place at the ankles by ankle bells. A fine tunic coat reaches to the knees and is enhanced by the use of garlands. The king usually has an ornamental high crown, pyramidical in shape, broad at the head and tapering upwards. The crowns vary according to the character being portrayed. The King and most of the noble characters, besides wearing elaborate head-dresses, have fine decorative epaulettes (*Bhuja Kirties*) that stand out impressively, necklaces with rose-like pendents (*Patakas*), earrings (*Karna Kundalam*), and neck scarves that flow in front and are held in place with the waist belt. They all use wigs and moustaches of hair, and in some cases even beards.

The make-up also varies for different characters. Generally, Kings and noble characters have their faces painted red and white, with yellow and blue markings. Saints, like Narada, have a make-up of red, white, yellow and green paints; and Vishnu in the character of Narsimha (incarnation as the Man-Lion), uses a wooden mask. Asuras (demons) and Yakshashas (female demons) have painted masks, the former using a mixture of yellow and red, and the latter green, blue, white and red, to distinguish them.

Satyabhama is the leading character of the Bhama Kalapam, and is also the consort of Sri Krishna; therefore she is always very beautifully dressed and ornamented. She has her long heavy braid of hair fully decorated with a jewelled strip that covers the whole length of it, and this includes ornaments in the shape of the incarnations of Vishnu. She wears, according to tradition, different ornaments for each day of the week, and these are usually replicas of those worn in ancient times by famous queens. Using a brocaded *Saree* and blouse (*Cholie*), Satyabhama has a jewelled waist belt (*Vaddhanam*), an ornament that outlines the forehead with a gem-studded centre-piece; side ornaments on the head shaped like a crescent moon and the sun; flowers in her hair, bell-shaped earrings dangling from a floral ear-top; and many bracelets and ankle bells complete the ensemble.

The Gopi in the Golla Kalapam dance drama, is prettily dressed in a bright

Saree, her hair in a top knot that is encircled with a garland of tiny conch shells. She uses pearl necklaces, and carries a basket on her head in which pots of milk and curds are placed.   And as she moves, her many bracelets make soft music.

YAKSHAGANA

In Andhra, as previously mentioned, the old dance dramas known as the Bahu Nataka, which portrayed the ten different types of what was known as the *Shiva-Leelas* or Legends of Lord Shiva, gradually developed into the Yakshagana. This form spread to other parts of the country, and was performed as Yakshagana in Andhra, Tamil Nad and Karnataka; as Lalita in Maharashtra; as Bhavai in Gujarat; Yatra in Bengal; and as Gandharva Gana in Nepal.   In each area, costumes and make-up varied according to tradition and regional taste.   In Tamil Nad and Karnataka, there is probably a general resemblance of costume and make-up.   In the troupe I saw from Karnataka, true to tradition, only men took part.   They wore for the most part rich waist cloths draped over the legs like trousers, folded over at the ankles and tied with the conventional dance bells. Over this, they had a deep blue or green or coloured jacket worked with beads on the shoulders, front of the sleeves and on the jacket front.   The breast pieces crossed on the chest were worked with coloured stones, with a front panel piece also embroidered in gold and coloured stones.

The head-dresses varied here also, with different characters using different crowns that sparkled with the inset stones or the use of peacock feathers.   The large crowns were round, oval, fluted or pointed and in size were about twice the height of the face.   From the back of these enormous headdresses, a white drapery floated and spread out fanwise at the back, its ends tucked into the waist on either side.   Many armlets, bracelets, necklaces and rings adorned their persons.   The faces were painted in mask-like fashion, with varying tints and characteristic strokes to indicate the various characters.   Rice paste was the basis as in Kathakali and no beard was used at all.   Usually moustaches are made of real hair.

Their themes being taken from the *Mahabharata*, the *Ramayana*, and the Krishna legends, heroes like Bhim and Yudhister, the famous Pandava brothers, have the face painted yellowish pink, with red on the cheeks, and white near the corners of the eyes and along the bridge of the nose.   Moustache and beard are of hair.

The romantic figures and musicians and singers, and the hero of the play, have their faces similarly painted as the above two noble characters, but they do not wear beards, and the headdresses are different.   The demon king wears a huge white beard and moustache; two large white blobs of rice flour are applied on the bridge and tip of the nose and on either side of the face, coming round half the forehead, the eyes and just under the cheek bones.   Near the cheek bones, the spot is decorated with red.

There are then the Red and Yellow demons.   The former has a red face and black moustaches, with a green and black painted beard on chin tip, streaks of white below and above the eyes and drawn from the nose outwards.   On the nose, he has a white triangle, and an enormous 'V' in green on his forehead. The Yellow demon is painted yellow, and wears a white paste beard, a huge white blob on his nose and two enormous semi-circles of raised white flour from nostrils to forehead on either side.   His eyes are decorated with heavy white designs.

As the dancers whirl with great speed, leap and float by in a sort of flying movement, the whole effect is very picturesque and fantastic.

Now that the various styles of the classical dance have been described in detail, together with their accompanying music and costume, we must turn our attention to the folk dances of India. The dance as expressed by rural and tribal India is both varied and tremendously alive throughout the country. Nature plays a vital role in influencing these vast and multifarious folk dance forms, which are closely associated with religious veneration, seasonal occupation and celebration.

14. Folk Dances of India

WHEREAS THE classical dances in India tend to be subject to a definite order, a recognised strict form, and a complicated system of gesture language, footwork, bodily movements and rhythm, the folk dances are generally quite spontaneous and are the creation of the people's imagination and desire for artistic and emotional expression. Displaying no inclination towards a rigid form, the whole depiction of folk art is guided more by the subject of the songs that either glorify Nature, express traditional occupations or offer devotion to the deities. Seasonal and religious, they have a sense of freedom, with regional affinities and differences, embodying within each material outward manifestation, a warmth of expression, and a charm and beauty that are refreshing by their very untutored quality.

Here we find a true analysis of the creative urge of the people in general that has come down through the ages by way of actual performance and remembrance of song and motif, its survival unsupported by the written word, and stabilised because of its tremendous sociological impact and basis. Through these arts, custom and tradition have been established; and with their continuance, India is the richer. With national consciousness of the arts growing from day to day, many of these beautiful expressive dances are coming to urban audiences and are being received with the enthusiasm and success they deserve. Now they are taking their rightful place along with the classical dances in the furtherance of our cultural heritage.

At the very outset I may mention that the number of folk dances in India is legion. I have selected a representative number from each region of the country, south, east, north, west and the centre, which will convey just how varied and unique they are, often having subjects in common.

SOUTH INDIA

1. *KOLATTAM*. Playing and dancing with little lacquered sticks held in the hands is popular throughout India. In the Kolattam, danced in Madras State

(Tamil Nad), young girls using lacquered sticks dance in celebration of the birth-day of Rama, hero of the *Ramayana*. On this auspicious day, flowers are strewn and young girls dressed in brilliant coloured *Sarees*, their hair wound with jasmine, dance in festive spirit.

Forming into squares or circles, and hitting their sticks criss-cross, they advance and move round and round, clapping their sticks up in front and below, as they bend to the right and to the left. Suddenly, they move backwards and forwards; turn one towards the other and beating their sticks sideways and in the centre, move round and round.

Then they leap forward on the toes, stepping back, and thus making many pretty and complicated patterns. This is a folk dance the popularity of which has come to the city and it is practised in home and schools. Very enjoyable for the young, it would take the same place as country dancing in the West. Other varieties of the Kolattam have accompanying religious or philosophic songs or lay stress on the beauty of musical composition.

2. *PINNAL KOLATTAM.* This is another type of Kolattam performed in Madras State, and we find that the dancers are doing here a Maypole as well as carrying painted sticks. A number of coloured streamers are attached to the top of a pole by means of a hook, and eight dancers go round and round, each one holding one streamer by the end. Winding the streamers into a pretty plaited rope, they move in circles and squares and lines, placing the toes forward and back; reversing and going first in one direction and then in another, they beat their sticks at the same time and keep changing their places.

Having woven the plaited rope, the dancers move in reverse and unwind the strands, at the same time circling, crossing one another's paths, kneeling and coming to position opposite one another. There is an accompanying song and chorus that speaks of the tapping of the sticks in rhythm, of the twining of the streamers, of happy youth and of the happy dance.

3. *VASANTA ATAM.* In springtime, when the trees come to blossom, and the air is crisp with the perfume of flowers, the peasants of South India dance to celebrate the birth of Nature. Their palms coloured with turmeric, and dressed in orange *Sarees* with vivid contrasting borders, girls and young women fore-gather before the village deity and crown her with garlands.

Little boys and girls bring mango buds and sing in chorus to the accompani-ment of cymbals, hand claps and the small round drum, the *Dholak*. They sing and dance extolling Barathi, Mother Goddess of the Earth. Men carry sticks, five feet in length with gold painted knobs and hung with crimson flowers and mango leaves, to form a background to the dance, the movements of which are in tune with the words of the song of praise. Young girls placing the vermilion dot on their foreheads, bow and turn round, circling with flat of foot and using some pretty gestures that denote joy and pleasure. As each girl pirouettes, she joins once again in the big circle. The stepping is simple in a metre of four.

4. *THE KUMMI.* This dance usually takes place in Tamil Nad during the Hindu New Year of the South which falls in January, just after the celebration of the Pongal festival. Cattle are beautifully caprisoned in crimson and gold, their necks hung with burnished brass bells and garlands of flowers, their foreheads touched with vermilion. Considered sacred to Shiva and to Krishna, these animals are taken in procession to the accompaniment of music and drumming. The festival lasts three days, when new rice is cooked, and prayers

Plate 89

Folk dances of South India. (1) Pinnal Kolattam, Madras. (2) Kolattam, Madras. (Courtesy, Publications Division, Government of India.)

Plate 90

1

2

Folk dances of South India. (1) Kaliyat-
tam dance, Kerala. (2) Sacred folk dance
of Kerala. (Photos, Darshan Lall.)
(3) Pulayarkali dance of Kerala. (Photo
copyright, Mohan Khokar.)

3

Plate 91

1

2

3

Folk dances of South India. (1) Solo dancer in a typical posture from the Ootam Tulal of Kerala. (2) Close-up showing make-up and head-dress of the Ootam Tulal dancer. (3) The Sari dance of Kerala. (Photos copyright, Mohan Khokar.)

Plate 92

1

2

3

4

Folk dances of South India : (1) The Karagam of Tamil Nad. (2) The Peacock dance of Tanjore, Tamil Nad. (Photos, Darshan Lall.) (3) The Huttari, the harvest dance of Coorg, Karnataka State. (4) The Suggikunitha, the harvest dance of Mysore. (Photos copyright, Mohan Khokar.)

are offered to Vishnu, the Merciful Aspect of God, to Ganesha the elephant-headed God, Giver of Good Fortune, to Indra, Lord of Heaven and to Gouri, Goddess of Plenty. Groups of young girls dance with varying steps and clapping hands, using little mincing steps in circles upon circles. Then they do three steps from side to side, jump and pirouette. The dance is accompanied by songs that do not necessarily bear on the subject on hand. As in all village dance and song, there is a joyous and a serious side. After worship and prayer for the occasion, there is dance and song in happy celebration. The Kummi takes several forms in Tamil Nad. There is the Flower dance done to a song that extols the beauty of many blossoms, the Housewife's dance, performed to a playful song telling of household chores, the joyful Mavilakku Kummi, the Milkmaid's dance, the Sarasvati Kummi and the National Song Kummi dedicated to Tamil Nad, to name a few.

5. *DUMMY HORSE DANCE-PLAY OF TANJORE—FOLK DANCE DRAMA.* One of the most picturesque and unquestionably interesting performances is the Dummy Horse Dance-Play done in rural South India near the temple towards autumn. Heavily attired in colourful costumes, dancers stand in a frame of a horse made of paper, cloth and light wood, brilliantly painted and draped. Each animal weighs about 120 pounds, and the dancers have to be very skilled to balance themselves perfectly, as they dance for hours together on wooden legs that work inside the framework, to the rhythm of music and drums. Dancing in front of the deities, using expressive gestures and relevant facial expressions the dances interpret themes from mythology. An interesting fact today is that the dancers are also introducing the old traditional music in the mythological subjects, and modern music compositions with popular appeal for social subjects. Historical themes are also a popular feature. Among the varied themes are the following.

a. *Ram Shastri.* This is a famous Mahratta historical subject of Western India, and the hero is Ram Shastri. He was an upright man and adviser in the State. He put an end to corruption and evil and set order in proper functioning. The dancer dresses in the Peshwa Mahratta costume of the period of Medieval India with a red and gold circular turban and flowing garments; and he rides on a white horse that has bright coloured tassels and a head-piece of red, a crimson neck-piece and blue draperies.

b. *Comic Interludes.* These are diversions in the more serious themes. The peacock and the zebra are most often impersonated and cause much merriment with their fantastic movements. The peacock has realistic colours common to the bird and wears a huge tail of feathers. The zebra has his stripes and is draped in blue and white.

c. *King and Queen.* These are characters of mythology. The dancers do not speak but use gestures and movements for interpretation. The king wears a grand crown, and his horse is jewelled and draped in red and green; while the queen has a dazzling crown, blue costume and she rides a horse that is draped in crimson and green.

d. *Draupadi and Bhima.* This famous Pandava hero and the beautiful princess Draupadi are characters from the *Mahabharata*, and are nearly always included in the selected subjects of the Dummy Horse shows. These two noble characters have white horses with beautiful decorated golden head and neck pieces, and royal blue draperies. The queen is dressed in velvet and spangles, with a small tiara. Bhima has a golden crown, a pale gold coat, and holds a mace in his hand.

e. *Shiva and Parvathi*.   Here is a subject from mythology and sacred legend. In this instance, the horse is replaced by the animal sacred to these deities. Parvathi rides on a white lion which is decorated with silver necklaces and blue draperies, and she is dressed in blue and gold.   Shiva rides on a white bull that has light blue draperies, and golden necklaces and head-piece.   The God wears a golden fluted crown and a jewelled stole over His golden garments.

This is really a colourful and picturesque show that combines the art of pantomime, drama and dance.   Decorative motifs are carefully selected and are appropriate to character. Vigorous movements done while manipulating these heavy animals, keeping time and interpreting the theme, the dancers have to work hard to keep up the tempo of the performance for several hours. These various characters described are the leads in the varied subjects that comprise these dance shows.

6. *OOTAM TULAL*.   This can be placed amongst the folk dance forms, for it is a type of pantomime dance akin to the classical Kathakali, and has been evolved by the people after the manner of Kathakali.   It is usually performed during the day in festival time by a single artiste and accompanied by a singer, a drummer and a cymbal player.

The performance commences with the customary loud drumming, followed by invocations chanted to Ganesha, representing wisdom and fortitude, and to Goddess Saraswati, representing Learning.   The story is then recited in simple lyrical verse, and the actor sings the songs which the musicians repeat; so that the dancer in this style constantly first sings the songs and then renders them in dance and mime, with appropriate hand gestures.

As in the Kathakali, episodes from the two great epics, the *Ramayana* and the *Mahabharata*, and from mythology are interpreted, the performance by this single performer going on for several hours.   He uses a mask of make-up on his face, composed of green paint and rice flour, red lips and the eyes are elongated and enlarged with antimony.   His jewelled crown, though less heavy and pretentious than in the Kathakali, glitters with coloured stones and tinsel, and his breast-piece and necklaces and bracelets sparkle.   The dancing in the Ootam Tulal is far less stylised than in the Kathakali, and the gesture language and *Abhinaya* less complete.   The dancer, during the intervals of the song and interpretation does a great deal of forceful stepping with postures and circling, and his facial expressions are very mobile.   It is quite amazing how this single performer can go on for hours interpreting some of the choicest and select excerpts of Malayalam literature.   Performing in the outer courtyards of the great temples, before a really understanding and appreciative audience, he is one of the central figures in the programmes of entertainment during festival time.

7. *KAIKOTTIKALI*.   This dance is performed by young women and girls in Kerala.   Forming a circle, they sing songs in chorus, keeping time with their hands.   The theme of the song is the well known story from mythology that once when Lord Shiva was in deep meditation on the loss of His Consort Sati, Parvati (who was Sati re-born after performing austerities) sought to win back the love of her Lord.   Shiva would not be aroused from His meditation.   Parvathi being attacked by a demon Asura, fell at Shiva's feet for protection.   At that moment, Kamadeva, the Cupid of Hindu mythology, drew his flower-decked

bow and shot an arrow at Shiva. Opening His eyes, the great God was filled with wrath and burnt Kamadeva to ashes with the power of His Third Eye.

Dressed in spotless white, the young women and girls form into the conventional circle and stepping round and round, clap one another's hands, slap their own hands together, and bend and go round. The rhythm of the song and dance is slow and measured, and the movements simple and graceful.

8. *SARI.* The Sari is generally performed during harvest time in the village in Kerala. Young women and girls dance in squares and lines in a group, dressed as usual in spotless white. To the accompaniment of a haunting melody, they use their arms and hands most effectively with many attractive movements and gestures. One notices immediately, that although it is a folk dance, there is emphasis on the rhythmic patterns of pure dance, with a wonderful studied syncopation between the technique and the beats of the *Madala* drum and cymbals. The stepping is well defined and varied, the dancers using the flat of feet and heels, stamping, moving to the right and left and forwards and backwards, and constantly utilizing the stance of placing the legs apart with knees greatly bent, a peculiar feature of the Kathakali pure dance sequences. The tempo of the performance is beautifully balanced, as it rises gradually to a climax of a faster pace and comes again and again in stages to the slower rhythms of action in general with which the dance began.

9. *TAPPATTIKKALI.* This dance is performed by young women and girls in Kerala during the festival when Lord Shiva is worshipped. Shiva as Mahadeva, honoured on this day, is the deity concerned, but the songs accompanying the dance are in praise of Shiva and Vishnu. One of the older women in the group commences the song and leads the dancers, the others repeating what she sings and following her movements. Circling round and round, and clapping their hands to the rhythm of their steps and the music, the dance is attractive and truly rural with the simplicity of footwork, the vivaciousness with which the movements are executed, and the expression of sweetness on the faces of the dancers.

10. *HARVEST DANCE OF THE KODAVAS.* Traditional dances are done in the area known as Coorg, a part of Mysore State, at harvest time. The men of the community gather in the fields and take part in the lively group dance, dressed in traditional long black tunics over white trousers, a sash tied around the waist, and picturesque white and gold turbans. They form into a great circle, carrying shields and long canes or sticks. To the accompaniment of singing and drums and pipes, played by the Erawa farm labourers, the dancers move round and round with forceful movements. Jumps, the raising of one foot, and balancing on the other, crossing of sticks and waving them in graceful yet strong strokes and swings, the dance is distinctly *Tandava* or Forceful in style, and speaks of the old days of chivalry amongst this martial race.

NORTH INDIA

11. *KAJRI.* The peasants of North India usually dance the Kajri during the rainy season, when they propitiate the Vedic God Indra, Nourisher of the Earth, and Agni, Quickener of the Seeds, and ask for their blessings for a successful harvest.

The dance movements follow the songs that are accompanied by the rhythmic beat of the round drum, the *Dholak*, and cymbals. There is the soft lullabye of a *Jhula* or swing that is moved in rhythm and is artistically decorated with flowers and coloured tassels. This is part of the festivities. As no particular hand gestures are indicated, usually clapping and buoyant singing denote joy and eagerness.

12. *NAUTANKI*. This old dance is traditional to Uttar Pradesh, and is a popular form of folk dance drama. The songs and main theme are recited in operatic style and are accompanied by the drum and music. Acting, dance movements, with circles and turns and movements of going backwards and forwards on the flat of foot, the dance dramas interpret the age old story of the Victory of Good over Evil as told in the *Ramayana* and the *Mahabharata*, in history and legend. Some of the themes are of a social character, though nowadays, these tend to be somewhat spoiled by the introduction of what is called something "modern".

13. *RAS LILA*. In Mathura and Brindaban in Uttar Pradesh particularly, where the legends connected with Sri Krishna, Radha and the Gopis and Gopas are most popular, numerous dances are performed based on the Krishna legends —the Ras Lila or group dance being the best known. To the accompaniment of songs telling of the childhood, boyhood, and early manhood of Sri Krishna, and the sound of drums and cymbals, and the flute, this popular type of dance is enacted during the days dedicated to Sri Krishna. Fine movements can be seen in these performances, many of the steps being common with those of the Kathak classical dance. Flat of foot, pirouetting, acting and mimicry play their part to an almost finished degree. The rhythms are excellent, and follow the quick movement of the dancers as they go forwards and backwards, stamp the feet, glide on the toes and use graceful arm movements with simple gestures. Playing the parts of the Gopis and Radha, now imitating them, now being shy and now lively, the expression of the dancers is full of freshness and charm.

14. *KARAN or WORSHIP OF THE HOLY TREE*. This occasion for the performance of the Karan or the worship of the Holy Tree, marks the happy period when the harvesting is over. In Shahabad in North India, the festival commences with fasting during the day. Then a branch covered with green leaves is cut from the tree, smeared with vermilion powder and butter and planted in the small compound or enclosure in front of the village hamlets. It is then decorated with flowers and garlands.

Following this, there is a worship ceremony, and then the offering of corn and molasses. The whole village takes part, with the performance of feats of strength and dancing. Women dressed in bright colours, with marigolds in their hair, and men wearing their best apparel, stand in a row and commence singing and dancing to the beat of the *Mandar* drum.

The men in their row move forward, till they stand face to face in a parallel row with the women's line. First they all move towards the right and then to the left, in a measured stepping of four steps, changing into a three-step movement, and pausing on the fourth step. All the while they gradually form into one great circle. The entire group then join together, turning round and bending and singing the songs of praise in chorus.

15. *KUMAON DANCE*. Up in the lovely Himalayan resort of Ranikhet in Uttar Pradesh, in the Kumaon Hills, group dances are done in celebration of the autumn festival of Dusserah. Only men take part, dressed in long white tunics, tight trousers and red sashes. Forming a circle and moving round and round,

facing one another at intervals, they move in a slow rhythm to the accompaniment of the *Dholak*, a long S-shaped trumpet and cymbals. Songs are sung speaking of the history and legend of the area, and the dance continues in a rhythm of eight beats, with the stress laid on the first and fifth beats. Now they circle again, with upraised arms, moving forward and crossing one foot before the other with a slight heave, and using the flat of foot, and now they intersperse movements with jumps and whirls. Sometimes, just two male dancers perform with forceful turns, brandishing swords with their right hands and holding shields in the left. The music blares forth, and the rhythm is strong as the dancers move faster and faster, now facing one another and now circling. Traditional, yet spontaneous, these dances have come down through the ages to celebrate festival and social events.

16. *THE JHORA*. Unlike the Kumaon dance proper, which is done entirely by men, the Jhora is a community dance and is done by both men and women, all castes joining in the celebration. It is a very lively dance done during festival time, and a great number of dancers participate, linking their arms and moving in a large circle as they advance with simple stepping. Dancing to a count of four or eight beats, they stand and bend, sit down, and then prance around in a merry alternation of movement and counter-movement. Life and joy seem to spring from this lively performance and draw the whole crowd into the spirit of joyousness.

17. *THE CHAPPELI*. This is one of the romantic dances of the Kumaon Hills, the Himalayan area of Uttar Pradesh. The dance is often performed at weddings and in springtime. Depicting as it does the spirit of romance, dancers perform in twos, holding a mirror in one hand and a coloured hankerchief in the other, which they gracefully wave, as they advance forwards and backwards in rhythmic stepping. Now it is lively, now gentle and romantic, and is accompanied by romantic songs and the *Dholak*.

18. *DANCES OF HIMACHAL PRADESH*. In this beautiful part of the Himalayas, there are several charming folk dances done by both men and women regularly, either together or separately. On the borders of Gharwal and its mountain villages, there is the Thali dance, done entirely by the Jaunsar women, and which is a very graceful performance. They hold brass trays, and forming into a circle, move forwards and backwards, with little slow steps, singing the while in chorus. It is in happy celebration of stringtime and festival. In the Jadda and the Jhainta festival dances, men and women participate with a great deal of freedom of both movement and rhythmic stepping. While the Thora dance again is in commemoration of the ancient days of chivalry when men danced before going into battle. The dance is very forceful, full of firm stepping, and as the men brandish their swords, they move faster and faster to the accompaniment of the *Nagara* drums and curling trumpets.

19. *DANCE OF THE SHEPHERDESSES*. In Chamba, another beautiful part of Himachal Pradesh in the Western Himalayas, there is the charming pastoral dance of the Gaddi women or shepherdesses. This dance, often called the Peasant Dance of Chamba, is done in two groups, composed of two circles, which go round and round with measured stepping and pretty hand gestures, to the accompaniment of a little catchy tune in fine rhythm. The songs are sung in chorus as the dancers perform; bending to either side, one set of women sing a line of the song and the others repeat it in chorus. With the light stepping, and the

lowering and raising of arms, as the wrists turn and the fingers form the shape of flowers or the opening of the bud into blossom, the dance takes on a delightfully appealing air of gaiety.

The men dance too, but they make a group of their own and their style is naturally *Tandava*, with a much faster tempo. Moving in a great ring, and going round and round at a good speed, this dance is popular at the annual fairs and at festival time. Singing accompanies the dance, and the songs tell of the legends of old or of the heroic days when men were warriors and the old bards came to the village to tell of their stirring exploits.

20. *KULU DANCES.* The Valley of the Gods is the name by which Kulu is known, because of the hundreds of silver-headed deities that are placed on beautifully decorated palanquins and taken in procession during the weekly fairs and festivals that occur in this lovely little valley in East Punjab, Western Himalayas. The biggest festivals are held in spring and autumn at Dusserah time. In mid-May, the Gods are taken to visit the Goddess Tripura Sundari, the patron Goddess of the village of Naggar, Kulu's summer capital. On this occasion, the silver heads of the Gods are carried on richly draped palanquins resplendent in crimson and gold, with scintillating umbrellas overhead. Another procession headed by the dancers and their musicians approach from the opposite side and both processions meet at the temple square. Thousands of people dressed in brilliant costume collect to watch the celebrations, and booths are erected. Then the Gods are placed in front of the temple entrance.

The men dancers, dressed in the traditional tight white trousers and tunics, with bright bordered shawls and black plumed caps lavishly draped with blue primulas and yellow Basanti (jasmine), begin their performance. Forming into the conventional circle, and holding a handkerchief in their right hands, they wave it with supple wrists and move round and round in a stepping of eight beats. Sometimes, there is a slight change, and there are four steps taken with a pause on the fifth, and three more steps with the flat of foot. Then suddenly, as the great group pauses, two or three dancers come into the centre of the circle and commence dancing with brandishing swords; then they circle these weapons very fast, round and round in the air, with great skill. The dance is accompanied by the *Dholak*, the resounding tones of the large silver-mouthed bell-shaped trumpets and small clarionets. As the musicians sing, they recall the old days of chivalry and romance and speak in praise of the deities. Moving from the rather slow and measured dance at the commencement, the entrance of the sword dancers raises the tempo of the performance till it reaches a climax.

The entire scene is colourful, with the dancers in their picturesque regalia, the resplendent Gods and the people in their bright shawls; all set against a backdrop of the beautiful Himalayan scenery and snow-capped peaks. Often these dances are performed when a farmer wants a rich harvest, and he has the principal deity carried for worship to his field. Dancing follows the ritual. The same performance that is seen at the fairs can be witnessed on such occasions.

21. *THE ROUF.* This lively dance is done essentially by women in Jammu (State of Jammu and Kashmir) and takes place usually on festival days during the harvesting season. The dancers form into two rows, about fifteen girls in each, and form a sort of chain by placing their arms across one another's backs. Walking gracefully in rhythmic stepping and moving forwards and backwards, the dancers sing in accompaniment. Each row of girls takes up the refrain as the

other starts the line. Dressed in bright skirts and draperies, with heavy ornaments of silver, their faces laden with smiles and animation, the dance is very attractive.

22. *THE HIKAT*. This is another dance done in Jammu, to the accompaniment of the performers' own singing. Groups of young girls and boys dance the Hikat for the sheer joy of expressing the exuberance of life. Their hands held crosswise, pairs of dancers circle round and round in a fast spin; their heads and bodies bent backwards, the girl's right hand is clasped in the boy's right hand and her left hand in his left hand. They face each other and move in perfect precision in a dizzy spin; a feat requiring good balance, perfect timing and the very precise moving of the feet close together as they go round and round.

23. *THE BHANGRA*. This is the most popular and best known dance of the Punjab, performed on all festive occasions. Forming into the usual large circle, the dancers start going round, so that during the performance as many dancers as wish to can join in the circle from time to time even if they have not joined at the start. The drummer takes his place in the centre of the circle, and as he plays his rhythmic beats, he every now and then gives the signal to the dancers to increase their speed. The three dancers who stand just behind the drummer lead the movements, and as the performance unfolds, there are lively movements of whirling round and round, beating of feet, clapping of their long sticks; and as they get into the spirit of the dance, they cry "Hoi Hoi" (Up, Up) to raise the excitement and fun of the dance, as they leap into the air. Then at intervals, there is a short pause in the dancing, and a *Dholla* or a *Boli*, which is the traditional folk song of the Punjab, is recited in fine rhythm. Following this, the dance starts once again.

This popular dance has its usual season, which commences with the sowing of the wheat and concludes with the Baisakhi festival when the wheat is harvested. The dance is done only by men and is performed every full moon in some open field of the village, to the accompaniment of song and the *Dholak*. Full of life and rhythm, backed by resounding songs and drum beats, the men dressed in a bright coloured waist cloth like a sarong and turban, and black waistcoat studded with sparkling buttons, this dance is not only spectacular, but is the national community dance of the Punjab.

A similar type of Bhangra is danced by men of the Dogra (warrior) community of Jammu.

24. *THE GIDDHA*. Just as the Bhangra is done entirely by men, so the Giddha is done exclusively by the women of the Punjab at festival time and during the sowing and harvesting of the wheat crop. With a long tradition behind it, this dance is noteworthy for graceful movements, and the lovely simple melody that accompanies it. Forming into a circle, the women go round and round, waving their arms and supple wrists, raising the arms and turning and moving forwards and back. Dressed in a bright *Shalwar Kameez* (wide trousers and tunic), with contrasting scarves, they make a pretty picture in this old pastoral dance of the region.

25. *HOLI or THE CARNIVAL OF COLOURS*. All over North India, the ushering in of spring with the throwing of colour, accompanied by dance and song, is the cause for much celebration and merriment. In Uttar Pradesh, for instance, women gather together in groups and with long syringes in their hands, dance gracefully with lively stepping, and turning round and round as they advance, work their sprays, casting multi-coloured powders in all directions. Dressed

in vivid colours, as they sway and bend sideways and forwards, taking small four step movements, the colours of the powders make a veritable rainbow.

Groups of men in a separate batch of their own commence singing loudly and dancing, creating a maze of colour as they move, their clothes covered with patches of purple, indigo, vermilion and crimson. The peasant women do not join with the men, but celebrate separately, dancing and singing in chorus—their fast movements and clapping hands extolling Mother Earth and the beauty of bud and blossom.

Throughout Rajasthan in central North India, Holi, the springtime celebration, is observed with great rejoicing. The Jhumar or Ghumar is a popular dance done by the women of Rajasthan on days like Holi and other festive occasions. Decked with flowers and scintillating jewels, the light glistening on their bright full skirts, bodices and draperies, the dance takes on a lively and colourful character. Commencing in a quick quartette of steps, emphasising each third beat in the rhythm of seven, they retreat and circle quickly in opposite directions. Swaying their hips and raising and lowering their face veils, they sing in chorus in accompaniment to the dance.

The men celebrate by themselves on the streets and on the village green. They become loud and noisy, the dance and song becoming quite boisterous. Thus the holiday spirit spreads far and wide.

26. *DIVALI DANCES*. During this festival of the New Year, the women of Rajasthan celebrate with dance and song. The most popular dance is the Jhumar or Ghumar, the graceful performance already described under the Holi dance celebrations.

27. *THE GINAD*. Rajasthan is an area where there are innumerable forms of the folk dance done during the various festive occasions. The Ginad is a very popular community dance performed in the Sekhwati region of Eastern Rajasthan, and is danced by people of all castes. They join together and perform in the period of about fourteen days before the spring festival of Holi. Gay and joyous, with the spirit of friendship, this dance can be seen in every group of tenement houses, to mark the commencement of the coming festival of the Carnival of Colours.

28. *GANGORE or THE FESTIVAL OF FLOWERS*. This picturesque celebration peculiar to Rajasthan is dedicated to Goddess Parvathi, also known as Gouri, the Yellow Goddess, emblematic of the ripened corn. The ceremonies begin when the sun enters Aries, the beginning of the Hindu New Year in Rajasthan. Barley is sown in a small trench, and artificial heat is applied till it germinates. The images of Gouri and Ishwara (Shiva) are made in clay and placed side by side. Women and girls then join hands and dance round the barley trench, invoking the blessings of Gouri, the Bountiful One, to bless their husbands. After a few days, the image of the Goddess is taken in procession to the lake. She is gorgeously dressed and ornamented. The women form a circle and dance round the deity, moving rhythmically in a one-step pattern, holding hands and going round and round while singing in chorus.

With graceful bending and swaying, their full skirts tiptilting around them, and keeping time with clapping hands, the dance continues in picturesque form. The hymns of praise dedicated to the Goddess that they sing are enhanced by the clang of the cymbals. Gangore is essentially a woman's festival, and the dance is done exclusively by them in a procession of their own. Flowers abound in their hair, in their garlands, in the garlands adorning the Goddess, and in the lavish floral tributes that are cast into the lake as the deity reaches it and is immersed with ancient ritual.

29. *HARVEST DANCES*. Immediately following the Festival of Flowers, when the peasants are eager to lay the first fruits of the golden corn before Prithvi, representing Mother Earth, in thanksgiving for a successful harvest, these dances take place.

Colourfully dressed, the peasant women enter the scene with circles of gay movements and form the conventional ring, with clapping hands. They sing praises to Surya, the Divine Aspect of the Sun, and bow to Goddess Prithvi. Then they show in gesture and movement, the cutting of the ripe corn, make it into bundles to carry on their heads, thresh and pound the grain, winnow it and finally place it in baskets. The dance further describes with gesture laden song, the making of *chhappaties* (flat, round, baked wheat bread) and ends with fast chasing movements and quick stepping.

The dance is usually done to a timing of eight counts, with the stress laid on the first and fifth. It commences with the coy veiling of the eyes, and moving round in circles. Then each movement is done to the speed of the main count and repeated at double the speed, with the emphasis placed each time on the right foot. There is a slight jumping movement where the dancers work along from side to side, and then continue for the most time in a straight line forwards and backwards. Finally, they cluster into a deep circle and move inwards and outwards like a great flower closing and opening. Their wrists are supple, their gestures easy and clear, as they sing in chorus to the accompaniment of clashing cymbals.

One of the songs, in a rough translation, goes like this:

"The breeze is blowing gently, so gently,
The corn is waving gently, so gently,
The sun is shining, the girls are smiling,
The scythes are cutting; the bracelets are jangling,
Ohé! la-la-la-la-la-la,
Jai Prithvi! My bundle is the heaviest.

"The black mud is sinking gently, so gently,
The river is flowing gently, so gently,
Red skirts are clinging, anklets are clinking,
Jewels are gleaming, bodies are bending,
Ohe! la-la-la-la-la-la,
Jai Prithvi! My bundle is the heaviest.

"The grain is being pounded gently, so gently,
The bread is baking gently, so gently,
The red flames are leaping; the young girls are dancing,
The men are relating, tales so entrancing,
Ohe! la-la-la-la-la-la,
Jai Prithvi! My bundle is the heaviest."

30. *KRISHNA DANCES*. The festive days connected with the Krishna legends are celebrated in Rajasthan with pomp and music and dance. One of

the interesting dances is the Jhulan Leela, or the Play of the Swing.   It is celebrated to commemorate the birthday of Sri Krishna, and is the occasion on which
the baby image of the Lord is placed in a cradle and rocked, while girls representing the Gopis or milkmaids sing and dance.   It is an early autumn festival
when the fields are like carpets of gold, and new birth is the theme of the main
song, as the girls rock the decorated cradle adorned with flowers, leaves and
tassels.   Clasping hands, the girls dance around the swing, moving with slow
measured steps, and gradually increasing the speed to the melodious rhythm of
their songs.   Cajoling with pretty gestures, swinging lightly round and round,
the songs are sometimes composed spontaneously, and sometimes traditional
songs are used.

One of the created songs, in a rough translation, goes like this:

"Little Baby Krishna I rock You in a cradle,
Under the shady Banyan tree,
Whose green crisp leaves are playing cymbals with each other;
So go to sleep my Little Darling.

"Little Baby Krishna, I have fastened Your cradle with silken strings;
And made for it a silver stand,
Decorated with tassels and malika flowers;
So go to sleep my Little Darling.

The breeze blows over the scented flowers,
And with the perfume fans Your eyelids,
The Gopis with tinkling anklets,
Are bringing your curds and butter,
So go to sleep My Little Darling."

31. *GOPIKA LILA*.   An original dance of the Gopis is performed in
some of the villages of Rajasthan during the local festivities in honour of Sri
Krishna.   It deals with the coquettish play of the milkmaids who on passing a
stream, place their water jars down and get ready to bathe.   Dancing as they
form a group, they feel the water with the tips of their toes and withdraw in mock
fear of the cold.   Then unbinding their hair, they enter the water and bathe.
Just as they finish, it begins to rain, and so they rush for shelter avoiding the
teasing humming bees.   Then dress, and soon the showers pass and the peacocks
come out and dance in joy with outspread tails.   The movements of the Gopika
Leela are fast and are done in the most popular eight beat timing, with the emphasis on the first and fifth counts; the original movement and gestures follow the
chorus song, and the dancers swing their hips, move forwards and backwards
clapping their hands.   Finally, moving apart, they   e together again and go
round and round very quickly, their stepping imitati   the mincing gait of the
peacock.

32. *KHAYAL*.   Just as there are the dramatic da.. · dramas found in the
classical forms in certain regions of India, so there are also folk dance dramas
in India.   The Khayal is one of these peculiar to rural Rajasthan.   Lore and
legend form the themes and as in the case of the classical dance dramas, here too,
only men participate, the feminine roles being played by very young men or grown
boys.   This old dance drama can be traced back to the 16th century A.D., when

Plate 93

Folk dance of North India. The Dangi dance of Chamba, Himachal Pradesh. (Photo copyright, Mohan Khokar.)

1

Folk dance of North India. The Sangla dance of Mahasu District, Simla Hills. (Photo copyright, Mohan Khokar.)

2

Folk dance of North India. The Chauphala-Kedar dance of Garhwal. The performers hold yak-tail whisks which they wave in the dance. (Photo copyright, Mohan Khokar.)

3

Folk dance of North India. The Kulu springtime dance, Kulu Valley, the Punjab.

4

Plate 94

1

Folk dance of North India. Bhangra
dance of the Punjab. (Photo copyright,
Mohan Khokar.)

Folk dance of North India. Bhangra
dance of the Punjab. (Photo, Darshan
Lall.)

2

Plate 95

1

Folk dance of North India. The Ghumar
dance of Rajasthan. (Photo copyright,
Mohan Khokar.)

Folk dance of North India. The Chhaja
dance of Jammu. (Photo, Darshan Lall.)

2

Plate 96

1

Folk dances of Western India.
(1, 2) The Garba, (Courtesy,
Indian National Theatre,
Bombay. Photos, Rajdatt.)

2

Folk dances of Western India.
The Krishna Bhajan dance,
Limbdi, Gujarat. (3) In the
lotus formation playing cymbals. (4) In the flower formation. (Photos, Author.)

3

4

art and its varying forms were at their zenith in Rajasthan. Inspired by legend, history and social events, and the charming love story of Dhola and Maru, the traditional lovers of Rajasthan, these dance dramas have a rich repertoire of themes. Various folk troupes from the Bhawai community have been formed and they commence to tour the State, giving their performances, after the rains are over. Powerful movements, mime and chanting characterise these performances which are done to the accompaniment of drums, stringed instruments and cymbals. Colourful costumes, a strong point among the people of this region, and decorative effects add great attraction to these old-world dance dramas.

15. Folk Dances of India—
Continued

WESTERN INDIA

33. *DHANDYA RAS*. In the region called Limbdi in the State of Gujerat, folk dancing has been systematised into a unique form, with a technique of footwork and display of figure movements. The men dance among themselves, performing all night to the accompaniment of the drum, songs and cymbals in the village. The Dhandya Ras is their most popular group dance, done by twenty-four men who hold short lacquered sticks. The song accompanying it tells of one of the important episodes from the epic poem the *Ramayana*, embracing the banishment of Prince Rama, the abduction of Sita, the war against Ravana and the victorious return home to Ayodhya of Rama and Sita. Singing in chorus, the dancers form an intricate series of movements, first with a rhythmic six-stepping, holding hands and moving round in a circle. Then, increasing the speed, they beat their sticks and each dancer makes a swift pirouette; after this they beat one another's sticks, and wave them with supple wrists over and over; change places and move in a complete circle; and finally, form into an inner and an outer circle.

All the time the speed is gradually rising and the dancers change to a very beautiful movement, in which the outer circle of dancers bend and cross their sticks and the inner circle of dancers cross their sticks above their heads. Then they cross and criss-cross exchanging places, and move again into a big circle, till the outer circle of dancers comes inside and the inner circle moves outside. Finally, the dancers form a bridge with their sticks in twos, moving opposite to one another, while every alternate man dances between, making a running circle with moving bridges. They squat, turn, and then run in the opposite direction. As the dance speeds up, rising in tempo in a quick change of three-stepping, turns and leaps, with the formation of these various patterns, they all sit down in groups of four in their places after every series of two patterns, in order to get some rest. The chorus however continues, and without any perceptible jerk, the movements of the dance once more flow on from the sitting position into the dance itself. The dance is very vigorous, and the timing is kept on a pair of drums, with certain pronounced beats being made to give the rhythm a very catchy, lithe and lilting syncopation that seems to add a tune to the drum beats and enhance the poetic metre of the songs.

34. *GANAPATHY BHAJAN.* The same dancers from Limbdi in Gujerat dance the famous Ganapathy Bhajan sacred song dance. It commences with a prayer song in honour of Ganapathy or Ganesha, the Giver of Good Fortune, and is also performed in a group by men only. It is conducted with each dancer holding a pair of cymbals and playing them as he moves. The prayer song calls on the deity to save the world from sorrow and grant good fortune; and requests the God to remove all pain and sadness from His worshippers and grant them peace. The light of their lives (the Soul) is like a flame, and they place it as they would the sacred fire (*Arati*) before Him in all humility.

Forming themselves into a circle in a sitting position, the dancers commence playing their cymbals with uplifted hands in sheer joy and fervour. One dancer comes into the centre and leaps rhythmically, then sitting down, throws his legs out and somersaults with somewhat the movement of a strutting bird. This movement is then repeated by a couple of others who exchange and inter-exchange a red scarf each time they whirl and leap.

Another dancer then enters the circle and dances on one foot only, with the other up-raised—all the while playing his cymbals and swaying backwards and forwards. And in the centre he moves and jumps forming a pivot for the dancers in the circle round him who sway and play their cymbals in a beautiful harmony of rhythmic beats.

35. *KRISHNA BHAJAN.* This is a light dance theme performed by men only, the performers being the same group from Limbdi in Gujerat State. The song tells of how the Gopis had gone, according to legend, to the banks of the Jamuna river at Brindaban (Uttar Pradesh) to fetch water, and seeing Sri Krishna standing there, were filled with rapture and adoration of Him. But they complained that He could not understand their love. While they sang, Sri Krishna's eyes were filled with a Divine pity for them, and His tears flowed with little sounds like "har-ra-ra-ra-ra-ra." Going to the forest under the Kadamba tree, the Gopis then danced in a group, which filled them with an inner joy in complete compliance with His Divine Will. In the play of the dance, Sri Krishna pulled their veils which tore delicately, making a sound like rustling leaves, "Par-ra-ra-ra-ra-ra."

In this group dance, the men perform entirely in a sitting position. Playing their cymbals and swaying their bodies rhythmically, they make various figure forms, as they move forwards and backwards, and form into a star shaped group. Now they form a rowing boat, now they lie backwards and form into the star shape again. Now they make a circle that sways, and now they form a circle in reverse. Beautifully timed and moving their bodies rhythmically, they play their cymbals, marking their religious fervour by the rising tempo that the dance reaches as it proceeds to its climax.

36. *RAS LILA.* The women of Limbdi in Gujerat State have their own group dances in which only they participate. One of these is the ever popular theme of Sri Krishna dancing with Radha and the Gopis. On full moon nights they dance this famous dance to the accompaniment of the melody of the sweet

toned bamboo flute and the *Dholak* drum for rhythmic timing. This dance done in circles with great charm and verve is also danced on the birthday of Krishna and at the Divali and Holi festivals.

37. *SOCIAL DANCES.* In the pretty villages near Limbdi in Gujerat State, young farmers' wives and peasant women dance this simple spontaneous type of dance mostly centering around village life. Amusing songs accompanied by a coquettish dance with teasing movements, fast stepping, circling and swaying, bending backwards and forwards, the dancers use gestures telling of the singing of the Koyil (cuckoo) in the pretty villages of Warla and Ginajari, where there are many flowers that delight housewives; but where there are no brooms for sweeping their floors to their despair!

Another group dance done in the traditional circle with song and clapping hands says, "Ah! the village fair is filled with lines of coloured bangles, glass and ivory and lac; what a beautiful jingling sound they will make on the slender wrists of the little wife as she busily grinds her corn. Ah! the jingling and the tinkling will sound like the cow-bells as the animals return in the evenings from the fields. Ah! the colours of the bangles will be shimmering like the stars on the blue waters and the moon on the golden corn."

The dances are simple, with simple four-step movements, a few gestures to indicate objects mentioned in the songs, with attractive bright costumes, good looking animated faces and gay singing that add greatly in charm as the dancers go on endlessly circling and clapping their hands to the rhythmic beat of the *Dholak* drum.

38. *THE GARBA.* It is believed that most of the dance forms of Saurashtra, a part of Gujarat State, can trace their origin far back in antiquity to the time of Sri Krishna who is believed to have ruled in this part of the country for nearly a hundred years. It is said that it was the Assamese princess Usha, granddaughter-in-law of Sri Krishna who popularised the Garba Lasya Nrtya in Saurashtra; that Sri Krishna himself gave the Ras Leela to them.

At the beginning of Aswin (September-October), comes the Dusserah festival, preceded by a nine-day celebration of Navratri. Villages give thanksgiving at the end of the monsoon rains with song and dance in which men and women, girls and boys, join in joyfulness. Village girls carrying decorated pitchers and pots of clay go from house to house ushering in the festival by dancing around the household "Garbi," the ornamented pot containing offerings and hung at the doorways. Later, they celebrate by dancing around Goddess Mataji, Giver of Plenty and Prosperity. The songs are light and filled with joy. The dance stepping is simple and is done by a group of dancers going round and round in circles, bending to the right and left and forwards, stamping the feet in a rhythm of four counts, and clapping their hands in sweeping gestures. During the Holi spring festival, these dances are very popular also, but then the themes centre around the Krishna legends, the little incidents of everyday village social life and the entrancing beauty of spring. Usually in the song, one of the girls with a good voice leads the first line and the others follow in chorus. This popular folk dance has been introduced into the cities, and is a favourite item at Gujarati gatherings and stage performances. In the cities, the themes of the dances are a little more sophisticated and the songs are composed to tell of the modern young girl, her fancies and her education, etc. But most popular of all are the Krishna legend themes. At all times though, the colourful costumes and lovely

old prints of the textiles, the sweetest of melodies, the grace and freedom of movement, are redolent of a charming old world atmosphere. A popular Garba song runs like this:
Yeshoda, the mother, says of the child Sri Krishna—

"Find Sri Krishna's earrings, they are lost—
They are golden with strings of silver;
No one can look as beautiful as He in them;
And so I search each street,
And go from house to house looking everywhere.

"There is nothing but a beautiful pearl in them,
Here am I churning the buttermilk,
While Sri Krishna leans over me, His
Arms around my neck, and feeling so distressed—
The earrings are lost
Therefore I search and search——"

39. *DANCE OF WORSHIP*. This is a simple and dignified dance performed in honour of the Goddess Randal, titular deity of some of the villages in Gujarat. Goddess Randal is a favourite with women, and on the day dedicated to her, women erect a bower with a seat on which is placed a piece of cloth and a figure is drawn on it with seeds and corn. A bowl is placed over the figure, and a coconut with two eyes painted in black collyrium with a nose in red lac is decorated with silk and silver. Lamps are kept alight for several nights, and then the girls gather around and sing songs of praise, interpreting the meaning of the words in dance and mime. The dance consists of slight swaying done to the rhythmic pulsations of the song metre.

40. *THE TIPPANI*. This is a community group dance in which the Koli village women excel, and it is a variation of the Garba and Gheraiya dances. But it is distinctive as it is done with the play of *Tippanis* or long sticks that have rounded bases and are tied with bells at the top. Flashing round and round in circles, moving their *Tippanis* in perfect rhythm as they beat the floor, turning and manipulating the sticks dexterously, this is a vibrant dance form full of colour and deft movement.

41. *GANESH CHATURTI DANCE*. During August-September, there is the religious festival dedicated to Ganesha or Ganapathy, the elephant-headed God of Wisdom and Fortitude. After the Pooja ceremonies, when the images are taken in procession to be immersed in the sea or river, the whole of Maharashtra celebrates with song and entertainment. Throngs of people follow the processions, and young men and boys forming two long parallel lines and holding each other with arms crossed over one another's shoulders, dance and sing to the accompaniment of cymbals. Getting their arms free, they bend and clap or play their cymbals, doing a fast jumping four-step of two feet forward and then back. The parallel line advances sideways for some time and then forming into a circle dance in a series of patterned movements, with the stepping changing also in the combinations and permutations of syncopated footwork. The rhythm is very catchy, and the dancing goes on and on in one fast pattern of movement and then into another and another; the dancers bending and circling with force-

ful turns of the entire body, and now waving the arms, now stretching them forwards and downwards in a constant rush of movement and pattern. The dance is very stirring and emotional, the drummer playing at high tempo. Women attach special significance to this festival as Ganesha was so specially devoted to his mother, the Goddess Parvathi.

42. *THE LEZIM DANCE.* This fascinating rhythmic dance performed with the *Lezim* or small mallet is the most popular in Maharashtra, and one can see it during festival time, performed in public squares and along the streets with processions. Groups of young boys and girls holding these *Lezims* in their hands do a very fine series of figure movements while they sound their *Lezims* to the accompaniment of the drum that beats rhythmically its metre of eight counts. Advancing, hopping, sitting, turning and going backwards as they bend; forming squares and lines and sometimes circles, the dance goes on for a long time in perfect unison of movement and play of the *Lezims* with the resounding drum beats. Like the Ganesha Chaturti festival dance, the Lezim dance is full of verve and as it proceeds, the tempo increases, creating a very beautiful pattern of sounds and movements. The dance is popular during the Gokul Ashtami festival in honour of Sri Krishna's birthday.

43. *DAHIKALA or THE DAHI HANDI DANCE.* This is another popular folk dance of Maharashtra performed to celebrate Sri Krishna's birthday, and tells of the legendary episode of Krishna's pranks when during His childhood he stole in mischief his favourite dish, which was fresh curds. Here again, the dance goes along with processions and shows the quick impish movements of the gay and innocent youthful doings of a much loved and mischievous child. Songs and cymbals and the *Dholak* accompany this lively dance.

44. *THE DASAVATAR or BOHADA.* Dance dramas peculiar to various regions of India are popular dramatic performances that have come down through the ages and withstood changing times. This interesting old folk dance drama form follows its own system and takes place on an improvised stage. The subjects are for the most part taken from mythology and legend, and the performance invariably commences with the *Sutradhar* or State Manager calling on and invoking Ganesha or Ganapathy, Saraswati, and finally Vishnu and His ten Incarnations of Matsya (the Fish), Kurma (the Tortoise), Varaha (the Boar), Narsimha (Man-Lion), Vamana (the Dwarf), Parasurama, Ramchandra, Krishna, Buddha, and Kalki.

Following this, the drama takes place. The subjects of these performances are usually selections from the *Ramayana* and the *Mahabharata*. They may include the war scene between Rama and Ravana; the legend of Narsimha and Hiranyakasipu; the story of Bhim, the powerful Pandava prince, and so on. Vigorous dance techniques, lyrical chanting and recitations telling of the incidents in a narrative form, and stirring accompaniment of the drum and cymbals, create a truly dramatic dance form in the folk dance idiom of Maharashtra.

45. *TAMASHA.* This is the operatic folk dance form of Maharashtra, with a certain amount of dancing in it. The players sing and narrate the story with mime and in between there is dance. The men do forceful martial movements, going up and down and using their arms with strong thrusts. The women sing in a high voice and their dancing is quick, concise, and staccato, with rhythmic pauses to accentuate the gusto. Chorus and solo, alternately high pitched and low voiced, vivid mime and brilliant costume, give it a character that is quite unique.

Plate 97

1

2

Folk dances of Western India. (1) The Tappa dance of Saurashtra, Gujarat.
(2) The Dhandya Ras of Saurashtra, Gujarat. (Courtesy, Indian National Theatre,
Bombay. Photos, Rajdatt.)

Plate 98

1

Folk dances of Eastern India. The Masked
Mystic Lama dance from the Mystery Play of
the Eastern Himalayas as done in the monastery
at Darjeeling. (Photo, B. Bhansali.)

Folk dances of Eastern India. (1) Men dancers of the
Kashi Hills in Assam in the Nongkrem dance. (2) The
women dancers in the Nongkrem dance. (Courtesy and
photos, Films Division, Government of India.)

2

3

Plate 99

1

Folk dances of Eastern India. (1) The Ghumara or drum dance of Orissa. (2) The Chadaya or festooned stick dance of Orissa (Photos copyright, Mohan Khokar.)

2

Plate 100

1

2

3

4

Puppets. (1) The Tollubomalattam or Shadow Play of Andhra Pradesh ; a leather puppet in the character of the *Vidhusak* (2) The *Kathputli* or puppets of Rajasthan representing Amar Singh Rathaur and Dwarapal (door-keeper). (3) The Bomalattam or puppets of Andhra Pradesh representing the Nayaka and Nayika (symbolic of lovers). (4) The Bomalattam or puppets of Madras representing Hanuman (*left*) and Rakshasha (*right*). (Courtesy and photos, Bharatiya Natya Sangh, New Delhi.)

EASTERN INDIA

46. *THE JATA JATIN*. This is a type of dance peculiar to that part of Bihar known as Mithila. Grown-up girls and young housewives gather together in the courtyards on full moon nights during the rainy season and dance from midnight till dawn. This charming old-world dance interprets the romantic story of the lovers Jata and Jatin, who were separated and had to undergo many hardships and sorrows, before they were freed from the machinations of the wicked boatman who kidnap-ped the beautiful Jatin.

Accompanied by the drum and singing, the dancing is done in a great circle, with simple stepping and bodily movements, as well as expressive mime that tells this epic story of true love. As the dance reaches its climax, the story unfolds the fateful episode when the wicked boatmen kidnapped the girl Jatin. This is actually done in the dance by one of the dancers who breaks through the circle and laying his hands on the heroine, makes as though carrying her off. The dance goes on interpreting the story and ends on a happy note as the romantic episode comes to a happy ending.

47. *SPRINGTIME DANCES*. All over North India, and in many other parts of the country, springtime is a season for celebration and song and dance. In Bihar, not only is Holi celebrated with gay song and dancing in groups, but this is the season of the flowering of Nature, when the ancient Ba festival is celebrated. People decorate their homes with fresh flowers and leaves and commemorate the day with dancing and singing for three whole days. These gay happy dances are noted more for the spontaneous movements of joyousness and the spirit of happy "getting-together" than for any special technique.

48. *THE BAISAKH BIHU*. This is really a non-religious dance celebrated in early spring, sometime about the middle of April (Baisakh), and performed on the occasion of the Bihu festival, after the harvesting. Gifts are exchanged, and boys and girls gather in parties and dance in groups together to the accompaniment of the drum and song and chorus. This charming community dance of Assam is an annual affair and is attended with a great deal of enthusiasm, for the boys and girls are then allowed to mingle freely together while they dance and celebrate.

49. *THE KHEL GOPAL*. Here we have again a dance that centres around the Krishna legends. The dance is really quite complex, and details several episodes, ending with the great Maha Ras group dance. It begins with the time when Krishna was young, dancing with his companions the Gopas. Suddenly they are attacked by the wicked demon Bakasura. Krishna fights the monster in a duel and slays him, and then He and the Gopas dance in triumph. The dance then becomes more lively as a group of Gopis come to join the celebration. As they dance with joy, another wicked demon Shankhasura comes on the scene and tries to attack them. The dancers being interrupted, break up their circle, whereupon Krishna once again engages the evil creature in battle and slays him too. This is the occasion for further happy celebration with the great Maha Ras, in which Krishna, the Gopis and the Gopas join. The dance ends with the dancers representing the ten *Avatars* of Vishnu, as the Gopis leave.

There is much spectacle and drama in this Krishna Lila or Play of Krishna in dance form. The movements are lively as all group dances tend to be, with patterned stepping, light and graceful interludes when the Gopis are participating, and *Tandava* or Forceful in the sections where Krishna slays His adversaries. Accompanied by the *Khol* drum, with its bass and falsetto tones beautifully offsetting one another, and cymbals and song and chorus, this group dance is a popular feature in Assam.

50. *RAKHAL LILA.* This dance is also connected with the Krishna legends, and depicts the dance of the Gopas or cowherds who danced and played with Sri Krishna during his childhood and youth. Large groups of young boys dressed in bright apparel perform this dance during Holi and the spring festival time. Performing in the open fields, it is gay and full of abandon, mischievous and full of fun. Lively fast stepping, mime and a quick tempo, characterise this dance of Assam, and tells of the many episodes connected with the old legends that speak of Sri Krishna's youthful pranks and frolics.

51. *DHOL AND TAFAR DANCE.* Vigorous dances are common amongst the various types of folk dances found throughout the country. But when the performers play on the round drum and the *Tafar* or octagonal tambourine as they dance, the art becomes both rhythmic and technically fine. Rhythm plays an important part in this dance, which is performed in the month of November, when there is the great Temple Car Festival. Amidst throngs of people gaily clad and music and drums, the great Temple Car or *Juggernaut* is pulled through the streets in procession.

52. *THE TABAL CHONGBI.* Holi, the festival of the Carnival of Colours, is the occasion for much rejoicing and fun throughout India. In Assam, it is celebrated with dance and song just as it is in other parts of the country. One of the popular Holi dances is the Tabal Chongbi or Dance of Leaping in the Moonlight. Boys and girls holding hands dance together with light and graceful stepping, accompanied by the drum, in the traditional large circle. The dance is gay, interspersed with swings and swaying, and moves round and round to a lively rhythm. The spirit of spring and the ecstasy of full moon time pervade the whole performance.

53. *CANOE DANCE OF THE SURMA VALLEY.* This is a very unique performance. Boats are prepared for racing, and great excitement prevails as a dancer stands up in the middle of his craft and commences his movements while he sings. Accompanied by the rhythmic beat of the drum and cymbals, the dance is a prelude to the actual boat race. Suddenly, as the signal is given for the race to start, the dancer balancing precariously continues his movements in perfect timing for as long as he can, all the while spurring on the rowers by his wonderfully supple and flowing movements. Peculiar to Assam, this dance is the occasion for huge crowds of enthusiastic people to gather and witness not only the ever popular sport of boat racing, but the dexterity and skill of the dance associated with it.

54. *NONGKREM DANCE.* This is a ritual dance of the Khasi people of Assam. A large group of about twenty-four men, dressed in ceremonial costume and decorated with shells, perform this stirring sword dance with very forceful movements. The dance becomes more and more spectacular as the tempo increases. Interspersed with jumps, whirls and powerful swings of the arms, it denotes a dance of martial people who are hunters by profession.

In this celebration, the women often dance with the men after the latter have laid aside their swords. Then the dance takes on a different character, becoming lively and languorous in turn and in tune with the pulsating drum beats. Beautiful costumes and rich golden crowns and heavy jewels worn by the women enhance the spectacle, as they flash and sparkle when the women dancers turn round and step forwards and backwards, slowly and gracefully.

Later, the men resume their dance with their swords, displaying their skill with these weapons. Then the women form a separate group, and continue with their quiet and graceful movements, taking steps forwards and backwards, interchanging places in lines and turning round—indeed, in striking contrast to the stirring movements of the men.

55. *KATHI.* This dance, done by men in Bengal, corresponds to the Dandhya Ras of Western India. A group of men, each holding a pair of short sticks and accompanied by the rhythmic beat of a small drum called the *Madhole*, begin to sing in chorus, each one hitting his own stick together in perfect timing. Then every other dancer stands opposite the man on his right and there is a play of sticks, hands and sticks crossing and re-crossing, and then beating their own sticks in counts of four and eight.

This is followed by the whole ensemble turning so that every other dancer goes through similar movements with his left hand partner. And all the time, the criss-crossing and patterns of clashing sticks continues, the dancers never stopping going round in the huge circle. The dance now moves into a fine fast tempo, with quick stepping, graceful bending, and turning of the body to the lilting melody. In the sound of the beating of the sticks in perfect synchronization with the drum beats, the movements of the dancers and turns of their heads in beautiful rhythm, there is a beauty of team work apparent all through. In between the pauses of the moving circle of dancers, solos are done by a man leaping into the centre, and performing some excellent acrobatics while he simultaneously beats his sticks and maintains perfect timing.

56. *JATRAS.* These are the dance dramas of Bengal that date back to over 400 years, and are performed by strolling players. Operatic in style, the themes centre round the Krishna legends. Only men take part, and boys play the feminine roles as in the traditional Kathakali of Kerala. They utilize a simple and lucid technique of acting and dance that combine to unfold the story and are accompanied by some of the most beautiful melodies, song and play of musical instruments. These sacred songs and lyrics are chanted in operatic style with chorus and the dance dramas employ mime for interpretation with dance between to give them the technical finish.

57. *KIRTAN DANCE.* Associated with the worship of Vishnu, these dances have a deeply religious flavour. All the people of the village in certain parts of Bengal, both young and old, join in this dance which is done to the accompaniment of the *Mirdanga*. The dancers go round and round in circles, raising and lowering their hands, and there is a sort of ecstasy in the movements as they play their cymbals and the beautiful chants and chorus of the lyrical sacred songs fill the air. As the dancers sway and play their cymbals, they appear to be in a trance-like concentration of dance and worship.

58. *BAUL DANCES.* These are purely entertainment dances and are performed at any time of the year by wandering bands of dancers who make a living by dancing in the courtyards of houses or in the villages, for the amusement and delight of the people. Accompanied by a small drum and song, these dancers of Bengal step in lively movement with the rhythmic beats that emphasise both movement and stepping.

59. *MASKED DANCES OF BENGAL.* In these interesting dances, the performers wear masks made of mango wood, plastered with clay and then painted with black features. Their themes are religious, in that they perform subjects from the Krishna legends, the various phases of Nature like the movements of rivers, and sacred legends connected with Lord Shiva. The dance commences in a slow and stately tempo, and gradually gathering speed, the dancers advance with facile interpretive mime and gestures to the rhythmic accompaniment of the drum, cymbals and songs.

Very stylised and dramatic because of the masks and the characteristic mime, these dances are of both sociological and historical value.

60. *COMMUNITY DANCING.* There are many attractive folk dances found in Orissa State, where boys and girls gather in the village of an evening and dance for sheer joy to the beat of the drums, particularly at harvest and spring-time. Songs accompany these spontaneous dances and are based on local legends, the life of the people, and very often quaint humour. These are not organised dances, and therefore the stepping is light and easy; and in the movements of pattern, changes and improvisations are made from time to time with a wonderful sense of harmony and rhythm. These community dances form part of the social life of the people and are therefore important from the sociological and group systems.

61. *HARVEST DANCES OF ORISSA.* In these dances of Orissa, Mother Earth is worshipped in celebration of the harvesting of a good crop. Men and women dance in separate groups. The movements are slow and graceful, done to the accompaniment of a plaintive song. Forming lines, bending and swaying, sometimes imitating the processes of cutting the corn, taking or gathering of the sheaves, and soothingly passing their hands over the ears of corn as if caressing them, the women dance in the true spirit of thanksgiving. The men, for their part, bend and kneel, turn and move round with shuffling steps or in a faster metre of three steps, going round and round in perfect harmony of both stance and stepping.

Several such harvest dances are done, sometimes accompanied by a song that is sung in chorus, and sometimes with the men and women dancing to the rhythm of drums and cymbals. The patterns of these dances are more descriptive than design making, and are purposeful as well.

62. *BAHAKA NATA or SANCHAR.* This is the drum dance of Orissa, and is performed either by a group of forty men or in duet form. In the latter form, the dance commences with one dancer drumming on the *Mirdanga* and the other playing cymbals. The drummer sings some songs of invocation to the Gods, and this is repeated by the cymbal player, the *Bhayaka* or drummer dancing as he plays the rhythmic timing on his drum. The stepping is fast and patterned and changes as he varies his drum rhythms. This is followed by more songs, which are beautiful lyrics of ancient Orissan origin, that relate episodes from the *Ramayana* and the *Mahabharata*. Sometimes, the drummer introduces romantic and witty songs and then the rhythms become very lively and the stepping fast and free.

In the group form, the Bahaka Nata is performed by twenty drummer-dancers and twenty cymbal players. A marvellous rhythm of cross playing, of timing and harmony, is achieved in which the patterned stepping changes greatly and frequently, as the men go round, walk in lines, move in a swaying posture and advance. It is a stirring sight as the colourful costumes and turbans of the men offset by bright ornaments and peacock feathers move in a flash of colour in the constantly varying designs of dance formations and beating and stamping feet.

63. *DANDA NATA*. Among the many folk dances of Orissa, the ritualistic Danda Nata is distinctive. Performed in the month of April during the Chaitra Parva festival, only the men take part. The dance begins with the Parva in which the principal dancer, colourfully dressed in bright skirt and shirt, dances with patterned stepping as he advances and retreats and moves sideways, holding a coloured stole that is draped around his shoulders.

The stepping and movements have a great deal more of variety than is found in most folk dances, and about sixteen different types are introduced to the resounding play of the *Dholak* drum and the *Mahuri*, Orissa's particular type of wind instrument. This principal dancer is then followed by the *Binakaria* or lute player, and as he dances and sings songs of praise to the deities, the little bells attached to his lute tinkle in harmony. This solo is notable for its diversity of steps on the heel, flat of foot, stamping and side stepping in counts of three, four and six.

In this performance, the old traditional custom of the feminine roles being played by boys or very young men is followed. Now, as the next dancer, known as the *Thetal* or intermediary enters, he emerges dressed as a woman. His solo dance is presently joined by two or three more such dancers; and finally, the whole group of dancers comes and sing songs, enacting episodes from the *Ramayana* and the *Mahabharata*. Each dancer plays the part of one of the characters in the story. As they perform this part of the dance which is really now developing into a dance drama, the songs which each dancer sings are repeated in chorus by a group of singers who are accompanied by the *Dholak* and the *Mahuri*.

The Danda Nata is unique in that it is a synthesis of pure dance, song and drama, and may well be compared to the Yatras of Bengal in certain respects. Its popularity makes it a conspicuous feature of many other seasonal festivals in Orissa.

64. *HUMO BAULI*. This is a joyous group dance performed by young unmarried girls at festival time. The dance starts with the chanting of rhythmic dance syllables by the dancers, who then break into song as they move slowly round with simple stepping and postures, bending and turning, and graceful walking. The dance represents the joy of living, the love of song and rhythm, and is a dedication to the spirit of celebration.

65. *GHANTA MARDALA*. This rather stirring and lively dance of Andhra is also a drum and cymbal group dance in which a number of men participate. Syncopating harmony of the drum beats and clashing cymbals mark the rhythms of this fast stepping performance, as the dancers move round and round and in lines. Following the first introductory songs, are introduced episodes contained in the epics, the *Ramayana* and the *Mahabharata*. The large group of dancers move and play, changing their rhythms frequently; and as they proceed with the performance, it gradually rises in tempo, the steps changing quickly with the patterns of movement scintillating like light and shade to the wonderful and finished play of the *Mirdanga* and cymbals.

66. *HARVEST DANCES OF ANDHRA*. These are popular and common throughout the country, and in Andhra there are many varieties that are performed at sowing and harvest time. Men and women dance separately and celebrate

these joyous seasonal occasions with appropriate songs and dances that ring with praise and propitiation for Bharati, Mother Earth. Very colourfully dressed, their ornaments flashing in the sun, the pretty women link hands and go round and round in circles, singing and interspersing their rounds with claps and gestures of prayer and thanksgiving. The dances are slow and dignified, but keep in close touch with the rhythm of the songs. Bracelets and anklets tinkle musically as their feet and arms are stretched, bent, raised and lowered. When the men dance in their own groups, there is more of adandon and gaiety; and the songs resound as they ring forth to the music of the drum and flute. Going round and round, leaping and jumping, twirling and stamping, the dance is full of exhuberance and vitality.

67. *STICK DANCE*. Like the Dhandya Ras of Gujerat and the Kathi of Bengal, Andhra has its lacquered short stick dance done by men in celebration of various festivals. Usually twenty-four men dancers participate in this, and to the beat of the *Mirdanga*, they form squares and circles, hitting their partner's sticks and then their own in a veritable maze of patterns. The dance begins at a slow tempo and gathering speed, it gets faster and faster as the men hit their sticks and move forwards and backwards; now standing and going round, now sitting and turning and coming back into position. The themes of the accompanying songs vary, sometimes being based on the Krishna legends, and sometimes in praise of the particular village deities. Often the songs change to gay and sparkling, romantic and humorous themes and then more dancers join the group, making it very large and spectacular. Criss-crossing their sticks, forming one design and then another, the dance goes on and on; and as the dancers pause on a particular note, soloists enter the centre of the ring and perform feats of jumping, turns and somersaults. Then once again the group carries on and the dance proceeds with the beating of sticks and the movement of going forwards and backwards.

PUPPETS

As has been seen from some of the preceding chapters, India possesses some rare and unusual types of stylised indigenous drama and dance, which have survived through the centuries and are being performed today in various part of the country. It has also been shown how masks, for instance, form an expressive instrument for some of the dramatic dance modes. These are usually painted representations of actual characters and animals as visualised by the people of each region. In the Kathakali dance dramas of Kerala, we find a highly stylised and unique mask built on the face with the delicate use of rice powder and paints. This gives each actor distinctive recognisable features, producing a uniformity of personality for all performances. The sensitive and beautiful Chau masks of the Seraikela dance dramas of Bihar, made from papier maché; the wooden and papier maché masks of the Sahi Jatra of Puri in Orissa; the Yakshagana dance dramas of Andhra, Karnataka and Tamil Nad; as well as the phantasmagorial painted wooden masks of the Lama Monk Dancers in the mystery plays performed in the monasteries of Ladakh, Lahoul, Spiti (Western Himalayas) and Sikkim (Eastern Himalayas), have all been purposefully planned and executed to re-enact subject and personalities from mythology, legend and history, and to enhance dramatic effect.

In India, the success and tremendous appeal that masks produced on audiences, gave rise to a sister art. Small village groups, with an accent on spontaneity and realism, introduced marionettes to supplement masks and take the place of the large numbers of actors or performers utilized in urban theatres. Many of these marionettes or puppets were real works of art. In addition, many people contributed their artistic attainments towards the making of these dolls. Those skilled in doll making and carving gave of their talents; painters did the faces; dresses and ornaments were made by those qualified in this, and the stage properties were made by other groups. Hence it became a community art and entertainment. Together with puppets came another art, the expressive Shadow Plays, which had the added advantage of being able to cater to larger audiences. Painting pictures as of dreams, they enhanced dramatic effect and created the illusion of reality, wherein the grotesque and wicked could be made to appear more terrifying, and the gentle and sweet more effectively soft and delicate.

We have innumerable examples in India of the effective use of both doll puppets and the more elaborate leather cut and painted puppets used in the Shadow Plays. There are the elaborately dressed and ornamented Orissa String Dolls, the Putli Khel of Bengal, the Kathputli of Rajasthan, the Bommalattam wood and cloth string dolls of Tamil Nad, and the puppets that appear regularly in Kerala and Kerala puppet shows. The finely cut, designed and painted transparent leather puppets used in the Shadow Plays of the Tolu Bommalatta (the Play of Leather Toys) of the Puppet Theatre of Andhra, the century-old transparent deer and goat skin Bommalatta puppets of Tamil Nad and the Pavai Koothu of Kerala, make interesting and fascinating study. In fact, puppets have formed a vital part of our folk art from time immemorial and therefore are a valuable contribution to the dramatic and dance folk forms in India. Each region has its own style of puppet theatre, interesting techniques of manipulation, presentation, story value, song rhythms and costume. Like the dance dramas, they too use singers and story narrators who elucidate the descriptive and dialogue features in the play, supported by music and the drum. The subjects too as in the dance dramas cover mythology, the epics *Ramayana* and the *Mahabharata*, and the *Puranas*. Another common factor is the use of mime.

In the actual dance, it is the living performers who utilize the science of *Abhinaya*, with the use of hand gestures and facial expressions to interpret the story and songs or lyrics; and in the puppet shows, a special vocabulary of just the most necessary words has been evolved through the years for easy facile interpretation. Actions and words are made to coincide perfectly in a recognised code—the puppet doing the appropriate and specially worked out actions for the particular words. This is certainly a strong part of pantomime which is so evident in some of our dance drama forms.

In the themes covering mythology, history, legend and romance, there is scope for actual dance to be introduced in these puppet plays. Here we find the beautifully conceived Court dancer and dancing girls of the Rajasthan Kathputli shows which have medieval history as their favourite subjects; and we have actual simple folk dances and even something of the *Tillana*, *Jatisvaram* and the *Alarippu* introduced in the puppet shows of Tamil Nad.

From the simplest and naive yet rather beautifully conceived modes of the wandering puppeteer and his own particular methods of presentation, who puts up a village show calling his audience by beat of his miniature drum, to the more elaborate shows of the actual Puppet Theatres, one finds a fund of knowledge being imparted together with entertainment from traditional lore and sacred story.   Lighted by large flickering oil lamps made of clay and cotton wicks, the small improvised mat in the village square with the puppet master operating his modest paper puppet just as effectively as the rural theatre stage and lovely string, rod, glove or shadow puppets, with its puppet master will bring to life a world of battles and adventure, romance and history, and tales that are of the realm of dreams.   In this world of make-believe, characters play and dance and mime; the movements, grouping, the entries, and the stylised actions, all true to a traditionally conceived and planned pattern, have catered to rural audiences through the centuries with a continuous history.

Apart from the fact that the art of puppetry provides valuable cultural material in the form of both drama and folk art, as well as being a community craft, it has now come to inspire urban dance drama.   In the contemporary scene, it has proved its adaptability for wonderful effects, different and exciting.   A very successful and laudable experiment is the Dance Ballets by the Little Ballet Troupe, who have so beautifully translated the modes of the doll puppets into the performance of human dance drama.   In their two ballets the "Ramayana" and the "Panchatantra," dancers dressed as puppets, dance and perform as these manipulated dolls do, and the effect is fascinating and original.   Movements, mime, costumes and decor take on an old-world and almost dream-like character, and the whole effect is one of beauty and charm.

In describing these sixty-eight representative forms of the folk dances of India, only half of rural India's dance modes have been covered.   The other half constitutes the tribal dances prevalent in our country.   These latter embrace the dances of our oldest inhabitants who have incorporated into their dances their own social traditions and environmental conditions, as well as the common heritage which they share with peasant India.   A brief survey of the most representative of the tribal dances of India will further elucidate the richness of India's many existing dance themes and their manifold techniques.

16. Tribal Dances of India

TRIBAL DANCES, like the folk dances of India, are full of the same spontaneous freedom and natural grace. They are also seasonal and religious like all rural dances and may be considered the sister dances of peasant India. Living and moving in natural surroundings they are vivid, temperamental, strong, often primeval, and filled with the zest of living; costumed for the most part in colourful apparel, these oldest of India's inhabitants have brought to posterity a rich heritage of dance, song and music that are pregnant with their sociological, psychological and historical backgrounds since centuries past. There are among these our tribal people, groups that can trace their origins to almost ten to fifteen thousand years ago.

I have described some of the representative folk dances existing in the various regions of India. Now, in detailing some of the representative tribal dances of our country, a more general picture will be had of the dance in its manifold and more spontaneous forms and expressions, dances that are ancient in origin and beautiful in conception.

Dance, as one of the creative expressions of a people closely associated with the land, and living in regions that have different environments and backgrounds, has still an indestructible link in tradition and trends of thought. Nature is always the strongest inspiration for them all, coupled with custom, and a religious heritage that has much in common.

NORTH INDIA

1. *DANCE OF THE VANJARAS or GYPSIES.* The gypsy is a member of a nomadic tribe found throughout the world and India is not without these picturesque people. The Vanjaras of Rajasthan and Western India, and the Lambardis of the south-east are among them.

It is believed that in ancient times, the Vanjaras were traders, living a hard but full life, carrying salt, opium, and corn on their cattle and camels to far distances.   Now, they are found in little groups, ruled by their "chiefs", living largely a family life of sorts and are farmers tending their herds of cows and buffaloes. They have their own particular deities, and are in some mysterious way absorbed in the worship of Nature.

But their life never seems to be settled, for the fiery blood of their ancestors still runs in their veins, and a love of the nomadic way of life for the sheer adventure of it still appeals to them.   When the springtime festival of Holi is celebrated throughout India, the Vanjara women dance to express their gladsome ardour for budding Nature.   The dance is usually done to a metre of fourteen counts, with the emphasis on the third and last beats.   The Vanjara musician, while drumming on his *Dholak*, introduces many little complicated tones, and the girls forming into the familiar circle, come together, some clapping their hands, and others beating short coloured sticks.   To the sound of the drum, they commence chanting in shrill voices, bending to right and left.   Suddenly, they form into a square and advance forwards in a fast running movement, turning back again and hitting their sticks criss-cross.   Their feet mark four quick steps, two slow and four faster again with slight pauses in between.

Once again they run round, their wide skirts tossing around them, and they continue their weird chanting, their heavy silver ornaments swinging over their cheeks.   Breaking once more into more vigorous running steps, tripping towards one another in a row, backwards and forwards, crossing their feet, the tassels at the end of their braids fly out as they move.

One of their favourite songs accompanying the dance and sung in chorus has a charming flow of cadence and mode of metrical arrangement.   Though difficult to translate, I was able to get the general trend:

> "How pretty is my heavy dark hair,
> How pretty are my sun-scorched arms,
> How pretty are the swinging jewels on them;
> I look at the tanks and the wells full of water
> I look at my poor little thirsty animal.

> "While my cows are quietly grazing,
> I braid my thick knotted hair,
> While my buffalows are quietly chewing,
> I thread pearls into the tassels
> That are fixed to the ends of my heavy dark hair.

> "The pearls have come from the seas and the rivers,
> Long days have we toiled to buy them,
> My silver is shining and weighs exactly
> As much as the neck bells of my cow."

2. *HOLI DANCE*.   The Bhils of Mewar in Rajasthan celebrate this springtime Carnival of Colours with a fascinating dance.   Lighting a great fire, and throwing handfuls of grain as an offering to their particular Goddess, men and women join together in dance round the fire.   The men carry short sticks in their hands, and as they circle slowly round and round, they beat these one against another, to the beats of the drummers who stand in the centre.   Commencing in a

slow tempo, the dance increases in speed and the men begin to shout with enthusiasm. At the same time, they beat their sticks faster and move with three steps forward, turn, and take three steps forward again. Now the women join in the fast moving circle, singing shrilly. As the dance gets wilder and wilder and reaches its climax, the men join hands as they stand in a circle, and the women climb on the men's clasped hands till a woman stands on each man's shoulders, holding the hand of the next woman. The whole circle goes round to the accompaniment of the song—a fast moving, tremendously vibrating spectacle filled with verve and the primeval forces of a people filled with the ecstasy of the love of Nature.

3. *ROMANTIC DANCE.* The pretty dances of the Santhals who live in the forest-clad hilly plateau of Chotta Nagpur in Bihar are very picturesque. The areas that these tribal people inhabit stretch as far as the border districts of Bengal in the east and to Orissa to the south. These dances are of a romantic nature and are usually performed on full moon nights. The men sway and dance holding a painted banner and playing on the drum and other musical instruments.

The girls assemble under a large Banyan tree near the rice fields, after having decked themselves with flowers, their bright coloured *Sarees* tucked above their knees, their silver anklets clinking. There is a slow rustling of the high corn, and the dancing commences against the background of their rustic, artistically shaped and rounded homesteads. Standing in a row, two and two together, their arms linked, the girls start moving and bending gracefully in imitation of the swaying corn stalks, to and fro, to and fro, to the rhythmic sound of the drums and pipes.

Then they lower themselves, bending the knees, turn round slowly and stand up; go forwards and backwards shuffling along, nodding their heads and linking arms and clapping alternately.

The men stand in a row in front at some distance and some of them play on the bamboo flute and the drums accompanied by the songs. There is a matchless beauty in the wonderful rhythms and the perfectly synchronising movements set against the glory of the full moonlight. Living in an organised tribal group, these people also have beautiful pastoral dances done at harvest time and when the indigo crop is picked. Women dance in a semi-circle, clapping hands and linking arms alternately, swaying slowly and gently and then gradually forming into a ring.

The men do the famous hunters' dance, which is full of strength and vigour, depicting the act of getting ready for the hunt with bow and arrow, stalking the animal, and finally shooting it. Mime and slow strong stepping, measured movements and syncopation of the metre of the drum beats, mark this ancient tribal dance.

4. *THE MAGHA.* Not far from where the Santhals live in the Chota Nagpur plateau in Bihar, there are the ancient Hos tribal people whose main occupation is agriculture. They are worshippers of Nature and the elements, and their chief deity is Dasauli who is propitiated with the Magha ritualistic dance. The God is believed to have his abode in the thick Sal tree groves and he gives protection to the people, their cattle and their lands. The dance is performed to the accompaniment of the *Dholak,* the pipe reeds and songs. Men dance in a slow rhythm, chanting and stepping round and round and back and forth. Then young girls form into a semi-circle with arms linked and move from side to side, taking one step forward, one back, kick one step and bring the two feet together.

Gradually they form into one great circle and go round and round, first clockwise and then anti-clockwise. The dance is slow and a bit monotonous, but the movements are graceful and rhythmic; however the costumes and the charm of the girls more than compensate for the monotony of the actual dance.

5. *INVOCATION DANCE.* The deity Dasauli is again invoked by dance and song by these tribal people in Bihar when the seed is sown at the time of the celebration of the Hero festival. Songs of praise sung with strength and power fill the air as the dancers, forming into the familiar line, begin to move in a circle, and as they dance, they request the deity to bless them with an early and rich harvest. In all these dances the stepping consists mainly of a shuffling movement on the flat of foot and going round and sideways, forwards and backwards and the stamping of feet. Sometimes they make a little heaving movement as they raise themselves and swing on the toes of one foot forward.

The Invocation dance is generally followed sometime afterwards by a dance of Thanksgiving to celebrate the Jomnama festival which comes as soon as the harvesting is over. This is a joyous dance and the songs and rhythms are therefore more lively. The spirit of gladness is evident throughout the dance, and as the women clap their hands and beat their feet, bending and turning, the men come forward and retreat with joyous abandon, some drumming hard and the others gaily advancing with jumps and kicks and turns.

6. *SARHUL.* This is a martial dance of pure tribal origin and setting, danced in summer time by the Oraons who live in Chota Nagpur in Bihar. The dance commences with the men blowing horns; then a group of young women form into two or three rows and dance together. The men also form two or three rows and dance beside them. Standing hand in hand, the women come forward, stamping their feet, running to and fro and sometimes stamping or swinging their feet at the end of each group of four steps. The men meanwhile move slowly up to the girls and back again. Then finally, they all form into one large circle and dance round and round, the men bringing up the rear.

7. *THE KARAMA.* This dance of the rainy season done in mid-August, between the transplanting and harvesting of the crops, is performed by the Kols of Chota Nagpur in Bihar. A branch of the Karam tree is cut and planted in the village dance ground. Accompanied by song and the drum, girls and boys carrying short sticks on their shoulders dance round the branch invoking the deity to grant them a good harvest. Slow and earnest, the girls imitate a hopping bird after taking a step and a half, then they bend low and raise one leg, and come back into position, singing and clapping their hands. The boys leap towards the girls and go round in a fast turn. Those dancers who are drumming and playing the wind instruments and flutes move forward towards the group of girls and then retreat. It is a picturesque dance as the rhythms are good and there is a sort of order as the three stances of the dancing, in three sets, with the girls, the boys and the boy-dancer-musicians move in a pattern of stepping and varied movements.

8. *KOL DANCE.* The Kols of the Chota Nagpur plateau in Bihar dance another ritual dance at the topical time of the planting of the seed, when they desire to invoke the deity in order that the seed will grow and flourish. The men and women dance together, the former leading all the movements and at particular signals from them, the women standing in a line, change their pattern of movement, body postures and positions, moving forwards and backwards

in parallel lines. Accompanied by drummers and clarionet players, the women now bob up and down, move sideways, and to and fro, winding between one another. And all the time their feet are shuffling and stamping in perfect timing. Finally, they all kneel and betimes beat the earth gently as though beseeching Mother Earth to nourish the newly planted seed. The dance ends with the dancers going round and round in circles. Very pretty, like some ancient ritual in the worship of Nature, the whole ensemble of dance and dancers bring to life in their fervour and bright costume and ornaments, a page from antiquity.

CENTRAL INDIA

9. *KARMA DANCE OF THE GONDS*. The Gonds, an ancient pre-Aryan people, live in the Maikal Hills at the eastern end of the Satpura ranges in Mandla, north-east Madhya Pradesh, and in the frontier districts of Orissa and Andhra. They are Nature-loving people, and have many dances done in dedication to their deity Bhimsen, at harvest and festival time, marriage celebrations and for the sheer joy of living. As the time approaches for showing the seed, they have all night sessions of singing and dancing, and the Karma is one of the most important dances.

Linking their arms, young women commence dancing in a straight line, then forming rectangles, they sway rhythmically as they face a group of men drummers, instrument players and singers, and at intervals bending and moving forwards up to the men and back.

The men form a separate circle and dance vigorously with strong movements and stepping. As the dance increases in tempo, the women circle round the men, moving to and fro. And as in the Bhil dance done at the time of the Holi festival, there is a movement, when some of the men dancers climb on the shoulders of the other men dancers and move round and round. When this feat is over, they take their places in a long line and wind round and round like a game of "oranges and lemon." The dance is full of spirit and enthusiasm.

10. *FESTIVAL DANCES*. The Maria-Muria Gond tribals of south-west Madhya Pradesh have some interesting community and ceremonial dances that commence as usual in the late evening and go on all night. Among the festival dances there are those dedicated to their deities, seasonal dances, ritualistic dances, and those that are specially meant for marriage celebrations and festive occasions. The Festival dances are a mass celebration, when something like several hundred girls dance together at night, creating a scene of thrilling beauty, in a setting of natural charm lit by blazing torches. Accompanied by several musical instruments like the horn, drums, flutes and clarionet, girls and boys assemble from a number of villages, elegantly dressed, and celebrate with dance and song. The performance is very picturesque and gay, with the lines of girls, the groups of boys, and the singers performing with great vigour. The dancing goes on till the early hours of the morning, ushering in festival time.

11. *VARIED DANCES OF THE GONDS*. Among the many varied dances of the Gonds of north-east Madhya Pradesh are those associated with social and group life. One can name the Nava Rani dance performed on the full moon night in honour of their presiding deities, Sakti and Danteshwari; and the Dewari and Chait Dances that are danced in springtime and to usher in summer. At the time of the sowing of the seed, the Godo dance is performed and the Goncho

is done to request the Goddess of Rain to grant them nourishment for their crops. Again, young men and women dance the whole night to honour Goddess Lakshmi, Giver of Fortune and Plenty, with the Lakshmi Jagar dance. On this auspicious occasion, the girls decorate the sacred image with flowers, place the deity beneath the Shemel tree and dance on and on throughout the long hours, with devotion and earnestness.

12. *THE KARMA DANCE OF THE BAIGA*. Like the Gonds, the Baigas also dance the Karma. The Baigas, who live in Madhya Pradesh, are considered the most ancient tribal people of India. They are the true lords of the soil and believe that they have been created the guardians of the forest and of all wild life. They are considered better dancers than the Gonds, and they possess a large variety of dances. Their romantic lyrical songs speak of a great love of natural beauty, therefore their natural tendency is to sing and dance at all seasons and when in love.

When the Baigas dance the Karma, the women form a line and the men perform in a group. Dressed gaily with large turbans set with peacock feathers, they make a brilliant picture beside the women in their bright shawls, beautiful silver jewelry and the peacock feathers in their hair. To the accompaniment of the *Dholak* drums, which are played with sticks, and the resounding songs, they dance in lines and circles, stamping, tripping, and moving to and fro. There are many variations of the Karma as done by the Baigas, such as, the Tadi Karma, the Lahaki Karma, the Khalha Karma, the Jhumar Karma and the Jharpat. Each type of the Karma has its special characteristics and is accompanied by different songs, drums and rhythms. The *Mandar* long drums are popular in some of the Karma variations.

13. *THE RINA*. During the New Year festival of Divali, the Baigas of Madhya Pradesh dance the Rina. This popular women's dance goes on towards January which is the marriage month. And it is often performed by the women of one village in a sort of challenge competition with the women of another village. Stepping slowly, they form into the familiar double line and then move till they stand back to back in two lines; they go again into a large circle, kneel and bend and sway, dancing on and on as the tempo of the drums constantly changes. Finally, with the spirit of the dance filling them with gladness, each woman performs in solo.

14. *THE BILMA*. Here is another popular dance of the Baigas, generally danced at marriage celebrations to the beat of the long *Mandar* drums. Men and women dance together in perfect harmony as they bend low and then step up and down increasing the tempo of their stepping. It is full of temperament, and as the women circle prettily, the men jump and bend and dance along merrily. The accompanying chorus is full of rhythm, loud and gay.

15. *THE SUA*. Baiga women in the village of Binjhwar of the district of Raipur in Madhya Pradesh are very fond of this ritualistic-imitative dance which is also known as the Parrot dance. According to one of their old legends, the daughter of Raja Hemanchal had a pet parrot which she loved very much. The princess was so good and so beautiful that she became deified and has been worshipped since ages past as Gaura. Because she loved her pet parrot so much, devotees make an image of a parrot, place it on rice and flowers in a basket on the dance grounds and dance around it. It is significant too that the parrot is considered the bird of learning in Indian folk-lore and the mediator between lovers. In this essentially feminine dance, the women dance at a slow tempo as

they move in a line, and at the same time they jerk their heads in bird-like fashion in imitation of this bird and cry shrilly in remembrance of it.

16. *THE TAPADI.* Once again we, have a dance in which Baiga women specialise. Forming into the regular lines facing one another, they clap and move rhythmically, singing in chorus for accompaniment. Swaying, moving to and fro, the clapping hands beating regularly, the dance goes on in even tenor. But it has a charm of its own.

17. *THE SAILA.* In this fast and rhythmic dance, it is the Baiga men who perform. It is done by the Baigas of the Dindori district in Madhya Pradesh, and includes the stick dance, the Danda Pata. The Saila dances are vivid and exceptionally good as an art and entertainment as well as a form of exercise. The dance generally takes place at the end of the rainy season and throughout the cold months. Just as the Baiga women in their enthusiasm for the dance, have competitions when they perform the Rina, so the Saila inspires the Baiga men to excel in the art of the dance and challenge other villages to a competition.

The dance is full of life, with the men walking, shuffling, bending and stamping their feet, skipping and advancing as they move faster and faster to the increasing beats of the drum. Like the Karma, it comprises many varieties, such as the Thadi Saila, the Baithak Saila, the Chamka Kudna Saila or Hunter's dance, the Artari Saila, the Shikai Saila, and the Chakramar Saila or Lizard's dance. Each one has certain characteristics of its own, with slightly different theme and movements, some with pantomime.

18. *THE MANDRI.* The Murias of Bastar in Madhya Pradesh dance this on festive occasions, and particularly at marriages. The dance commences with a group of boys carrying ritualistic offerings and gifts and conducting the bridegroom to the ceremonial place. In this light and happy dance, there are a variety of movements with boy and girl dancers and drummers participating to move in patterns with running steps and circles, then changing direction, kneeling and bending and jumping. The movements of the drummers as they dance and manipulate their drums is fascinating, sometimes playing with one hand only, and sometimes with both.

19. *RELIGIOUS DANCES.* These dances of the Murias of Madhya Pradesh are closely associated with group and tribal life and custom and are dedicated to ceremonial, family celebrations, the group deity and the particular deity of the various *Ghotuls* (dormitories in which young men and young girls live separately). Many of these dances are the ever popular stick dances and are as much festival dances as religious dances. Men dancers with drums hung from their shoulders dance with force and verve, moving forwards and backwards, as a group of girls form their own circle and a third group of small boys in their circle dance and play on the small *Turburi* drums near the line formed by the men. There is a rhythmic unison about the three ensembles, as the different groups each dance in their own style and stepping.

20. *THE CHHERTA.* The Murias of Bastar in Madhya Pradesh like the Baigas love to sing and dance, and they also have many varieties of both the arts. Among the dances are the stick dances performed with patterned figures, rhythmic stepping and accompanied by song, like the Dhandya Ras of Gujerat. For the most part, these dances are accompanied by drums of many kinds, but often only songs are used, along with gongs, flutes, an indigenous type of stringed instrument, horns and a type of guitar.

The Chherta is one of joy, done by girls and boys from one *Ghotul* visiting a neighbouring village and dancing in front of each house. The chief dancer wears a mask, peacock feathers in his head-dress, and is generally the comedian of the show. As he acts and mimes, the others dance in gay and lively fashion, forming the usual curved line, their arms around one another's shoulders, bending and stamping their feet and increasing the speed, zig-zagging and circling, moving to and fro in an unending spirit of *joie de vivre*, as many improvisations are done in fun and play.

21. *HAR ENDANNA.* The Murias of Bastar in Madhya Pradesh do this light and charming dance of fast tempo, usually during the New Year at Divali and at marriage celebrations. The site is the grounds of the *Ghotul* or near the marriage pavilion. In a lilting change of movements, boys and girls hold hands or link arms and dance round and round in a circle, changing direction from time to time and then moving to and fro.

22. *HULKI DANCES.* Here again is a favourite dance of the Murias of Bastar in Madhya Pradesh. These are dances of sheer fun and enjoyment, and are performed by boys and girls going from one village to another and dancing together. There are many varieties of Hulki, each having steps and formations, songs and rhythms, of their own.

23. *KARSANAS.* These again are dances of fun and recreation, and take place in the *Ghotuls* of the Murias. Fast and energetic, these social dances are often imitative; and in the many varieties of the Karsanas, there are for instance, the Nature dances of the Crane, performed by a group of girls, the extraordinary designed Flower dance also done by girls with dexterity and a sense of fine balance. The latter is slow in contrast to the former which is faster and lively.

24. *THE BISON DANCE.* The Murias of Bastar in Madhya Pradesh perform this picturesque vigorous dance of joy and invocation during marriage celebrations. The men wear a colourful head-dress consisting of a pair of bison's horns, crowned by a tall tuft of peacock and bird's feathers, with strings of cowrie shells hanging from its edge to lightly screen the face. The women wear a round flat hat stuck with feathers, and use many ornaments to offset their simple white and red draperies. Forming into an inner circle, with their left hands on their neighbour's shoulder and holding a long stick in the right hand, the women beat their sticks on the ground rhythmically, stamping their feet, turning and bending and ever moving round. The men with large long drums suspended around them, form a great outer circle, drum loudly and lustily as they circle round and round, turning and changing their steps in a fast tempo. As the dance goes on round and round with changes of movement and turns, there is a flash of colour. It is joyous, dynamic and ritualistic.

25. *DANCES OF THE BHILS.* The Bhils of Madhya Pradesh are fond of song and dance. The men dance the Dagla for sheer enjoyment and exercise, and the women dance the Pali together with the men. This is more vigorous and lively, with fast turns and circles, and the stepping is done on the flat of foot, on the toes and with running and skipping steps.

26. *DANCES OF THE BHANJARAS.* The Bhanjaras or gypsies of Madhya Pradesh dance the Langi to celebrate the Rakhi Purnima festival or Coconut Day in Sawan (July-August) to the accompaniment of songs dedicated to Varuna, God of the Waters. It is also danced to honour Goddess Kali. When the women dance, the men accompany them with songs, first singing in honour of the deities

Plate 101

Tribal dances of Bihar. (1) Oroan men and women performing
the famous Karma dance. (2) The Oroans performing the Jadur
dance.   (Photos copyright, Mohan Khokar.)

Plate 102

1

Tribal dances of Madhya Pradesh. (1) Group of men in the Bison Horn dance of the Maria Gonds. (2) Group of women in the same dance. (Photos, Darshan Lall.)

2

Tribal group dance of the Marias of Madhya Pradesh. (Photo copyright, Mohan Khokar.)

3

Plate 103

1

Naga dances of Assam. (1) A dancer takes a great leap of joy in the Warrior group dance. (2) Walking in their ceremonial dress, the Naga dancers form a circle in their famous Warrior dance. (Courtesy, Films Division, Government of India.)

Plate 104

Naga dances of Assam. The Naga Spear dance as performed in Imphal. (Photo, Darshan Lall.)

and then honouring one of their great heroes, Prithviraj Chouhan.

The lively Phag dance is done during Holi, and in this the men carry swords, as they march and advance, go in fast whirls and retreat, brandishing their weapons. The accompanying songs tell of the old days of dashing adventure.

Among the lighter themes, the women dance the Lota, and the Saundarya. In the Lota dance, they cleverly balance pitchers full of water on their heads as they go round and round, move backwards and forwards, alternating the tempo with slow and fast rhythms, without spilling a single drop of water.

In the joyous Saundarya, which like the Lota dance can be done at any time of the year, the women form two rows facing one another, clasp hands, swing back and forth and circle.

17. Tribal Dances of India— Continued

EASTERN INDIA

27. *KIRATARJUN DANCE.* The Paikas are an old and interesting tribal people who live in Orissa State and have some old historic dances. Some of them depict the episodes from the epics, the *Ramayana* and the *Mahabharata*, but their best known subjects are taken from mythology and legend. In the very powerful and fast moving dance, the Kiratarjun, the story of Kirat's victory over Arjuna is portrayed. It is stately, with bold and defined steps, postures and mime conveying the idea of heroes and warlike attitudes.

In the Garudbahan dance, the dancers depict the story of how Garuda, the special mythological bird and vehicle of Lord Vishnu, battles for recognition as an equal of the Lord. But finally gives up the idea when he realises that it is God Himself whom he is trying to overcome and compete with. Here again, there is dignity and poise in the dance, with strong movements, postures and martial stepping that all lend a sense of power and final obeisance to the Lord.

28. *THE MAYA SHAVARI.* This is a complicated and difficult theme that is interpreted through group dance, and may almost be called a rural-tribal dance drama. It tells of the legend that in Satyayug, during the churning of the ocean, Vishnu disguised as the beautiful Mohini (symbolic of Delusion), tempted Lord Shiva. Parvathi, Consort of Shiva, was so angry that she disguised herself as Shavari and getting together some companions went in search of Sri Krishna to tempt Him in return. Charmed by her beauty and gentleness, Krishna followed Parvathi to Mount Kailash, the abode of Lord Shiva, who was about to slay Krishna, when Parvati disclosed what she had done. Krishna then understood Parvathi's ruse.

In this dance the people try to show that Gods too have human weaknesses and qualities and understand them, and in impersonating these many characters in the dance, they exhibit the arts of both mime and pure dance. Characterisation is excellent, and the naive and honest feelings about the relationship between human beings and the deities they honour and worship is portrayed with feeling and humour.

29. *KARAMA*. In the Mayurbhanj area of Orissa State, the Bhoomiya tribal people have a number of dances, among which one of the most popular is the Karama, which is danced on the eleventh night of the month of Bhadon (springtime), on what is called the day of the Ekadasi. "Karama" means "good fortune" and this festival is celebrated in honour of Lord Shiva, and prayers are offered to Him to grant a good harvest and prosperity. A tree is cut and planted in the village, and under it is placed an earthern pot containing paddy (unhusked rice) and other grains symbolic of good luck. After performing this preliminary ceremony, the people fast, and then they dance all night to the accompaniment of drums and songs of praise. The dancing is decorous and full of devotional earnestness as is shown by the dignity with which the stepping is done to a simple rhythm rising to a vigour and then toning down to a milder degree as the theme unfolds. The Karama dance in fact is common to many of the tribal people and is closely connected with the invocation for good harvests amongst them all.

30. *THE JADUR*. The Bhoomiyas dance this also for good results in the cultivation of their crops. The deity in whose honour it is performed is the tribal God Baru Bonga. People gather on the nearest hill and offering their rice drink called Pachuvraj to the deities, they pour some of it on the fields for their better growth. Then they all form a long line, and dance their way down the hill, ending the performance of joy and happiness in the village.

31. *COMMUNITY DANCES*. All tribal people have these social dances which are for enjoyment and recreation, and in Orissa State, there are several of them. Boys and girls from several villages often gather of an evening in harvest and springtime sowing of the fields, and dance in sheer joy, to the beat of the *Mandari* drums. Songs based on the local legends, the life of the people, and quaint humour accompany these performances. Though the dances are not organised, the stepping is patterned, falling into a natural rhythm back and forth, round and round. There is much fun and laughter as the leader introduces his own improvisations which the others have to follow or drop out of line. Sometimes, one village challenges another to a dance competition, and the performance goes on for hours on end, setting a high standard of composition and endurance.

32. *COURTSHIP DANCES*. The Bhuiyas are an interesting and colourful tribal people, inhabiting Orissa, and have a unique dance in which the girls and boys dance together in happy mood. The entertainment commences with the boys going with presents and flowers to the village near by and playing their drums and pipes. The girls come out and greeting the visitors, accept the gifts. They give them hospitality and then they all dance together.

The dances go on till near sunset and the fast movements are exciting and full of patterned stepping. The boys line themselves opposite the girls, who dance forwards towards them, and retreat. Only one line advances at a time, while the members of the other line stand still and keep the time with clapping hands. The girls now change their line into a curve and the boys advance and retreat. Moving to and fro in one direction, the curving line of the girls undulates, while the line of boy dancers now changes also to a curve and moves the same way, but in the opposite direction. Clasping hands, one line bends forwards, the other line standing still but clapping the time, and then the other line does the same. And so on and on it goes, alternately moving and standing still and clapping, one line leading and the other repeating to the incessant drum beats and songs.

Sometimes, at the end of such a session of dancing, betrothals take place, bringing a romantic end to this dance of youth.

33. *HARVEST DANCES*.   The Bhuiyas enjoy harvest time and they celebrate this with song and dance, just as other rural and tribal people do all over India.   Bharati Mata, Mother Earth, is worshipped and in the celebration, men and women dance in separate groups.   The movements are slow and soft, done to the accompaniment of a plaintive rhythmic tune.   In the women's dance, the lines of graceful bending, swaying, turning and moving to and fro with stamping feet, there is a primeval touch of beauty.   Sometimes they show gestures and movements of the actual processes of gathering of the sheaves, caressing the earth as though enticing it to give forth fruit, and happiness at the good harvest.   The men in their group form a line and bend and kneel, turn and jump, carrying out shouts of glee as they whirl in the air and fall on their feet in perfect timing to the drum beats.

Sometimes, as a variation in these dances, the men and women join together at this stage of the dance, the men kneeling and the women bending and doing a soft movement of cutting the grain.   The leader of the men's line, who carries a palm leaf, fans the ground with it to the accompaniment of songs of praise to Bharati Mata.

34. *HOLI DANCE*.   The Bhatra tribal people of Orissa celebrate the spring festival of the Carnival of Colours with great fun and dance and music.   The men go out in hunting parties and when they return at nightfall, they join with the women in dancing and singing.   One line of the verse is sung by the men on one side, to be followed by the women on the other side.   The song tells of the great days when hunting was an important occupation of the men and many brave and adventurous deeds were done.   After this, the men and women take short sticks and dance in groups of four, criss-crossing their sticks, beating them one against the other's and going in squares and circles.   Taking at the same time three steps forward, turn and retreat for three steps, then moving forward three steps again.   The tempo increases slightly as the dancers form their varying patterns, and finally there is an interchanging of the groups.   The dance is very colourful and bright, with the silver ornaments of the women flashing as they move and the many-hued turbans of the men stuck with peacock feathers in them, swaying as the dancers shake and toss their heads.

35. *KARAMA DANCE (I)*.   This colourful dance is done by the Binjhal, Kharia, Oraon, Kisan and Kol tribals of Sambalpur District in Orissa.   It is a ritual dance done in honour of the tribal deity Karamrani, the Giver of Good Fortune and children.   On the eleventh day of the full moon in the month of Bhadra (Aug.-Sept), boys and girls begin by singing and dancing and beating drums. They cut a branch of the Karam tree or Sal, and planting it in the village dance ground, dance around it.   After having performed the ritualistic ceremony and prayers having been said by the priest, this dance takes place.   When the Binjhal people dance the Karama, a group of men dancers, each carrying a mirror in one hand, form two rows and move to and fro to the rhythmic beat of the earthern *Madal* drum, the cymbals and song.   First, the dancers dance in solo, each one doing a dance of his own, and each soloist moving in harmony with the rest. This is followed by the men dancing in two's, while sitting down, facing one another

and hitting the heels of their outstretched legs on the ground, bending their bodies and swinging to and fro. As they move, their ankle bells mark the time beats. This is followed by the dancers standing up in two's with their left hands on one another's shoulders. Twisting, moving with quick even steps forwards and backwards and sideways, they create a strange and fascinating picture. Bright shirts and multi-coloured turbans that have peacock feathers fixed in them in tiers, and many flashing ornaments, add greatly to the whole ensemble.

After the men have finished their dance, the girls stand in a semi-circle either holding hands or with their arms so placed that they encircle one another's shoulders, or stand arm-in-arm, or with the arms crossed behind and in front. They commence by swinging to and fro. Now they bend in front, now back, now to one side and now to the other, like flowers swaying in a breeze. Then coming to a position of being bent almost double and forwards, they bend their knees and cross hands and clap rhythmically. As the tempo of the dance increases, the dancers form into a large circle and move into lines to the accompaniment of different songs—the most important lyric sung being the one addressed to the deity that grants rain. Sometimes, girls and boys dance together in the Karama, forming separate lines. The dance is full of lively stepping, stamping, beating of the left foot forward and back, and a repetition of this with the right foot, then circling and clapping. The dance goes on all night, and in the early morning, they remove the branch of the Sal tree which has been planted, and taking it in procession to the nearest tank or stream, cast it in the waters.

KARAMA DANCE (II). This dance though performed by more than one of the tribal groups, is differently done by some of them. The first one is done by the Binjhals in the manner described above. The Kharias, Kisans and Oraons commence the dance by a large group forming a circle in which both men and women participate. The front of the line is occupied by the men, next the women, then young girls, and the children at the end. The dancers at first move round holding hands and stepping with intricate footwork; and as the rhythms change, they move their bodies rhythmically, and change to placing their arms around the shoulders of their neighbours with crossed hands. As they change the positions of their arms, the dance continues. And they dance with flat of foot and on the toes, raise the left foot back and advance; move forwards and backwards and to the right and the left. The dance goes on, increasing in tempo, and those who cannot keep up with the pace, drop off, till only the best dancers are left. They now make patterns of steps, going round and round and to and fro, till the climax is reached. Then the whole performance is decreased in tempo and comes to a slow and even stepping and rhythm.

36. *SUA DANCE.* After the season of the Karama dance comes another period of dancing among these tribal people of Sambalpur in Orissa. Young girls, filled with the spirit of adventure and romance, visit a number of villages, singing and dancing to the accompaniment of Gond tribal musicians and drummers. They stop at each village, dance and sing, enjoy the hospitality of their hosts, stay the night, and next morning they go on to the next village and repeat the performance. This romantic type of dance and song goes on for many days and the girls derive a great deal of enjoyment in this way.

The dancing is simple but lively, and takes the usual shape of the girls forming into the line with their arms linked and moving sideways and forwards and backwards. Now it is a straight line, now curved into a semi-circle, now it goes into one big circle and now it opens up.   Stamping and shuffling, raising the feet alternately as they move sideways and bend forwards, the dance is as lilting as the songs that accompany it.   Pretty costumes and hair-do's add greatly to this attractive dance that is the acme of youthful gaiety.

37. *DESI KARAMA*.   This dance is one of the very few solo performances to be found among the tribal people, who generally enjoy dancing in groups and with men and women participating, even though they might dance in separate lines or groups.   The Desi Karama is done by the Ganda and Pana people of Orissa State.   One dancer sings and dances to the accompaniment of the drummer.   Bending forwards, turning from side to side, whirling, acting and mime, show that the soloist must be quite an adept.   The songs which he sings are considered to be very sweet in melody, and tell of the old legends and myths of the area.   As the *Madal* drums his rhythms, the dancer appears to be lost in a world of movement and rhythm all his own.

38. *DALKHAI*.   The Dalkhai is a festive dance done by young girls of the Binjhal, Saura, Kuda and Nirda tribal people of Sambalpur in Orissa State, and is usually performed during the autumn festival of Dusserah, at the springtime festival and at harvest time.   Forming into the usual line which is later changed into a semi-circle, girls commence by singing songs appropriate to the occasion. Accompanied by two or three different types of drums and wind instruments, the *Dhol* drummer dances with the girls in a strenuous and varied series of changing movements and steps.   Waving their hands, taking them to the sides and in a sweeping gesture, as they hold a piece of cloth that is suspended from the shoulders, they gyrate rhythmically.   Now they bend their knees, now they lean forward, their bodies half bent; now they twist their hips and torsos; and now they stamp and side step.   The dance is enhanced by the drummer achieving perfect timing and unison of beats between his own playing and those of the other drummers, and at the same time, keeping in step in all its variety with the girl dancers.

39. *THE GHOORMA*.   This rather fascinating clay-drum dance performed by men of the Binjhal, Khonda and Sawa tribal people at marriages, at Dusserah time and on other festive occasions, is quick and stirring.   Slinging the drums around their shoulders and then fixing them to their waist-bands, the dancers play their drums as they parade with a stylised walk into a pattern of circles.   Accompanied by two other drums and songs, the dancers step forwards and backwards, bending and tossing their heads, stamping their feet and kicking one foot back as they form into circles.   This is followed by the drummers playing a series of very beautiful drum syllables to get the dancers to commence dancing again. Because, after their first series of dance movements done in circles, they form into a line, while the accompanying singer sings songs in praise of Saraswati, Goddess of Learning, and other deities.

With the sound of the patterned drum syllables, the dance steps get more varied with a great deal of bending and turns and swift whirls.   Now, there is a softened tempo, and there is a prayer-song recitation from the *Ramayana* and the *Mahabharata*, and the *Puranas*, each verse ending with a dance sequence. The picturesqueness of the dance is made peculiarly different by one of the dancers carrying a long bamboo pole with movable wooden figures of two men, fixed atop of it.   And he dances along with the other dancers as they bend forwards and backwards, bend in half to the front, sit down, and then resume dancing all in one long dance sequence.

40. *RING DANCE.* The familiar formation into a circle or ring and dancing is also seen in this dance of enjoyment and recreation, done by the women of the Oraon tribals of Orissa. It is usually performed during all festivals and during the spring and autumn celebrations. Making a circle formation, the women place their arms at the back of their neighbours and clasp the hands of the next but one dancer. Thus firmly held, they go into a semi-circle and again into a full circle, at the same time raising one foot back while the other is placed forward. Then bending their knees, and with a rocking movement, they advance in a circle. Now bending forwards, now back, they unfold into a semi-circle again, and end up in the formation of a ring that goes round and round.

41. *THE KOISABADI.* Once again we find the ever popular and nationwide stick dance being done by the Bhuiyas, Gonds and Gaudas of Sambalpur District in Orissa State. The men carry sticks about two feet long and forming into a line at first, they go into squares and double lines, facing one another as they step back and forth, hitting their own sticks and then those of their neighbours and those standing across. The patterns of movement and criss-crossing of the sticks continue with increasing speed and accuracy, to the accompaniment of singing, which the leader starts, to be followed by the chorus. At the end of every verse, the dancers cry with gusto "Haijo", "Laijo", and then move once again into their designs of rectangles, squares and double lines. The steps match the beating of the sticks very skilfully, and there is a fine rhythm of movement and striking of sticks. The themes of the songs that accompany the dance are based on the romantic Radha-Krishna legends.

42. *WARRIOR DANCE.* The Nagas are a virile and colourful people living in the interior of Assam, some in the hills, and some on the plains with their dense forests and tropical vegetation. Picturesquely dressed in great plumed head-dresses and carrying swords and staves, they form into an enormous circle and go round and round. At the same time they chant, and turning and whirling, they move in a three-step measure. Only men take part and it is a marvellous sight to see these men with their splendid physique and rippling muscles taking their great leaps into the air, squatting, turning, bending and marching, as they circle in slow and forceful stepping. The light flashing on their waving weapons, their virile movements powerful and strong, combine to create the effect of Nature and the wide open spaces at their best.

43. *SPEAR DANCE.* Not unlike the Warrior dance, this very spectacular and thrilling dance of the Naga people is full of a rare primeval grace. Carrying long spears and forming into the great line that eventually changes into an enormous circle, the dancers sing and chant as they move. The dance commences with the brandishing of the spears with raised arms over their heads and then with striking postures of strength and sureness, they cast their weapons at an invisible enemy. The whole movement of poised body, raised left foot and the weight cast on the right foot is marvellous. The posture is repeated with every so many steps of walking and stalking, crouching and ending with a great leap. The dancers then change their tactics and quickly make a thrust at themselves with speed and grace and just as beautifully parry each his own thrust with skilful cunning. The dance is one of the hunter, and is full of the deftness and accuracy required for a hunter's skill with his natural weapon—the spear.

44. *DANCE OF IMITATION.* The Zemi tribal people of the Nagas living in the forest clad areas of Assam have these dances since they live so close to

Nature. No wonder the movements of some of the animals, birds and even insects, inspire the sense of rhythm and dance in man. With these influences, the Zemi Nagas have the Dance of the Bee and the Dance of the Hornbill. Strangely enough, these two creatures are the exact opposite of each other in movement and size and habits; one being so tiny and active and the other so large and slow. In these two very different dances, one can trace the ability of the human to impersonate delicacy and swiftness with as much ease as solidarity and a kind of clumsy grace. In the Dance of the Bee, there are quick, fleeting movements with small, fast, running steps and gestures that bespeak of a creature that flits and flies; but in the Dance of the Hornbill, there is the more precise defined stepping, with waddling from side to side, and head movements and gestures that indicate a creature whose natural habit is to fly abruptly, move with calculation, and generally appear to be somewhat top-heavy owing to the size of its beak.

45. *THE KHAMBA LIM*. This may well be called the Harvest dance of the Zemi tribal people of the Nagas, living in the Cachar Hills of Assam. These people are rather different to the Nagas who inhabit the hills in their way of life and customs. The Zemis have a number of interesting dances which are done to the accompaniment of songs, horns and drums. When the harvest season is about to commence, these hardy people dance in joy and hope for having reaped a good crop. Men dancers form a line and the women form another line of their own as they move to and fro, forwards and backwards, with simple steps that consist mainly of stamping, shuffling and going round and round. Then the two lines change places, the men taking the place where the women's line was, and the women moving into their place. But the dance continues without the lines being broken up, and the dancers go past one another with smooth and graceful steps.

46. *THE NRUIRA LIM*. This dance is also done when the harvest season is about to commence, and is really meant to depict a cock fight. In this popular sport found in many villages, and also in Tribal India, there is great fun and excitement. Young girls and boys form a group, the boys standing opposite the line made up by the girls, and just for the fun and amusement of it, they go through a series of movements that would take place in a real cock fight. Jumping forwards, raising their hands and pushing their heads forwards, then leaping back and forth, the dance is just one of those social affairs participated in by the young.

47. *THE BAMBOO DANCE*. The Kuki Nagas do this interesting dance that demands both skill and a sense of perfect timing. Four long bamboo poles are placed across one another to form a square that can be opened and closed again. The accompanying drummers sit near the end of the square, and as they commence their rhythmic beats, the dancers skilfully hop on one foot outside the crossed sticks when the square is closed and then inside when it is opened. This dance is generally done by girls, and it becomes more intricate and complicated as two or more dancers compete in the clever hopping in and out of the crossed poles as the square is opened and closed. During the course of the dance, drummers increase the tempo and the dance accordingly gets faster and faster. It is really a sight to see the rapid and skilful hopping that is done as the poles are moved faster and faster.

48. *SHIVA DANCES*. These dances are done in honour of the great God Shiva, and His other aspect Shakti, at the festivals of the Boro tribal people who

inhabit the plains of Assam. These agriculturists who love their land, always celebrate with song and dance on auspicious days connected with their occupation. The Habajani dance is done by them after marriage ceremonies, and the Baisaku and Bihu dances take place in spring, with the planting and harvesting of the crops. First they beseech the God for a good harvest, and later they make a thanksgiving. These dances are devotional and ritualistic and of ancient origin.

Another ancient dance representing victory in battle, is the Nat Puja dance, in which the men carry swords and dedicate themselves to Lord Shiva, who will grant them success in their undertakings. This dance too is one of ritual and devotion to the deity, with full faith that He will bless them with prosperity.

WESTERN INDIA

49. *HARVEST DANCE*. The Adivasis of Gujerat also dance in joyous celebration and in thanksgiving at the harvesting of the crops. Men and women dance together but in separate groups. Usually the men perform the ever popular stick dance in which they form into the usual two lines and start hitting one another's sticks, and then their own sticks in accompaniment to the loud drum beats of the *Dholak*. Stepping gaily up and down, now turning and now sitting, now interchanging places with their neighbours, and now turning round and jumping, this dance is rhythmic and fast, and like most stick dances is patterned and lively, the tempo increasing and leading the performance to a fine climax.

The women's dance is slower and placid. They form into a semi-circle and sometimes into two semi-circles facing each other, and move towards one another and back again, to and fro, sometimes clapping and sometimes linking arms and swaying from side to side. The song accompanying the dance is plaintive and punctuated with shrill notes that give it a peculiarly ringing lilt.

50. *HOLI DANCE*. The Adivasis also dance at Holi to usher in the spring festival of the Carnival of Colours. The dance is not so colourful and gay as its counterpart in other parts of India among the rural and tribal peoples, but it is significant in the rather charming songs that are sung; and the dance though monotonous is spontaneous. Going round and round with clapping hands, and bending and shuffling along, it is old in origin and theme.

SOUTH INDIA

51. *DANCE OF THE TODAS*. The dance of the Toda people who live in Ootacamund, in the Nilgiri Hills of Madras State, is very ancient in origin, with its roots in ritual and worship of the sun. Toda settlements hang like bee-hives above the rolling downs, and have their own conical cathedral in which the Sun deity is represented by a hewn stone. Their songs are generally sung in chorus, one woman starting the line and the others joining in the strain. It is believed to resemble the sound of a swarm of bees that comes from a distance over the valley, getting louder and louder as it approaches one.

Usually it is the men who dance in groups on the days that are dedicated to the Sun deity. Holding hands and forming a circle, they go round and round with the movements repeated over and over. Now they are bending forward with a slow stepping on the flat of feet, and now they are doing a two-step and working forwards and backwards, always in a circle. But the sight of these men bending in the dance with joyous whoops of delight, their bearded faces alight, their slim figures draped in shawls, reminds one for all the world as though the seven dwarfs of Snow White were off on a spree!

52. *DANDARIA DANCES*.　Here once again is the stick dance done by the Gond tribal people who live in Hyderabad in Andhra Pradesh.　Groups of dancers comprising men and women, dressed in their most colourful costumes, go from one village to another and exchange visits on special festive days, to dance and sing together in happy celebration.　The visiting men dance with the men and the women dance with women only.　The men perform the now familiar stick dance, standing in lines and squares and changing places and beating their sticks criss-criss-cross.　The women do the same in their group, and it is great fun to see the two groups in their pattern of steps and hitting sticks moving in designs and changing designs, to the resounding drum beats and the songs.

53. *SOCIAL DANCES*.　These simple popular dances of the Bhanjaras or Lambadis, the gypsy tribals who live in Hyderabad in Andhra Pradesh, are associated with their household tasks, cultivation and sowing, planting and harvesting.　These colourful people, whether they live in the north or centre or south of India, have a very brilliant colour sense, and the costumes of the women are very picturesque: wide skirts in bright colours, with contrasting embroidery and tiny inset scintillating mirrors, bright *Cholis* and draperies, they create a startling picture as they dance.　Their technique is actually very simple.　Forming into a great circle, the women go round and round singing shrilly, and accompanied by the *Dholak* and horn.　Their many bracelets clinking to the rhythm of their steps, they clap and turn their hands in simple gestures that depict their agricultural tasks.　They form into a double line and advance and retreat, now holding hands and bending forwards, now resting their hands on the back of their heads and going backwards.　These are merry lively dances, typical of the happy-go-lucky temperament of these simple people.

　　　These fifty-three examples of some of the tribal dances of India are representative of the many interesting forms of terpsichorean art prevalent in the country. The subject is comprehensive, and indeed vast in variety, indicating how imporgant a part dance and song play in the social, religious and sociological life of the people.

　　　Now that a general picture has been given of the Dance in India in its various classical, folk and tribal modes, it will be fitting to write of the Revival of the Dance in our country since its renaissance as a national art, and mention some of the leading personalities who have during the years contributed such valuable service in giving it its proper place and perspective.

Plate 105

1

Naga dances of Assam. (1) A distinctive dance of celebration. (2) The Warrior's dance. (Photos, Darshan Lall.) (3) A lively group dance performed by young Naga men and women. (Photo copyright, Mohan Khokar.)

2

3

Plate 106

Naga dances of Assam. (1) One of the picturesque group dances of celebration performed by Naga men and women. (2) The Çock dance. (Photos, Darshan Lall.)

Plate 107

1

Tribal dances of Andhra Pradesh. (1) A Lambardi (Gipsy) woman taking her position in the dance. (Photo, Darshan Lall.) (2) A group dance performed by Lambardi women, Hyderabad (Dn.). (Photo copyright, Mohan Khokar.)

2

Plate 108

1

2

(1) The late Madame Menaka, the distinguished dancer, in an expressive mood in the *Abhinaya* from the Kathak dance ballet, the "Krishna Lila". (2) Madame Menaka and her partner, Ram Narayan Misra, in a scene from the "Krishna Lila" ballet. (3) Madame Menaka (*centre*) and her group of dancers in the "Menaka-Vishwamitra" dance ballet. (Photos and courtesy, Major-Gen. S. S. Sokhey.)

3

18. Revival of the Dance

As EXPLAINED in Chapter I, the dance was mentioned in some of the *Vedas* as an art associated with worship and ritual, and therefore it was clothed in sanctity. It occupied this position of dignity throughout the period known as the Golden Age of the Aryans. Princesses and women of culture counted dancing as an accomplishment and a cultural asset, and they studied the art very seriously. Its prestige is believed to have continued throughout the Brahmanical period from about 1000 B.C. to about 500 B.C., during which there was the emphasis on Pantheism, a doctrine which taught that the whole Universe must be identified with God. Sacred books, the *Upanishads*, were written about 800 B.C., setting out to expound and explain the precepts and ritualistic teachings of the four *Vedas*. Dance was symbolically associated with the Gods in their Divine dances that represented picturesque parable modes.

With the establishment of Pali Buddhism in 500 B.C., in its search for truth, there was a concentration on the purely spiritual aspects of life, and the dance as an art began to gradually decline. Members of the higher strata of society and family members were forbidden to dance, or to sing or to play on musical instruments. The dance therefore lost almost all its religious sanctity and position of honour, and it practically fell into disuse as a purely cultural and religious art expression, becoming instead a form of entertainment for the Royal courts. In this period too, the Apsaras or celestial nymphs mostly appear in bas relief as temptresses who came to earth to disturb saints in their meditation.

However, with the decline of Buddhism in India, and the rise of reformed Brahmanism, men reverted to the Upanishadic teachings. The lyrical and heroic epic poems, the *Ramayana* and the *Mahabharata*, (the former with its heroic incidents, the attention paid to the grandeur of Nature and the fine sentiments and emotions of the human heart, revealed to the sage Valmiki; and the latter consisting of a series of religious, moral, metaphysical, philosophical and political discourses told through poetic narrative, revealed to the Sage Vyasa); and the *Puranas* (eighteen in number), comprehensive encyclopaedic details comprising discourses and discussions on theology, mythology, the arts and sciences, philosophy and history and politics and law with a unity of purpose and theological thought, became widely acknowledged and taught. Many beautiful dance dramas and dance subjects came to be based on the stories of the *Puranas*. And with the merging of so many centuries of thought, the numerous references to the classical dance being a great and noble art came to light. In the Gupta period (A.D. 326 to 500) for instance, it was discovered that dancers were honoured and elevated to a position of esteem. Panini, one of our most eminent ancient grammarians in the 5th century B.C., speaks of the *Natas* or dancers and mentions about their having to study the *Nata Sutras* or the Handbooks for Dancers. Now with the spread of the teachings of the *Ramayana* and the *Mahabharata* and the *Puranas* once again, dance and music were revived as great arts, and they came again into prominence, reaching their height about the 1st and 2nd centuries A.D., and continued so for almost a thousand years.

In the South, we find that Tamil poets in their writings have preserved much of the beauty and importance of the dance. To them we owe a debt of gratitude for their marvellous descriptions of the dances of the Gods, Shiva, Parvathi, Lakshmi, Sri Krishna, Kali, Balaram and Indra. The dance played an important part in the cultural and spiritual life of the Tamils, from earliest times in fact, and there are hundreds of references to Tamil classical dances in the writings that have come down to posterity. The *Silappadikaram* ("The Epic of the Anklet"), for instance, placed about the 2nd century A.D., glorifies the beauty and expressiveness of the dance.

Later, during the Chola dynasty (9th century to 13th century A.D.), a period that tells of a highly developed civilization in which the theatre, dance, music, architecture, painting, poetry and cultural festivals, formed part of the daily life of the people of every class and occupation, there was a great impetus given to the dance. The Chola kings won immortal fame by their great temple building activities, and for instituting the system of dancers in them. They encouraged the thousands of beautiful sculptural works executed in these places of worship and the arts which they built. The temples thus became the centres of both religious devotion and of the arts and learning; and innumerable examples of sculpture, painting and of frescoes representing the dance can be found within their portals. In some of the larger temples, theatres or *Natya Mandirs* were built, where dance and drama were performed under the most aesthetic and exalting conditions. Dance was thus restored to its former place of importance and honour.

When the Nayak kings ruled over a part of the South, they too encouraged the arts and gave shelter to the groups of dancers, musicians and Bhagavatulus who migrated from Andhra, and helped them settle in the Tanjore District in what was then known as Achatapuram, named after one of the distinguished Nayak kings. In Andhra and Orissa, too, this return to the recognition of the cultural and devotional aspects of the dance and music, greatly helped to reinstate them to a place of honour and real appreciation. Temples in Orissa had their dancers and their mode was ritualistic and devotional. Beautiful dance sculptures began to appear in the various temples in Orissa, Andhra, Madhya Pradesh, and all over the South. These have served to enlighten succeeding generations as to the importance and the beauty of dance as an art in these various regions.

In the north, the early classical dance became the forerunner of the Sanskrit drama. Ujjain and Kanouj were the centres where the Sanskrit theatre took root and flourished. Gifted bards regularly recited verses in the open air beneath the canopy of the sky or spreading trees, or within the courtyards of the temples. They enlarged their repertoire by reading extracts from the *Ramayana* and the *Mahabharata*, with their fine lyrical passages and sacred history. From the stage of reciting bards, the ancient Prakrit plays were created, followed in turn by the Sanskrit plays. For Prakrit was the language of the people at large in those days, and Sanskrit was the language of the lettered. Starting with Saumilla and Bhasa and followed by Sudraka, Kalidasa, Bhavabhuti and Harsha, sublime and romantic ideals came to be expressed more and more in drama form, and became in fact a part of the many facets of life as it was lived then.

For example, in *Shakuntala* and *Puruvurasa and Urvashi*, both of which were written by Kalidasa, we are given wonderful pen pictures of life and events of his time. The former is vivid, with interesting sidelights on the social structure of his days; the latter depicts the definite turn to something akin to musical opera, with its poetic fancies, where emotion and speech are given to animal and plant life. Again, in Kalidasa's *Malavika Agnamitra* and in Vishakadalla's *Mudree Rakshasas*, there are distinct allusions to the political ideals of the time. Later, metaphysics and humour were introduced, and the dance also came to be dramatised. Plays like *Malavika Agnamitra* laid stress on the beauty and techniques of the dance. At the same time, musical sketches like the *Banas*, and amusing one act monologues became popular. *The Toy Cart*, another famous Sanskrit play, built its theme around the dancer Vasantasena.

Though the best Sanskrit dramas were written sometime between 200 B.C. and the 10th century A.D., the actual production of plays was at its zenith between the 8th and 15th centuries A.D. Dance and drama were enacted in the temple theatres (*Devasthan* or *Natya Mandir*) and also in the music rooms of the palaces of kings, where a special place was set apart for such performances. The theatre was a square structure built in front of the temple, beautifully sculptured, with ornate ceiling, and a high roof crowned with golden domes. It was divided into three sections, namely, the green rooms or dressing rooms, which were to the west; the auditorium to the east; and the centre raised to form the stage. Two entrances opened from it at the back to the dressing rooms, and between these sat the musicians.

Plays and dance performances took place on lunar holidays and during coronations, marriages and festivals. The king sat in the centre on his throne, his entourage on his left, and persons of rank and learning on his right. Men and women sat separately. The auditorium was large enough to seat a very large number of persons. The perfume of roses and incense filled the air; and sparkling gems, brocaded silks and colourful costumes gleamed in the vast auditorium which was circular in shape, permitting everyone a perfect view of the stage. Young maidens dressed in gossamer silks waved plumed fans, and armed guards leant majestically at the back, keeping watch. The spacious and elegant stage, supported by richly decorated pillars, and adorned with green foliage, garlands of flowers, coconuts and banana saplings, faced the deity. The temple sculptures provided the rich background, the embossed silk curtains permitted the change of scenes while burnished lamps illuminated the artistes and settings.

The actors were generally descended from a long line of *Sutas* who were court bards and minstrels, even though kings themselves acted sometimes, and queens and princesses and ladies of culture danced. Dancers were very well educated and took to the art with serious purpose. At a young age, they learnt besides dancing, dramatics, perfume-making, painting, music, singing, grammar and the art of conversation. In addition, it was essential that they learned to read and write and knew the essentials of Indian philosophy. No wonder the classical dance reached great heights in both performance and artistry.

In the villages in India, along with legend and lore, the recitation of the *Ramayana* and the *Mahabharata* and original humorous sketches and songs became popular. Puppet shows came to acquire a new significance as did the exquisite Shadow Plays, figuring largely in such festivals as the Ram Lila, the Krishna Lila, and the spring and autumn festivals. Side by side, dancing was always done, springing as it did from the natural expression of the people; further, dance also interpreted drama and was often performed along with it. These performances brought to light the vast material inherent in the cultural, social, historical and religious life of the people.

I have described the conditions under which the dance in ancient India flourished, and during its zenith when the theatre in India was in its heyday. As happens in all countries and among all peoples, the vicissitudes and prosperity of life deeply affect art at all times. It has been the same in India. Change of thought, outlook, culture, circumstances and attitudes have all left their indelible marks on the position of the dance from time to time. Up and down, it has vibrated between favour and disfavour, finally ending in an art that became confined to a particular group of people who passed it on to posterity as a hereditary art. For a long time after this and in the process of its nation-wide decline into the background as a cultural feature of importance, most of the well planned stage techniques of the old fabulous days of theatre-craft were forgotten, and drama and dramatic performance too became haphazard, but for the few families who preserved them.

One of the greatest drawbacks of this was the fact that the regular theatre as such ceased to function actively all over the country, and dance and drama no longer had good theatres where they could be performed exclusively. India is still suffering from the lack of such theatres. Dance and drama have most often to be performed in movie houses or lecture-cum-theatre halls.

The history of the revival of the theatre in India has not been without its struggles and vicissitudes, and though great men have come forward within the last century to re-create some semblance of the old Sanskrit days, and instil into it the permanency and some of the artistry it once enjoyed, only a small measure of success has been achieved—mainly due to lack of good theatres in sufficient numbers. In Bengal, the stage has perhaps more than in any other State in India reached a really highly artistic and dramatic standard, and only great persistence and a strong desire to overcome all disabilities have achieved this.

The villages fortunately have suffered little from the prejudices and disadvantages of the cities and towns. Excellent dramas, sketches, dances and dance dramas have continued to be staged, even if they be in a modest way. Using the natural talents of the people, and the village green if necessary for these performances, it is in rural India that dance and drama have taken their deepest roots. Around the village green, or on the rough stage erected under spreading trees, whose gracious shade lent the setting and the site a beauty all its own, there grew a spirit of intimate understanding and candour amongst the performers and the spectators.

Kathakali, the classical dance dramas of Kerala in south-west India, for instance, had the greatest advantage in that it grew up in the villages. It was performed by the people for the people of the village. Children, adults, one and all, came to understand and appreciate each nuance of this highly skilled and dramatic dance form, following story and gesture with perfect sympathy and pride. When some of these troupes came to perform in the cities, they chose the grand pillared courtyards of the temples for their settings. This provided the artistic congeniality necessary for enacting the grand spectacle of the dance dramas to their fullest degree. Picturesque costumes and grandeur of movement, with dramatic acting, were highlighted by the many flares or dozens of flickering oil lamps. At the same time, the spaciousness and the atmosphere of the familiar temple surroundings helped them feel at home as they performed. But in the cities it is a different matter, and neither the Kathakali dancers nor folk dance troupes feel happy or comfortable on the inadequate stages which are generally available.

In 1961, when the Tagore Centenary was celebrated, it was decided by the Government that a good and adequate theatre should very soon be built in each of the leading cities in commemoration of one who contributed so richly not only to literature but also to the various arts. Meanwhile, the Bharatiya Natya Sangh or Theatre Centre of India, which is affiliated to the Theatre Centre U.N.E.S.C.O., and has affiliated branches in the various State capitals, organised a Theatre Architecture Exhibition with a view to invite suitable designs for our coming national theatres. This no doubt furnished new ideas and constructive suggestions for what should be the best type of theatre for present-day India and its particular needs. The Drama Competition organised by the Bharatiya Natya Sangh about 1953, certainly proved that there is a great need for numerous good theatres without delay. More than 1000 entries were received and the various regional groups between them staged plays in thirteen languages.

* * * *

As far as the dance in India is concerned, many great names figure in the course of its revival and re-establishment on a permanent footing. The late Dr. Rabindranath Tagore, poet and Nobel prize winner for Literature, artist, writer and painter, first conceived in a really big way, the idea to glean portions of the vast material available in dance, from the various regions where it was being performed, and present it artistically and sympathetically to audiences.

In South India, more than anywhere else, dancing was organised, fresh and vigorous in its renaissance and was understood and appreciated greatly, owing to the regular performances of Bharata Natyam and Kathakali. This was the position, in spite of the fact that there still existed a prejudice against family members studying the art or performing on the stage. Kathakali was practically confined to Kerala and village audiences; while Bharata Natyam, Orissi and Kuchipudi were performed mainly by the Devadasis and the Kuchipudi professional dancers respectively.

As far back as 1917, during his visit to Sylhet in Assam, Poet Tagore witnessed the dance of Manipur, and with his artistic foresight, he was able to recognise in the art the basis for the revival of the dance for larger groups.   He was charmed by its lyrical beauty, romantic themes, graceful movements and the unique costumes, so he brought dancers and teachers from this region back to his cultural centre at Shantiniketan and had them impart their knowledge to the pupils of this famous institution.

He then wrote a play which was to be interpreted into dance drama form, called "The Worship of the Dancing Girl," and Gauri Devi, the talented daughter of India's celebrated painter Nandalal Bose, played the leading role of the dancer. She was perhaps the first non-professional to appear in Calcutta on the stage as a dancer in this period of the revival of the Indian dance.   The dance drama was a tremendous success and Gauri Devi was hailed as a dancer of great talent, and the accompanying soft and alluring melodies used along with the songs of Manipur created a sensation.

Just as he had simplified and sweetened many of the classical melodies, making them more understandable to all, by creating the famous "Bengali music," which in time became so popular in India, Poet Tagore gave to the Indian dance also that savour of sweetness and soulful expression with much grace required to stir a people estranged from their own classical art.   At first the Tagore School of Dance was mainly based on the graceful dance of Manipur with its traditional themes.   But later on, Bharata Natyam and Kathakali were introduced, when the poet brought teachers from the South who taught these two schools in Shantiniketan.   Thus the Tagore school became a creative art based on the very best traditions of some of the main styles of the classical dance.

Many leading cities in India, such as Bombay, Calcutta and Madras, had the opportunity of witnessing some of the highly artistic performances, as the dance began to flow uninterrupted once again into the circles from whence it had been so long denied a place.   I recall with vivid pleasure "The Kingdom of Cards," "Redemption," and "Chitrangada," the last named being a romantic story from the annals of Manipur.   From India, the Tagore troupe toured England and Europe and took the art of dance and dance drama to very wide and appreciative audiences.   In 1936, when I visited Shantiniketan as a guest of the poet, I was able to fully appreciate the fine work being done under the most desirable conditions of art and culture.   As I was accompanied by my teacher Nabhakumar Singha of Manipur, and was able to get suitable South Indian accompaniment there, I was able to give a small recital for the poet and the residents of Shantiniketan, and in return was rewarded with a beautiful little dance ballet staged by the Tagore troupe in their really delightful theatre.

Two other great artistes who have helped place Indian dancing on the map, both at home and abroad, are the late Madame Menaka, an accomplished and cultured lady from Bengal, and Uday Shankar, also hailing from Bengal.

Madame Menaka specialised in the Lucknow Gharana or school of Kathak under distinguished *gurus*, and organised the first ballet company in India, taking as her partner Ram Narayan Misra of the Bindadin Maharaj Gharana.   And through her solos, duets, group dances and ballets, she brought to the Indian stage wonderful compositions embodying the rich choreography and the fullness of *Abhinaya* possible in this school of the dance.   Indeed, a real transformation was brought about by her in the presentation of this ancient dance style, not only as an art but in the beauty of her costumes, the excellence of decor and the special quality of the varied *Raga* melodies she utilised.   Later, Madame Menaka

Plate 109

Uday Shankar Company. (1, 2, 3, 6, 7) Scenes from the Uday Shankar Company's classical ballet, "Shiva-Parvati." (4) A folk dance and (8) a dance of Rajasthan. (Photos, A. L. Syed.)

Plate 110

1

2

Ram Gopal, the celebrated dancer, (1) Showing the
Vira Rasa (heroic mood) as portrayed in one of his
Kathakali dances. (2) A posture from the *Sandhya
Nrtta Murti*, Shiva's Yogic Evening dance. (Courtesy,
Ram Gopal.)

Plate 111

Guru Gopinath, the famous Kathakali teacher and dancer, in one of his early dance portrayals as Shiva.

2

Dance ballet "Usha Anirudda" in Kathakali technique, produced by Darpana, Ahmedabad. (2) Chattuni Panicker as Sri Krishna (*centre*) brings a reconciliation between Anirudda and Bana. (3) The three characters, *left to right*, Anirudda, Sri Krishna and Bana. (Courtesy, Mrinalini Sarabhai.)

3

Plate 112

1

2

3

4

(1) Shirin Vajifdar in the ballet "Birth of Urvashi." (Courtesy, Shirin Vajifdar.) (2) Ragi▨ Devi as Parvati in the ballet "Parvati-Parinayam" (Marriage of Parvati). (Photos, Hamiltc▨ Studios, Bombay.) (3) Hima Devi in the character of a Gopi from the dance ballet "Th▨ Yashoda," produced by the Hima Kala Kendra, Bombay. (Photo, Modern Photos, Bombay▨ (4) Dance ballet "Gita Govindam," produced by Darpana, Ahmedabad; Mrinali▨ Sarabhai as Radha (centre) is being dressed by her Sakhis (companions) before sh▨ goes to meet Shri Krishna. (Courtesy, Mrinalini Sarabhai.)

studied the Manipuri, and Kathakali dance schools under famed masters and enriched her repertoire.

Her close friendship with the late Madame Pavlova only served to increase her deep and abiding love of the dance. And through such ballets as the "Krishna Lila," the "Deva Vijaya Nritya," the "Menaka Lasyam" and the "Malavika-Agnamitra" dance drama (in which she incorporated Kathak, Bharata Natyam, Manipuri and Kathakali), she interpreted drama through dance, achieving true beauty of creative expression within the orbit of the pure classical techniques. In 1936, she won for India and the classical dance three Honour Prizes, taking pride of place among the 17 International ballet groups that participated in the International ballet Olympiad held in Berlin that year. In addition to her many successful performances throughout India, this gifted dancer visited Burma, Malaya, Indonesia and all the capitals of Europe, where she created a new world of artistic achievement. In 1938, Madame Menaka established the Nritalayam School of the Dance at Khandala in Maharashtra State, where a number of young dancers, such as Damayanti Joshi, Malati Pandeya, Shirin Vazifdar and Kamal Kartikar studied and appeared in her ballets with success. To the very last Madame Menaka worked ceaselessly, giving her all for the furtherance of the dance—an art to which she was dedicated with a lifelong devotion.

Uday Shankar's name is known throughout the four continents, and he has achieved a unique place amongst dance lovers all over the world. His special talents of a creative order have been instrumental in bringing to light the hidden beauties of the Indian dance through perfectly conceived dance ballets. His genius in presentation, supported by probably the finest orchestral accompaniment heard in the dance world in India, is history now. The Uday Shankar School of the Dance is one of creative work, based on the Manipuri and Kathakali dance techniques primarily, and embodying the expressive gesture language, wonderful rhythms, varied subjects and dramatic forms of both these schools.

Influenced by his gift for painting, line and colour, and his study of sculpture, these arts have much to do with the sheer beauty of his compositions. His early association with Madame Pavlova, when he composed and danced in her "Radha-Krishna Ballet," introduced the expressive ideals possible in the Indian dance. Charm of posture and choreography marked his compositions and he has been most successful in creating something very unique and poetic through his presentations of both classical and folk dancing. The stage in India has greatly gained by his contributions and his many appearances all over India. Indeed, he gained the praise of critics and audiences in England, Europe and America not only for the artistic performances he gave year after year in these countries, but for his gift of being able to convey through his art the true message and meaning of the Indian dance.

In his famed "Shiva-Parvathi Dance Ballet," he brought to audiences the richness of Kathakali with its peculiar admixture of pure classical techniques and the art of pantomime, presented in the magnificent dramatic ballet form. Besides his classical ballets, based on leading subjects from mythology, Uday Shankar was the first to experiment seriously with modern themes, using the folk and classical idioms in a synthesis of choreography and mode to interpret life today. His "Rhythm of Life" and his "Labour and Machinery" are concrete examples of this. His creative genius has gone further in his famous shadow plays like the "Ramayana," presented on a large and magnificent scale in colour, where the characters come alive with all the reality and form of actual dance, yet retain the dream-like wonder of characters performing in ephemeral cavalcade.

Uday Shankar's talented partner and wife, Amala Shankar, has contributed a great deal of charm and artistry as well as ability to her husband's performances. Specialising in the Manipuri techniques, she has danced in solo and in the leading roles in his ballets. Specially noteworthy is her latest performance in his ballet "Samanya Kshati," created on one of the well-known poems by Tagore, and performed in the many leading cities of India in connection with the Tagore Centenary. With a rare grace, understanding of the true motives of the dance art, fluency of movement and technique, Amala rightly takes her place as one of our leading dancers.

Srimati Rukmani Devi of Adyar, Madras, is another well-known name in India. She has organised and furthered the scope of Bharata Natyam, the classical dance of South India, not only in the traditional form which is done in solo, but has also utilised it for the creation of dance drama and ballet. At the Kalakshetra Art Centre, which she has established in Adyar, the classical dance of Bharata Natyam and Kathakali are sedulously learnt and presented on the stage in their pure forms in a series of programmes. Her special work in giving a thorough training in the classical dance not only from the technical point of view but also from the cultural and historical angles has done much to make the understanding of the dance more deep and lasting for her students and dancers in India. Herself an accomplished Bharata Natyam dancer, her contribution to the renaissance of the dance in India has been outstanding. Her dance drama "Kumarasambhava," dealing with the Shiva-Parvathi theme, is a classical example of how perfectly she has used Bharata Natyam for interpreting in dance form a truly sublime and philosophical subject. Written originally in Sanskrit by the immortal dramatist Kalidasa, this lyric is a piece of sheer poetic beauty and is supported in the dance by interpretive song in the South Indian classical music style. Srimati Rukmani's Kathakali dance episodes and her folk dances arranged in groups bring to the stage today the popular village forms of the South in their classical and rural modes. Other outstanding dance dramas which have won laurels for this distinguished artiste are the immortal "Gita Govindam," Jayadeva's mystic lyrical poem of the Radha-Krishna idyll, and "Ramayana," based on the famed epic poem.

Besides dance, Srimati Rukmani Devi has established a very good weaving centre at Kalakshetra, where this ancient art is given full scope. Excellent *Sarees* and other textiles, reproducing ancient designs and introducing many new and exotic patterns, are being produced and have become popular for their aesthetic value.

Poet Tagore in the east of India, and Poet Valathol, the grand old man of Kerala in the south-west, have both worked valiantly for the cultural permanancy of the dance. Valathol's name is known throughout South India and especially in his own State for his fine poetic writings, and in the field of the dance for starting and establishing the Kalamandalam Dance Academy in Cochin (Kerala) where he organised the correct and detailed training for Kathakali dance under well-known experts. Intensive courses are available, and dozens of known dancers of today who perform Kathakali, owe their excellent knowledge to this institution, which has also been responsible for presenting Kathakali dance dramas in their original and pristine form and techniques with conspicuous success on the stages of most of the leading cities of India. In recognising the full impact that the revival of Kathakali in a big way would make on the cultural renaissance in India, the late Poet Valathol showed great insight and understanding. Poet, writer, aesthetist, and cultural ambassador, he has become the symbol of all that stands for art and culture in his home State.

The three sisters Cita, Chitra and Lata Pooviah who hail from Coorg, South India, are among the early pioneers in the dance renaissance of India, who spent years of intensive study of the Kathak school, under famed *gurus* like Jai Lal. With their cultural background, high academic qualifications and their love of the arts, they were able to give full scope to their talents in the performance of this famous style of the classical dance. I had occasion to see several of their highly artistic recitals, and it was a pleasure to be introduced with so much finesse to the pure dance modes and the beauty of the *Abhinaya* of Kathak, which they portrayed with such skill, inner feeling, grace and artistry. Lovely costumes, subtle and fascinating interplay of mood to express the dramatic content, and perfection of the techniques brought to audiences in Bombay and the major cities of India, not only delight and enjoyment, but a lasting conception of the meaning and spiritual intentions of the classical dance.

Cita Pooviah has in addition taken her doctorate in India on Dance Research, and made a valuable contribution towards the enhancement and appreciation of Kathak in the United States by her series of lecture demonstrations on the art, and her comparative discourses on the Western and Indian classical dance arts.

Another well-known name in the world of the Indian dance is Ram Gopal, who is known amongst connoisseurs as a born dancer. He has mastered the techniques of Bharata Natyam and of Kathakali with a serious purpose and depth of understanding, and made a deep study of Kathak also. Presenting these schools in both solo and ballet form, he has been able to depict the best traditions of the Indian classical dance to large audiences both in India and abroad. Artistically arranged and performed with every detail of technique and interpretive quality perfectly balanced, he has contributed much towards the preserving of these dance forms in their purity, giving them their correct perspective and value in the world of international dance.

Indeed, some of Ram Gopal's dances like "Dharani," a dance ballet in three acts in Bharata Natyam style, an exquisite symbolic subject which takes us back hundreds of years to the ancient atmosphere of the age-old temples of the south; he plays the role of a boy attendant in the temple. Among his other outstanding dance subjects done in solo in the Bharata Natyam technique are the "Natanam Adinar," the Dance of Shiva; the Garuda Dance depicting the sacred eagle of Vishnu in Kathakali style; and the "Sandhya Nrittya," the Evening Dance of Shiva, done at eventide with the setting of the sun. They all show his flawless technique and understanding of the underlying spirit of the classical dance.

For a number of years now Ram Gopal has been living in England, where he has made several successful appearances in some of the leading theatres, including his many brilliant and spectacular performances with his new enlarged Company in Britain's Royal Festival Hall, all of which have gained him unqualified praise. During his appearances in the Far East, Japan, the Phillipines, the Americas, Scandinavia, France, Switzerland and Britain, he has brought an understanding of the highest concepts and artistic ideals of India's classical and folk dances to tens of thousands of people in these various countries. He has taken great pains to present the four main schools of Bharata Natyam, Kathak, Kathakali and Manipuri in their pure forms, both in solo and as dance ballet. And among his recent productions that have gained him the highest honours are "The Legend of the Taj Mahal," and "The Rajput Serenade of Love," in which he has utilized Kathak and the folk dances of North India.

Mrinalini Sarabhai, another distinguished dancer who has earned both name and fame for the Indian dance, hails from South India. She is the Director of Dharpana, a dance society, which is sponsored by the Karmakshetra Educational Foundation of Ahmedabad. Her creative work in the classical and folk dance forms and the presenting of these modes in solo and ballets have won her acclaim. And she has most successfully presented these not only in India, but in the United States, South America, Britain, Europe and South-East Asia. Performing Bharata Natyam, Kathakali, Manipuri, Orissi and Kuchipudi in their traditional solo modes, and utilizing each school in its purity for the various themes of her dance ballets, Mrinalini has been both creative and artistic, revealing the delicate and dramatic differences between the various styles that are to be found in our classical dance in the various regions of the country. Today, with her intensive work at her dance centre at Ahmedabad, she continues to create new themes and train many new and talented artistes.

I enjoyed seeing her "Kirat Arjuna," a theme from mythology, and her "Vasanta Vijayam," gleaned from legend, both danced in the Kathakali style with her partner Chattuni Pannickar and her troupe of dancers; the charming "Abhi Sarika," a romantic story of young lovers, using the Bharata Natyam style, and the classical story of "Vasavadatta," attractively portrayed in folk techniques. Her latest ballets "Git Govinda," the immortal lyrical subject by Jayadeva, telling of the Radha-Krishna idylls, and "Sita Kalayanam," the story of the marriage of Rama and Sita from the *Ramayana*, show that Mrinalini's gifts for creating and arranging ballets using the classical modes is exceptional. As the performances unfold, bringing to life the beauty of story and interpretation, supported by perfection of technique and enhanced by costume and decor, one is transported into the realms of myth and legend with all their fascination and allure. Gifted, deeply versed in the classical and folk modes, Mrinalini has brought honour to India and a recognised place for the Indian dance wherever she has performed.

There are many famous dancers who have consistently staged excellent performances of the classical dances of India, and who possess a long and proud tradition of dance and music in their families. The name of Balasaraswathi stands out as one of the greatest exponents of the Bharata Natyam of the South. Herself the grand-daughter of the great singer and *Veena* player Dhanam, and daughter of the celebrated classical singer Jayamma, she has carried on the tradition of artistry, dedication, and perfection and the interpretation of lyric and song through dance. To watch her perform is to truly experience and appreciate the full worth of this great school; her sheer artistry unfolding itself in a richness of posture and expressive interpretation becomes a vivid drama in itself. I have had the privilege of seeing her several times in Madras, Calcutta, and Bombay, and each time I had the feeling anew that here was an artiste who not only danced perfectly, but became the very personification and spirit of this ancient art when she danced. A simple stage indeed for her performance, with no glamour of the fine settings or decor, yet one forgot all this as she transformed herself from a living person into living drama with each expression or turn of her head;

in each movement of gestural explanation of the lyrical passages she so impressively portrayed.

Now sad, now quizzical and angry, now dissuading and eager, now disdainful and questioning, her expressions changed at will. And one felt one could watch her for hours as she told through dance the various dramatic episodes so beautifully described in the classic lyrics.

In her *Abhinayam* of the *Varnam*, danced to the plaintive strains of *Bhairavi Raga*, in the lyric that tells how a lovesick maiden entreats her lover and pursues him to pour out her love for him, she is superb. And she excels in the *Padams*. I recall several, such as the one in which Uma is taunted for loving Shiva who is depicted in one of his legendary forms as a poor mendicant, and therefore according to the maid, unworthy of Uma's love. And again, as she interprets a devotional song in praise of Nataraja, the Dancing Shiva and patron deity of the Bharata Natyam; or the appealing interpretation of a girl overcome with envy, who expresses her feelings of jealousy and hatred for her rival, and bemoans her own cruel fate. Or the beautiful passages from the *Git Govindam*, telling of the Radha-Krishna idylls in allegory, with their expressions of love and devotion, happiness and sadness. In fact, Balasaraswathi is at her best in the *Abhinayam*, a supreme artiste and exponent of this art, and she remains so today.

The late Kalayani sisters are names to be remembered as two great exponents of Bharata Natyam, who helped keep alive and create a permanent place for this school by their perfect expositions done with a rare understanding and artistry born of tradition.

Sri E. Krishna Iyer, lawyer, patriot, a model city father, editor, author, actor and singer, is one of the great pioneers and cultured exponents of the Bharata Natyam and the Bhagavata Mela dance dramas. What Tagore did for the Manipur dance and Valathol for Kathakali in Kerala, E. Krishna Iyer has done for Bharata Natyam and the Bhagavata Mela dance dramas in the South. Trained under the famed Natyacharya Melatur Natesa Iyer in these two styles of the classical dance, from 1925 he fought a historic battle for seven years and brought about a permanent and successful renaissance of the classical dance and dance drama in South India.

He was one of the founders of the Music Academy of Madras (1928), and started its journal, and has been the moving spirit in reviving folk music, the indigenous puppet shows and more than thirty varieties of folk dance. During his thirty years dedicated to art and service, Sri E. Krishna Iyer has discovered, guided and encouraged new talent in the dance and brought it to prominence; among them are Ram Gopal, Balasaraswathi, Kumari Kalanadhi and Varalakshmi of Kumbakonam. He now heads the Bharatiya Natya Sangh, Madras, an institution for the furtherance of Indian music, dance and drama.

In addition to the many well-known dancers who by their performance have helped stabilise and establish the revival of the classical dance in India, many distinguished *gurus* have preserved the art throughout the generations in their families and brought credit to the dance through their pupils. In the South, Bharata Natyam owes its prestige to personages like the late Ponniah Pillai, Meenakshi Sunduram Pillai of the village of Pandanallur in Tanjore District, with his inexhaustible knowledge of the art; Putappa, Guribai of Baroda, Muthukumaran Pillai, and Chokilangam Pillai, Muthuswamy Pillai, Kandappa Pillai, Kuppiah Pillai, and Ramiah Pillai, to name a few. And in more recent times, one can name Sri Govindraj Pillai, founder of the Sri Rajarajeswari Bharata Natya Kala Mandir, one of the foremost dance academies in Bombay, and Sri Ramani of Matunga.

Because these teachers and exponents have passed on the art through generations, the dance has been preserved in its purity in various aspects of its technique. We see the Bharata Natyam performed in the Pandanallur strong statuesque manner with its precision of finesse and clear cut line; and the Vavhuvlur style, showing how the dance can also be perfectly performed in a more delicate, *Lasya* and gracious manner, each style having a special appeal of its own. The former with its straight lines and postures like temple sculptures come to life, combining great speed and intricate movement in the technique; and the latter also technically brilliant but more feminine and reminiscent of the mythical nymphs described in Indian myth and legend.

As one thinks of the many personalities who have contributed to the dance and its permanency in its revival, many dancers' names come to mind. Ragini Devi, artiste and devotee of the classical techniques of Bharata Natyam and Kathakali, is a shining example. First to re-discover and present Kathakali dance drama for audiences in other parts of India, she made many successful and highly acclaimed all-India tours with her troupe. She has lectured on the dance at the Universities of Banares, Madras, Calcutta, Andhra and Anamalai, as well as in colleges in Baroda, Delhi, and Karachi. After her successful performances in London, she was invited to give a course of lectures on the Indian dance at the London University, later performing in Europe and the United States. She has helped knowledge and understanding of our dance art by her lectures with demonstrations at the Universities of Columbia, Cornell, Pennsylvania, and Minnesota, in the United States. Her performances through the years have been marked by a deep understanding of the philosophical concepts of the dance, and have inspired many young dancers to seriously study it, not the least among them, her brilliant and talented young daughter Indrani.

In the Kathakali school of the dance, several names of great masters have already been mentioned in the chapter dealing with Kathakali. Among other well-known dancers from Kerala who have done credit and honour to the art are Mahadevan, who danced in the Uday Shankar company for many years and whose splendid performances won him name and fame in India, America and other countries of the world; Kavingal Chattuni Pannicker, partner of lovely Mrinalini Sarabhai, who has delighted audiences throughout the world with his great technical ability, histrionic talent and artistic expression of Kathakali in its many nuances; Kalamandalam Krishna Nair, another product of Kerala, who has specialised in Kathakali and also danced with the Mrinalini Sarabhai company; and Raghavan who possesses the personality, disciplined training, craftsmanship and excellent performance of this highly dramatic school of the dance. He has danced with conspicuous success in the leading cities in India and has partnered Ritha Devi on her successful dance tours in West Germany and other countries of Europe.

Guru Gopinath, who also hails from Kerala, comes from the house of Perumanar which had a long tradition in Kathakali and is the younger brother of Champakulam Pachu Pillai, noted for his roles of the Red Beards (*Chukanna Tadi*). Guru Gopinath's grand-uncle, Sanku Pillai, had amongst his disciples many dancers who ultimately became masters of the art. Trained in the best traditions of Kathakali, therefore, under such eminent *gurus* as Paramu Pillai, Mathur Kunjupilla Pannikar (scholar and exponent), *guru* Changanoor Raman Pillai, and Kunju Kurup and Kavalappara Narayana Nair while at the Kalamandalam centre at Kerala, *guru* Gopinath has won laurels wherever he has performed. For over three decades he has taught and performed Kathakali, imparting its highest ideals to over a thousand pupils through his schools; the Shri Chitrodaya Dancing School at Travancore, under the patronage of the Maharaja of Travancore, was started by him and he and his talented wife Tangamoni directed it for nine years, imparting the techniques of Kathakali and Mohini Atam to a large number of ardent students. In 1945, Guru Gopinath established his own dance centre, the Natana Niketanam at Madras, and then later organised a Kerala Kalamandalam in Delhi, for the study and performance of this great art. Now he also directs the Vishwa Kala Kendra at Ernakulam in Kerala, an international dance and cultural centre.

Among his memorable performances that I have seen, are his wonderful interpretations of the characters of Arjuna and Sri Krishna before the battle of Kurukshetra and the war itself; and the theme of King Mahabali and Vishnu as the dwarf Vamana. Indeed, as one watched these and other performances one was enveloped with the moral teachings of these sacred subjects as the vivid reality of the acting, technique and inimitable art of pantomime revealed the best traditions of Kathakali.

Turning to the Kathak school of the classical dance, the great names associated with its revival and development have already been mentioned in the chapter on this school. In the Lucknow school, among other well-known names of exponents and dedicated artistes may be mentioned, Gauri Shankar, Jai Kumari, Kalayan Das, Krishna Kumar, Pundit Sitaram Misra, Guru Ram Dutt Misra, Ram Narain Misra, Ratan Shankar, Briju Maharaj and Gopi Krishna. In the Jaipur school, well remembered names are Chunni Lal and his two sons Jai Lal and Sunder Lal, Durga Prasad, Jaya Kumari, Sohanlal Radhey, Hira Lal and Sheo Datta, to name only a few.

Sitara Devi, daughter of the distinguished *guru* and composer Maharaj Sukhdeve, is our most brilliant and accomplished of women dancers in Kathak, which art she has mastered to its fullest degree. Technically brilliant, a master of the *Parans* in which she combines both virtuosity and charm, Sitara is also a composer, and in each of her many performances she introduces a new and revealingly thrilling mode of Kathak and its interpretation. Her lucid performance and depiction of the Shiva, Krishna and Kali *Tandavas* bring forth the beauty of special techniques with emotional interpretation, equally appealingly as her splendid expositions of such features as her *Tarana*, her varied *Thoras* and *Tukdas* and her fine performances of the *Nrtyas* with their combination of both technique and dramatic content. Indeed, in this great dancer one finds a deep and sincere desire to carry on and discover and present Kathak in its best traditions which her family have done for generations.

Damayanti Joshi is another well-known dancer of Kathak, who has become popular with audiences. Combining speed, precision, and versatility in her performances, she has through the years maintained the high standards which this school demands for its most effective interpretation.

Many illustrious names have been mentioned in the chapter on the dance of Manipur, who have preserved and spread the tenets and performance of this school. It must be mentioned here that among those who have learned the art and been responsible for its understanding and appreciation outside Manipur are the four Jhaveri sisters, Nayana, Ranjana, Suverna and Darshana. They have not only mastered the techniques but have completely entered into the spirit of this classical dance art as though born to the traditions, displaying their ability and deep love of its many modes. Intrinsically pure in performance, strictly following code and precept, their graceful, beautifully staged performances, both in solo and group and ballet form, have earned them a very special place in the Manipur dance in India, Japan and other South-East Asian countries where they have performed with conspicuous success, and have been recognised in Manipur itself as real ambassadors of the art. I have enjoyed through the years their interpretation of the *Chali*, the *Bhangi Parengs*, with their special *Lasya* characteristics and alluring grace, as well as their fine performance of the various Ras Lilas. Specialising in composition and utilizing this school in its pure and pristine beauty, they have done equally well in dance ballets such as "Usha Haran," a subject from mythology in which the first attempt was made to produce a ballet in pure Manipuri style; "Raj Nartaki," a classical subject woven around the dancing girl Amarapalli; "Chaitanya Mahaprabhu," a dance ballet telling of the life and devotion to God of this great Saint of Bengal; and in 1961 in connection with the Tagore Centenary celebrations, they enacted in ballet the poet's work entitled "Bhanu Shingher Padavalli," a subject based on the Radha-Krishna idylls.

In the dance of Kuchipudi, besides the masters and *gurus* who have been mentioned in the chapter on this school, one must remember the veteran Natyacharya, the late Vedanta Lakshminarayana Sashtri of Kuchipudi, as being the best known. Pendala Satyabhama of Pithapuram and Chittajallu Venkataraman of Marempalli, were women dancers of distinction and the very best exponents of the Kuchipudi school; and Shri Challa Bharatastram Lakshmayya of Kotakonda, now very old, made his name with his marvellous interpretation of the *Abhinayam*, particularly in the role of Satyabhama in the dance drama "Bhama Kalapam." Other well-known names in the classical dance of Andhra are Vempati Satyan, Vedantam Raghavayya, Pasumurti Krishnamurthy; Korda Narsimha Rao, who is a Natyacharya of distinction and dances with Indrani in her Kuchipudi items and is the founder and director of the Shri Nritya Bharati Dance Centre; and Kanchanmala who has made her name for her grace and special performance of this school.

Chinta Krishnamurthy, the greatest living authority on Kuchipudi today, is the son of the great master Chinta Venkataramaiah. He has been working ceaselessly and actively to further the cause of this important school of the classical dance through his centre, the Venkatarama Natya Mandali. He is now the president of the Sangeet Natak Akademi of Andhra Pradesh.

Banda Kanaka Lingeshwara Rao, who has been responsible for the spread of Kuchipudi by introducing it to the modern stage, is an authority and Natyacharya of Kuchipudi. Author, writer, dramatist and actor of distinction, Banda Kanaka Lingeshwara Rao has been responsible for the establishment of the Sri Siddhendra Kalakshetram dance school at Kuchipudi where the art is taught to a large number of pupils in its best traditions. He has added much valuable information about this school of the dance by his intensive research in the history and techniques of Kuchipudi.

Vedantam Satyanarayana Sarma, youngest winner of the Presidential Award, whose marvellous enactment of the roles of Satyabhama in the dance drama "Bhama Kalapam," Usha in "Usha Parinayam," and several other stellar roles in some of the famed Kuchipudi dance dramas is a dancer of great ability and versatility. Master of the difficult techniques, he excels in the deeply emotional and dramatic part of this ancient classical school, lending the dance dramas distinction, beauty of mode and special appeal by his wonderful convincing performances. Indeed, this artiste's perfect artistry and superb technique makes him one of the finest exponents of the art.

Turning to the classical dance of Orissi or Odissi, besides the distinguished names mentioned in the chapter on this school, the art has been preserved and spread by the efforts of well-known Natyacharyas and dancers. Kalicharan Patnaik, Natyacharya, composer, drama and dance ballet producer, writer and research specialist from Cuttack, is well known. His valuable collection of manuscripts on the art, his intense study and writing, and his special compositions give him a unique place in Orissi. Dhirendranath Patnaik is another personality closely associated with Orissi and the spread and understanding of its special style. Natyacharya Deba Prasad Das, dancer and exponent who performs with Indrani in her programmes on Orissi, Pandit Ram Gopal Misra, Mayadhar Rout, Dayanidhi Das and Ragunath Datta, are all teachers of Orissi who have devoted themselves to the study and imparting of the purity of Orissi to serious students and lovers of the dance; and among gifted dancers are Kumari Sanjuta Misra, Jayanti Ghose, Kumari Angarbala Roy and Balakrushna Das.

In mentioning the many notables who have contributed towards the true interpretation and firm establishment in each of the main schools of the dance, one can name with pleasure some well known dancers who are keeping the torch of India's classical dance art alive by their performances.

Shanta Rao, noted exponent of the Mohini Atam of Kerala, and one of the foremost interpreters of Bharata Natyam and Kathakali, has brought distinction and credit to this our ancient art. She has a vital strength that lends itself admirably to these styles in their pure and pristine forms.

Indeed her interpretation of the stirring *Natanam Adinar*, the gentler graces of the *Tillana* and the mosaic-like beauty of the *Jatisvaram*, discloses a strict adherence to the form and technique of Bharata Natyam in its manifold and subtle intricacies. Yet, she introduces with each performance a fresh and brilliant touch of artistry and versatility. In her *Abhinayam*, whether it be in the gracious philosophical *Varnam* and *Kirtanams* or the tender emotions of the *Padams* and *Sabdam* in Bharata Natyam, we find her interpretation full of dramatic mood and intention. Shanta Rao was one of the very first artistes outside Kerala to specialise in the Kathakali and Mohini Atam, in both of which she excels. Her portrayals in the Kathakali bring to life the strength and dramatic character of this school with its powerful clear-cut movements and wonderful characterization. I have watched with pleasure her superb performances of Mohini Atam in which she always succeeds in completely carrying away her audiences with her. She has graced the stages in the important cities of India, as well as in South-East Asia, Europe, America and Israel, winning well deserved laurels for her attainments and for the great classical dance of India.

Indrani (Rahman), daughter of the well-known dancer Ragini Devi, has danced since childhood. Specialising in Bharata Natyam, Orissi, Kuchipudi and Mohini

Atam, she has been a pioneer in being the first artiste to present both Orissi and Kuchipudi dance dramas in their abbreviated form outside their places of origin. Graceful, technically well versed in the various classical schools, she has held her audiences captive with her sensitivity, delicately defined interpretations and accomplishments.

Interpreting Bharata Natyam in its manifold beauties of the classical interplay of dance patterns in different *Talas* and dance melodic patterns in some of the most appealing *Ragas*, Indrani expresses a beauty of flow and form in movement and posture. Equally well she interprets the *Abhinayam* with its rich vocabulary of gesture and emotional acting. She can perform the Bharata Natyam with great grace and finesse, and then transform herself as she interprets Orissi and Kuchipudi. Her "Orissi Suite" and the "Natangi," the former invocation dances, and the latter showing the pure dance with its joyous movements reflecting the plastic beauty of the temple sculptures are offset by her gentle appealing interpretation of episodes from the *Git Govinda*, the immortal poem by Jayadeva, which tells of the philosophical love between Krishna and Radha. Once again she transforms herself as she interprets the *Sabdas* and *Darus* from the dramatic subjects of Kuchipudi in the brilliant Shiva-Lila, showing the ten manifestations of this form of God; the "Manduka Shabdam," describing the kingdom of the Frog Maiden Mandodari and as she distracts Ravana with provocative charm. Performing with Narsimha Rao and Baliram, once again she depicts the famous subjects of "Daksha Yagnya" and "Chamundeshwari Shabdam." The former is highly dramatic depicting as it does the powerful dance of Shiva when Sati throws herself into the sacrificial fire when spurned by her father Daksha, and the tragic enactment by Sati; the latter tells of the awesome dance of Durga as she destroys the demon Mahisha.

Indrani has danced throughout India and the world, in Europe, U.S.S.R., South-East Asia, America, Canada, the Caribbean, Africa and Australia, as a soloist and with her ensemble of dancers.

Vyjantimala, a gifted young dancer, is also India's first lady of the screen today. She has specialised in Bharata Natyam and the folk dances of South India. Hailing from the South herself, she finds herself at home in the lovely lyrical modes of the classical dance, in which her emotional acting and dramatic interpretation are best expressed, just as much as in the fine technicalities which she presents with all the aplomb of a finished product of this school. Today, she has a dance school in Madras, where members of her troupe and other young students learn both the classical and traditional folk dances. Vyjantimala is another accomplished Indian dancer who has won laurels for her country by her performances in India and abroad.

Yamini Krishnamurthi is another young artiste who has dedicated herself to this ancient art of the dance in India, and become an adept in Bharata Natyam, Kuchipudi and Orissi. Delicately built and vibrant in her interpretations, she portrays with true artistry the fine and subtle distinctions between these three styles of the classical dance. It is a treat to watch her display with equal ease the stately beauty and statuesque qualities of Bharata Natyam with its patterned intricate movements; the lyrical plasticity and flexions and bends of Orissi; and the gracious dramatic flow and poise of Kuchipudi. Selecting her programmes to allow herself ample scope to show her attainments, Yamini excels in the interpretation of such themes as the "Krishna Sabdam," showing the "Nayaka-

Nayaki Bhava," the "Bhama Kalapam," the "Navarasa" and the "Tarangam" from Kuchipudi.   In Orissi, her "Bhumipranam," the invocation dance, and the "Pallavi" portraying the plastic lyricism of this school are a delight: and she contrasts this with the fine *Abhinayam* in the love theme from the *Git Govindam*. She has played the leading role of Visvamohini in the Kuchipudi dance drama "Ksheera Sagara Mathanam," the mythological subject built around the legend of the Churning of the Ocean.   This role gives her the distinction of being the first woman to play in a Kuchipudi dance drama, which are traditionally only enacted by men.

Hailing from Andhra, Yamini won a Government scholarship for further studies in the dance and studied at the Kalakshetra Dance Academy in Madras as well as under several distinguished *gurus*.   This rising young dancer has not only danced in the leading cities of India, but also in Burma and Nepal and Australia.

Ritha Devi is another dancer with considerable talent, understanding of the art, and very much alive in the field.   Art critic and dancer, she combines knowledge of the subject with many fine performances to her credit.   Ritha Devi has specialised in the Manipur school and Bharata Natyam and is also well versed in Kuchipudi and Kathakali.   In her numerous recitals she has shown her command both of the varied techniques as well as the *Abhinayam* of these four schools of the dance.   When she interprets some of these famous subjects from the Manipur school, such as the Lai Haraoba, and the Radha-Krishna-Gopika themes, one is impressed by her graceful flexibility of movement, and the full beauty of this most *Lasya* style.

With equal ability she can interpret the strong modes and moods of the Kathakali school in her portrayals, for instance, of Putana of the Krishna legends, the *Rakshasha* woman who was sent to kill the divine child by feeding him her breast, and who dies herself instead.   And her fine interpretations of the dramatic, descriptive and emotional trends of the Kuchipudi dance drama *Sabdas*, such as the "Manduka Shabdam," the theme of the Frog Maiden Mandodari diverting the attentions of Ravana, and the mood changing to show Ravana falling under her spell and carrying her away to Lanka.

I have followed with interest and admiration this gifted young dancer's achievements ever since she first embarked on this very difficult and demanding profession.   With great endurance and determination to go on studying and practising long hours, she has blossomed into one of our leading dancers.   Here is another artiste who has enhanced the understanding and appreciation of the Indian dance amongst large audiences in India, England, Europe and other countries of the world.

Kumari Kamala is one of our best known gifted young dancers who has specialised in Bharata Natyam.   Very versatile, she has the supple delicate physique enviable in any dancer.   Endowed with great natural grace and flexibility of body and limbs, she uses these to perfectly unfold this highly technical and dramatic style of the classical dance.   Her intricate patterned pure dance compositions portrayed in the *Tillana*, the *Jatisvaram* and the *Varnam* have earned for her a justifiably high place in the world of the Indian dance.   She has graced many of the prominent stages in India and has successfully danced in solo recitals in England and Europe.   Kumari Kamala is not only excellent in performing with skill and virtuosity the pure dance of Bharata Natyam, but she portrays the *Abhi-*

nayam with equal charm and ability, bringing a new and appealing note to each interpretation, whether it be the coy Nayaki expressing her love and devotion to Krishna, or the devotional prayer theme to God. With subtle expressions and mood she can move her audience from joy and gladness to sadness and sorrow, or to the dignity of religious devotion. In the role of Kuruvanji she portrays with equal ease and sympathy the dual roles of Madanavali and the scintillating gipsy Mohini.

Srimati M. K. Saroja is one of our most gifted and distinguished young dancers. Seeing her perform is sheer delight, for not only is her *Abhinayam* full of expression and deeply moving, but her great sense of rhythm and the lovely sculpturesque modes of her techniques, bring to life the full beauty of Bharata Natyam. Her marvellous control and delicacy of movement, her expressive gestures and grace place her amongst our leading dancers. Saroja dances in the pristine purity of the early Devadasi style which embodies the full lyrical content of the classical dance, and she has delighted audiences in more than 500 recitals, having also toured for three years as a star dancer with the celebrated Ram Gopal.

Kumari Sudha Doraiswamy, well known to Bombay audiences, has blossomed into an accomplished young dancer. A beautiful girl, graceful and devoted to her art, she brings a freshness and allure to her performances, whether it be the classical Bharata Natyam and Kuchipudi schools or folk dances. Meticulous in each portrayal and adhering to purity of style, we find in Kumari Sudha one of those artistes who combine versatility and artistry.

Young Roshan Kumari, adept in the Kathak school of the dance, has come to the forefront by sheer talent. Supple, brilliant and precise, she excels in the intricacies of pure dance which she performs with great verve. And she is equally good in the gentler emotional interpretations of that important school of the dance.

Charming Shirin, Roshan and Khorshed Vazifdar have delighted audiences with their artistic performances in India, England, Europe, South-East Asia and Ceylon. Specialising in Bharata Natyam, Kathakali and Kathak, they have performed both in solo, and group and ballet form with conspicuous success through the years. Their dance ballets "The Terrible Boon" (Vishnu as Mohini dancing to destroy Bhasmasura), "Transposed Heads" (a fantasy from legend), "The Birth of Urvashi," and "Triumph of Life," were notable for their fine choreography and composition. Dedicated, accomplished and artistic, these gifted sisters have introduced a special flair and appeal in the presentation of their dance and dance ballet performances. Their school, the Nritya Manjari at Bombay, has trained and continues to train scores of young dancers in the Kathak and Kathakali techniques. Roshan continues the dedicated work in South India, having specialised in Bharata Natyam and Mohini Atam.

Ragini, Padmini and Lalitha, the sisters from Travancore, are well known for their many Bharata Natyam performances. Dancing with perfect coordination of movement and interpretation, they have performed both in solo and together, adding to the picturesque presentation of this school. The Mohini Atam and folk dances have also figured in their dance programmes.

Kumudini and Shevanti are two other dancers of note who have devoted themselves to the Indian dance. They have danced successfully in India and abroad and have studied under and performed with Ram Gopal, the celebrated dancer, in England, Europe and Asia.

As we try to enumerate the many dancers who are coming into the field and who have performed after serious study under distinguished *gurus*, we discover that the number is large and growing daily throughout India. Rani Karna, exponent of the Kathak school, who has delighted audiences in Delhi and the North; Chandralekha, Anjali Hora, Kumari Radha and Kumari Meenakshi, who have specialised in Bharata Natyam and contributed of their talents, are some of the other names. Two young dancers, Siloo Irani and Prasanya Pannikar, presented not long ago in a *Jugalbandi*, organised by the Pracheen Nritya Niketan, an interesting programme to show the similarities and common rhythms of the two schools of Kathak and Bharata Natyam respectively. Opposite the *Alarippu* and the *Natanam Adinar*, important stages of the Bharata Natyam, were performed the *Amad*, *Thora* and *Paran* of Kathak. *Tatkar* formed the main theme. Guru Shankar recited the Kathak *Bols* or rhythmic syllables and these were repeated by Guru Krishna Pannikar in syllabic forms of the Bharata Natyam *Jatis*; each closely followed by the *Tablah* and the *Mirdanga* respectively. Thus fine Kathak pure dance patterns were illustrated against the picturesque *Jati-adavus* from Bharata Natyam. And successive series of *Thoras* or verse syllabic recitations in the Kathak style, each ending on the *Sum* and ready to commence on the first beat, in Kathak, and the patterned sequences of Bharata Natyam each ending with a complicated *Thirmana* or finale, pointed out the mode of perfect synchronization between the foot rhythms and the drum beats, a common factor of all Indian dance styles.

There are various associations and groups also who have contributed much valuable work in the field of the dance and dance drama. The Indian National Theatre is the foremost Dance and Theatre Group in India, functioning in Bombay, Delhi, Calcutta and Madras, and has been responsible for staging several excellent dance ballets covering a wide variety of themes, solo dance performances of well-known dancers and also introducing to Indian audiences Indian folk dance groups and foreign ballet companies.

Among the productions I have enjoyed are "Narsingha Mehta," the story of a saint of Gujarat who dedicated his whole life to the good of humanity, directed by Yogendra Desai, with the use of Manipuri dance techniques and the Kathakali gesture language, with folk dances introduced in the village sequences. The whole dance ballet was accompanied by a fine choral orchestra. "Grow More Food," was another dance ballet presented by the Indian National Theatre, arranged by the dancer and choreographer Parvathi Kumar. This social subject was produced in a mixture of classical and folk techniques, and had a humorous commentary with cross-cuts of choral music describing the dialogues and introducing the characters. "Mirabai," the classic story of the Rajasthan princess who became a devotee of Sri Krishna and sang and composed her immortal sacred songs dedicated to Him, had the main techniques done in the Manipur dance style and the Kathakali gesture language, with full choral orchestra accompaniment. "Raj Nartaki," a classical subject from mythology, and "Rhythm and Culture," a dance ballet giving a survey of Indian culture from pre-historic times to the present day were two other outstanding productions. In the latter dance ballet, Manipur, Bharata Natyam, Kathak and Kathakali techniques were introduced, with folk dancing in the rural sequences. Both these ballets were directed by *guru* Bipin Singha, the noted teacher of Manipur, and Yogendra Desai.

The Bharatiya Kala Kendra of Bombay, theatre section of the Bharatiya Vidhya Bhavan, has staged several interesting dance ballets with students from their own dance academy as well as with other well known artistes. I recall "Jai Somnath," which dealt with a dancer dedicated and attached to the historic temple of Somnath in Gujerat. Kathakali dance techniques played the major role, with Bharata Natyam and Manipur dancing introduced in relevant portions. Here too choral accompaniment was the added attraction. Another unique ballet was "Tana Riri," the delightful vignette woven around the *Dipak Raga* (which has the power to create fire), and the *Megh Raga* (which can bring rain). The story tells how India's celebrated musician of medieval times Tansen was filled with an inward fire after singing the *Dipak Raga* and was later restored to health by the cooling showers that descended when two simple village girls sang the *Megh Raga* in the early morning.

The Hima Kala Kendra is an interesting group headed by the dancer and dramatist Hima Devi, talented niece of the distinguished dancer, the late Madame Menaka. Hima has qualified in dramatic art from the Royal Academy, London, and she has brought to the Indian stage many fine experiments in theatre craft. Exponent of Bharat Natyam, Kathakali and Manipur dance techniques, Hima Devi has given several dance recitals as well as produced, directed and played the lead in some outstanding dance ballets. In "The Birth of a Nation," depicting the dawn of freedom in India, she introduced some of the main classical techniques. "Chitra" dealt with a romantic episode from the annals of Manipur, and her "Light of Asia" interpreted in dance ballet form the life of the Buddha. Aesthetically produced, with special romantic effects, chanting and recitation, this stirring and devotional theme was enthusiastically received whenever it was presented. In this connection it may be mentioned that the late Mira Devi, mother of Hima Devi, was one of the early pioneers in the dance world of India, who performed extensively in her own country and abroad, bringing a fresh and charming interpretation to the art by her original work and compositions. Hima Devi has travelled widely, and has performed in several countries in the East and the West, where she received unadulterated acclaim.

The Little Ballet Troupe, Bombay, started by the late Shanti Bardan, has been unique in that this artiste who was highly gifted and imaginative, first conceived the idea of producing dance ballets which were enacted and danced by performers who interpreted their roles by impersonating puppets. Starting at first with straight ballet, Shanti Bardan produced "The Discovery of India," based on Jawaharlal Nehru's book. It brought out the highlights of the subject through various classical techniques. But the great success of this gifted dancer and composer lay in his beautifully produced ballets "Ramayana," and "Panchatantra." Uniquely costumed and utilizing an original technique of stage craft and decor, the dancers moved like puppets, their costumes and masks symbolising these charming marionettes. Now headed by his wife Gul Bardan, the Little Ballet Troupe continues the valuable work, having produced "Megh Doot," ("Cloud Messenger") by Kalidasa, and a tour in Europe where they won an international award in Paris for the most artistic and original presentation in dance ballet for their "Ramayana."

The Roop Kala Kendra of Matunga, Bombay, has rendered much valuable service by helping to stage excellent Bharata Natyam, Kathakali, Manipuri and Kathak recitals, particularly helping young dancers to make their debut. Its affiliated cultural centres in Madras, Delhi and Calcutta, have also contributed much by their spirit of dedication to the dance art.

Plate 113

1

2

Dance ballets by the Little Ballet Troupe, Bombay. (1) Dance ballet "Ramayana"; Ravana (*right*) and Jatayu (*left*) fight. (2) A pair of cranes from the ballet "Panchatantra". (3) Another scene from the ballet "Ramayana" with Rama, Lakshman and Sita in the Panchvati forest with the birds. The characters in these ballets impersonate puppets. (Courtesy, Little Ballet Troupe, Bombay.)

3

Plate 114

1

2

3

The Ram Lila ballet produced by Narendra Sharma. (1) Ram and Sita take leave of King Dasratha before going to Banvas. Queen Kaikeyi stands in the background. (2) Surpa naka tries her charms on Rama, to the great discomfort of Sita. (3) Ravana and the bird Jatayu in combat. (Photos copyright, Mohan Khokar.)

The Kala Kendra of Delhi is yet another organisation which presents and assists artistes to stage regular programmes of dance and music. Briju Maharaj, the famous Kathak exponent, has under its auspices produced and directed and played the leading part in some fine dance ballets, among them, "Kumara Sambhaba," a subject from the Shiva legends, and "Malti Madhav," a well-known Sanskrit drama. Excellent choreography and perfect interpretation as well as good presentation won him the unstinted praise of audiences both in Delhi and Bombay.

Four other groups in Bombay that are doing constructive work in the advancement of the dance are the Nritya Dharpana, and the ballet units of Yogindra Desai and of Sachin Shankar. In Calcutta, among other groups, the Indian Revival Group has much to its credit.

In the context of dance ballet and dance drama production, we find that there are some dancers who believe that dance productions make an impact on audiences even when two or more styles are intermingled. I have seen several such productions, and have found them interesting, primarily because of good presentation, decor, pleasing musical accompaniment, and the original work entailed. But the point remains, that even if such experiments increase the urge for original work, one must not forget that with the fusion of the techniques of the various schools, the particular distinctive characteristics of each one is lost in the melee, and there is also the likelihood that after a time the dancing becomes monotonous.

In my opinion, the best approach in the interests of both dancers and in preserving the purity and unique techniques of each school of the dance, would be to arrange the dance drama or ballet so that the different schools can be smoothly introduced in an unadulterated form to suit a particular sequence or context it best fits, and where it can be seen to the best advantage. This will certainly afford all the necessary variety of composition, choreography and mode. It will also encourage artistes who have studied the various schools of the dance to work together in harmony and present each style in its purity. As an example, the recent dance drama "Chitra," produced by Hima Kala Kendra, fulfilled these necessities fully, with dancers performing pure Manipuri, Kathakali, Bharata Natyam and Kathak in the various stages of the story, with folk dance in the village scenes.

I have enjoyed performing my solo numbers in a straight recital, but there is a special joy in planning a dance interpretation of story through ballet, and co-operating with other dancers. My first opportunity came when Mrs Bapsy Sabavala, who has done so much in the interests of social welfare, asked me and my group to take part in the production "A Rajput Village from Dusk to Dawn," which was being organised by her and directed by Karl Khandalavala, the well-known author and art critic. Being a subject set in North India, we interpreted it through the folk dances of Rajasthan and Saurashtra, introducing Kathak classical dancing in relevant places.

We had a group of expert folk dancers from Saurashtra visiting at the time, as they had been brought down by my husband to build an entire village in the outskirts of Bombay for a film he was producing, and also dance and act in it. Their authentic costumes, their marvellous rhythmic dances, already described, the Dandhya Ras and the Krishna Bhajan and Ganpathy Bhajan dances proved ideal for the theme which depicted the village in festival time. My group of dancers, Rukmani and Kamalini Khatau, Romilla Shroff, Sunanda Vijaykar and Sumita Pakvasa and I performed some of the folk dances of Rajasthan and a stick dance learned from the Saurashtrian dancers, while between scenes we had three Kathak dancers perform.

Again, the late Mrs. Phiroza Wadia, gifted and artistic, well known in Bombay for her interest in social welfare, produced with Karl Khandalavala as Director of Production a three-piece dance ballet. Our group were the main dancers supported by a cast of eighty.

The first ballet was based on the story of "Nala and Damyanti," a subject from the Epics, and was to be set against a background representing the Ajanta frescoes. The idea was to recreate these famous mural settings of the Buddhist period and enact this famous romantic story from ancient Indian mythology against them. We used the Bharata Natyam dance style for interpreting the story, and in the court scenes the spectacular Kathakali solo items like the Garuda Dance with the special picturesque costume. In this way, not only was it possible to have different dance schools in their pure form, but the music also had to be in keeping and afforded much variety.

In the second ballet, "Pilgrim Sundaramurti," devotee of Lord Shiva, a subject represented in many South Indian bronzes and sculptures, we were supported by a cast of thirty. Three Kathakali dancers interpreted this tragic story of the pilgrim who had to renounce marriage and remain a devotee of Lord Shiva. Bharata Natyam was introduced in solo when a Devadasi performed before the Shrine.

The third ballet comprised story-scenes from Rajasthan miniatures depicting themes from the Krishna legends. The dance decor represented twelve such vignettes, and each was interpreted in dance, against an immense picture set with members of the cast who posed to support the dancers. Full use was made of the folk dances of Rajasthan and Saurashtra, particularly the dances of Holi and the Ras Lila seen so often in the miniatures. We also danced in the Manipur style in solo and group to interpret some of the famous Krishna legends told through the paintings. Finally, there was a Kathak solo in the Jaipur school.

In this concluding chapter, I have tried to recount to some extent how far dance has been revived as a national art in India. Since Independence, many more solo artistes and groups have had the opportunity to dance abroad in various countries of the world. Ancient forms of the classical dance such as Orissi and Kuchipudi have come to be known and performed outside their particular regions. The folk dances have been given a recognised place in our national life, equally with the tribal dances. Every year they are presented in the Republic Day parade and have been seen by tens of thousands of people. Consequent to this, many of these groups have been able to perform on some of the stages of the leading cities of India. India however still suffers from a lack of sufficient theatres for the exclusive use of dance and drama. It is heartening to see that in honour of poet Tagore and his great contributions to art and culture, the Government has built a theatre in each of the State capitals, as part of the Tagore Centenary celebrations, known as the Rabindra Bharati Theatres. But though this is an encouraging sign, this effort can only fulfil the crying need for more theatres to only a small extent. It is unfair to expect Government to provide all the theatres which India needs, and as in other countries all over the world, wealthy citizens

Plate 115

"Pushpa Anjali" Dance Ensemble, produced by the late Mrs. Phiroza Wadia. Scene from the dance ballet "Nala-Damayanti"; the three chief dancers in the centre foreground, *left to right*, Rukmini Khatau, Enakshi Bhavnani, and Kamalini Khatau. The stage decor and costumes were inspired by the Ajanta frescoes. (Photo, D. R. D. Wadia.)

Plate 116

1

"Pushpa Anjali" Dance Ensemble, prod
by the late Mrs. Phiroza Wadia. (1) Scene
the dance ballet "Shiva-Sundramurti";
dancer in the foreground, Gopal Pillay
Garuda. (2) Scene from the dance b
"Rajput Miniatures"; chief dancer in ce
foreground, Enakshi Bhavnani as Radha
four Gopis. (Photos, D. R. D. Wadia.)

2

must make their contributions in national interest, by creating endowments for the building of such theatres. Bombay has already given the lead in this direction with four such theatres in the city.

As the number of theatres increases, it will become possible for more recognised dance and drama impressarios and associations to regularly present whole seasons of dance, drama and music. It is only when these arts become a regular established national feature that they will achieve their fullest fulfilment, and create the strongest bonds of unity through culture.

Appendix

1. *MARKARA-SANKRANTI or THE KHUMBA MELA*. This festival of the Winter Solstice falls in mid-January, when the Sun enters a new sign. In Northern India, the Hindu solar year closes with the Winter Solstice, followed immediately by the New Year. In Tamil Nad, it marks the Tamil New Year. In Central and Western India it is observed as Till Sankrant when the Sun enters Capricon.

2. *MAHASHIVA RATRI*. Observed in February, this festival is dedicated to Lord Shiva and is associated with the conversion of Lubdhaka the hunter who became a devotee of Lord Shiva and was carried in a celestial chariot to Lord Shiva's abode.

3. *VASANTA PANCHMI*. This festival takes place in Magh (January-February) and marks the first day of spring. It commemorates the day on which Kamadev, the Hindu Cupid, was burned to ashes by Shiva with His Third Eye for having disturbed Him in His meditation. Followed immediately by Holi.

4. *HOLI*. The spring festival of the Carnival of Colours is observed on full moon night in Phalgun (February-March), when people play with coloured water and powder. In South India it is known as Kama Dahan and commemorates the day on which Kamadev was burned to ashes. In Bengal it is dedicated to Goddess Saraswati and is known as the Saraswati Pooja.

5. *CHANDON JATRA*. This takes place in Baisakh (April-May) in Orissa and is dedicated to Jagannath, Vishnu as Lord of the Universe.

6. *RAKSHA BANDAN*. This festival falls on the full moon day of Sravan (July-August), when Sachi, consort of Indra, Lord of the Firmament, tied an amulet (*Rakshand*) on his wrist to help him defeat his enemies. Rajput women tied amulets (the *Raksha Bandan*) on the wrists of their brothers who gave them gifts in promise of protection in time of danger. The custom is observed today almost all over India. In Western India, it is known as Rakhi Purnima or Cocoanut Day, when amulets are presented by sisters to brothers, and offerings are made to Varuna, God of the Waters.

7. *NAG PANCHMI*. This festival is observed on the fifth day of Sravan (July-August) and is dedicated to Shesah Naga, the great Serpent on whom Lord Vishnu is believed to rest during the intervals of Creation.

8. *JHOOLAN JATRA.* This festival takes place in Sravan (July-August) in Orissa, when the image of Lord Vishnu is placed on a decorated swing in Vaishnava temples and attended by the Maharis (Devadasis) and Gotipuas (temple boy-dancers).

9. *GOKUL ASHTAMI.* This festival takes place in Sravan (July-August) and celebrates the birthday of Sri Krishna, incarnation of Lord Vishnu, Second of the Hindu Trinity and the Merciful Aspect of God.

10. *ONAM FESTIVAL.* This is observed in Kerala in Chingam of the Malayalam year (August-September), in remembrance of good King Mahabali who once ruled over Kerala, and lost his kingdom because under his rule it rivalled the blessedness of heaven itself. But Lord Vishnu granted him a boon to visit the earth each year when he would be remembered by the people with rejoicing.

11. *GANESH CHATURTI.* This festival takes place on the fourth day of the waxing of the moon in Bhadrapada (August-September) to celebrate the birthday of Ganesha (Ganapathy), the elephant-headed God, Remover of obstacles and spiritual son of Lord Shiva and Parvathi.

12. *DUSSERAH.* This national festival takes place in Asvin (September-October). Commencing with the Navratri which is the beginning of nine nights dedicated to Goddess Durga in Her various revelations; the festival also commemorates the victory of Prince Rama over Ravana. It is therefore of special significance to warriors since time immemorial. In Bengal, the festival is known as Durga Pooja.

13. *DIVALI.* This Festival of Lights marks the Hindu New Year, and falls in Kartika-Agrahayana (November-December). It commemorates the day Prince Rama was crowned King of Ayodhya, and also the day on which King Vikramaditya was crowned. The day is dedicated to Lord Vishnu, Preserver of Mankind, and His consort Lakshmi, Goddess of Fortune.

14. *CAR FESTIVALS.* These celebrations are peculiar to temples all over India that have the sacred *Rath* or ornamental wooden chariots which are used for taking the particular temple deity in procession on the day dedicated to Him.

Glossary

Abhanga. Posture of slightly bending the figure to either side.

Abhinayam, Abhinaya. Interpretation of emotional expression.

Abhinaya Chandrika. Classical treatise on the Orissi dance.

Abhinaya Dharpana. Classical treatise on gesture and emotional expression.

Abhinaya Nritya. Stage in the Orissi dance performance.

Abhisar. Showing emotional expression and interpretation in the Ras Lilas of Manipur dance.

Achala Svaras. Immoveable tones in Indian music.

Achauba Bhangi Pareng. A basic dance composition in the Manipur school in *Lasya* or Feminine style.

Adavus. Basic foundation and unit of the dance step patterns and postures in the Bharata Natyam school.

Adavu-Jati. A combination of *Adavus.*

Ahamaragam. Form of Bharata Natyam.

Alap. Musical mode in slow tempo.

Alarippu. First stage in the Bharata Natyam dance performance.

Amad. First stage in the Kathak dance performance.

Ananda Nritya. One of the stages in the Orissi dance performance. Same as the *Tarijham.*

Angahara. A combination of six or eight *Karanas* or basic dance postures.

Apsaras. Heavenly nymphs who dance with divine grace.

Arati dance. Performed by the Chau Masked dancers of Bihar.

Ashtapadis. Invocatory and benedictory lyrics.

Astra Danda. Sword dance performed by the Chau Masked dancers of Bihar.

Atibhanga. A posture with an exaggerated bend.

Avanagh. Drums.

Bahaka Nata (Sanchar). Folk drum dance of Orissa.

Bahu Natakas. Indigenous musical dramas of Andhra Pradesh.

Baisakh Bihu. Folk dance of Assam.

Bala Gopala. Sri Krishna.

Balarama. Brother of Sri Krishna.

Bamboo Dance. A folk dance of Assam.

Batunata. One of the stages in the Orissi dance performance.

Batu Nritya. One of the stages in the Orissi dance performance.

Baul Dances. Folk dances of Bengal.

Bee Dance. A folk dance of Assam.

Been. A musical instrument of North India.

Belis. Fundamental bodily positions combined with basic dance movements on which the Orissi dance style is based.

Betat. Musical instruments in which the strings are plucked.

Bhagavata Mela Natakam. Sacred dance dramas performed by a group of Brahmins.

Bhagavat Gita. Sacred teachings of Sri Krishna. The Song of God.

Bhagavatar. A devotee of God who worships the Almighty through sacred song in Tamil Nad.

Bhagavatulu. In Andhra the Bhagavatars were known as Bhagavatulus.

Bhairava. A *Raga* melody.

Bhairivi. A *Ragini.*

Bhajans. Sacred songs addressed to God.

Bhaka Nata (Sanchar). A folk dance of Orissa.

Bhakti. The cult of worship of God through devotion and love.

Bhama Kalapam. Best known dance drama in the Kuchipudi school.

Bhangas. Rhythmic balance of the body.

Bhangis. The principal dance positions more highly elaborated in Orissi.

Bhangi Parengs. Essence of pure dance compositions in the Manipur school.

Bhangra Dance. A folk dance of the Punjab.

Bharata Muni. Author of the great Sanskrit classical treatise on dramaturgy, the *Natya Sastra.*

Bharata Natyam. One of the main schools of the classical dance, Tamil Nad.

Bharati. Goddess of the Earth.

Bhavai. A form of dance drama in Gujerat.

Bhil Dances. Tribal dances of Madhya Pradesh.

Bhoga Melan. Professional women dancers of Andhra Pradesh.

Bhumi Pranam. Invocation and beginning stage in the Orissi dance performance.

Bihu Dance. Tribal dance of Assam.

Bilma Dance. Tribal dance of Madhya Pradesh.

Bol. Word syllables on the drum in the Kathak dance.

Boli. Traditional folk song of the Punjab.

Bommalatam. Puppets of Tamil Nad.

Brahma. Creator and First of the Hindu Trinity.

Brahmana Melas. Groups of Brahmin *gurus* and experts of the dance.

Brindavan Bhangi Pareng. A variation of the Achauba Bhangi Pareng dance composition in the *Lasya* or Feminine style of Manipur.

Canoe Dance. A folk dance of Assam.

Carana or Khanda. End of every four lines of the song in the Kathakali dance drama.

Chait Dance. A tribal dance of Madhya Pradesh.

Chala Svaras. Moveable tones of notes in Indian music.

Chali, Chari or Chalan. Style of walk in Orissi.

Chandra. The Moon God.

Chapeli. A folk dance of Uttar Pradesh.

Chaturanga. A dance composition in Manipur school with song, verse, *Svara* passages and word composition.

Chau Masked Dancers. Classical dancers of Bihar Seraikela.

Chaupada. Type of classical dances done by the Raja Nartakis, professional secular dancers of Andhra.

Chenda. A drum used in the Kathakali dance dramas.

Chherta Dance. A tribal dance of Madhya Pradesh.

Chindi. A type of Bharata Natyam, Tamil Nad.

Chollu. Rhythmic word syllables played on the *Mirdanga* drum.

Community Dances. Folk dances of Orissa.

Courtship Dances. Tribal dances of Orissa.

Dadra. Love lyrics interpreted in the Kathak dance.

Dagla Dance. A tribal dance of Rajasthan.

Daksha. Father of Goddess Parvathi.

Dalkhai Dance. A tribal dance of Orissa.

Dance of Worship. A folk dance of Gujerat.

Danda Nata. A folk dance of Orissa.

Danda Pata. A tribal stick dance of Madhya Pradesh.

Dandaria Dances. Tribal dances of Andhra.

Daruvus, Daru. The entrance dance of each character in the Kuchipudi dance dramas in which he or she introduces himself or herself by starting with song, followed by pure dance interludes, postures and hand gestures.

Darbari. A *Raga* melody.

Darupada. Type of classical dance performed by the professional Raja Nartakis or secular dancers in the Nayak durbars in Tamil Nad.

Dastavatarabhinayam. The portrayal of the ten *Avatars* or incarnations of Sri Krishna in the Kuchipudi dance drama of Bhama Kalapam.

Daughter of Himavan. Goddess Parvathi, consort of Shiva.

Deepak. A *Raga* Melody.

Devadasis. Handmaidens of God.

Devasthan. Temple theatres.

Devi. Goddess Kali.

Dewari Dances. Tribal dances of Madhya Pradesh.

Dhamar. Lyrical subjects from the Krishna legends interpreted in the Kathak dance.

Dhandya Ras. A group stick folk dance of Gujerat.

Dhola, Dhol. A folk drum.

Dhrumal. Group dance of Manipur performed by men in *Tandava* or Forceful style, using from fourteen to one hundred drums.

Dhrupads. Lyrical compositions in praise of the deities interpreted in the Kathak dance.

Dhwaja. Flag festival of Indra, Lord of the Firmament.

Dilruba. A stringed instrument of Bengal.

Druva Paravisika Druva. Satyabhama's introduction song and dance at the beginning of the Kuchipudi dance drama, Bhama Kalapam.

Dummy Horse Play of Tanjore. Folk dance dramas of Tamil Nad.

Durga. A Goddess, twin aspect of Lord Shiva.

Festival Dances. Tribal dances of Madhya Pradesh.

Ganapathy, Ganesh. Elephant-headed God, spiritual son of Shiva and Parvathi.

Ganapathy Bhajan. A folk dance of Gujerat, danced with the playing of cymbals.

Gandharva Gana. The Yakshagana dance drama as performed in Nepal.

Gandharvas. Heavenly musicians.

Ganesha Sabda Svarpata. Dramatic dance item in the Orissi dance performance.

Ganesh Vandana. First stage in a Kathak dance performance.

Garba. A folk dance of Gujerat.

Garuda Dance. Dance representing the Garuda bird, sacred to Lord Vishnu, as done in the Kathakali dance dramas.

Garud Bahan Dance. A tribal dance of Orissa.

Gath-Bhava. Finely chanted lyrical songs that are interpreted in the Kathak dance.

Gatis. Lyrical compositions of the *Abhinaya* of Kathak dance.

Geetam. Devotional songs.

Ghan. Cymbals.

Ghanta Mardala. A folk dance of Andhra Pradesh.

Ghazal. Beautiful love song interpreted in the *Abhinaya* of the Kathak dance.

Gheriya. A folk dance of Maharashtra.

Ghoorma. Clay Drum Dance of the tribals of Madhya Pradesh.

Giddha Dance. A folk dance of Punjab, performed by women.

Ginad. A folk dance of Rajasthan.

Git Govindam. "Song Celestial," by poet Jayadeva, telling of the philosophical love of Krishna and Radha.

Godo Dance. A harvest tribal dance of Madhya Pradesh.

Goncho Dance. A harvest tribal dance of Madhya Pradesh.

Gopas. The cowherds who were Sri Krishna's childhood playmates.

Gopika-Lila. The Ras Lila, symbolic of the yearning of the souls of mankind to become one with God.

Gopurams. Temple tower-gateways in Tamil Nad.

Goshtha or Gopa Ras. Tandava style dance drama of Manipur based on the Krishna legends.

Goshtha Bhangi Pareng. A basic dance composition in the *Tandava* or Forceful style in the Manipur dance.

Goshtha Brindavan Pareng. A variation of the Goshtha Pareng, *Tandava* or Forceful style in the Manipur dance.

Gouri. Goddess of Plenty.

Gotipuas. Boy dancers attached to the temples in Orissa.

Gurus. Teachers.

Har Endanna Dance. A tribal dance of Madhya Pradesh.

Harvest Dance of the Kodavas. A folk dance of Coorg, Mysore State.

Hastak. A characteristic posture in the Kathak dance.

Havest Dances. Popular folk dances of many regions of India.

Hikat Dance. A folk dance of Jammu.

Hindole. A *Raga* melody.

Holi Dance. A dance common throughout India done during the spring festival of Holi, the Carnival of Colours.

Hornbill Dance. A folk dance of Assam.

Humo Bauli Dance. A folk dance of Assam.

Hulki Dances. Tribal dances of Madhya Pradesh.

Imitation Dance. A tribal dance of Assam.

Indra. God of the Firmament.

Invocation Dance. A tribal dance of Bihar.

Ishta Deva Bandana. One of the stages in the Orissi dance performance.

Jadda Dance. A folk festival dance of Himachal Pradesh.

Jadur Dance. A tribal dance of Orissa.

Jagarana Nritya. Invocation and salutation to Mother Earth in the Orissi dance performance.

Jata-jatni. A folk dance of Bihar.

Jatis. Time units in the dance.

Jatisvaram. One of the stages in the Bharata Natyam dance performance, with emphasis on time and musical score.

Jhainta. A folk festival dance of Himachal Pradesh.

Jharpat Dance. A tribal dance of Madhya Pradesh.

Jhoora Dance. A community dance of Himachal Pradesh.

Jog. A *Raga* melody.

Kai Kottikalli Dance. A folk dance of Kerala.

Kajri Dance. A folk dance of North India.

Kalasam. The dramatic finale in the Kathakali school, which comes in the pure dance sequences.

Kali. A Goddess, twin Aspect of Lord Shiva.

Kaliya. The wicked serpent monster overcome by Sri Krishna.

Kamadev. The Cupid of Indian mythology.

Kumaon Dance. A folk dance of Uttar Pradesh.

Karanas. The basic Alphabet of Postures on which all dance is based in the classical schools.

Kari. Type of make-up in the Kathakali dance dramas, generally used by female demons.

Karsanas. A tribal dance of Madhya Pradesh.

Kartal Cholom. Group dance in Manipur in *Tandava* or Forceful style, with men dancers playing on *Kartals* or large cymbals.

Kartikeya. God of war and spiritual son of Shiva and Parvathi.

Kathak. The classical dance school of North India.

Kathi. A type of make-up used in the Kathakali dance dramas, usually used by wicked characters like the enemies of the Gods.

Kathi Dance. A folk dance of Bengal done with sticks.

Kavita. Lyrics with word syllables based on the legends of the Gods, interpreted in the Kathak dance.

Kelika. The dancers who performed solo classical dances of the secular type in Andhra.

Keli-kottu. Loud drumming played to announce the Kathakali dance drama performance.

Khamba Lim Dance. A tribal harvest dance of Assam.

Khanda. Every four lines of the song in the Kathakali dance dramas

Khayal. Folk dance dramas of Rajasthan.

Khel Gopal. A folk dance of Assam.

Khol. A folk drum.

Khubakishei. Lasya or Feminine clap group dance performed by girls in Manipur.

Khurumba Pareng. Another variation of the Achauba Bhangi Pareng composition in *Lasya* or Feminine style of Manipur.

Kirtiprabandha. Dance composition of Manipur school, with lyrics, song, *Svara* passages and word compositions.

Koisabadi Dance. A tribal dance of Madhya Pradesh.

Kolattam. A folk dance of Tamil Nad, South India.

Kol Dance. A tribal dance of Madhya Pradesh.

Krishna Lila. A folk dance of Rajasthan.

Krishna Atam. Dance dramas of Kerala.

Kshetragna Padas. Benedictory and invocatory songs of praise to God composed by the saint Kshetragna Yogi of Andhra and interpreted in the Kuchipudi dance dramas.

Kuchipudi. The classical dance drama of Kuchipudi, Andhra.

Kudiyatam. Old Sanskrit dramas of Kerala.

Kummi. Classical dance done by women in Kerala, based on the Kathakali techniques.

Kunja Ras. Group dance drama of Manipur based on the Krishna legends, in *Lasya* or Feminine style.

Kuruvanji. A classical dance ballet performed in Bharata Natyam techniques in Tamil Nad.

Lahaki Karma Dance. A tribal dance of Madhya Pradesh.

Lahaki Saila Dance. A tribal dance of Madhya Pradesh.

Lai Haraoba. Ancient ritualistic Shaivite dance drama of Manipur.

Lakshmi. Goddess, consort of Vishnu.

Lakshmi Jagar Dance. A tribal dance of Madhya Pradesh.

Lakshyana. *Abhinaya* or emotional expression and interpretation in the Orissi dance.

Lama Monk Dances. Masked mystic dances of the Buddhist Lama monks of the monasteries of the western and eastern Himalayan areas of India.

Langi Dance. A dance of the gypsies of Rajasthan.

Laya. Speed, rhythm.

Laya Venyasams. Technique of patterned rhythms in the Kuchipudi dance dramas.

Lezim Dance. A folk dance of Maharashtra.

Madalas. Drums.

Madhole. A type of drum.

Madomabela Dyutam. Type of secular classical solo dance done by the Raja Nartakis of Andhra.

Mahabharata. One of the famous epic poems of ancient India.

Mahadeva. Lord Shiva.

Mahajanaka Jataka. Ancient Buddhist sacred story.

Maha Ras. The great group dance drama of Manipur classical style, based on the Krishna legends.

Maharis. The Devadasis or handmaidens of God, attached to the temples in Orissa.

Maiba, Maibi. Priest and priestess in the ritualistic dance of the Lai Haraoba of Manipur.

Maleppu Chital. The Jasmine Flower Dance performed in the Krishna Atam dance dramas of Kerala.

Malkaus. A *Raga* melody.

Mandar. A folk drum.

Manjiras. Small cymbals.

Manjira Cholom. *Lasya* or Feminine group dance of Manipur done by girl dancers playing on small cymbals.

Mardalam. A type of drum.

Masked Dances. Folk dances of Bengal.

Matras. Sub-divisions of the main metrical timing.

Mutrika. The combination of two *Karanas* or basic postures forming the Alphabet of Postures.

Muyalagam. The evil dwarf crushed under the foot of Lord Shiva in His dance of the Nataraja.

Meenakshi. Goddess; another name for Parvathi.

Meend. Created tonal notes in Indian music.

Megh. Malahar. A *Raga* melody.

Meju Vani. Dancers in Andhra who specialised in the interpretation of *Padams*, songs of love or romantic mood.

Minukku. A type of facial make-up used by women characters in the Kathakali dance dramas.

Mirdanga. The classical drum, oval in shape and played on either side, while the instrument is kept on its body.

Mitra. God of the Sun.

Mizrab. Plectrum used for plucking the strings in Indian music.

Mohini. Vishnu in the guise of this Goddess and symbolic of Delusion.

Mohini Atam. Classical dance done by women in Kerala.

Moirang Parva. One of the duets in the Lai Haraoba dance drama of Manipur.

Moksha. Salvation.

Mother of the Three Worlds. Goddess Uma.

Mukti. The finale of a dance sequence in the Orissi dance performance.

Muvva Gopala Padams. The poetic love lyrics dedicated to Sri Krishna, composed by Bhakta Kshtragna of Kuchipudi, Andhra.

Nadanta. The mystic dance of Shiva as the Nataraja.

Nagara. A type of drum.

Nagasvaram. A type of Indian clarionet from South India.

Narada. The ancient sage.

Nata Lakshmanan. Forceful postural stances done by men in the Kuchipudi dance dramas.

Natangi. One of the stages in the Orissi dance performance, and same as the *Tarijham.*

Natanam Adinar. The Dance of Shiva as done in the Bharat Natyam.

Nataraja. Shiva in His famed Cosmic Dance.

Natas. Dancers.

Nata Sutras. Handbooks for dancers.

Nat Puja Dance. A folk dance of Assam.

Nattuva Melas. The *gurus* (teachers) and experts of the dance in Andhra.

Nattuvanars. The *gurus* and experts of the classical dance in Tamil Nad.

Natya. The combination of both dancing and acting.

Natyacharyas. Dance teachers who are experts.

Natya Melas. Professional women dancers of Andhra, who formed a group known as the Natya Melas.

Natya Sastra. The great treatise on dramaturgy by Bharata Muni, in Sanskrit.

Natvara. Krishna, the Divine Dancer. A dramatic sequence performed in the Kathak school.

Nautanki. A folk dance drama of Uttar Pradesh.

Navarani Dance. A tribal dance of Madhya Pradesh.

Nayaka-Nayika Bhava. The mood symbolic of the yearning of human souls to become one with God, the Infinite.

Nitya Ras. Group dance drama of Manipur based on the Krishna legends.

Nonkrem Dance. A folk dance of Assam.

Nrtya. Dance with emotional expression and mood.

Nrittaratnavalli. A treatise on the classical dance written on palm leaves by the Andhra scholar Jayapa Senani in the 13th century A.D.

Nrtta. Pure dance.

Nruira Lim Dance. A tribal dance of Assam, representing the cock fight.

Nupura. Ankle bells.

Ootam Tulal. A solo dance based on the Kathakali performance of Kerala.

Orissa String Dolls. The puppets of Orissa.

Orissi or Odissi. The classical dance of Orissa.

Paathya. Lyrical compositions based on the theme of a dance drama and rendered in a particular form called *Paathya.*

Pada Bhedas. Various ways in which the feet can be used in the Orissi dance school.

Padabhinayam. Elaborate footwork.

Pada Kila. The solo secular classical dance done by the Raja Nartakis of Andhra.

Padams. Finely chanted lyrical songs of love or romantic mood interpreted in the Bharata Natyam.

Pallavi. The main theme or burden of the song interpreted in the dance Bharata Natyam.

Pandanallur. One of the styles of Bharata Natyam. It gets its name from the village of that name which has produced some of the greatest exponents and *gurus* of this school.

Paran. Pure dance in Kathak.

Parija. *Abhinaya* or emotional expression and interpretation in the Orissa dance performance.

Parvathi. Goddess, consort of Lord Shiva.

Patra Prabesh. Entrance of the dancer at commencement of the Orissi dance performance.

Pavai Koothu. Puppets of Kerala.

Phag Dance. The Springtime dance of the gypsies of Rajasthan.

Phul Basant. Duet dance of love done in springtime by the Chau Masked Dancers of Bihar, Seraikela.

Pinal Kolattam. A folk dance of Tamil Nad.

Pindibhandas. Completed whole bodily movements achieved from particular sequences of the dance.

Pranaya Kalahan. The episode of Satyabhama declaring herself more beautiful than her Lord Krishna, in the Kuchipudi dance drama Bhama Kalapam.

Pravesha Daru. The song with which each character introduces himself or herself in the Kuchipudi dance dramas.

Prithvi. Goddess of the Earth.

Pung Cholom. Group drum dance of Manipur done in *Tandava* or Forceful style, with dancers playing drums as they dance.

Puranas. Ancient philosophical treatises.

Purappadu. Commencement of the Kathakali dance drama, in which the pure dance style and technique are performed.

Puthli Khel. Puppets of Bengal.

Radha. Beloved of Sri Krishna.

Raga. The traditional melody into which the Indian musician has woven his improvisations, and it is a selection of five, six or seven notes distributed along the scale.

Raja Nartaki. Professional secular dancers who used to perform in ancient times in the royal courts and at social gatherings.

Rajaraeswari Natakam. One of the forms of the Bharata Natyam as performed in Tanjore, Tamil Nad.

Rakhal Lila. A folk dance of Assam.

Rama. The hero of the *Ramayana* and prince of Ayodhya.

Ras Lila. Sacred group dance with characters representing Krishan, Radha and the Gopis.

Ravana. The wicked king of Lanka (Ceylon).

Rechakas. Special foot, waist, neck, and arm movements with hand gestures.

Rina Dance. A tribal dance of Madhya Pradesh.

Ring Dance. A tribal dance of Orissa.

Rouf Dance. A folk dance of Jammu.

Sabdas. Dramatic lyrics based on the theme of the Kuchipudi dance drama being enacted, and rendered in a particular musical form called *Paathya.*

Sabdam. Rendering in gesture language and emotional acting of a devotional lyric or song. One of the stages of the Bharata Natyam performance.

Sadir Atam. The old name for the Bharata Natyam dance.

Saila Dance. A tribal dance of Madhya Pradesh.

Samagama. The act of Sri Krishna relenting and returning to Satyabhama in the Kuchipudi dance drama Bhama Kalapam.

Sama Veda. One of the four *Vedas*, the sacred books of the Hindus.

Sanchar. The folk drum dance of Orissa.

Sanchari Bhava. A series of mental pictures of conceptions created with many aspects of the main motif of the lyric, through variations of interpretations as shown in the *Abhinayam* of the classical modes.

Sandhya Nritya. Shiva's Evening Dance performed on the Himalayas.

Sangeet. One of the stages in the Kathak dance performance, stress here being on time and musical notation.

Sangitaratnakara. A Sanskrit treatise on music by the great authority Sarangadeva.

Sarangi. A stringed instrument of North India.

Saraswathi. Goddess, consort of Lord Brahma.

Sari Dance. A folk dance of Kerala.

Sastras. Fundamental scriptural treatises and teachings.

Saundarya. Gipsy dance of Rajasthan.

Savatula Kayyam. An additional episode in the Kuchipudi dance drama Bhama Kalapam, when Rukmani is presented to Sri Krishna as His bride, in order to increase the suffering of Satyabhama.

Shakti. The active principle or energy of the Gods, which is feminine and symbolically called the consort in Hindu mythology.

Shanai. A type of clarionet used in North Indian music.

Shepherdess's Dance. A folk dance of the Punjab Hills.

Shiva. Third of the Hindu Trinity, Destroyer of Evil and Creator of Good.

Shiva Leela Natakams. The ten Shiva legends.

Shiva Linga. The symbol of Lord Shiva.

Shiva Sabda Svarpata. The dance of Shiva and its interpretation as done in the Orissi school.

Shulapani. Lord Shiva.

Silpa Sastras. The handbook for craftsmen.

Sita. Wife of Rama, hero of the epic poem the *Ramayana.*

Sitar. A stringed musical instrument in North Indian music.

Slokas. Sacred hymns.

Social Dances. Folk dances of Gujerat.

Sokkam. Type of Bharata Natyam done in a particular temple in Tamil Nad.

Spear Dance. A tribal dance of the Nagas of Assam.

Springtime Dances. Folk dances of North India.

Sri Raga. A *Raga.*

Srutis. Quarter tones in between two consecutive notes, to make more minute degrees of pitch. There are twenty-two *Srutis* in all.

Stick Dance. A folk dance of Andhra.

Suddha Maddala. Pure drumming on *Madala* drums at the commencement of a Kathakali dance drama performance.

Sukracharya. Ancient sage who was an authority on the thirty-two *Silpa Sastras* or handbooks for craftsmen.

Suraguru Natakam. A type of Bharata Natyam done in a particular temple in Tamil Nad.

Surya. Sun God.

Sushir. Wind instruments.

Sutradhara. Stage manager.

Svaram, Svara. Musical notation.

Swara Pallabi Nrtta. One of the stages in the Orissi dance performance.

Swarmala. Dance composition of Manipur school with stress on time and musical score.

Tabal Chongbi Dance. A folk dance of Assam.

Tablahs. A pair of drums.

Tadi Karma Dance. A tribal dance of Madhya Pradesh.

Tadi Saila Dance. A tribal dance of Madhya Pradesh.

Tafar Dance. A folk dance of Assam.

Tihai. The finale done at the end of pure dance sequences in one of the stages of the Orissi dance performance.

Tala. Rhythmic timing.

Tallina or Telana. Dance composition of the Manipur school.

Tamasha. A folk operatic form of dance in Maharashtra.

Tana. Original and novel combinations of tone utilizing pure vowels or pure sound within the allotted scale of the *Raga* being sung or played.

Tandava. Forceful, strong.

Tandavas. Descriptive dance compositions on Shiva, Krishna or one of the deities interpreted and danced in Kathak.

Tappattikali. A folk dance of Kerala.

Tarabs. Resonance wires in Indian musical instruments.

Tarana. Pure dance in Kathak with intricate rhythms.

Taranga Nritya. Interpretation of invocatory and benedictory songs of praise to God.

Tarangas. Invocatory and benedictory songs of praise to God.

Tarijham One of the stages in the Orissi dance performance.

Tarina. A variation of pure dance composition in the Manipur school.

Tat. Stringed musical instruments played with a bow.

Thanpura. Musical instrument for keeping the melody in the correct key.

Thata. Introduction to the technique of the Kathak dance performance.

Third Eye. Third Eye of Lord Shiva, symbolic of spiritual intuition.

Thirmana. Finale to the pure dance sequences in the Bharata Natyam performance.

Thithi. A wind bag instrument with reed mouth-piece to embellish the tonal runs in music, Andhra.

Thoras. Verse compositions of rhythmic syllabic words in the Kathak school.

Thora Dance. A folk dance of Himachal Pradesh.

Tillana. One of the stages in the Bharata Natyam dance performance.

Tippani Dance. A folk dance of Maharashtra.

Todas Dance. A tribal dance of South India.

Todyam. Devotional dance done behind the raised curtain in the Kathakali dance drama prelude.

Tolu Bommalata. Play of leather toys, literally, actually the Shadow Plays of Tamil Nad.

Tribhanga. The triple bend in posture, in which there is the emphasis on the curvature of the hips.

Trikhand Manjura. Ritualistic and devotional salutation to Mother Earth, the Gods, and the *guru* in the Orissi dance performance.

Turburi. Small tribal drums of Madhya Pradesh.

Twashtri. Another name for the Sun God.

Ukuttas. Rhythmic syllabic words recited and played on the drum in the technique of the Orissi school.

Uktaprat-Yuktaka. Intricate dance sequences to show the particular attributes of the character coupled with emotional acting, as shown in the Kuchipudi dance drama Bhama Kalapam.

Ulukhal Ras. Group dance drama of Manipur based on the Krishna legends.

Uma. Goddess, consort of Lord Shiva.

Upanishads. Sacred books that explain the precepts of the Vedas.

Usha. Goddess of the Dawn.

Valmiki. The Sage to whom the epic poem the *Ramayana* was revealed.

Vamana. The dwarf incarnation of Lord Vishnu.

Vanjaras Dance. A dance of the gypsies of Rajasthan.

Varied Dances. Tribal dances of Madhya Pradesh.

Varikolam. Type of Bharata Natyam done in a particular temple in Tamil Nad.

Varnam. The most highly elaborate stage of the Bharata Natyam performance, literally meaning "colour."

Varuna. God of the Waters.

Vasanta Atam. A folk dance of South India.

Vasanta Ras. Spring festival group dance drama of Manipur.

Vavhuvlur. A particular style of the Bharata Natyam of Tamil Nad.

Vayu. God of the Wind.

Veena. India's most ancient and celebrated musical instrument used in South India.

Vighnaraj Puja. One of the stages in the Orissi dance performance.

Virabhadra. Shiva in his most powerful aspect.

Vishnu. The Merciful Aspect of God, and Second of the Hindu Trinity.

Vishwakarma. The Architect of Heaven.

Vyasa. The sage to whom the epic poem the *Mahabharata* was revealed.

Warrior Dance. A tribal dance of the Nagas of Assam.

Yajur Veda. One of the four *Vedas*, the sacred books of the Hindus.

Yakshaganas. Dance dramas of Andhra Pradesh, which have their counterparts in Tamil Nad, Mysore, Maharashtra and Nepal.

Yatra, Jatra. Dance drama or musical plays with dance in Bengal.

Yoga. Science and deep study of body and mental control.

Yoga Sutra. The Sanskrit treatise on the science of *Yoga*.

Bibliography

AGARKAR, A. J. *Folk Dance of Maharashtra.* Bombay, 1950.

AIYANGAR, S. KRISHNASWAMY. *Ancient India.* London, 1911.

AMBROSE, KAY. *Classical Dance and Costumes of India.* London, 1951.

ANAND, MULK RAJ. *The Dancing Foot.* Delhi, 1957.

ARCHER, W. G. (Introduction and Notes). *Kangra Painting.* London, 1952.

ARNOLD, EDWIN. *Gita Govindum.* London, 1885.

— *The Mahabharata.* London, 1883.

BANNERJI, JITENDRA NATH. *The Development of Hindu Iconography.* Calcutta, 1941.

BANNERJI, PROJESH. *Dance of India*, 5th enl. and revised Edition. Allahabad, 1942.

— *The Folk Dance of India.* Allahabad, 1944.

BATRA, RAI BAHADUR, R. L. *Science and Art of Indian Music.* Lahore, 1945.

BATTACHARYA, BRINDAVAN CH. *Indian Images.* Calcutta, 1921.

BHADURI, MANJULIKA and CHATTERJI, SANTOSH. *The Art of the Hindu Dance.* Calcutta, 1945.

BHARATA MUNI. *Natya Sastra*, Vols. I and II. (Sanskrit.)

BHARATIYA NRITYA KALA MANDIR, PATNA. Bulletin No. 1, 1958.

BOWERS, FAUBION. *The Dance in India.* New York, 1953.

— *Theatre in the East*: A Survey of Asian Dance and Drama. London, 1956.

CHANDA, P. RAMPRASAD. *The Beginnings of Art in Eastern India, with Special Reference to Sculptures in the Indian Museum.* Calcutta, 1927.

CHATTERJI, SANTOSH. *Devadasi—the Temple Dancer.* Calcutta, 1945.

CHAUDHURI, SUDHANSU. *Konarak.* Introduction and Annotation by O. C. Gangoly. Calcutta, 1956.

COOMARASWAMY, ANANDA KENTISH. *The Dance of Shiva and Fourteen Other Essays.* New York, 1918.

— *History of Indian and Indonesian Art.* London, 1927.

— *Introduction to Indian Art.* Madras, 1927.

— *Rajput Paintings* (16th to 19th Century). London, 1916.

— *Aims of Indian Art.* London, 1908.

— *Selected Examples of Indian Art.* London, 1948.

— *The Indian Craftsman.* London, 1909.

— *Indian Music.* London, New York, 1917.

— *Viswakarma.* Examples of Indian Architecture, Sculpture, Paintings and Handicrafts Chosen by the Author. 1st Series—100 Examples of Indian Sculptures with an Introduction by Eric Gill. London, 1912-1914.

— *Archaic Indian Terracottas.* 1928.

— *The Arts and Crafts of India and Ceylon.* London & Edinburgh, 1913.

CROOKE, WILLIAM. *Popular Religion and Folklore of North India.* Allahabad, 1894.

DAVEL, KRISHNAJI BALLAL. *The Hindu Musical Scale and Twenty-two Shruties.* Poona, 1910.

— *The Ragas of Hindusthan.* Poona, 1918-23.

DAYAL, LEELA (ROW). *Manipuri Dances*; *Lasya Lahari.* Bombay, 1951.

— *Nritta Manjari*: The 62 Fundamental Sequences of Bharata Natyam. Calcutta, 1948.

DESAI, KANU. *Git Govinda*. Ten Pictures of a Mystic and Poetic Interpretation of Radha's Love for Krishna. Ahmedabad, 1952.

DE ZOETE, BERYL. *Dance and Drama of Bali*. London, 1958.

— *The Other Mind*, A Study of Dance in South India. London, 1953.

DICKENSON, ERIC. *Kishangarh Painting*. (Edited by Karl Khandalavala). New Delhi,1959.

DUTT, GURUSADAY. *The Folk Dances of Bengal*. Ed. by Ashok Mitra. Calcutta, 1954.

ELWIN, VERRIER. *Folk Songs of the Maikal Hills*. Madras, 1944.

— *The Baiga*. Bombay, 1939.

— *The Muria and Their Ghotul*. Bombay, 1947.

FREDERIC, LOUIS. *Indian Temples and Sculpture*. Introduction by Jean Naudou. Translated by Eva M. Hooykaas and A. H. Christie. London, 1959.

GANGOLI, O. C. *Ragas and Raginis*, A Pictorial and Iconographic Study of Indian Musical Notes Based on Original Sources. Calcutta, 1934-35.

— *South Indian Bronzes*. Calcutta, 1914.

— *Indian Terracotta Art*. Calcutta, 1959.

GHOSH, MANMOHAN. *Abhinaya Dharpana* (Translation).

GHURYE, G. S. *Bharatanatya and Its Costume*. Bombay, 1958.

GOPINATH and RAMANA RAO, S. V. *The Classical Dance Poses of India*. Madras, 1955.

GRIFFITHS, JOHN. *The Paintings in the Buddhist Cave Temples of Ajanta, India*. London, 1896-97.

HAVELL, ERNEST BINFIELD. *Ideals of Indian Art*. London, 1918.

— *The Himalayas in Indian Art*. London, 1924.

— *A Handbook of Indian Art*. London, 1920.

— *Indian Sculpture and Painting*. London, 1928.

INDIA. Ministry of Information & Broadcasting, Publications Division. *Folk Dances of India*. Delhi, 1956.

— *Indian Dance*. Delhi, 1955.

— *Kangra Valley Painting*. Introduction by M. S. Randhawa. 1954.

— *Architecture and Sculpture of India*. Delhi, 1956.

INDIA. Tourist Department, Ministry of Information & Broadcasting, Publications Division. *The Dance in India*. Delhi, 1958.

HENDLEY, T. H. "Indian Jewellery," *Journal of Indian Art*, Vol. 12.

HORROWITZ, PROFESSOR E. P. *Indian Theatre*. 1940.

IYENGAR, C. R. SRINIVASA. *Indian Dance*; *Natya and Nritya*. Madras, 1948.

IYER, E. KRISHNA. *Bharata Natya and Other Dances of Tamil Nad*. Baroda, 1957.

IYER, K. BHARATHA. *Kathakali, the Sacred Dance-Drama of Malabar*. London, 1955.

KEITH, SIR A. B. *Religion and Philosophy of the Vedas*. Cambridge, U.S.A., 1925.

KALA VIKASH KENDRA SOUVENIR, 1958. *Dance and Music of Orissa*:

(a) "Sculptural Representations of Music and Dance in Orissa" by Dr. Krishna Chandra Panigrahi.

(b) "Orissa Buddhism and Orissi Dance" by Dr. Nabin Kumar Sahoo.

(c) "My Impressions of Orissi Dance" by Professor Mohan Khokar.

(d) "Principal Bhangis of Orissi Dance" by Kalicharan Pattanaik and Priyabrata Goswami.

(e) "The Mahari" by Sadasiva Ratha Sharma.

(f) "Hand Gestures in Orissi Dance" by Direndranath Pattanaik.

(g) "Pataka Hasta in Sangita Abhinaya Dharpana" by Kalicharan Pattanaik.

(h) "The Puppet Play as Prevalent in Orissa" by Dr. Kunjabehari Das.

(i) "Raga Malabashri" by Kalicharan Pattanaik.

(j) "Musical Instruments in Orissan Architecture" by Sadasiva Ratha Sharma.

(k) "Tandava Poses in Orissan Sculptures" by Sadasiva Ratha Sharma.

KALA VIKASH KENDRA. Bulletin 1. "Folk Dance and Music of Orissa, Sambalput," by Direndranath Pattanaik. Calcutta, 1959.

KAR, CHINTAMANI. *Classical Indian Sculpture* 300 B.C.—A.D. 500. London, 1950.
— *Indian Metal Sculpture.* London, 1952.

KHANDALAVALA, KARL. *Pahari Miniature Painting.* Bombay, 1958.

KHASTGIR, SUDHIR RAJAN. *Dances in Lino-cut.* Dehra Dun, 1945.

KOTHARE, BALAJI. *Hindu Holidays.* Bombay, 1904.

KRAMRISCH, STELLA. *Indian Sculpture.* Calcutta, 1933.

LAMERI. *The Gesture Language of the Hindu Dance.* New York, 1951.

MACDONNELL. *India's Past, Her Literature, Language, Art and Antiquities.* London, 1927.

MACKENZIE, D. A. *Indian Myth and Legend.*

MUNSHI, K. M. *Saga of Indian Sculpture.* Bombay, 1957.

NAIDU, VENKATA NARAYANSWAMI, NAIDU, P. SRINAVASULU, and PANTULU, ONGOLE V. RANGAYYA. *Tandava Laksanam or The Fundamentals of Ancient Hindu Dancing*, being a Translation into English of the Fourth Chapter of the Natya Sastra of Bharata Muni. Madras, 1936.

NANDIKESVARA. *The Mirror of Gestures, being the Abhinaya Dharpana of Nandikesvara*, translated into English by Ananda Coomaraswamy and Gopala Krishnayya Duggirala. Cambridge, 1917.

PANDEYA, AVINASH C. *The Art of Kathakoli.* Allahabad, 1943.

POPLEY, H. A. *The Music of India.* Calcutta, 1950.

PREMKUMAR. *The Language of Kathakali*, A Guide to Mudras. Allahabad, 1948.

RAGINI DEVI. *Dances of India.* Calcutta, 1953.
— *Nritanjali*, An Introduction to Hindu Dancing. New York, 1928.

RAM GOPAL. *Rhythm in the Heavens*, An Autobiography. London, 1957.
— *Indian Dancing.* London, 1951.

RANDHAWA, M. S. *Kangra Paintings of the Bhagavata Purana.* New Delhi, 1960.

ROSENTHAL, E. *The Story of Indian Music and Its Instruments.* London, 1928.

SPREEN, HILDEGARD L. *Folk Dances of South India.* With the Assistance of R. Ramani. Bombay, 1945.

SAMBAMOORTHY, P. *South Indian Music.* Madras, 1941.

SANYAL, AMIYA NATH. *Ragas and Raginis.* Bombay, 1959.

SARANGADEVA. *Sangitaratnakara of Sarangadeva*, translated into English with detailed notes by Dr. C. Kunhan Raja. Madras, 1945.

SASTRI, H. KRISHNA. *South Indian Images of Gods and Goddesses.* Madras, 1916.

SHAH, PROFESSOR K. T. *South Indian Bronzes.* Bombay, 1930.
—*The Splendour that was Ind.* Bombay, 1930.

SHIRALI, VISHNUDAS. *Hindu Music and Rhythm.* Paris, 1939.

SINHA, BIPIN. *The Dance of Manipur.*

SOUVENIR ON KUCHIPUDI NATYA SEMINAR. Hyderabad, 1959.
(*a*) "Kuchipudi School of Dancing" by Vissa Appa Rao.
(*b*) "The Dance Art in Andhra Pradesh" by Vissa Appa Rao.
(*c*) "Bhama Kalapam of Kuchipudi" by Saiva Krishnamurthi and M. Sangamesam.

STOOKE, HERBERT J. and KARL KHANDALAVALA. *The Laud Ragmala Miniatures*; a Study in Indian Painting and Music. Oxford, 1953.

STRANGEWAYS-FOX, A. H. *Music of Hindusthan.* Oxford, 1914.

TAGORE, SIR SOURINDRO MOHUN. *Six Principal Ragas*; with a brief view of Hindu Music. Calcutta, 1877.
— *Six Ragas and Thirty-six Raginis of the Hindus.* Calcutta, 1887.
— *The Twenty-two Srutees of the Hindus.* Calcutta, 1886.

TANDRA DEVI. *Village Theatres.*

TODD.   *Annals of Rajasthan.*   Vols. I and II.

TRAVANCORE, RAJA RAMA VARMA OF.   *Balarama-Bharatam* (A Treatise on Dancing).   Travancore Trivandrum, 1904.

VAKIL, KANAYALAL H.   *Rock-cut Temples around Bombay at Elephanta and Jogeshwari, Mantapeswar and Kanheri.*   Bombay, 1932.

VARMA, K. M.   *Natya, Nrtta and Nrtya.*   Their Meaning and Relation.   Calcutta, 1957.

VASYDEVA, PUDUVAL R.   *The Art of Kathakali.*   Trivandrum, 1933.

VENKATACHALLAM, GOVINDRAJ.   *Dance in India.*

WATSON, J. F.   *Textile Manufacturers and the Costumes of the People of India.*   London, 1866-67.

WAUCHOPE, R. S.   *Buddhist Cave Temples of India.*   Calcutta, 1933.

WOODROFFE, SIR JOHN (Arthur Avalon).   *Garland of Letters.*   Madras, 1922.

— *Tantra Tattva; Principles of Tantra*, Part I.   London, 1914.

YAGNIK, R. K.   *The Indian Theatre.*   London, 1933.

YAZDANI, GULLAM.   *Fine Arts, Architecture, Sculpture and Painting.*   London, 1953.

Index

255